HER OWN LIFE

AUTOBIOGRAPHICAL
WRITINGS BY
SEVENTEENTH-CENTURY
ENGLISHWOMEN

EDITED BY
ELSPETH GRAHAM, HILARY HINDS,
ELAINE HOBBY AND HELEN WILCOX

Routledge
Taylor & Francis Group

LONDON AND NEW YORK

First published 1989
by Routledge
2 Park Square, Milton Park, Abingdon, Oxfordshire, OX14 4RN
711 Third Avenue, New York, NY 10017

Reprinted in 1992, 1994, 1996, 1998, 2002

Transferred to Digital Printing 2005

Routledge is an imprint of the Taylor and Francis Group, an informa business

First issued in hardback 2015

British Library Cataloguing in Publication Data

Her own life: autobiographical writings by
seventeenth-century Englishwomen.
1. England. Social life 1600–1700.
Biographies. Collections
I. Graham, Elspeth,
942.07'092'2

Library of Congress Cataloguing in Publication Data

Her own life: autobiographical writings by seventeenth-century
Englishwomen/edited by Elspeth Graham . . . [et al.].
p. cm.
Bibliography: p.
Includes index.
1. English literature–17th century. 2. English literature–Women
authors. 3. Autobiography–Women authors. 4. Women–England–
History–17th century–Sources. I. Graham, Elspeth.
PR1127.H38   1989
820.8'09287–dc   89–6220

ISBN 978-0-415-01700-8 (pbk)
ISBN 978-1-138-16801-5 (hbk)

CONTENTS

———————— ⚜ ————————

ACKNOWLEDGEMENTS

We are grateful for the co-operation of curators and librarians at the following places: Abbot Hall Art Gallery, Kendal; Beinecke Collection, Yale University; The British Library; Cambridge University Library; Friends' Library, London; The Huntington Library; Kent County Archives; Liverpool University Library; Nottingham University Library; John Rylands Library, Manchester; Dr Williams's Library, London. The extracts from Anne Clifford's *Diary* are published with the kind permission of the Rt. Hon. Lord Sackville.

We would also like to thank the following for their scholarly and practical assistance: Maureen Bell, Elizabeth Birrell, Jim and Margaret Boulton, Colin Buckley, Steven Davies, Charles Fleischmann, Glen and Ave-Fenella Graham, Kathryn Harriss, Sylvia Harrop, Ian Harvey, Lesley Ling, Philip Lloyd, Tom O'Malley, George Parfitt, Kathryn Perry, Gill Robinson, Caroline Root, Lyndal Roper, Gary Scanlon, Shirley Seaton, Jan Sellers, I. A. Shapiro, Simon Shepherd, Jackie Stacey, Ann Thompson, Jeffrey Wainwright, Linda Walker, Pam Watts, Valerie Wayne, Christine White, Allan Wilcox, and the Research Committees of Liverpool University and Manchester Polytechnic.

Finally, we happily acknowledge the support given to this project in its early stages by Merrilyn Julian, and the enthusiastic encouragement of Janice Price and Adèle Price in seeing it through to completion.

The editors and the publishers would like to thank the following for permission to reproduce the photographs contained in this book: Plate 1, reproduced by courtesy of Abbot Hall Art Gallery, Kendal, Cumbria ('The Great Picture' is on view in the Great Hall at Appleby Castle, on loan from Abbot Hall Art Gallery); Plate 2, by permission of the Syndics of Cambridge University Library; Plates 3 and 4, by permission of the British Library.

INTRODUCTION

'Why hath this lady writ her own life?':
some origins of autobiography

Dozens of seventeenth-century women wrote autobiographical texts that have survived, and those included in this anthology represent only a small, if representative sample of what could be here.[1] Women authors of the period came from many walks of life, from Mary Simpson, a poor woman of Norwich, whose *Faith and Experience* (1649) was published by her church minister after her death (he explains in his dedicatory epistle that she could not write, but spoke about her life and beliefs on her deathbed whilst someone else recorded them); to Lady Ann Fanshawe's manuscript addressed to her son, an account of 'your father and my life'.[2] Such women also spanned between them a diverse range of religious and political positions, including Catholics like Lady Lucy Knatchbull and Elizabeth Cellier, and the Quaker narratives of Dorothy Waugh, Hester Biddle, and Sarah Blackborow.[3]

The development of autobiography in the seventeenth century and the subsequent rise of the novel have often been associated with the origins in that same period of bourgeois individualism, which made possible and promoted a focus on individual experience (Watt 1957; McKeown 1987). Certainly a wide variety of genres came to be used to write extensively about personal beliefs or activities. These include the frequently-cited collections of letters by Dorothy Osborne, Constance Fowler, Rachel Wriothesley (Lady Russell), and Dorothy Sidney (Countess of Sunderland),[4] as well as a spectrum of lesser-known texts, such as Mary Trye's, Hannah Wolley's and Louise Bourgeois's accounts of their activities as healers (Bourgeois 1656; Trye 1675; Wolley 1674). Another factor in the increased production of such writings in these years is the breakdown of state control over the press during the civil war, which made publishing more possible for women, as well as for men previously excluded from print.[5] Hester Shaw, for example, wrote two autobiographical pamphlets in 1653 concerning the theft of her money by her church minister, and Mary Blaithwaite, a parliamentary pamphlet-seller, recorded her persecution by Cumberland royalists (Shaw 1654a; 1654b; Blaithwaite 1654). Varied as this collection aims to be, it merely scratches the surface.

The extracts included here from Anne Clifford's diary closely approximate the structure and concerns we might expect a woman of her class to have. A near-daily record, its surprises lie in her tenacity. It is a private document, and is therefore quite distinct from the other texts we reprint. Most of the surviving autobiographical writings of the period were written with publication or manuscript circulation in mind, and were made possible or necessary by a variety of circumstances which, while specific in each case, reveal interrelating patterns. An important source of women's autobiographies in the period, for instance, is the published pamphlets of radical sectaries. Acting from what they believed was direct contact with God, many were led to engage in public preaching and the disruption of church services: activities that frequently resulted in their arrest and imprisonment. It therefore comes as no surprise to find that a good number of Quaker pamphlets, and some Baptist ones, published in the 1650s and 1660s were written from prison, and that their autobiographical element is strong, women explaining the origins of their behaviour and describing the events that preceded their conversion and/or imprisonment. Many of these activists' tracts, like *Anna Trapnel's Report and Plea* (1654), have a direct political purpose, aiming to influence the reader's understanding not only of their personal behaviour, but also of the wider social implications of accepting their messages as God's. Others, like Katharine Evans and Sarah Cheevers's *A Short Relation* (1662), not only argue for their release from gaol but also aim a particular message at the like-minded reader: 'a child of wisdom may understand', they say (p. 120). It was not only resistance to the church and government that produced the need for such appeals. Later in the century *A Vindication of Anne Wentworth* (1677) also reacts against oppression. Commanded, Wentworth says, by God, she has had no choice but to describe her eighteen years of suffering at the hands of her husband; God told her to leave her husband and church when they opposed the 'public meaning' of her work: that she represents a class of the oppressed, her husband a class of oppressors.[6]

Such texts, then, are not the personal anatomizing that we might expect to find in autobiography. They are public documents, with a social purpose, and Anna Trapnel tells us that her *Report and Plea* is based in part on the stories told her by others, not the sole product of her own (and God's) ideas. In this public, social dimension they are closely linked to another central source of autobiographical writings of the day, the conversion narrative.[7]

The published conversion narrative recording a woman's or man's spiritual and profane development became a popular form during the seventeenth century. Those joining radical sects, especially the Baptists, were required to give a public account of how they came to believe they were numbered amongst the elect, and why they should be admitted to membership of a specific congregation. (This process is described in some detail in the extract included here from Susanna Parr's *Susanna's Apology* (1659). She also explains the sectaries' convention of voting to select their minister and to decide questions of dispute within the church.) A collection of such declarations of faith, made by both women and men, was published in 1653 by John Rogers, and it is of interest that in his comments on the narratives he has selected he notes that the distinction between the elect and others is not one founded on gender or other social distinctions: 'The difference that is to be made is already proved to be between the precious, and the vile, the clean and the unclean; and not to be a difference of sexes, ages or relations.' (Rogers 1653: 563). Also, although he maintains that men within the church should have some greater freedom than women, he specifically defends women's right to vote on matters of church policy and to hold church offices (see also Walker 1652). In such an organization, women were likely to find their voices.

It is scarcely surprising, then, that several of the autobiographies included here can be classified as conversion narratives. Sarah Davy's *Heaven Realized* (1670) is in some ways particularly representative, being based in part on a diary kept to assess signs of her election or damnation, a practice much recommended by some sects.[8] Davy (like Hannah Allen) describes feelings of isolation and depression that beset her before she found spiritual peace and assurance of her salvation, but it is important to remember when reading such accounts that they are not reducible simply to individual experience. A specific pattern of doubt, false security, renewed (often agonizing) doubt, and eventual true assurance characterizes not only Allen's and Davy's accounts but many of the narratives published in the period. A drive to suicide also frequently occurs in such stories, as does a stubborn refusal to listen to words of comfort (Watkins 1972). The sinner could not be sure she was saved unless her experiences paralleled to a large degree those of her peers, and she would be predisposed to recognize the popular pattern of emotions and compulsive actions. We also find that many of these narratives were published posthumously, offered by their editors, who were usually clergymen, as an example to other sectaries of proper godly behaviour. Only those that could be interpreted as proper models would find publication in this way.[9]

The conversion narrative not only required a certain pattern of experience, but also provided an author with a framework through which to assess and find important the things she did and felt: Sarah Davy appeals to God to give her a 'right understanding' of things that have happened to her, and her editor has divided her text into 'appropriate' sections. In a text not anthologized here, however, Jane Turner explains that the conversion narrative framework need not be as totally determinate as such a description might suggest. She shows that the relationship between doctrinally-required interpretation and experience is dialectical, neither experience nor interpretation taking absolute precedence:

> Though some persons have much knowledge as to principles, and but little experience, yet none can have experience of that they do not understand, either in principle before they had that experience, or else they have learned that principle by experience; for (as I said before) all experience is either an effect of knowledge, or by it we learn knowledge, otherwise it cannot be experience.
>
> (Turner 1653: 199)

The emotions and incidents described in these anthologized texts, therefore – Hannah Allen's despair after the death of her husband, Sarah Davy's falling in love with another woman – are not wholly reducible to the framework that permitted their composition. This is particularly striking in the case of Anne Wentworth's pamphlet, which uses the language of the conversion narrative – the requirement on her to 'declare my experiences' – to write and publish a text recording her reasons for leaving her Baptist church and her husband.

This duty to account for one's soul's growth and salvation also

4

informs the only verse autobiography included here. An Collins explains at length that her writing is for her 'private use', to record instances of God's grace, and that it is properly confined to spiritual matters. Similar claims were made in two contemporary books of autobiographical devotional verse, the anonymous *Eliza's Babes* (1652), and Elizabeth Major's *Honey on the Rod* (1656). We can also see that it was probably the confidence and attention to self commended by Baptists that made it possible for Susanna Parr's *Susanna's Apology* to be written in vindication of her leaving her Baptist church.

Whilst the appeal against oppression and the conversion narrative can be seen as the major autobiographical forms of the period, not all the texts in this collection fall into or relate to these categories. Two of them, Margaret Cavendish's 'A true relation of my birth, breeding and life' (1656), and Mary Carleton's *The Case of Madam Mary Carleton* (1663a) can more helpfully be seen in relation to the contemporary growth of the romance. Margaret Cavendish's account of her life was published as part of a book of romances, and Mary Carleton's makes wide use of romance conventions to make credible her assertion that she is a German Princess. This juxtaposition alerts us to the fact that in that period, at least, no clear dividing line can safely be drawn between published fiction and fact, inventiveness and truth: many contemporary romances, like Defoe's later novels, are presented as autobiographical to justify what might otherwise be seen as an irreligious publication of 'lies'. Like the texts written from oppression or imprisonment, Carleton's *The Case of Madam Mary Carleton* appeals to the reader as arbiter, seeking to change her/his understanding of the author's experiences and influence her/his assessment of justice; Margaret Cavendish, meanwhile, like Alice Thornton, whose autobiography was written for manuscript circulation, is concerned to vindicate her modest reputation whilst telling her story. The self presented in the text is one created with the reader in view.

The variation in origins of these writings has particular effects on their style as well as their content. Where Mary Carleton's narrative parodies romance convention, most of the works included here find their vocabulary in the bible and/or church practices. Katharine Evans and Sarah Cheevers's *A Short Relation*, for instance, weaves in and out of bible incidents and quotation, as they record their conversations with God and compare their experiences with those of various biblical characters. Similar features are found in *Anna*

Trapnel's Report and Plea and in Joan Vokins's *God's Mighty Power Magnified* (1691), and the writings of Sarah Davy and Anne Wentworth are saturated with scriptural quotation and echo. Since they were writing for a public of bible-owners and readers, such language serves to make their narratives more accessible, as well as giving a broader meaning to their activities. Less radical religious positions, like those occupied by Susanna Parr or An Collins, are more chary of such prolific use of bible texts. None the less, despite Parr's scathing rejection of the enthusiasts' behaviour and withdrawal from her Baptist church, her description of the death of her child and its spiritual interpretation is rich with scriptural echoes (p. 110), as is An Collins's celebration of her union with her Saviour (p. 64).

Remarkable and varied as these autobiographical writings are, it would be a mistake to imagine that they represent a predominant form of women's published texts in the period. Katharine Evans and Sarah Cheevers were imprisoned by the Inquisition for bringing printed prophecies to Malta, and they, Anna Trapnel, Anne Wentworth, and Joan Vokins are only a tiny fraction of the number of women to publish such religio-political texts in the period. Many also wrote and published meditations on religio-political themes. An Collins, whose *Divine Songs* (1653) includes prose meditations, was also not by any means the period's only woman poet, a wealth of love poetry (or more accurately, anti-love poetry) appearing after the Restoration. Margaret Cavendish was particularly prolific, publishing not only romances and poetry but plays and philosophy, and she was certainly not the only woman to do so, as the recent revival of interest in Restoration women playwrights is revealing. Towards the end of the century, too, women turned their hands to defending female control of medicine, midwifery, and cookery, and began to write books defending women's right to practise and make money from such ancient skills, as well as to publish polemics defending female ability and (near) equality with men.[10] We hope that this collection will stimulate interest in other women's texts of the period.

'Harlot's brood': the historical context

Relationships between women and men in the seventeenth century could be defined by reference to a whole complex of interlocking and interdependent ideas, definitions, conventions, and statutes, whether concerning law, religion, society, philosophy, or nature. Ideas from each category were seen to reflect and reinforce the others, for all were based on notions of order or hierarchy, and all were concerned to ascribe men and women to their rightful places within these hierarchies.

Women, within these orders, were subject to men. T.E., in his book *The Lawes Resolutions of Womens Rights* (1632), explores the nature of this subjection in relation to the marriage partnership:

> in this consolidation which we call wedlock is a locking together. It is true, that man and wife are one person, but understand in what manner.
>
> When a small brook or little river incorporateth with Rhodanus, Humber or the Thames, the poor rivulet loseth her name; it is carried and recarried with the new associate; it beareth no sway; it possesseth nothing during coverture. A woman as soon as she is married is called 'covert'; in Latin 'nupta', that is, 'veiled'; as it were clouded and overshadowed; she hath lost her stream. I may more truly, far away, say to a married woman, her new self is her superior, her companion, her master . . .
>
> All [women] are understood either married, or to be married, and their desires are subject to their husbands; I know no remedy, yet some can shift it well enough. The common law here shaketh hand with divinity.
>
> (1632: 124–5, 6)

Here secular law is following divine law, which is also manifested in natural law; all underline the notion that women have no identity of their own, but are subsumed in the persons of first their fathers and then their husbands. If, in the light of this, Margaret Cavendish's fear of being effaced from history if she should die and her husband remarry can be credited as being by no means unfounded or fanciful, then perhaps both Anne Wentworth's and Mary Carleton's fears for their lives, consequent to their marriages (see pp. 186, 189, and 133), should not be dismissed as mere rhetoric.

These 'natural' or divine hierarchies related to very precise ideas about the 'nature' of women: being composed primarily of cold and wet humours,[11] they were subject to 'a changeable, deceptive and tricky temperament' (Davis 1975a: 124). They were also much more libidinous creatures than men: Thomas Becon instructed girls from the age of 14 to strive to 'suppress that lust and desire in them'.[12] In women, then, these 'lower' passions ruled the 'higher' ones of reason and intellect, which were the province of the male. The danger, it was thought, was that if women were given a free rein, they would try to reproduce this physiological 'disorderliness' in society, by dominating men. This was another justification for the production of manifold exhortations, prescriptions, instructions, and warnings: for the 'good' woman was not the 'natural' woman, but simply the one who managed to contain her baser nature. In this, she differed little from other members of the animal kingdom; her docility was the result of expert training:

> She submits herself with quietness, cheerfully, even as a well-broken horse turns at the least turning, stands at the least check of the rider's bridle, readily going and standing as he wishes that sits upon his back.
>
> (Whateley 1617; 1975: 43)

These prescriptions were particularly plentiful concerning the marriage relationship, and were manifested not only in legal documents, but also in marriage manuals and domestic conduct books. The characterization of marriage as a 'necessary evil', associated with St Paul and the Catholic church, had been modified by Protestant, and more particularly Puritan, commentators, who instead lauded it as an honourable, dignified, and natural union between men and women, sanctioned by God: Milton termed it 'the crown of all our bliss/Ordained by thee' (1968: 656). But within this blissful union men and women had quite distinct parts to play. A woman was to be modest, chaste, submissive, deferent, loyal, and silent unless spoken to: these elements comprised her 'honesty', a recurrent term used to describe the appropriate demeanour of a wife: 'a woman hath no charge to see to, but her honesty and chastity. Wherewith when she is informed of that, she is sufficiently appointed.'[13] The man's first duty was to God, the woman's to God's will as transmitted through the person of her husband: 'she must regard him as God's deputy . . . the image and glory of God' (Whateley 1619: 193, 195). William Gouge, in his conduct book *Of Domesticall Duties* spelt out the implications of this: 'She may do nothing against God's will, but many things must she do against her own will, if her husband require her' (1622: 337). And it was the possibility of a contradiction inherent in this statement, duty to God set against duty to one's husband, that proved to be the arena in which so many of the debates and controversies were played out, in particular by women involved in the radical sects and their opponents. For if a man forbade his wife to perform a godly duty, she was to pray for guidance and follow God: their spiritual equality was here to supersede their temporal inequality. It was this argument that was to prove so significant for Anne Wentworth in her justifications for having left her husband (see p. 187).

It is important not to assume, however, on the evidence of these documents alone, that women in seventeenth-century Britain were uniformly downtrodden and submissive. These texts were, after all, written by men, and were highly prescriptive rather than simply descriptive; they were elucidating an ideal that was doubtless never achieved. This is not to say, of course, that the 'reality' was necessarily more favourable than this ideal: Richard Baxter, a Presbyterian divine, offers an unsentimental account of women's lot in the marriage relationship:

> Women especially must expect so much suffering in a married life, that if God had not put them into a natural inclination to it, and so strong a love to their children, as maketh them patient under the most annoying troubles, the world would ere this have been at the end, through their refusal of so calamitous a life. Their sickness in breeding, their pain in bringing forth, with the danger of their lives, the tedious trouble day and night which they have with their children in their nursing and their childhood; besides their subjection to their husbands, and continual care of family affairs: being forced to consume their lives in a multitude of low and troublesome businesses. All this and much more would have utterly deterred their sex from marriage, if nature itself had not inclined them to it.
>
> (Baxter 1672: 481)

This seems a long way from Milton's image of marriage as 'the crown of all our bliss', and is a useful reminder that we have access to contrasting images of women's lives, and thence to different ideologies, if not to the 'realities', to women's experiences themselves.

Women's position in relation to the law is similarly ambiguous. T. E. was able to write, apparently quite unequivocally:

> women have no voice in Parliament, they . . . have nothing to do in constituting laws, or consenting to them, or interpreting of laws or in hearing them interpreted at lectures, leets or charges, and yet they stand strictly tied to men's establishments, little or nothing excused by ignorance.
>
> (T. E. 1632: 6, 2)

This does not, however, seem to have been strictly the case. Women, in the sway of their baser passions, were not held to be directly responsible for their actions: it was the men 'in charge' of them who bore the final reponsibility. It seems that this allowed women a degree of licence of which they did not fail to take advantage:

> In England, in most felonious acts by a married woman to which her husband could be shown to be privy or at which he was present, the wife could not be held entirely culpable. If indicted, she might be acquitted or receive a lesser sentence than he for the same crime . . . Small wonder

that the Star Chamber grumbled in 1603 that some women who had torn down enclosure fences were 'hiding behind their sex'.

(Davis 1975a: 146)

Throughout the seventeenth century women are found participating in bread and grain riots and tax revolts, protesting against enclosure and taking an active part in London's 'mob'. Nor were their activities confined to these protests: they petitioned Parliament on such diverse matters as the decline of trade and the civil war;[14] as members of the sects they preached, prophesied, wrote, and published, travelling extensively to testify to their faith (see Evans, Cheevers, and Vokins in this volume) and often coming into conflict with the law as a result of these activities. Constrained by the law and by social expectation within their marriages, many chose to travel with women friends (Vokins) or alone (Trapnel), and to do so with defiance rather than compliance: as Trapnel says, when confirming in court that she is not married, 'having no hindrance, why may not I go where I please?' (p. 81). Nor were the popular images of women suggestive of meekness or subservience: even the 'negative' ones of the scold, the husband-beater, or the lascivious widow indicate the threat men felt was posed by women who did not comply with the idealized image. Moreover, research into popular festivals has shown that in some places women had their own festival day, at Hocktide, when 'they blocked the streets and bound male passers-by', and even their own fair (Reay 1985a:11; see also Davis 1975a; 1975b). Far from being the unquestioningly deferent, passive, and silent creatures praised in the conduct books, women consistently challenged many elements of the status quo.

Implicit in this diversity of challenges is a recognition that 'women' in the seventeenth century no more formed a homogeneous group than they do now: women active in the London mob, for example, would not have been of the Duchess of Newcastle's class. Such material differences are important not only as evidence that such challenges were not the preserve of only one class, but also because of the implications that they had for the circumstances under which women wrote, matters of literacy, and the reception of their writings.

Literacy rates are extremely difficult to determine. 'Literacy' is taken as the capacity to sign one's name, a skill that could be, and often was, taught separately from other writing skills. Reading, too, was taught separately, prior to writing, so that although it is likely that the capacity to read was more widespread than that to write (since many would have ceased being educated before the teaching of the second skill (Spufford 1979: 412)) it is difficult to estimate the relationship between the two. Moreover, although class differences tend to be taken into account in discussions of male literacy, women are often grouped together without this consideration. Various estimates of women's literacy have, however, been made. Barry Reay suggests that 10 per cent of women and 30 per cent of men could sign their names at the time of the civil war (1985: 4), and Spufford cites figures that concur with this estimate:

> Between 1580 and 1700, 11 per cent of women, 15 per cent of labourers and 21 per cent of husbandmen could sign their names, against 56 per cent of tradesmen and craftsmen and 65 per cent of yeomen.
>
> (Spufford 1979: 409)

Presumably this 11 per cent would divide into similar proportions along class lines as for the men: the higher the social class, the greater the likelihood that women could sign their names. Demographic differences, too, were significant: Cressy suggests that even in the 'relatively advanced dioceses of Norwich and Exeter', more than four-fifths of the women sampled were unable to sign their names, whilst in London the illiteracy rate for women deponents dropped from 78 per cent in the 1670s to 52 per cent in the 1690s (Cressy 1980: 128, 147). He suggests that, in general, relatively rapid advances in literacy were made towards the end of the century:

> By the time of the accession of George I it is likely that the inability to sign was confined to 55 per cent of the men and 75 per cent of the women. This compared to 70 per cent illiteracy among men and 90 per cent among women at the time of the civil war.
>
> (Cressy 1980: 176)

Nor are class and literacy rates the only variables that have to be taken into account in attempting to situate women's lives and activities: the social, political, and religious climate in the seventeenth century was also notoriously changeable. The civil war, the protectorate and commonwealth, the emergence and influence, if only temporarily, of the radical sects, and the restoration of Charles II all marked out and contributed to a series of profound changes in this climate.

The implications and radical nature of the changes and challenges that accompanied the civil war and its immediate aftermath are hard to overestimate. Here too social class was important, as one of the factors determining allegiance to the king or to parliament. Richard Baxter analysed these divisions:

> A very great part of the knights and gentlemen . . . adhered to the King . . . Most of the tenants of these gentlemen, and also most of the poorest of the people, whom the other called the rabble, did follow the gentry and were for the King. On the Parliament's side were the smaller part (as some thought) of the gentry in most of the counties, and the greatest part of the tradesmen and freeholders and the middle sort of men, especially in those corporations and counties which depend on clothing and such manufactures.
>
> (quoted in Hill 1961: 105)

The general social distinctions between the factions, he suggests, are clear: the 'middle sort of men' and, according to other contemporary commentators, 'very many of the peasantry' (Hill 1961: 105) were aligned with Parliament against the royalist gentry and those dependent on them, their tenants and retainers.

Even a bare outline of some of the political events of these years can give an idea of the impact they had. The 1640s saw the demise of the Star Chamber, the Court of High Commission, the Councils of Wales and of the North, episcopacy, the church courts, the House of Lords, and censorship, and the executions of the Earl of Strafford, the Archibishop of Canterbury, and the King. New administrative bodies included the county committees, which had the power to call 'errant ministers and politically suspect landlords' before them, and to deprive them of their parishes and lands. The testimonies of women, artisans, and labourers before these committees, concerning the competence and political respectability of their hitherto superiors, were now permissible. Tithes were never abolished, but many people just stopped paying them. There were enclosure riots in at least twenty-six counties between 1640 and 1644. 'Popular agitation forced the pace of the English Revolution' (Reay 1984a: 4–5, 6).

This contributed to an atmosphere in which the radical religious sects could flourish and gain influence. Although some separatist groups had their origins much earlier, it was not until the 1640s that they began to proliferate:

> With only a handful of separatist churches, and perhaps a population of 1,000 separatists in 1641, London could by 1646 boast thirty-six gathered churches; while by 1670 London Quakers alone possibly numbered between 8,000 and 10,000.
>
> (Reay 1984a: 12)

Despite the large number of sects that developed, they did have a number of concerns in common. The most important of these was an emphasis on the immediate contact of the individual believer with the divine, unmediated by any priest. Along with this went a modification or rejection of the distinction between laymen (and sometimes laywomen) and clergymen, and rejection of the notion of a national church, and thus also entailed hostility to tithes, which paid the stipends of the clergy of the Church of England. The sects do, however, have separate histories and a number of significant differences between them, which it is also important to appreciate if many of the nuances of the autobiographical writings included here are not to be lost.

The first Independent congregation is generally credited as that established by Henry Jacob in London in 1616, although other separatist congregations had existed since the reign of Elizabeth. 'Independency' was a loosely applied, generic name under which a number of different separatist congregations were grouped, but this term did not so much indicate a federation as serve as a catch-all for a collection of splinter groups, with different and sometimes opposing priorities, interpretations, and emphases. In common with each other, though, were their arguments that the state should have no power in ecclesiastical matters, and that each congregation should be separate, managing its own affairs without the interference of external, national ecclesiastical bodies. Their stress on the spiritual equality of all allowed some women to debate these issues in print and sometimes to preach.

The General and the Particular Baptists have, despite their similar names, quite distinct origins and histories. The General Baptists originated from exiled separatist groups in Holland; they believed that Christ died for all, not just an elect. More numerous were the Particular Baptists, who arose from splits within an Independent church in the 1630s, and held a Calvinistic belief in restricted atonement: only the elect, foreordained by God, would be saved. Generally, both groups were opposed to infant baptism, believing the only true baptism was through immersion, freely chosen by the individual. Congregations were still self-governing, so that it is difficult to generalize on such matters as their attitudes to women preachers and writers.

The Fifth Monarchist movement had its origins in the millenarian ideas circulating in the 1640s, predicting the imminent second coming of Christ and the establishing of the New Jerusalem on earth, or, more precisely, in England. Most importantly, it involved a notion of the centrality of prophecy, the reading and interpreting of the scriptures as a guide to the understanding of current and future events. When these two elements came together, and the prophecies of people such as Anna Trapnel and Vavasor Powell, both Fifth Monarchists, interpreted the scriptures in relation to current political events, it becomes clear why they were experienced as so threatening. The movement began to gain momentum in 1651, when a number of prominent Baptists and Independents drew up a list of objectives and beliefs. They argued for non-hierarchical organization amongst the saints – God's elect – and took as a basis for action a literal interpretation of the prophecies of Daniel and Revelation. This entailed not only the belief in the imminent arrival of King Jesus, but also that it was the duty of the saints to eliminate any hindrances to this, using physical force if necessary. This sanctioning of the use of violence (rather than any actual manifestations of violence) also contributed to the widespread alarm and opposition to the movement. They were at their most influential in 1653, when there were a number of Fifth Monarchist sympathisers in the Barebones Parliament (see pp. 71, 73). After its dissolution at the end of that year they continued to voice their opposition to Cromwell and the Protectorate, but after two unsuccessful uprisings in 1657 and 1661, the movement declined and had disappeared by the end of the century.

The Quakers originated in the north of England in the early 1650s. By 1656 they had moved south and gained in numbers and influence, particularly in Wales, Gloucestershire, and Cornwall. They came together principally from the New Model Army and from other radical groups such as the Ranters and Baptists. It was only after 1660 that the movement took a quietist and pacifist stance, before this being one of the most radical and outspoken groups. They argued against tithes, the supremacy of the clergy, and the restoration of the monarchy, as well as refusing 'hat honour'[15] and insisting on using 'thou' (rather than the more respectful 'you') to all, irrespective of their position in the social hierarchy. They relied on the 'inner light' of God within them as their ultimate guide, above even the scriptures, and this enabled women to justify their writing, prophesying, and travelling, despite the disapproval and hostility of many men. Unlike most of the other sects, the Quakers survived the restoration and the persecution that followed it, albeit in a more restrictive and conservative spirit: the autobiography of Joan Vokins, included here, shows much greater concern with the internal workings of the movement and its ability to retain its members than Quaker women's writings from before 1660, when there was a much greater tendency to debate such matters as tithes, the clergy, and the irrelevance of the universities.

The delineation between sects, however, was not as clear-cut as these outlines may suggest. People moved from one to another, seeking the surest way to experience God's grace; sects split and reformed and changed direction – George Fox, one of the leading Quakers, described many Friends' groups as originating from 'shattered Baptist communities' (see Whiting 1931: 88); groupings merged or crossed over until it is hard to differentiate between them: the Fifth Monarchists, for example, were largely drawn from Baptist and Independent congregations, and never really separated from them, often continuing to meet within their existing churches. This flux and fluidity evidently confused people at the time too: it perhaps accounts for Anna Trapnel being labelled 'a Quaker' in the print included here (p. 72).

These sects and groupings were notable, to a greater or lesser degree, for the numbers of women active within them. Bernard Capp, in his book, misleadingly titled The Fifth Monarchy Men, notes that 'in the church lists which have survived, women easily outnumbered men' (Capp 1972: 82); more than 7,000 women put their names to a Quaker petition against tithes presented to Parliament in 1659 (Forster 1659: 1); and it seems that high numbers of women were common in other sects as well, commentators often noting that they were made up of 'chiefly women' or 'most silly women' (Thomas 1958: 45). Nor was women's involvement in religious dissent something entirely new; there are numerous instances of women in the fifteenth and sixteenth centuries being brought to trial for their religious activities (Thomson 1965). The innovatory aspect, therefore, was not that women were involved in the sects, but the scale of that involvement.[16]

The significance of the sects for women, though, does not lie only in the numbers involved; it is the nature and implications of their activities that need to be stressed, for their concerns were not narrowly 'scriptural' in the way the word might be understood today. Their concern with religion was also a concern with politics, with the present and future state of England. The link between politics and religion was not simply metaphorical, but the two coincided in a much more fundamental way, in their common concern with how men and women should live in relation to each other, God, and the civil authorities, all of which were in a hierarchical relationship with each other but whose internal structures of authority and subservience were also seen to mirror each other. The family was a 'little church' or 'little state'; Calvin saw the subjection of the wife to the husband as a guarantee of the subjection of both of them to God (Haller 1941–2: 250; Davis 1975a: 128): the power of God, the King, and the husband were understood to reflect and thereby to reinforce each other. Religion, then, was inescapably at the heart of the revolution, for all the parties involved, in one interpretation or another: it was 'both the legitimising ideology of the rulers and . . . the revolutionary idiom of the ruled' (Reay 1984a: 3). To challenge the structures and hierarchies of established religion was to strike at the foundation of the social and political hierarchies of the time, as contemporary commentators such as Thomas Edwards were well aware: 'if a toleration [of the sects] were granted', he said, '[men] should never have peace in their families more, or ever after have command of wives, children, servants' (Hill 1972: 310–11). Anna Trapnel, then, was rather stating a commonplace than exaggerating when she said that 'one depends upon the other, rulers upon clergy, and clergy upon rulers' (see p. 77). By playing such a significant part in the sects, women were not only entering public debates in significant numbers for the first time, but they were entering debates that were concerned with the fundamental structures and destiny of British social and political life.

'Myself I sought to know': definitions of autobiography and the self

It is clear from the shared features of many of the texts included in this collection that a motivation for the women who wrote them was to make the truth about themselves known. And repeatedly we find the texts have been entitled (whether by the women themselves or by their original editors) a 'true relation', 'a vindication', a 'plea', or a 'record', all of which suggest factuality or a demand to be believed. With different degrees of explicitness, these women wrote and were perceived by their contemporaries as writing, with the intention of speaking themselves in order to make that self heard and known. This intention coincides with a modern sense of what autobiography is. The etymology of the word and everyday usage suggest that it can be defined as a life of the self who is writing (hence our title, *Her Own Life*, taken from the words of Margaret Cavendish).

But although it may be clear that autobiography takes its form from an articulation of the self, definitions of autobiography are, in fact, notoriously hard to draw up. Many of the implicit concepts on which innocent-seeming definitions depend prove tricky when they come under scrutiny. The question of 'truth', so vigorously asserted by many of the women whose writings are included here, can be problematic to the modern reader. Then, the concepts of a 'self' and a 'life' also present difficulties. Do we assume a fully constructed self who pre-exists the autobiography, who then expresses that self in writing? Or is that self constructed in the process of writing? What is the nature of the 'life' we expect to find in this sort of writing? And what is the relation of a 'self' to a 'life'? Clearly, to insist too simply that autobiography is the narration of a life is to fall into the dangers of 'that notion's facile presumption of referentiality', as Domna C. Stanton puts it (Stanton 1987: vii).

Now that autobiography is beginning to be much written about as well as read[17] (in the seventeenth century the most famous and popular autobiographies were sometimes 'literally read to pieces' (Bunyan's autobiography, see Webber 1968: 271) and today autobiography has a large and keen readership) these problems have increasingly demanded consideration. One of the areas in which autobiography has attracted much attention, for instance, is as an historical source, useful in giving insight into lives and ways of thinking that is not to be found from official documentation or public records.[18] Part of our impulse in making this collection of seventeenth-century women's autobiographies is, indeed, connected with this urge to recover women's experience and sense of themselves. But as all the texts in this collection reveal, a transparent account of experience cannot be found in autobiography. Obviously it is necessary to make choices and therefore exclusions in writing a life, so the act of writing involves a patterning and thus an interpretation.[19] More than this, though, experience and the relation of experience cannot be easily separated. We all tell the story of ourselves all the time and this is part of the experience of life, not simply a secondary reflection of it. The experience of living a life also involves inhabiting a structure of meanings and feelings which is culturally as well as personally specific.[20] It would be difficult to read many of the texts here out of the context of meanings which informed the lives of seventeenth-century women.

To read, for instance, Evans and Cheevers's account of imprisonment in the Inquisition in Malta for factual, documentary evidence would leave us baffled. Or to read it merely in twentieth-century, secularized terms without some understanding of Quaker belief and practice would leave us with a sense that it was merely bizarre and that Evans and Cheevers were dotty. A text such as this not only reminds us of the dangers of anachronism, but (as in the story of Mary Carleton where conventions of meaning in romance were exploited with material effect) it illustrates, too, how a struggle over meaning can be part of an actual, material struggle. When Katharine Evans is apparently dying because she refuses to accept food from her gaolors, her willingness to die is an act of resistance in itself, but there is a contest, too, over the meaning of death. What death signifies becomes a struggle taken up between Sarah Cheevers and the friar, arguing over the weak, almost dying body of Katharine Evans (p. 122). The autobiography, as a whole, is part of an attempt to make their meanings 'stick'.[21]

The system of meanings – linguistic, doctrinal, social, even literary – that these accounts reveal is often, then, as much part of the texture of experience as an effect of writing. Although, obviously, written forms are determined by the conventions of writing which are used and by the purpose to which the text is to be put, absolute distinctions between lived experience and a written articulation of the self are hard to maintain, especially when, as is the case with most of our texts, the act of writing was an act expected and designed to have an effect in the world. Sometimes this effect is the offering of a life story as an example or as something to be interpreted, as is the case with the conversion narratives (which are sometimes referred to as 'hermeneutic autobiographies') of Hannah Allen, Sarah Davy, and Joan Vokins. Sometimes the effect involves a setting right of the record as in Alice Thornton's defence of her reputation, Margaret Cavendish's assertion of her identity, or Anne Wentworth's vindication of her decision to leave her husband. Yet this begins to imply that all constructions of a 'self' are in some sense 'fictional'.[22] There are hazards in collapsing our categories of life and text too far. To see lives simply as texts is to deny the actuality of lives lived. After all, Mary Carleton was, in the end, executed; Alice Thornton did give birth to nine children, only three of whom survived to adulthood.

Many of these questions concerning how we understand the relation of lives and writing in autobiography depend on a concept of the 'self'. All the texts included in the collection not only take the writer herself as subject matter, but imply, or more often, directly address a reader. Twentieth-century readers can easily share the sense these seventeenth-century women had of the necessity of an audience if a self is to be articulated. Many current descriptions of the construction of the self work with this sort of notion. For instance, the French psychoanalyst, Jacques Lacan, whose theoretical writing has had a strong influence on one strand of recent thinking about literature, gender, and sexuality, summarized the way psychotherapy works: 'The subject begins the analysis by talking about himself [sic] without talking to you, or by talking to you without talking about himself. When he can talk to you about himself, the analysis will be over' (Lacan 1966: 373; trans. Wilden 1972: 21). It is necessary, Lacan is suggesting here, for all of us, if we are to have full subjectivity, to be able to produce ourselves as the content of our utterances – to be our own subject matter. But what we say of ourselves must also be understood by someone; we cannot be considered to be speaking ourselves if we are speaking into a void or meeting incomprehension. We need to construct ourselves in relation to others. This involves arriving at agreement over meanings – both referential and emotional – that can be shared. We are, then, deeply implicated in culture, since it is in the symbolic systems of culture and specifically in language, that meanings are negotiated and made available. Lacan's remarks depend on an assumption that language always takes the form of dialogue and that the 'self' is best understood as a 'subject' who is determined by the cultural systems she or he is born into, and so is subject to them. But the subject is also in control of and able to create meaning and is the source point for meanings (like the grammatical subject of a sentence, on which the sentence's meaning is predicated). Without a subject, symbolic discourses, and therefore human society, could not exist any more than a subject can exist outside symbolic systems. Lacan's description of the psychoanalytic process can usefully be applied not only to the way that our constant self-articulations in everyday life function, but more specifically here to autobiography since this is clearly a form that takes its shape from precisely this speaking of a self and speaking to others. The non-recognition of women as full legal subjects in the seventeenth century perhaps gives a particular significance and urgency to women writing the self and being recognized.

So, since Lacan's account does not depend on a concept of an absolute and fixed identity which can be revealed to a greater or lesser extent, but implies instead a sense of full subjectivity that depends on negotiation of relationship and symbolic systems, it is perhaps an attractive model when we try to disentangle issues of 'self', 'life', and 'writing'. But it might also bring us back, yet again, to problems of the relegation or denial of the material.[23] In some recent American (and British) writing a more conventional sense of 'self' has been reasserted and developed. Theorists such as Kohut, Hartmann, Modell, and Kernberg define their concept of the 'self' by distinguishing it from the ego (a psychic element or agent which gives a sense of 'I' or 'me'). For them, the self is 'the whole person of an individual, including his [sic] body and body parts as well as his psychic organization and its parts',[24] so it is 'a content of the mental apparatus but not one of its constituents, i.e., not one of the agencies of the mind' (Kohut 1971 in Layton and Schapiro 1986: 2). 'Self' theorists concentrate on the need each of us has to become individuated and to recognize others as separate. In the life of any individual, formation of a sense of self and its resilience later on, depends on early negotiations of self defined against and in relation to others, where the 'other' takes the form of an object of various emotions. Many of these theorists work with a strong sense of external reality distinct from the psychic reality of the individual and tend to see society and culture as a product of the aggregated personalities of individuals. For many of them, creativity, especially writing, performs the function of restoring or re-creating a sense of self and re-negotiating self–object relations. Although this sort of thinking does not account for the interdependence of cultural systems and the 'self' with the same precision as in Lacanian theory, the idea of writing as a re-creation of the self and its objects can easily be related to the writing of autobiography where this is quite explicit.

Questions such as these about how to perceive a 'self' or subject in relation to the text that articulates it, are presented in another way when focusing on women's articulations of themselves. In collecting together texts written by women we assume that these writers *do* have a gendered identity that precedes the act of writing and is central to their experience. Such a notion of the gendered self that is not merely a product of the text seems crucial.[25] But even here it has to be remembered that not only were women's writings in the seventeenth century often written according to models developed in dominant and therefore masculine traditions but were quite materially affected by the interventions of male editors and publishers.

Attempts to define autobiography by establishing a history of it as a literary genre have also raised problems about how the self in autobiography is constructed. Very often such histories have omitted women's autobiographies.[26] And those attempts to elaborate a theory

20

of what distinguishes women's from men's autobiographies seem, so far, to offer only partial or inadequate accounts. The suggestion that women's autobiographies are typified by presentations of the self defined in relation to others depends on an implausible idea that men's do not, or implies that women have a more reactive and consciously relational sense of self than men (Mason 1980). This may often be true, but cannot be taken as a general statement. Nor can the notion that women 'write in discontinuous forms and . . . emphasize the personal over the professional' (Jelinek 1980: xii). The variety of 'selves' presented in this collection alone suggests that these ways of differentiating women's and men's writing are too schematic. In general, there is no single pattern in the way selves are articulated. Perhaps the most common structure we expect to find today is a linear one, beginning with childhood and following a life through change and development. This structure is one that becomes particularly influential from the seventeenth century onwards, but it is by no means the only one. Autobiographies, written then or now, can vary enormously in pattern, in focusing on a wide sweep of experience or on a single issue, and in the degree to which introspection or attention to activity in the world is important. Autobiography is certainly revealed by the texts included here as a diverse, complicated, and sophisticated form.

In the end, autobiography is perhaps fascinating not because it can be *explained* by any of the available theories, psychological, historical, or literary, but because it *raises* questions about 'self', writing, 'experience', and literary convention with particular intensity. But there are other, maybe less esoteric, pleasures that attract us to autobiography, too. Reading seventeenth-century autobiography allows us the pleasure of access to a historically different world in an intimate way. There are pleasures that come out of identification or of empathy with others' sense of life, and also those of recognizing difference between the personalities, the social and cultural environments of their writers, and between the seventeenth century and now. For in these seventeenth-century texts we find much that is strange and demands efforts of understanding and imagination. But we find, too, many concerns that we share. We recognize our own inheritance in the writings of these seventeenth-century women.

'My condition is unparalleled' distinctions and connections

When reading the autobiographical work of the seventeenth-century

21

women included in this anthology, the initial impression is probably of enormous differences between them. 'My condition is unparalleled', writes Hannah Allen (p. 203), and it could be said that each woman writes her own story precisely because she is unique or, as Margaret Cavendish puts it, 'singular' (p. 96). The autobiographical forms chosen cover a wide range, from unpolished diary to crafted verse, from unstructured memoir to tailored romance. Even those women who write the rather more familiar narrative of conversion express their spiritual histories through personal defence, or meditation, or accounts of journeys, trials, and imprisonment. Perhaps this spectrum of forms is not surprising, since the women were experimenting with modes of expression for their own selves and circumstances, which comprised a variety of types and situations. In terms of spiritual allegiance, the writers in this collection span the Church of England through shades of non-conformity to the Quakers; in social class they range from the Countess of Dorset, Pembroke, and Montgomery (all in the person of Anne Clifford) to the shipwright's daughter from Poplar, Anna Trapnel. Margaret Cavendish, Duchess of Newcastle, writes contemptuously of the 'barbarous people' who destroyed her family home in the civil war (p. 92); those 'people' by allegiance would have included most of the other women in this anthology. On the subject of women they are further divided in ways typical of the seventeenth century. Evans and Cheevers clearly derive great strength from their friendship in adversity, and Sarah Davy enjoys an apparently lesbian relationship with her converter. However, these women do not escape the proverbial and stereotyped judgments of their own sex. Susanna Parr, in defending herself, pleads 'the natural and sinful infirmities' of her sex (p. 108), and Anna Trapnel turns the proverb lore ironically on her enemies when she accuses them of being 'like women, all speakers and no hearers' (p. 81).

What, then, do these texts have in common which makes it sensible and stimulating to put them together? In contrast to our previous perception of each woman's uniqueness, we may set the powerful impression that these women wrote autobiographically because they in fact felt similar to others, particularly their readers whom they could advise, admonish, or inspire. This approach to autobiography leads the writer towards the influence and safety of shared experience, biblical precedent, literary models, and spiritual example. There are, however, three further common features among the autobiographies in this collection which may be usefully considered here. First, regardless of differences of forms and personal viewpoint, they share a particular female perspective on experience and self-expression. For although the individual women may indeed be 'unparalleled', they are for the most part only able to define themselves by reference to the overpowering expectations and assumptions of womanhood made by seventeenth-century society. As in later women's autobiography, it often involves comparison with (and praise of) their own mothers, but the maternal is only one of a multiplicity of images of virtuous femininity against which the subject must measure herself. Susanna Parr's statement that she will 'compare [her] own heart with the rule' (p. 108) is revealing of an implicit comparison which is at the centre of all these texts. Fundamental, also, is an experience of some kind of oppression: in marriage, such as the 'unspeakable tyrannies' of Anne Wentworth's 'hard-hearted yoke-fellow' (p. 183); confinement in repeated childbirth (Alice Thornton), or in prison (Trapnel, Evans, and Cheevers); restriction of freedom through religious dogma (Susanna Parr); sufferings from chronic illness or depression (An Collins, Sarah Davy, Hannah Allen). The writing of autobiography may well be related to such a 'despairing condition' (Allen, p. 201) and the paradoxical 'labour' described by Sarah Davy, while writing about her misery, 'to keep my troubles to myself' (p. 172).

It would be wrong, however, to imply that the female perspective is a consistently gloomy one; the defiance and delights of these women are expressed in both small and large ways. The detail of clothes, for example, is emblematic of individuality at crucial moments in the texts of Anne Clifford, Mary Carleton, and Margaret Cavendish. At the opposite extreme, a number of the autobiographies are written in the aftermath of kinds of escape: for Joan Vokins by conversion to the Quaker faith, for Anne Wentworth by the rejection of her husband in favour of her 'heavenly bridegroom' (p. 187). Above all, despite much self-doubt and humility (themselves elements of the conventionally female), these women wrote 'their own lives' and in many cases published them, against the backdrop of a hostile world in which, as Cavendish feared, 'none cares to know' who these women were and what they did (pp. 98–99).

The autobiographical texts in themselves celebrate the existence of their subjects – I write myself, therefore I am – and the second major common feature is a high level of awareness of the actual writing process. Anne Wentworth finally broke with her husband because he threatened to destroy her writings and thus, by implication, her independent self; Susanna Parr paradoxically used the freedom of the written word in order to deny that right to women generally; Margaret Cavendish animatedly describes the process of assembling her 'ragged rout' of words into presentable marching order (p. 94). Nor is the writing of these autobiographies by any means a simple or spontaneous affair; the texts grow from carefully kept journals (Alice Thornton), commonplace books (Anna Trapnel), and letters (Mary Carleton, Joan Vokins). Their evolution and textuality are complex, and may be most clearly seen in the light of the varied inter-connections with other texts – these earlier versions by their own authors, the rumours and counter-stories which surround their subjects (extending to records of court proceedings and popular ballads in Carleton's case), and most crucially the bible, which intersects with the language and experience of the majority of these autobiographies. Here intertextuality extends beyond written creativity to a kind of personal relationship; to speak the word of the bible is to identify with the experience of the Jews and, as Vokins put it, share in the 'sweet refreshing life' that Christ 'communicates' to the individual (p. 212).

It may well seem to the modern reader that these autobiographies, despite their vivid female perspective and informing sensitivity to the issue of writing, are remarkably silent on many aspects of women's lives. 'I don't delight to stir in such puddles', writes Anna Trapnel (p. 77), speaking as it were for all of them in their reluctance to discuss, for instance, personal emotion and psychological depths. This probably has less to do with any notable differences between seventeenth-century women and ourselves, than with their moti-vation for writing autobiography. Anna Trapnel goes on to say that 'truth engageth me to let the world know' the facts of her experience (p. 77).

A frequently avowed concern with the truth is the third major unifying factor among these texts: their purpose is, as Margaret Cavendish puts it, 'not to please the fancy, but to tell the truth' (p. 99). This 'truth' often stems from an almost legalist desire for self-defence; there is invariably an existing 'text' to be answered or corrected, as the titles of Anna Trapnel's *Plea*, Anne Wentworth's *Vindication*, and Susanna Parr's *Apology* indicate. In other instances, the concern with truth is more ambivalently bound up with imagin-ation. An Collins sets her own 'truth' against the perceived 'unskil-fulness' of her verse (p. 57), while Mary Carleton's evident skill in romance writing complicates the notion of historical truth put forward by her text. There is clearly a rhetoric of truthfulness which is fundamental to autobiographical writing, but these works are unusually dominated by the need to persuade the self and the reader towards belief in kinds of truth – personal, experiential, doctrinal. This may well result from the fact that the women themselves experience, and resist, persuasion: the pressures from king and husband on Anne Clifford, the requiring of Susanna Parr to speak against her will, the tormenting of those in prison, the compelling 'long persuasions' of Hannah Allen by her aunt and Mr Shorthose (p. 208). All three unifying features are themselves united here. The particularly female experience of vulnerability to persuasion leads to a defensive desire for accuracy of reputation – the commodity of truth – a desire heightened by the women's awareness of their own textuality.

The circles of truth and fiction, self and self-image, experience and expression, simultaneously trap and release these seventeenth-century women. This is most evident in the endings of the autobiographies. Margaret Cavendish, for example, defines her own individuality in the last sentences of her memoir, but can only do so by reference to her father and husband – self-expression and patriarchy ironically converge. Others have more practical escape routes from their texts. Anna Trapnel ends the section of her work anthologized here by praying for her enemies (who may also be her readers); as Hannah Allen concludes she shares with more sympathetic readers the most 'comfortable' quotations she has found to sustain her in suffering (p. 209). Though each woman is, strictly speaking, 'unparalleled', their autobiographical writing reaches out for community with readers both then and now.

Notes

1 For studies of some of these texts, see Pomerleau 1980; Mason 1980; Mendelson 1985.

2 *The Autobiographies of Lady Anne Halkett and Lady Ann Fanshawe*, ed. John Loftis (Oxford 1979). Many manuscripts written by women from wealthy backgrounds have been printed in more recent times. These include Penington 1821; Mordaunt 1856; Rich 1847; 1848.

3 Lady Lucy Knatchbull was a Catholic nun. Parts of her narrative are contained in *The Life of Lady Lucy Knatchbull* (Knatchbull 1931). Cellier (1680) describes her own conversion to Catholicism and her visiting of Catholic prisoners in the late 1670s, leading up to the accusations of the Meal-Tub Plot. Dorothy Waugh's 'A relation' (1656) contains her description of her arrest and sentencing to the scold's bridle and whipping. Biddle (1682) and Blackborow (1660) both describe their adoption of Quakerism and their subsequent imprisonment.

4 Dorothy Osborne (1987) gives her views on courtship, marriage, and female independence. Constance Fowler's letters to her brother (Fowler 1815) record her loving feelings towards another woman, whom she conjures her brother to marry. Rachel Wriothesley, Lady Russell's letters concerning parliamentary gossip of the period 1672–82 were published in 1853, and Dorothy Sidney, Countess of Sunderland's letters about politics and affairs of

state in 1680 appeared in 1819. Margaret Cavendish's letters to her future husband William have also survived, published 1965.

5 The press was controlled through the strict licensing of the Stationers' Company, which limited the total number of printing presses and required texts to be registered before publication. Although this system never entirely prevented publication by those critical of the government, the outbreak of civil war in the early 1640s made a radical difference in terms of access to the press. See Plant 1965; Cranfield 1978; Siebert 1952.

6 Various women allude to the miseries of married life, including Mordaunt (1856) and Rich (1847; 1848). It appears though that Wentworth is unique in the symbolic interpretation she gives to such unhappiness.

7 Patricia Caldwell (1983) makes a related point, suggesting that women's conversion narratives such as Elizabeth White's *The Experiences* (1696) can be read as 'a female parable, an extended metaphor derived from the universal experiences of women's lives' (p. 8).

8 See also the *ms.* diary kept by a relative of Oliver Cromwell's, made as a 'help to memory' of God's goodness to her (British Library Add. Ms. 5858, ff. 213–21).

9 See also the circumstances of publication of Bell 1673; White 1696; Moore 1657; and the many collections of Quaker deathbed testimonies to deceased Friends. Although in other ways it does not conform to the conversion narrative format, a similar motivation is also claimed as justification for the posthumous publishing of Joan Vokins's *God's Mighty Power Magnified* (1691).

10 See Hobby 1988 for a survey of women's writing in the period; Greer *et al.* 1988 for a collection of seventeenth-century women's poetry; Morgan 1981 for plays, and various anthologies of Aphra Behn's writings, notably Behn 1989; Ferguson 1985 for some seventeenth-century polemics.

11 The body was understood to be composed of four humours or fluids (blood, phlegm, black bile (or melancholy), and yellow bile (or choler)); the variant mixture of these determined people's characters. Men and women were thought to have different combinations and proportions of these humours, which accounted for their different 'natures'.

12 Thomas Becon, from his 'Catechism' in *Worckes* (1564), quoted in Powell 1917: 156.

13 Juan Luis Vives, from his *Instruction of a Christian Woman* (first published in Latin 1523, and in translation by Richard Hyrde in c.1540), in Watson 1912: 34.

14 For more information about women petitioners, see for example, McArthur 1909 and Higgins 1973.

15 Taking off the hat in the presence of a social superior.

16 Although this too must be kept in perspective: Reay (1984a: 111) suggests that 'committed protestantism never captured the nation, and even at its peak organized dissent attracted only 6 per cent of the population'.

17 See, as examples of influential full-length studies or collections of articles: Weintraub 1978; Jelinek 1980; Olney 1980; Spengemann 1981; Stone 1982; Stanton 1987. There have also been several special editions of academic journals devoted to autobiography, including: *Genre* 1973, vol. VI, nos 1 and 2; *Modern Language Notes* 1978; *Prose Studies* September 1985, vol. 8 no.2; *Literature and History* Spring 1988, vol. 14, no. 1.

18 See, for instance, Pollock 1983 and Pollock 1987. These are interesting examples of how autobiography has been used to draw up a picture of parent–child relationships from 1500 to 1900.

19 Stanley 1988 argues that we all produce autobiography all the time in our everyday conversations. Written autobiographies only differ from this in that 'what appears in writing is very much simpler'. Her implicit points about selection and organization and the relation of literary autobiography to 'life' are interesting, but this remark underplays the complexity of written forms.

20 The phrase 'structures of feeling' is used throughout Raymond Williams's work. It is particularly important in Williams 1977, section II, ch. 9 where he defines his sense of the relationship between social and institutional change and the personal: 'we are concerned

with meanings and values as they are actively lived or felt' (p. 132). The idea that structures of meaning operate at both personal and wider cultural levels, informing the individual consciousness and unconsciousness as well as the social, which is central to much recent literary and cultural theory, is neatly summarized in Culler 1974: xiii.

21 See Thompson 1984: 132 and Cameron 1986: 84 on making meanings 'stick' in general. See Bauman 1983 for a fascinating analysis of seventeenth-century Quaker langauge theories and practices as social acts.

22 See Dodd 1987 on fictiveness and non-fiction. The dangers of seeing everything as textual can be inferred from worrying statements such as: 'the bases for historical knowledge are not empirical facts but written texts, even if these texts masquerade in the guise of wars or revolutions' (de Man 1983: 165). For a discussion of these issues see Louvre 1987.

23 This implication has often been drawn from Lacan's own writings and also from those influenced by him, such as Julia Kristeva. It is more pronounced in 'deconstructionist' and 'postmodern' theories, such as those of Derrida, Lyotard, and de Man.

24 Jacobson 1964: 6 summarizing the theories in Hartmann 1964. For a description of self-psychology and its relation to literature see Layton and Schapiro 1986.

25 Some theorists see a notion of masculine and feminine texts as more important than the gender of the writer, e.g. Kristeva 1974. To talk about 'women' is, of course, to raise issues about how gender is constructed and assigned. It is assumed here that 'woman' is a composite category – biological, psychic, cultural, and social.

26 There are no references to women in Mehlman 1971 and Spengemann 1980 and there are only single chapters in Olney 1980 and Stone 1982.

ENGLISH SEVENTEENTH-CENTURY CHRONOLOGY

Decade	National Life	Writing
1600	1603 Death of Queen Elizabeth Accession of James I	1604–5 *King Lear*
	1605 Gunpowder Plot	1605 Bacon, *The Advancement of Learning*
1610		1610 Jonson, *The Alchemist* 1611 *Authorized Version* 1616–17 Anne Clifford's *Diary*
	1618 Bacon Lord Chancellor Execution of Raleigh	
	Start of Thirty Years' War	
1620	1620 Pilgrim Fathers leave for America	
		1621 Burton, *Anatomy of Melancholy*
	1625 Accession of Charles I	
	Parliament dissolved	
1630	1633 Laud Archbishop of Canterbury	1633 Donne, *Poems* Herbert, *The Temple* (both posthumous)
	1636 Plague	
		1637 Milton, *Lycidas*
1640	1640–1 Long Parliament; fall of Strafford and Laud	
	1642–6 First Civil War, ending with surrender of Charles I to Scots	1642 Milton et al., *Apology for Smectymnuus*
		Browne, *Religio Medici*
		1643 Milton, *Doctrine and Discipline of Divorce*

	1648 Second Civil War	
	1649 Execution of Charles I	1649 Winstanley, *True Levellers' Standard*
	Commonwealth declared	
1650		1650 Marvell, *Horatian Ode*
		1651 Hobbes, *Leviathan*
	1652 'Pacification' of Ireland	
	1652–3 Dutch War	1653 An Collins, *Divine Songs and Meditations*
	1653 Cromwell declared Lord Protector	
		1654 *Anna Trapnel's Report and Plea*
		1656 Margaret Cavendish, *Nature's Pictures*
	1658 Death of Cromwell	
		1659 Susanna Parr, *Susanna's Apology*
1660	1660 Restoration of the Monarchy – accession of Charles II	
	1662 Act of Uniformity	1662 Katharine Evans and Sarah Cheevers, *A Short Relation of Cruel Sufferings*
		1663 Mary Carleton, *The Case of Madam Mary Carleton*
	1665–7 War with Holland	
	1665 Great Plague	
	1666 Fire of London	
		1667 Milton, *Paradise Lost*
		1668 Alice Thornton, *A Book of Remembrances*
1670		1670 Sarah Davy, *Heaven Realized*
	1672 Declaration of Indulgence	

1673 Test Act (withdrawal of
Declaration of Indulgence)

1677 A Vindication of Anne
Wentworth

1677 Aphra Behn, The Rover

1678 Bunyan, Pilgrim's Progress

1680

1681 Dryden, Absalom and
Achitophel

1683 Hannah Allen, Satan his
Methods and Malice Baffled

1685 Accession of James II

1688 Accession of William and Mary
after 'Glorious Revolution'

1690   1690 Battle of the Boyne
(end of James II's hopes)

1690 Locke, Essay Concerning
Human Understanding

1691 Joan Vokins, God's Mighty
Power Magnified

1694 Mary Astell, Serious Proposal
to the Ladies

1700 Congreve, Way of the World

EDITORIAL NOTE

The aim of this anthology is to make available to the modern reader substantial extracts from a range of autobiographical writing by seventeenth-century Englishwomen. The editorial principles by which we have worked in preparing the volume reflect this aim, in attempting to balance the integrity of the original texts with the requirements of their new readers.

The spelling and punctuation of all the extracts have been modernized, since to leave them unaltered would introduce a distancing impression of 'quaintness' for twentieth-century readers. However, we have attempted to maintain the original tone of the writings by keeping archaic spellings or grammatical forms in specific instances where modernization would have significantly changed the form or sound of the word (e.g., 'yea', 'hath'); similarly, we have not 'corrected' grammatical oddities. We have removed italics where these were used for proper names, reported speech, or quotation (using modern conventions of punctuation instead and supplying biblical references in parentheses), but italics have been kept where they imply stress or individuality of voice (as in the extracts from Sarah Davy and Anne Wentworth). Marginal notes in the originals have been transferred to the relevant point in the text, where they appear in parentheses. Dates have been normalized to follow the modern convention of the year beginning on 1 January, rather than 25 March. Notes are used to supply historical information, annotate particularly interesting biblical references, give explanatory glosses from contemporary writing or other works by the author, and to clarify seventeenth-century word meanings where appropriate.

Further details of editorial principles – for example, copytexts chosen, or decisions on modernization specific to a text – may be found in the textual notes which precede the work of each writer in the anthology.

Where we have found it helpful to cite seventeenth-century texts other than those anthologized here, we have modernized the quotations in keeping with the editorial principles outlined above. However, the original titles of such works have not been modernized, to facilitate further reference. Quotations from modern editions of seventeenth-century texts appear unaltered.

1

ANNE CLIFFORD

The Diary of Anne, Countess of Dorset, Pembroke and Montgomery, daughter and heiress of George Clifford, Earl of Cumberland, 1616–17

There are two surviving autobiographical texts of Lady Anne Clifford (1590–1676). The first is her assortment of day-by-day books, chronicles, memorials, and diaries, from which the following extracts are taken. The second is the 'Great Picture' which she commissioned in 1646 (see p. 36), a triptych which expresses the history of her family and her personal 'cause'. The centre panel depicts the members of her immediate family: her parents, the Earl and Countess of Cumberland (her mother, so present in the diary, stands nearer the centre than her father, who was often absent in her childhood), and her brothers, who died in infancy. In the side panels stands Anne Clifford herself: on the left, aged 15, in the year of her father's death (when she should have inherited the Clifford lands, which her father willed instead to her uncles); on the right, aged 56, contemporary with the painting of the triptych (the year in which she eventually succeeded to the land after the death of her uncles).

The picture is a statement of Anne Clifford's bold and tenacious belief (held over forty-one years, with some legal justification but against great odds) that she was, though female, the rightful heir to her family's estates in the north. This was clearly of greater significance to her than either of her two marriages, first to Richard Sackville, Earl of Dorset (the 'lord' who figures in the diary extracts) and, after his death, to Philip Herbert, Earl of Pembroke and Montgomery. The diminutive portraits of her two husbands hang behind Clifford in the right-hand panel of the triptych, almost as trophies of her past. She indeed spent much of her first marriage resisting the spend-thrift Dorset's wish to compromise with her uncles by renouncing her claim on the lands in return for a cash settlement; and when the defiant Clifford finally inherited her lands, she left her second husband and spent the rest of her life in her northern castles.

Lady Anne Clifford's *Great Picture*, the Clifford family triptych from Appleby Castle.

What strikes one first about both Anne Clifford's 'autobiographies' is the impression of strength of character – an individual woman holding out against the combined patriarchal forces of father, uncles, husbands, lawyers, churchmen, and even the king (as chronicled in the remarkable diary entries for January 1617). However, both texts are shot through with uncertainties, too. While the side panels of the painting show Clifford framing and containing her family, they also span those forty years of waiting upon the wills and judgments of others. The diary, perhaps written partly in order to explain and defend her stand, is fascinatingly complicated by vestigial loyalties to husband and to providence, and characterized by self-doubt as well as satisfaction, both intensified by isolation at Knole, the Sackville house in Kent.

Like most diaries, Anne Clifford's has the further ambivalence of self-expression in so modest and unpolished a form; fixing and interpreting the patterns of her own history (witness her interest in 'signs', anniversaries, and coincidences) yet suppressing the urge to self-analysis or contemplation (her description of herself as 'like an owl in the desert' on 12 May 1616 being a rare exception). The prevailing texture of her diary is juxtaposition which conceals links and ironies, as when on Easter Day 1617 she records how she and her husband had a 'falling out' soon after church, but adding, without comment, that she still wore her best white clothes throughout the day. At other points in the diary this mixing of items reveals, sometimes comically, the multi-faceted life of an aristocratic woman in early seventeenth-century England. In February 1617, for example, she comments in one entry on her daughter's nose-bleed and the king's speech in the Star Chamber; the next month she notes how the dog has 'puppied' while she herself has finished reading Exodus with her chaplain.

The following extracts from the diary for 1616 and 1617, when Clifford was 26 or 27 and married to the Earl of Dorset with one young daughter, are centrally concerned with two experiences: the death of her mother, and the prolonged dispute with Dorset over 'the business', an expressive euphemism for the legal wrangle which affected her personal and even sexual life (see 19–23 April 1617) so profoundly. As the entry for 29 May 1616 reveals, her mother's death also had a bearing on this matter; it was symbolically important to Clifford that her mother should be buried in the land which she herself was determined to inherit. A few years earlier, the poet Aemilia Lanyer had celebrated Anne and her mother as emblems of a virtuous female succession (Lanyer 1611), and solidarity among women is in fact an interesting feature of Clifford's diary. On 4 May 1616 she comments on the kindness of Lady Willoughby in 'the midst of all my misery', and the scenes at court in January 1617 indicate that Anne received secret support from the queen in her fight against the persuasions of king and husband. Both portrait and diary indicate also the significance of books in Anne Clifford's entertainment and self-definition;[1] experience and education together molded the powerful Clifford personality. As the sermon preached at her funeral finally asserted, Anne Clifford was consistent and unique: 'she was like herself in all things' (Rainbowe 1677: 53).

Note

1 Anne Clifford was surrounded by poets and their works: the side panels of the 'Great Picture' depict the books she was reading at the time of the two portraits, and include a miniature of her tutor, Samuel Daniel; the diary records her reading of Spenser and Sandys, among others, and the visit of Donne on 27 July 1617 after his Sunday morning sermon in Sevenoaks; during her second marriage, her personal chaplain at Wilton was George Herbert, whose *Temple* appears among the books in the later side panel of the triptych.

Textual note

The diary exists in an unpaginated manuscript at the Kent County Archives in Maidstone, not in its original form but in an eighteenth-century copy: MS Sackville of Knole U269/F48. The years 1603 and 1616–19 are recorded in this manuscript, which is characterized by a substantial number of marginal notes. Where these were clearly meant to be part of the original text, they appear in the main text below within square brackets. On the other hand, where they are in a different hand and supply information about people mentioned in the text, they appear among the notes. Annotation of other persons named in the diary has been kept to a minimum, in order not to clutter the text. The diminutive term 'coz.', often used in this period to refer to friends as well as family, is in fact employed by Clifford to refer to genuine relatives, and so has been consistently expanded to 'cousin'.

The diary was published in 1923 with an introductory essay by Vita Sackville-West; Anne Clifford's biography was written by George C. Williamson (Kendal, 1922; reprinted 1967).

---

from: The Diary of Lady Anne Clifford

February–May 1616

February 1616

Upon the 21st my lord and I began our journey northward;[1] the same day my Lord Willoughby came and broke his fast with my lord. We had 2 coaches in our company with 4 horses apiece and about 26 horsemen, I having no women to attend me but Willoughby and Judith, Thomas Glenham going with my lord.

Upon the 26th going from Lichfield to Croxall and about a mile from Croxall, my lord and I parted, he returning to Lichfield and I going into Derby. I came to my lodgings with a heavy heart, considering how many things stood between my lord and I. I had in my company 10 persons and 13 horses.

March 1616

Upon the 1st we went from the Parson's House near the dangerous moors, being eight miles; and afterwards the ways so dangerous the horses were fain to be taken out of the coach to be lifted down the hills. This day Rivers's horse fell from a bridge into the river. We came to Manchester about ten at night.[2]

Upon the 20th in the morning, my Lord William Howard with his son, my cousin William Howard,[3] and Mr John Dudley came hither to take the answer of my mother and myself, which was a direct denial to stand to the judges' award.[4] The same day came Sir Timothy Whittington hither, who did all he could do to mitigate the anger between my Lord William Howard and my mother; so as at last we parted all good friends, and it was agreed upon my men and horses should stay and we should go up to London together after Easter.

Upon the 22nd my lady and I went in a coach to Whinfell and rode about the park and saw all the woods.

[Upon the 24th my Lady of Somerset[5] was sent by water from Blackfriars as a prisoner to the Tower.]

Upon the 27th my cousin William Howard sent me a dapple grey nag for my own saddle.

Upon the 31st, being Easter Day, I received[6] with my mother in the chapel at Brougham.

April 1616

Upon the 1st came my cousin Charles Howard[7] and Mr John Dudley with letters to show that it was my lord's pleasure that the men and horses should come away without me. And so, after much falling out betwixt my lady and them, all the folks went away, there being a paper drawn[8] to show that they went away by my lord's direction and contrary to my will.

At night I sent 2 messengers to my folks to entreat them to stay. For some 2 nights my mother and I lay together and had much talk about this business.

Upon the 2nd I went after my folks in my lady's coach, she bringing me a quarter of a mile in the way, where she and I had a grievous and heavy parting.[9] Most part of the way I rid behind Mr Hodgson.

[As I came I heard that Sir John Digby, late embassador in Spain, was made V. Chamberlain[10] and sworn of the Privy Council. Not long after this my cousin Sir John Oliver was made Lord Deputy of Ireland in the place of Sir Arthur Chichester.]

Upon the 10th we went from Ware to Tottenham, where my lord's coach with his men and horses met me and came to London to the lesser Dorset House.

Upon the 11th I came from London to Knole, where I had but a cold welcome from my lord. My Lady Margaret[11] met me in the outermost gate and my lord came to me in the drawing chamber.

Upon the 12th I told my lord how I had left those writings, which the judges and my lord would have me sign and seal, behind with my mother.

Upon the 13th my lord and Thomas Glenham went up to London.

Upon the 17th came Tom Woodgatt from London but brought me no news of my going up, which I daily look for. [Upon the 17th my mother sickened as she came from prayers, being taken with a cold chillness in the manner of an ague, which afterwards turned to great heats and pains in her side; so as when she was opened, it was plainly seen she had an impostume.][12]

Upon the 18th Baskett came hither and brought me a letter from my lord, to let me know this was the last time of asking me whether I would set my hand to this award of the judges.

Upon the 19th I returned my lord for answer that I would not stand to the award of the judges, what misery soever it cost me. This morning the Bishop of St David's and my little child were brought to speak to me.

About this time I used to rise early in the morning and go to the standing[13] in the garden, and, taking my prayer book with me, beseech God to be merciful to me in this and to help me as he always hath done.

May 1616

Upon the 1st Rivers came from London in the afternoon and brought me word that I should neither live at Knole or Bollbroke.[14]

Upon the 2nd came Mr Legg[15] and told divers of the servants that my lord would come down and see me once more, which would be the last time that I should see him again.

Upon the 3rd came Baskett[16] down from London and brought me a letter from my lord, by which I might see it was his pleasure that the child should go the next day to London; which at the first was somewhat grievous to me. But when I considered that it would make my lord more angry with me and be worse for the child, I resolved to let her go, after I had sent for Mr Legg and talked with him about that and other matters, and wept bitterly.

[My Lady Margaret lay in the great Dorset House. For now my lord and his whole company was removed from the lesser Dorset House where I lay when I was first married. About this time died my Lord of Shrewsbury at his house in Broad Street.]

Upon the 4th, being Saturday, between ten and eleven the child went into the litter to go to London, Mrs Bathurst and her two maids, with Mr Legg and a good company of the servants, going with her. In the afternoon came a man called Hilton, born in Craven, from my Lady Willoughby to see me; which I took as a great argument of her love being in the midst of all my misery.

Upon the 8th I dispatched a letter to my mother.

Upon the 9th I received a letter from Mr Bellasis, how extreme ill my mother had been; and in the afternoon came Humphrey Godding's son with letters that my mother was exceeding ill and, as they thought, in sore danger of death. So as I sent Rivers presently to London with letters to be sent to her, and certain cordials and conserves.

At night was brought to me a letter from my lord, to let me know his determination was the child should go live at Horsley,[17] and not come hither any more. So as this was a very grievous and sorrowful day to me.

Upon the 10th Rivers came from London, and brought me word from Lord William that she[18] was not in such danger as I feared. The same day came the steward from London, whom I expected would have given warning to many of the servants to go away because the audits was newly come up.[19]

[Upon the 10th, early in the morning, I wrote a very earnest letter to beseech him that I might not go to the Little House that was appointed for me, but that I might go to Horsley and sojourn with my child. And to the same effect I wrote to my sister Beauchamp.][20]

Upon the 11th, being Sunday, before Mr Legg went away I talked with him an hour or two about all the business[21] and matters between me and my lord; so as I gave him better satisfaction and made him conceive a better opinion of me than he ever did.

A little before dinner came Matthew[22] down from London, my lord sending me by him the wedding ring that my Lord Treasurer and my old Lady[23] were married withall; and a message that my lord would be here next week, and that the child would not as yet go down to Horsley. And I sent my lord the wedding ring that my lord and I was married with. The same day came Mr Marsh[24] from London and persuaded me much to consent to this argument.

The 12th, at night, Grosvenor[25] came hither and told me how my lord had won £200 at the cocking match, and that my Lord of Essex and Lord Willoughby who was on my lord's side won a great deal; and how there was some unkind words between my lord and his side and Sir William Herbert and his side. This day my Lady Grantham sent me a letter about these businesses between my uncle Cumberland and me, and returned me an answer.

All this time my lord was in London, where he had all and infinite great resort coming to him. He went much abroad to cocking, to bowling alleys, to plays and horse races, and commended by all the world. I stayed in the country, having many times a sorrowful and heavy heart, and being condemned by most folks because I would not consent to the agreements. So as I may truly say, I am like an owl in the desert.[26]

Upon the 13th, being Monday, my lady's footman Thomas Petty brought me letters out of Westmoreland, by which I perceived how very sick and full of grievous pains my dear mother was; so as she was not able to write herself to me, and most of her people about her feared she would hardly recover this sickness. At night I went out and prayed to God my only helper that she might not die in this pitiful case. The 14th, Richard Jones came from London to me and brought a letter with him from Matthew, the effect whereof was to persuade me to yield to my lord's desire in this business at this time, or else I was undone for ever.

Upon the 15th my lord came down from London and my cousin Cecily Neville;[27] my lord lying in Leslie chamber, and I in my own. Upon the 17th my lord and I, after supper, had some talk about these businesses, Matthew being in the room; where we all fell out and so parted for that night. Upon the 18th, being Saturday, in the morning my lord and I having much talk about these businesses, we agreed that Mr Marsh should go presently down to my mother; and that by him I should write a letter to persuade her to give over her jointure[28] presently to my lord, and that he would give her yearly as much as it was worth. This day my lord went from Knole to London. [N.B. My lord was at London when my mother died, but he went to Lewes before he heard of her death.]

Upon the 20th, being Monday, I dispatched Mr Marsh with letters to my mother about the business aforesaid. I sent them unsealed because my lord might see them. [Upon the 20th went my child to West Horsley with Mary Neville and Mrs Bathurst from London. Mary Hicken was with her, for still she lain in bed with Lady Margaret.] My brother Compton[29] and his wife kept the house at West Horsley, and my brother Beauchamp and my sister, his wife, sojourned with them; so as the child was with both her aunts.

Upon the 22nd Mr Davies came down from London and brought me word that my mother was very well recovered of her dangerous sickness. By him I writ a letter to my lord that Mr Amherst[30] and Mr Davie might confer together about my jointure, to free it from the payment of debts and all other incumbrances.

[Upon the 24th, being Friday, between the hours of six and nine at night died my dear mother at Brougham, in the same chamber where my father was born; 13 years and 2 months after the death of Queen Elizabeth[31] and 10 years and 7 months after the death of my father, I being 26 years old and 5 months and the child 2 years wanting a month.]

Upon the 24th my Lady Somerset[32] was arraigned and condemned at Westminster Hall, where she confessed her fault and asked the king's mercy and was much pitied by all beholders. Upon the 25th my Lord Somerset was arraigned and condemned in the same place, and stood much upon his innocency.

Upon the 27th, being Monday, my lord came down to Buckhurst. My Lord Vaux and his uncle Sir Henry Neville and divers others came with him, but the lords that promised to go with him stayed behind, agreeing to meet him the next day at Lewes. [At this great meeting at Lewes, my Lord Compton,[33] my Lord Merdaunt,[34] Tom Neville, John Herbert and all that crew, with Walter Raleigh,[35] Jack Laurie and a multitude of such company, were there. There was much bull baiting, bowling, cards and dice, with suchlike sports, to entertain the time.]

Upon the 28th my Lady Selby[36] came hither to see me, and told me that she had heard some folks say that I have done well in not consenting to the composition.[37]

Upon the 29th Kendall came and brought me the heavy news of my mother's death, which I held as the greatest and most lamentable cross that could have befallen me. Also, he brought her will along with him, wherein she appointed her body should be buried in the parish church of Anwick; which was a double grief to me when I considered her body should be carried away and not interred at Skipton. So as I took that as a sign that I should be dispossessed of the inheritance of my forefathers.

The same night I sent Hamon away with the will to my lord who was then at Lewes.

Upon the 30th the Bishop of St David's came to me in the morning to comfort me in these afflictions, and in the afternoon I sent for Sir William Selby to speak to him about the conveyance of my dear mother's body into Northumberland, and about the building of a little chapel. [On the 30th at night, or the 31st, my lord was told the news of my mother's death, he being then at Lewes with all this company.]

Upon the 31st came Mr Amherst from my lord, and he brought me word that my lord would be here on Saturday. The same day, Mr James brought me a letter from Mr Woolrich wherein it seemed it was my mother's pleasure her body should be conveyed to what place I appointed, which was some contentment to my aggrieved soul.[38]

[Anne Clifford spent the second half of 1616 in Westmoreland, seeing to her mother's funeral, goods, and land. She returned to London in December and stayed there for Christmas and New Year; she notes that on New Year's Day the king 'kissed me and used me very kindly'.]

January 1617

Upon the 8th we came from London to Knole. This night my lord and I had a falling out about the land.

Upon the 9th I went up to see the things in the closet[39] and began to have Mr Sandys's book[40] read to me about the government of the Turks, my lord sitting the most part of the day reading in his closet.

Upon the 10th my lord went up to London upon the sudden, we not knowing it till the afternoon.

Upon the 16th I received a letter from my lord that I should come up to London the next day, because I was to go before the king on Monday next.

Upon the 17th when I came up, my lord told me I must resolve to go to the king the next day. Upon the 18th, being Saturday, I went presently after dinner to the queen, to the drawing chamber, where my Lady Derby told the queen how my business stood and that I was to go to the king; so she promised me she would do all the good in it she could. When I had stayed but a little while there I was sent for out, my lord and I going through my Lord Buckingham's chamber who brought us into the king, being in the drawing chamber. He put out all that were there, and my lord and I kneeled by his chair-sides when he persuaded us both to peace and to put the whole matter wholly into his hands, which my lord consented to; but I beseeched his majesty to pardon me, for that I would never part from Westmoreland while I lived upon any condition whatsoever. Sometimes he used fair means and persuasions, and sometimes foul means; but I was resolved before so as nothing would move me. From the king we went to the queen's side. I brought my Lady St John to her lodgings and so we went home. At this time I was much bound to my lord, for he was far kinder to me in all these businesses than I expected, and was very unwilling that the king should do me any public disgrace. [The queen gave me warning not to trust my matters absolutely to the king, lest he should deceive me.]

Upon the 19th my lord and I went to the court in the morning, thinking the queen would have gone to the chapel; but she did not, so my Lady Ruthven and I and many others stood in the closet to hear the sermon. I dined with my Lady Ruthven. Presently, after dinner she and I went up to the drawing chamber where my Lady D.,[41] my Lady Montgomery, my Lord Burleigh, persuaded me to refer these businesses to the king. About six o'clock my lord came for me, so he and I and Lady St John went home in her coach. This night the masque was danced at the court but I would not stay to see it because I had seen it already.[42]

Upon the 20th, I and my lord went presently after dinner to the court. He went up to the king's side about his business; I went to my aunt Bedford in her lodging, where I stayed in Lady Ruthven's chamber till towards eight o'clock. About which time I was sent for up to the king into his drawing chamber, when the door was locked and nobody suffered to stay there but my lord and I, my uncle Cumberland, my cousin Clifford, my Lords Arundel, Pembroke,

Montgomery, Sir John Digby. For lawyers there were my Lord Chief Justice Montague and Hobart Yelverton, the king's solicitor; Sir Randal Crewe was to speak for my lord and I. The king asked us all if we would submit to his judgment in this case. My uncle Cumberland, my cousin Clifford, and my lord answered they would, but I would never agree to it without Westmoreland. At which the king grew in a great chaff, my Lord of Pembroke and the king's solicitor speaking much against me. At last when they saw there was no remedy, my lord, fearing the king would do me some public disgrace, desired Sir John Digby would open the door, who went out with me and persuaded me much to yield to the king. My Lord Hay came to me, to whom I told in brief how this business stood. Presently after, my lord came from the king when it was resolved that if I would not come to an agreement, there should be an agreement made without me. We went down, Sir Robert Douglas and Sir George Chaworth bringing us to the coach. By the way my lord and I went in at Worcester house to see my Lord and Lady; and so came home this day. I may say I was led miraculously by God's providence, and next to that I trust all my good to the worth and nobleness of my lord's disposition. For neither I nor anybody else thought I should have passed over this day so well as I have done.

Upon the 22nd the child had her sixth fit of the ague[43] in the morning. Mr Smith went up in the coach to London to my lord, to whom I wrote a letter to let him know in what case the child was, and to give him humble thanks for his noble usage towards me at London. The same day my lord came down to Knole to see the child.

Upon the 23rd my lord went up betimes to London again. The same day the child put on her red baize coats.

Upon the 25th I spent most of my time in working, and in going up and down to see the child. About five or six o'clock the fit took her, which lasted six or seven hours.

Upon the 28th at this time I wore a plain green flannel gown that William Punn made me, and my yellow taffety waistcoat. Rivers used to read to me in Montaigne's plays, and Moll Neville in the *Faerie Queene*.

Upon the 30th Mr Amherst[44] the preacher came hither to see me, with whom I had much talk. He told me that now they began to think at London that I had done well in not referring this business to the king, and that everybody said God had a hand in it.[45]

[All this time of my being in the country, there was much ado at London about my business; in so much that my lord, my uncle

Cumberland, my cousin Clifford, with the chief justice of the council of both sides, on divers times with the king hearing it go so directly for me, he said there was a law in England to keep me from the land.

There was during this time much cock fighting at the court, where the lords' cocks did fight against the king's. Although this business was somewhat chargeable[46] to my lord, yet it brought him into great grace and favour with the king, so he useth him very kindly and speaketh very often to him than of any other man. My lord grew very great with my Lord of Arundel.

My sister Compton and her husband were now upon terms of parting, so as they left Horsley, she lying in London. It was agreed she should have £100 a year and he to have the child from her.]

[After the crisis in 'the business', the months of February and March 1617 are characterized by uncertainty and waiting, and by intermittent illnesses of her husband and daughter.]

April–June 1617

April 1617

Upon the 11th, my lord was very ill this day and could not sleep, so that I lay on a pallet. The 12th Mrs Watson came here, with whom I had much talk of my lord's being made a Knight of the Garter. This night I went in Judith's chamber, where I mean to continue till my lord is better.

The 13th my lord sat where the gentlemen used to sit. He dined abroad in the great chamber and supped privately with me in the drawing chamber, and had much discourse of the manners of the folks at court.

The 14th I was so ill with lying in Judith's chamber that I had a plain fit of fever.

The 15th I was so sick and my face so swelled that my lord and Tom Glenham were fain to keep the table in the drawing chamber and I sat within. Marsh came in the afternoon, to whom I gave directions to go to Mr Davis and Mr Walter about the drawing of letters to the tenants in Westmoreland[47] because I intend sending him thither. This night I left Judith's chamber and came to lie in the chamber where I lay when my lord was in France, in the green cloth-of-gold bed where the child was born.

The 16th my lord and I had much talk about these businesses, he urging me still to go to London to sign and seal; but I told him that my promise so far passed to my brother and to all the world that I would never do it, whatever became of me and mine.

Upon the 17th, in the morning, my lord told me he was resolved never to move me more in these businesses, because he saw how fully I was bent.

The 18th, being Good Friday, I spent most of the day in hearing Kate Buchin read the bible and a book of the preparation to the sacrament.

The 19th I signed 33 letters with my own hand which I sent by him to the tenants in Westmoreland. The same night, my lord and I had much talk of and persuaded me to these businesses, but I would not, and yet I told him I was in perfect charity with all the world. All this Lent I ate flesh and observed no day but Good Friday.[48]

The 20th, being Easter Day, my lord and I and Tom Glenham, and most of the folk, received the communion by Mr Ran. Yet in the afternoon my lord and I had a great falling out, Matthew continuing still to do me all the ill office he could with my lord. All this time I wore my white satin gown and my white waistcoat.

The 22nd he came to dine abroad in the great chamber; this night we played burley break[49] upon the bowling green.

The 23rd Lord Clanricarde came hither. After they were gone, my lord and I and Tom Glenham went to Mr Lune's house to see the fine flowers that is in the garden.

This night my lord should have lain with me, but he and I fell out about matters.[50]

The 24th my lord went to Sevenoaks again. After supper we played at burley break upon the green. This night my lord came to lie in my chamber.

This night, being Friday, I came to keep my fish days which I intend to keep all the year long. After dinner I had a great deal of talk with Richard Dawson that served my lady;[51] he telling me all the names, how the possession of Brougham castle was delivered to my uncle of Cumberland's folks, and how Mr Worleigh and all my people are gone from home except John Ruvy, who kept all the stuff in the baron's chamber (the plate being already sent to Lord William Howard's).

The 26th I spent the evening in working and going down to my lord's closet, where I sat and read much in the Turkish history[52] and Chaucer.

The 28th was the first time the child put on a pair of whalebone bodice.

My lord went a-hunting the fox and the hare. I sent William Punn to Greenwich to see my Lady Roxburgh and remember my service to Mr Q.[53] About this time, my lord made the steward alter most of the rooms in the house, and dress them up as fine as he could, and determined to make all his old clothes in purple stuff[54] for the gallery and drawing chamber.

May 1617

Upon the 1st I cut the child's strings off from her coats and made her use togs alone,[55] so as she had two or three falls at first but had no hurt with them.

The 2nd the child put on her first coat that was laced with lace, being of red baize.

The 3rd my lord went from Buckhurst to London, and rid it in four hours, he riding very hard, a-hunting all the while he was at Buckhurst and had his health exceeding well.

The 7th my Lord Keeper rode from Dorset House to Westminster in great pomp and state, most of the lords going with him, amongst which my lord was one.

The 8th: I spent this day in working,[56] the time being very tedious unto me as having neither comfort nor company, only the child.

The 12th I began to dress my head with a roll without a wire.

I wrote not to my lord because he wrote not to me since he went away. After supper I went with the child, who rode the piebald nag that came out of Westmoreland, to Mrs [xxxx].[57] The 14th the child came to lie with me, which was the first time that ever she lay all night in a bed with me since she was born.

The 15th the child put on her white coats and left off many things from her head, the weather growing extreme hot.

Mrs Ryder came here and told me Lord Sheffield's wife was lately dead, since the king went from York.

The 17th the steward came from London and told me my lord was much discontented with me for not doing this business, because he must be fain to buy land for the payment of the money which will much encumber his estate.

Upon the 18th Mr Woolrich came hither to serve me, he bringing me news that all Westmoreland was surrendered to my uncle Cumberland.

The 19th came my cousin Sir Edward George, who brought me a token from my Lady Somerset.

The 24th we set up a great many of the books that came out of the north in my closet, this being a sad day with me thinking of the troubles I have passed. I used to spend much time with Mr Woolrich in talking of my dear mother and other businesses in the north.

This time my lord's mother did first of all sue out of her thirds,[58] which was an increase of trouble and discontent to my lord.

The 25th my Lord St. John's tailor came to me hither to measure of me and to make me a new gown. In the afternoon my cousin Russell wrote me a letter, to let me know how my lord had cancelled my jointure he made upon me last June when I went into the north; and by these proceedings I may see how much my lord is offended with me and that my enemies have the upper hand of me. I am resolved to take all patiently, casting all my care upon God. His footman told me that my cousin Russell and my Lady Bedford were agreed, and my Lord Herbert and his lady, and that the next week they were to seal the writings and the agreement, which I little expected.

The 27th I wrote a letter to my lord to let him know how ill I took his cancelling my jointure, but yet told him I was content to bear it with patience, whatsoever he thought fit.

The 29th I wrote a letter to my sister Beauchamp and sent her a lock of the child's hair. I wrote a letter to my sister Compton and my aunt Glenham,[59] I being desirous to win the love of my lord's kindred by all the fair means I could.

The 31st Mr Hodgson told me my cousin Clifford went in at Brougham Castle and saw the house but did not lie there; and that all the tenants were very well affected towards me and ill towards them.

June 1617

The 3rd Mr Heardson came hither in the morning and told me that many did condemn me for standing out so in this business; so on the other side many did commend me in regard that I have done that which is both just and honourable.

This night I went into a bath.

The 6th, after supper, we went in the coach to Goodwife Sisley's[60] and ate so much cheese there that it made me sick.

The 8th, being Whit Sunday, we all went to church, but my eyes were so blubbered with weeping that I could scarce look up; and in

the afternoon we again fell out about Matthew. After supper we
played at burley break upon the bowling green.

Notes

1 *journey northward*: Anne Clifford and her husband, Richard Sackville, 3rd Earl of Dorset,
   travelled to Anne's mother, Lady Cumberland, at Brougham Castle near Penrith.
2 The manuscript proceeds directly from 1 to 20 March 1616.
3 *my cousin William Howard*: her husband's first cousin. [Note in manuscript.]
4 *direct denial . . . award*: Clifford and her mother refused to accept the legal judgment that
   her uncles, rather than Anne Clifford herself, should inherit her father's estates.
5 *my Lady of Somerset*: the Earl of Dorset's cousin, imprisoned because accused of complicity
   in the murder of Sir Thomas Overbury who had objected to her marriage to the Earl of
   Somerset.
6 *received*: took communion.
7 *my cousin Charles Howard*: 4th son of Thomas Howard Earl of Suffok, and therefore her
   husband's first cousin. [Note in manuscript.]
8 *a paper drawn*: The memorandum stated that 'this stay of mine proceeds only from my
   husband's command, contrary to my consent or agreement' (Williamson 1922; 1967: 90).
9 *grievous and heavy parting*: forty years later, Clifford erected a stone column at the site and
   instituted an annual distribution of bread and money to the local poor.
10 *V. Chamberlain*: Vice-Chamberlain.
11 *My Lady Margaret*: her daughter, born in July 1614. In 1629 Margaret married the Earl of
   Thanet, and their sons inherited the Clifford lands and title.
12 *impostume*: abscess or tumour.
13 *standing*: a hunter's station or stand from which to shoot game (*OED*: 4c).
14 *Bollbroke*: the second Dorset family residence, in Sussex.
15 *Mr Legg*: Mr Edward Legg, steward. [Note in manuscript.]
16 *Baskett*: Mr Peter Baskett, gentleman of the horse. [Note in manuscript.]
17 *Horsley*: West Horsley, Surrey.
18 *she*: Clifford's mother, who had been unwell since 17 April 1616.
19 *audits . . . up*: an indication of the precarious state of the family finances (increasing the
   pressure on Clifford to accept a cash settlement in lieu of the northern lands).
20 *my sister Beauchamp*: Anne, daughter of Robert Earl of Dorset, married to Lord Beauchamp,
   great grandson of the Protector Duke of Somerset. [Note in manuscript.]
21 *the business*: a term increasingly used by Clifford to imply the financial, legal, and emotional
   wrangle with her husband over her disputed inheritance (see p. 37). Clifford used the same
   word earlier in her diary to refer to the publicly unhappy marriage of her own parents: 'my
   mother' had to 'attend to the king about the business between my father and her' (July
   1603).
22 *Matthew*: Mr Matthew Caldicott, my lord's favourite. [Note in manuscript.]
23 *my Lord Treasurer . . . Lady*: her husband's grandparents.
24 *Mr Marsh*: attendant on my lady. [Note in manuscript.]
25 *Grosvenor*: gentleman usher. [Note in manuscript.]
26 *like an owl in the desert*: Psalms 102.6.
27 *my cousin Cecily Neville*: daughter to Lady Abergavenny, who was sister to Robert Earl of
   Dorset. [Note in manuscript.]
28 *her jointure*: the rights of Lady Cumberland to the estate of her late husband.
29 *My brother Compton*: Sir Henry Compton of Brambletye House (3rd son of Henry, 1st Lord
   Compton) married Lady Cecily Sackville daughter of Robert Earl of Dorset. [Note in
   manuscript.]

30 *Mr Amherst*: sergeant-at-law and queen's sergeant described by Thomas 1st Earl of Dorset in his will as 'his very loving friend Richard Amherst, Esq., high steward of all his manors, lands, and possessions within the county of Sussex'. [Note in manuscript.]

31 *death of Queen Elizabeth*: Clifford places her mother's death by means of significant reference points and anniversaries. The death of the previous queen was a personal memory; in her earliest surviving diary, Clifford notes that on 20 March 1603 'Mr. Flocknall, my aunt Warwick's man, brought us word from his lady, that the queen died about 2/3 o'clock in the morning. The message was delivered to my mother and me in the same chamber where afterwards I was married.'

32 *my Lady Somerset*: daughter of Lord Treasurer Suffolk, and first cousin to Richard 3rd Earl of Dorset. [Note in manuscript.] See note 5.

33 *my Lord Compton*: afterwards 1st Earl of Northampton. [Note in manuscript.]

34 *my Lord Merdaunt*: married Lord Compton's sister. [Note in manuscript.]

35 *Walter Raleigh*: in the manuscript this appears as 'Wat. Raleigh'.

36 *my Lady Selby*: of the Mote, Ightham. [Note in manuscript.]

37 *composition*: another proposed legal agreement by her husband, this time arranging for her mother to hand over her 'jointure' lands (see note 28) in return for annual cash payments.

38 *her body . . . aggrieved soul*: Clifford's mother was eventually buried in the parish church at Appleby in Westmoreland.

39 *closet*: her private chamber.

40 *Mr Sandys's book*: George Sandys, *A Relation of a Journey begun An. Dom. 1610 . . . containing a description of the Turkish Empire* (1615).

41 *my Lady D.*: probably Lady Derby, with whom (among others)-she had spent New Year's Day.

42 *the masque . . . already*: on Twelfth Night 'we stood to see the masque in the box with my Lady Ruthven'.

43 *ague*: a violent fever, particularly marked by successive fits (OED 2).

44 *Mr Amherst*: Jeffery Amherst, D.D., Rector of Horsemonden, brother of the sergeant. [Note in manuscript.]

45 *they began to think . . . hand in it*: contrast the entry for 7 February: 'Mr Oberton and I had a great deal of talk, he telling me how much I was condemned in the world and what strange censures most folks made of my courses.'

46 *chargeable* : costly; Dorset lost a lot of money in gaming with the king.

47 *letters . . . Westmoreland*: concerning the uncertain ownership of their properties following the death of Lady Cumberland.

48 *All this Lent . . . Good Friday*: she only fasted from meat ('flesh') on Good Friday.

49 *burley [or barley] break*: an outdoor game in which two couples were chased by a third and were able to 'break' partnerships in order to avoid being caught.

50 *This night . . . matters*: the long-running battle over lands and money evidently had a profound effect on their married life. It is perhaps significant that an early meaning of the word 'rape' was to take away land or goods by force (OED 1).

51 *my lady*: her late mother.

52 *the Turkish history*: see note 40.

53 *Mr Q.*: as yet unidentified.

54 *old clothes . . . stuff*: her husband wishes to have the hangings redone in purple. 'Clothes' may well mean 'cloths'; 'stuff' was no casual term but referred to woven (often woollen) fabric.

55 *strings . . . togs*: her daughter was learning to walk unaided; it appears that Clifford removed some special walking reins from the child's coat.

56 *working*: embroidery, the needle-'work' of leisured women.

57 Name removed from manuscript.

58 *sue out of her thirds*: Dorset was attempting to sue his stepmother for the third of a deceased husband's property allowed to his widow.

59 *aunt Glenham*: Anne, eldest daughter of 1st Earl of Dorset, married to Sir Henry Glenham, of Glenham, Suffolk. [Note in manuscript.]

60 *Goodwife Sisley's*: a Jane Sisley is listed as part of the Knole household, 1613–24, working in 'The Nursery' (Clifford, ed. Sackville-West 1923: lix).

2

AN COLLINS

Divine Songs and Meditations
London, printed by R. Bishop. Anno dom. 1653

'Your verses are more like you than your peckter [picture]', wrote Margaret Cavendish in a letter to her future husband in 1645 (Cavendish, ed. Grant 1965: 103). Cavendish's comment is based upon a commonly-held assumption that verses have the capacity to create a 'picture' of their writer, to animate the silent holder of the pen. This view is, however, a questionable one, and the presence of only one poet, An Collins, in this anthology[1] suggests the greater importance of other forms – diary, memoir, defence, prose prophecy – as media of autobiography for seventeenth-century women. An Collins's poetry appears here as autobiography not because all poetry is necessarily or primarily an expression of the individual, but because Collins's verse consciously pushes her self to its surface. In her opening poem, 'The Discourse', she writes of her poems as 'the image of her mind' which, being discovered by those to whom 'the author be unknown', would enable those readers to 'conjecture how she was inclined' (1653: 4; see p. 58). Earlier, in her poetic 'Preface', she calls the verses 'the offspring of my mind' (sig. A4[v])[2] which, in a female reworking of the argument of many male-authored sonnet sequences, would reproduce her characteristics and bear her stamp. The poems are meditations on the text of her own life, and share many of the functions of prose autobiography: self-analysis, confession, spiritual example. As Stanley Stewart suggests, Collins's verses 'are, in several respects, a form of the diary' (Collins, ed. Stewart 1961: ii).

Why, then, did An Collins choose to write in verse? Pleasure in poetic creativity seems to have been the initial reason. The 'delight' in her quiet life stemmed from channelling her 'enlargedness of mind, and activity of spirit' into verses which ensured her 'spiritual calmness' (sig. A1[r-v]):

> To be brief, I became affected to poetry, insomuch that I proceeded to practise the same; and though the helps I had therein were small, yet the thing itself appeared

unto me so amiable as that it inflamed my faculties to put forth themselves in a practice so pleasing.

('To the Reader', sig. A1ʳ)

This description of the almost passionate pleasure of poetry leads revealingly into the language of self-expression: her 'faculties . . . put forth themselves'. In 'The Preface' she goes on to explain that her 'morning exercise' of writing 'songs or counterfeits of poesies' also gave her the chance to 'vindicate' her 'former works' (sig. A3ʳ). This concern with the narrative of her life, however, is given an appropriately edifying context; the poems are

> set forth (as I trust) for the benefit and comfort of others; chiefly for those Christians who are of disconsolate spirits, who may perceive herein the faithfulness, love and tender compassionateness of God to his people.
>
> (sig. A2ᵛ)

Again like many an autobiographer, Collins asserts that what she is dealing with is 'the manifestation of divine truth' (sig. A2ʳ), so that the poverty of her poetic skill (as she perceived it) is seen as acceptable: 'Yet for their matter, I suppose they be/Not worthless quite, whilst they with truth agree' ('The Preface', sig. A4ᵛ). The familiar humility of the religious poet[3] is intensified here by the nakedly autobiographical function of the verse, whose value (in Collins's view) ceases to lie in its skill or even ultimately in its individuality; the author cites herself only in order to exemplify God's grace and draw her readers instead to 'read the scriptures touched in this book' ('The Discourse', 1653: 3; see p. 58).

It has, significantly, proved difficult to find out anything about An Collins's life other than that revealed in her autobiographical poetry. Her prefatory material speaks of her being 'restrained from bodily employments' and therefore leading a 'retired course of life' (sig. A2ʳ); she is 'confined' to the house not only by her femininity but also by abnormal physical 'weakness' (sig. A3ʳ). It is not at all clear what Collins's illness or condition was, but the poems refer to 'crosses' (see p. 58) and suffering of an apparently physical as well as mental kind. As for her religious and political sympathies, her 'Song composed in time of the Civil War' (1653: 63–6) is critical of the radical wing of the parliamentary movement, but her theological language identifies her as Calvinist.[4] Her prefatory epistle speaks of ordinary Christians as 'saints' who know of God's providence by experience (sig. A2ᵛ), and her poetic 'Preface' refers to God's goodness being demonstrated to his 'elect' by means of 'divers dispensations' (sig. A3ʳ); on the other hand, she finds comfort in 'prayer and the blessed sacrament' as well as from 'saving graces and God's holy word' (p. 60).

An Collins was, it would therefore seem, a middle-of-the-road believer who interpreted and found purpose in her uncomfortable and withdrawn life by means of biblical precedent and a vocation to poetry:

> Oh! What transcendent ravishing delights,
> What bliss unspeakable they do possess,
> Whose mirth to holy praises them excites,
> And cheers them to go on, in godliness.

(1653: 8; see p. 61)

Her one known volume of poetry, *Divine Songs and Meditations* (1653), is fascinating for its powerful testimony of her ability to transcend profound misery with the 'excitement' of 'holy praises'; the extremes of mood in the verse are indeed biblical in their intensity. This small collection of poetry also encompasses a variety of tones, from the narrative self-portrait and analysis of 'The Discourse' to the lyrical expression in the 'Songs' of a life intertwined with God's grace. The language of devotion, rich with Old Testament imagery of the female soul and the awaited 'beloved', is given a particularly self-conscious and vivid treatment by this poet who writes from an avowedly passive femininity. As 'Another Song' declares,

> Yet as a garden is my mind enclosed fast
> Being to safety so confined from storm and blast
> Apt to produce a fruit most rare,
> That is not common with every woman
> That fruitful are.

(1653: 57; see p. 68)

Her 'rare' state is in the end an enriching one; the 'enclosed garden' is, though restricted, an emblem of virginity and perfection. Her poetry asserts, in its honesty and its lyricism, her triumph in the battle to 'restrain discontent' (1653: 59). If the volume is a diary, it is a record of a particularly female accommodation of providence.

Notes

1 Other authors represented in this anthology, however, also wrote verses: Margaret Cavendish, Anna Trapnel, Anne Wentworth.
2 In books without page numbers the convention is to make reference to the printer's marks on each gathering (section) of the book. A4^v is the verso (second side) of the fourth sheet of gathering A.
3 See, for example, George Herbert's 'A True Hymn'.
4 My interpretation here differs from that of the editor of the brief extract from Collins's work in Greer et al. 1988: 148–54.

Textual note

This modernized text is based on the sole original copy of the *Divine Songs and Meditations* in the Huntington Library, California, shelfmark 54047. Approximately half the volume was reproduced in 1961 as Augustan Reprint

Society Publication no. 94, edited by Stanley Stewart (Clark Library, Los Angeles).

Collins's marginal biblical references have been transferred to the notes in order to avoid disturbance (whether visual or metrical) of the poetic text.

From: *Divine Songs and Meditations*

From The Discourse

You that endeared are to piety,
And of a gracious disposition are,
Delighting greatly in sincerity,
As your respects to godly ones declare;
For whose society you only care:
Deign to survey her works that worthless seem
To such as honest meanings disesteem.[1]

But those that in my love I have preferred
Before all creatures in this world beside,
My works, I hope, will never disregard,
Though some defects herein may be espied;
Which those that have their judgments rectified
Can but discern, yet not with scornful eye,
As their mild censures chiefly testify.

Unto the public view of everyone
I did not purpose these my lines to send,
Which for my private use were made alone;
Or as I said, if any pious friend
Will once vouchsafe to read them to the end:
Let such conceive if error here they find,
'Twas want of art, not true intent of mind.

Some may desirous be to understand
What moved me, who unskilful am herein,
To meddle with, and thus to take in hand,
That which I cannot well end or begin;
But such may first resolve themselves herein,
If they consider, 'tis not want of skill
That's more blameworthy than want of good will.

1 Then know, I chiefly aim that this should be
  Unto the praise of God's most blessed name,
  For by the mouths of sucking babes doth he
  Reveal his power and immortal fame;[2]
  Permitting children to extol the same:
  When those that were profound and worldly wise
  In ignominious sort did him despise.

2 Next in respect of that I have received
  Is nothing to that some have, I do confess,
  Yet he to whom one talent was bequeathed
  Was called to strict account, nevertheless,
  As well as he that many did possess;[3]
  From which I gather, they have no excuse,
  Which of ability will make no use.

3 Moreover this is thirdly in respect
  Of some near kindred, who survive me may,
  The which perhaps do better works neglect,
  Yet this they may be pleased to survey
  Through willingness to hear what I could say;
  Whereby they may be haply drawn to look,
  And read the scriptures touched in this book.

4 And lastly in regard of anyone
  Who may by accident hereafter find
  This, though to them the author be unknown,
  Yet seeing here the image of her mind,
  They may conjecture how she was inclined;
  And further note, that God doth grace bestow
  Upon his servants, though he keeps them low.

  Even in my cradle did my crosses breed,
  And so grew up with me unto this day,
  Whereof variety of cares proceed,
  Which of myself I never could allay
  Nor yet their multiplying brood destroy,
  For one distemper could no sooner die
  But many others would his room supply.

  Yea like the messengers of Job they haste,
  One comes before another can be gone;
  All motions of delight were soon defaced;[4]

Finding no matter for to feed upon,
They quickly were dispersed every one;
Whereat my mind itself would much torment
Upon the rack of restless discontent.

The summer's day, though cheerful in itself,
Was wearisome and tedious unto me,
As those that comfort lack, content or health,
To credit this may soon'st persuaded be,
For by experience truth hereof they see.
Now if the summer's day cause no delight,
How irksome think you was the winter's night.

'Twere to no end, but altogether vain,
My several crosses namely to express;
To rub the scar would but increase the pain,
And words of pity would no grief release,
But rather aggravate my heaviness,
Who ever chose my crosses to conceal
Till to my grief they would themselves reveal.

So (to be brief) I spent my infancy
And part of freshest years, as hath been said,
Partaking then of nothing cheerfully
Being through frailty apt to be afraid,
And likely still distempered or dismayed,
Through present sense of some calamity
Or preconceit[5] of future misery.

But as the longest winter hath an end
So did this fruitless discontent expire,
And God in mercy some refreshing send,
Whereby I learned his goodness to admire,
And also larger blessings to desire;
For those that once have tasted grace indeed
Will thirst for more, and crave it till they speed.

But that I may proceed methodical,
When first the restless wanderings of my mind
Began to settle, and resolve withal
No more to be disturbed with every wind,
If such a pleasing exercise did find,
Which was to ponder what worth each day
The sense of hearing should to it convey.

But living where profaneness did abound,
Where little goodness might be seen or heard;
Those consolations could be but unsound
Having to godliness no great regard:
Because that of the means I was debarred,
Through ignorance of better exercise
I then delighted pleasant histories.

Whereof the most part were but feigned I knew
Which notwithstanding I no whit despised,
Imagining although they were not true,
They were convenient being moralised;
Such vanities I then too highly prized:
But when profane discourses pleased me best
Obscenities I always did detest.

But all this while, the fumes of vanities
Did interpose between my soul's weak sight
And heavenly bliss, divine felicities;
Until that morning star so matchless bright,
The sun of righteousness, revealed his light
Unto my soul, which sweet refreshings brings
Because he comes with healing in his wings.[6]

Whose blessed beams my mind eradiates
And makes it sensible of piety,
And so by consequence communicates
Celestial health to every faculty,
Expelling palpable obscurity
Which made my soul uncapable of grace,
Which now she much desires for to embrace.

Perceiving well that nothing can afford
Her either final rest, or full content,
But saving graces and God's holy word,
Which is a means those graces to augment;
With prayer and the blessed sacrament:
Which means with reverence my soul affects
And former pleasing vanities rejects.

Together with unnecessary grief
Whose ill effects can hardly be expressed,
For certainly it argues unbelief

Which hinders many from eternal rest[7]
Who do not seek in time to be redressed;
Therefore I would establish inward peace,
However outward crosses do increase.

If cross disgrace or dismal accident,
Indignity or loss, befalleth me,
Immediately distempers to prevent
I called to mind how all things ordered be,
Appointed, and disposed, as we see,
By God's most gracious providence, which is,
I am persuaded, for the good of his.

Yet am I not so firm, I must confess,
But many times discomforts will intrude,
Which oft prevails to hinder quietness,
And by that means some sorrows are renewed:
Which hope will help me quickly to exclude:
So though distress continue for a night,
Yet joy returneth by the morning light.[8]

With confidence these favours will increase;
My soul hath recollected all her powers,
To praise the author of this blissful peace
Which no untimely cross event devours;
So permanent are the celestial flowers;
Those graces which are ever conversant
Where holiness combinds with true content.

Oh! what transcendent ravishing delights,
What bliss unspeakable they do possess,
Whose mirth to holy praises them excites,
And cheers them to go on, in godliness,
The very quintessence of happiness
As is attainable, or may be had
In this life present, which were else but bad.

There is a kind of counterfeit content
Wherewith some are deceived, 'tis to be feared,
Who think they need not sorrow or lament,
Being to sensual pleasures so endeared;
Whose minds are stupid, and their conscience seared,[9]
Else might they see all earthly delectation
To be but vanity and heart's vexation.[10]

To lightning, carnal mirth we may compare,
For as a flash it hastes and soon is gone,
Foretelling of a thunder clap of care;
It also blasts the heart it lighteth on;
Makes it to goodness senseless as a stone:
Disabling every part and faculty
Of soul and body unto piety.

But sacred joy is like the sun's clear light,
Which may with clouds be sometimes overcast,
Yet breaks it forth anon, and shines more bright,
Whose lively force continually doth last;
And shows most orient[11] when a storm is past:
So true delight may be eclipsed, we see,
But quite extinguished can it never be.

(*Divine Songs*, pp. 2–9)

[The remainder of the poem – another seventy-four stanzas – examines the 'grounds of true religion', those 'sacred principles' which Collins 'got by heart' (1653:9) in order to discover 'true delight'.]

A Song expressing their happiness who have communion with Christ

When scorched with distracting care,
    My mind finds out a shade
Which fruitless trees, false fear, despair
    And melancholy made,
Where neither bird did sing
    Nor fragrant flowers spring,
Nor any plant of use:
    No sound of happiness
Had there at all ingress[12]
    Such comforts to produce,
But Sorrow there frequents,
    The nurse of discontents,
And Murmuring her maid
    Whose harsh unpleasant noise
All mental fruits destroys
    Whereby delight's conveyed.

Whereof my judgment being certified
    My mind from thence did move,

For her conception so to provide
    That it might not abortive prove,
Which fruit to signify
    It was conceived by
Most true intelligence
    Of this sweet truth divine:
'Who formed thee is thine',[13]
    Whence sprang this inference:
He, too, that's Lord of all
    Will thee beloved call,
Though all else prove unkind;
    Then cheerful may I sing
Sith[14] I enjoy the spring,
    Though cisterns dry I find.

For in our union with the Lord alone
    Consists our happiness.
Certainly such who are with Christ at one
    He leaves not comfortless,[15]
But come to them he will
    Their souls with joy to fill,
And them to fortify
    Their works to undergo
And bear their cross also
    With much alacrity:
Who his assisting grace
    Do feelingly embrace,
With confidence may say,
    'Through Christ that strengthens me
No thing so hard I see
    But what perform I may.'[16]

But when the soul no help can see
    Through sin's interposition,
Then quite forlorn that while is she,
    Bewailing her condition;
In which deplored case
    Now such a soul hath space
To think how she delayed
    Her saviour to admit
Who shued[17] to her for it,

And to this purpose said,
'Open to me my love,
　My sister, and my dove,
My locks with dew wet are'[18]
　Yet she remissive grew,
Till he himself withdrew[19]
　Before she was aware.

But tasting once how sweet he is,
　And smelling his perfumes,[20]
Long can she not his presence miss,
　But grief her strength consumes:
For when he visits one
　He cometh not alone,
But brings abundant grace
　True light, and holiness
And spirit to express
　One's wants in every case;
For as he wisdom is,
　So is he unto his
Wisdom and purity,[21]
　Which when he seems to hide,
The soul, missing her guide,
　Must needs confused lie.

Then let them know, that would enjoy
　The firm fruition
Of his sweet presence, he will stay
　With single hearts alone,
Who [　　]²² their former mate,
　Do quite exterminate:
With all things that defile.
　They that are Christ's, truly,
The flesh do crucify
　With its affections vile.[23]
Then grounds of truth are sought,
　New principles are wrought
Of grace and holiness,
　Which plantings of the heart
Will spring in every part,
　And so itself express.

Then shall the soul like morning bright
　　Unto her lord appear,
And as the moon when full of light
　　So fair is she and clear,[24]
With that inherent grace
　　That's darted from the face
Of Christ, that sun divine,
　　Which hath a purging power
Corruption to devour,
　　And conscience to refine;
Perfection thus begun
　　As pure as the sun,
The soul shall be likewise
　　With that great blessedness,
Imputed righteousness[25]
　　Which freely justifies.

They that are thus complete with grace
　　And know that they are so,
For glory must set sail apace
　　Whilst wind doth fitly blow,
Now is the tide of love,
　　Now doth the angel move;
If that there be defect
　　That soul which sin doth wound,
Here now is healing found,
　　If she no time neglect;
To whom shall be revealed
　　What erst[26] hath been concealed,
When brought unto that light,
　　Which in the soul doth shine
When he that's most divine
　　Declares his presence bright.

Then he will his beloved show
　　The reason wherefore she
Is seated in a place so low,
　　Nor from all troubles free;
And wherefore they do thrive
　　That wicked works contrive;
Christ telleth his also,

For who as friends he takes
He of his counsel makes,
        And they shall secrets know:[27]
Such need not pine with cares,
        Seeing all things are theirs
If they are Christ's indeed;[28]
        Therefore let such confess
They are not comfortless,
        Nor left in time of need.

                              (*Divine Songs*, pp. 28–33)

A Song demonstrating the vanities of earthly things

Shall sadness persuade me never to sing
But leave unto sirens[29] that excellent thing?
No that may not be, for truly I find
The sanguine complexion to mirth is inclined.

Moreover, they may who righteousness love,
Be soberly merry, and sorrows remove,
They only have right to rejoicing always
Whose joy may be mixed with prayer and praise.

Wherefore rejoiceth the epicure?
As though his fading delights would endure,
Whereas they are ended as soon as begun,
For all things are vanity under the sun.[30]

Riches and honour, fame and promotion,
Idols, to whom the most do their devotion,
How fading they are, I need not to show,
For this by experience, too many do know.

They that delight in costly attire,
If they can compast[31] the things they desire,
Have only obtained what sin first procured,
And many to folly are thereby allured.

Learning is sure an excellent thing,
From whence all arts and sciences spring,
Yet is it not from vanity free,
For many great scholars profane often be.

Whoso hath studied geometry,
Or gained experience in geography,
By tedious labour much knowledge may gain,
Yet in the conclusion, he'll find all is vain.

He that hath studied astronomy,
Though his meditation ascend to the sky
He may miss of heaven and heavenly bliss
If that he can practise no study but this.

But they that delight in divinity,
And to be exquisite in theology,
Much heavenly comfort in this life may gain,
And when it is ended their joys shall remain.

What should I speak more of vanities,
To use many words when few may suffice,
It argueth folly, therefore I have done,
Concluding, all's vanity under the sun.

(*Divine Songs*,pp. 40–1)

Another Song

The winter of my infancy being over-passed
When supposed, suddenly the spring would haste
Which useth everything to cheer
With invitation to recreation
This time of year.

The sun sends forth his radiant beams to warm the ground,
The drops distil, between the gleams delights abound,
Ver[32] brings her mate the flowery queen,
The groves she dresses, her art expresses
On every green.

But in my spring it was not so, but contrary,
For no delightful flowers grew to please the eye,
No hopeful bud, nor fruitful bough,
No moderate showers which causeth flowers
To spring and grow.

My April was exceeding dry, therefore unkind;
Whence 'tis that small utility I look to find,

For when that April is so dry
(As hath been spoken) it doth betoken
Much scarcity.

Thus is my spring now almost passed in heaviness,
The sky of pleasure's overcast with sad distress
For by a comfortless eclipse,
Disconsolation and sore vexation
My blossom nips.

Yet as a garden is my mind enclosed fast[33]
Being to safety so confined from storm and blast
Apt to produce a fruit most rare,
That is not common with every woman
That fruitful are.

A love of goodness is the chiefest plant therein,
The second is (for to be brief) dislike to sin;
These grow in spite of misery,
Which grace doth nourish and cause to flourish
Continually.

But evil motions, corrupt seeds, fall here also
Whence springs profaneness as do weeds where flowers grow,
Which must supplanted[34] be with speed
These weeds of error, distrust and terror,
Lest woe succeed.

So shall they not molest the plants before expressed,
Which countervails[35] these outward wants, and purchase rest
Which more commodious is for me
Than outward pleasures or earthly treasures
Enjoyed would be.

My little hopes of wordly gain I fret not at,
As yet I do this hope retain; though spring be late
Perhaps my summer-age may be,
Not prejudicial, but beneficial
Enough for me.

Admit the worst it be not so, but stormy too,
I'll learn myself to undergo more than I do
And still content myself with this

Sweet meditation and contemplation
Of heavenly bliss,

Which for the saints reserved is, who persevere
In piety and holiness, and godly fear,
The pleasures of which bliss divine
Neither logician nor rhetorician
Can well define.

(*Divine Songs*, pp. 56–8)

Notes

1 *worthless seem . . . disesteem* : the poems will, she assumes, seem 'worthless' to readers who disapprove of 'honest meanings' in poetry, preferring complexity and artifice.

2 *by the mouths . . . fame* : Psalms 8.2, 'Out of the mouths of babes and sucklings hast thou ordained strength.' [Reference supplied in a printed marginal note.]

3 *he to whom . . . possess* : Matthew 25. 14–30, being the parable of the talents. [Marginal reference.]

4 *defaced* : put out of countenance, disappointed.

5 *preconceit* : anticipation.

6 *sun of righteousness . . . with healing in his wings* : Malachi 4.2. [Marginal reference.]

7 *hinders . . . rest* : Hebrews 3.19, 'so we see that they could not enter in [to their heavenly rest] because of unbelief.' [Marginal reference.]

8 *though distresss . . . morning light* : Psalms 30.5. [Marginal reference.]

9 *seared (or sered)* : dried up, callous.

10 *vanity . . . vexation* : Ecclesiastes 2.26. [Marginal reference.]

11 *shows most orient* : shines most brightly, like the sun rising in the east.

12 *Had . . . ingress* : could enter.

13 *Who formed . . . thine* : Isaiah 54.5, 'For thy Maker is thine husband.' [Marginal reference.]

14 *Sith* : since.

15 *leaves not comfortless* : John 14.18.

16 *'Through Christ . . . may'* : Philippians 4.13. [Marginal reference.]

17 *shued* : sued.

18 *'Open to me . . . are'* : Song of Solomon 5.2. [Marginal reference.]

19 *withdrew* : Song of Solomon 5.6.

20 *tasting . . . perfumes* : in the Song of Solomon the 'beloved' is associated with myrrh and sweet spices.

21 *So is he . . . purity* : I Corinthians 1.30 [Marginal reference.]

22 An illegible word appears in square brackets in the original at this point.

23 *They that . . . vile* : Galatians 5.24. [Marginal reference.]

24 *like morning . . . clear* : Song of Solomon 6.10. [Marginal reference.]

25 *Imputed righteousness* : Christ's righteousness attributed to the individual Christian soul.

26 *erst* : formerly.

27 *For who . . . know* : John 15.15. [Marginal reference.]

28 *all things . . . indeed* : I Corinthians 4.21–3. [Marginal reference.]

29 *sirens* : mythical sea-nymphs whose songs lured sailors to their deaths.

30 *all things . . . sun* : Ecclesiastes 1.2.

31 *compass* : encompass, achieve.

32 *Ver* : spring.

33 *as a garden . . . enclosed fast* : Song of Solomon 4.12, 'A garden enclosed is my sister, my spouse; a spring shut up, a fountain sealed.' Collins uses this famous passage, often taken as a reference to the church or the Virgin Mary, and translates it into a subjective statement of her own 'rare' condition.

34 *supplanted* : uprooted.

35 *countervails* : is of equal force, equivalent to.

3

ANNA TRAPNEL

*Anna Trapnel's Report and Plea. Or, a narrative of her journey
from London into Cornwall, the occasion of it, the Lord's
encouragements to it, and signal presence with her in it.*

*Proclaiming the rage and strivings of the people against the
comings forth of the Lord Jesus to reign, manifested in the harsh,
rough, boisterous, rugged, inhumane and uncivil usage of Anna
Trapnel by the justices and people in Cornwall, at a place called
Truro.*

*Whereto is annexed a defiance against all the reproachful, vile,
horrid, abusive and scandalous reports raised out of the bottomless pit
against her by the profane generation, prompted thereunto by
professors and clergy, both in city and country, 'who have a form of
godliness, but deny the power' [2 Timothy 3.5].*

*Commended for the justification of the truth, and satisfaction of
all men, from her own hand.*

*Printed at London for Thomas Brewster, at the Three Bibles, near
London House. 1654.*

It is no coincidence that 1654 was the year that Anna Trapnel published
four of her six texts.[1] It was a centrally important year for all Fifth Monarchists, in which they found themselves arguing once again from the sidelines of
political life rather than from the centre, where they had briefly found themselves for the duration of the Barebones Parliament in the second half of
1653.

In April 1653 the Rump Parliament had been dissolved, and in July
Cromwell had called a new assembly of men 'nominated directly for their
religious and moral virtues' (Capp 1984:171), which came to be known as
the Barebones Parliament. Amongst the 140 members were a dozen Fifth
Monarchists, and many other radicals; even Cromwell demonstrated the

71

HANNAH TRAPNEL,
A Quaker and pretended Prophetess

(From a scarce Print by Gaywood)

For an account of this extraordinary woman, see Heath's Chronicle, Cromwelliana & the High Court of Justice.

A misleadingly-captioned print of the Fifth Monarchist prophet Anna Trapnel. Gaywood was a well-known engraver whose work included portraits of Charles I, Oliver Cromwell and Charles II.

currency of their terms of reference by drawing on the millenarian prophecies of Daniel and Revelation in his inaugural speech. This grouping began to push for some, at least, of the reforms being demanded by the radical sects: tithes, law, and land reform were all on the political agenda. But by December the conservatives in the assembly, alarmed by this programme, contrived the parliament's dissolution. Power returned to the army, whose leaders produced a new constitution under which Cromwell became Lord Protector. For the Fifth Monarchists this was nothing short of betrayal. From being 'Gideon, going before Israel, blowing the trumpet of courage and valour', Cromwell had become a bull, running 'at many precious saints that stood in the way of him, that looked boldly in his face; he gave them many pushes, scratching them with his horn' (Trapnel 1654a: 6, 13). The saints, the Fifth Monarchists, had clearly become a party in opposition, conscious of facing a serious threat from a formidable political force.

This, then, was the immediate political backdrop to Trapnel's writing, her *annus mirabilis* of visions, prophesying, writing, and travelling, through which she agitated for her convictions and her interpretations of events, in preparation for the imminent arrival of King Jesus. She first came into the public eye in January 1654, when attending the examination of Vavasor Powell, a Baptist/Fifth Monarchist preacher and writer, by the Council of State at Whitehall (see p. 79 and note 20 below), at which she fell into a trance which lasted twelve days. During this time her extemporary and prophetic verses and prayers were recorded by a friend. Such activity did not go unnoticed by the authorities: on 7 February, Marchamont Needham reported to Cromwell that Trapnel's congregation was planning both to publish her prophecies, 'which are desperate against your person . . . and the government', and to send her on a mission 'to proclaim them *viva voce*'. Needham was right: two accounts of Trapnel's trance were soon published, *The Cry of a Stone* and *Strange and Wonderful Newes from White-Hall*; and shortly afterwards Trapnel set out for Cornwall, where her prophesying resulted, in March, in her arrest. An account of this journey, her arrest, trial, return to London, and imprisonment in Bridewell forms the narrative basis of *Anna Trapnel's Report and Plea*.

It is, however, much more than a narrative. The title alone suggests that the text should not only record, but also persuade: it is a 'plea' as well as a 'report'. This immediately puts the readership in a very active, discriminating relationship with the text, for they must decide whether the plea succeeds or fails.

Trapnel's aim in writing, stated quite explicitly in her prefatory 'To the Reader', is to set the record straight. 'I go not about to vindicate myself, but the truth', she writes, and immediately the truth, which is the truth of God's word, is set in opposition to her 'self'; the former is dependent on the absence of the latter.[2] None the less, in one way or another her 'self' intrudes throughout. Despite closing her preface by stressing that she will 'relate the truth without addition', a later passage suggests a much more complex apprehension of just what constitutes this 'truth':

> though I fail in an orderly penning down these things, yet not in a true relation of as much as I remember, and what is expedient to be written. I could not have related so much from the shallow memory I have naturally, but through often relating these things they become as a written book, spread open before me, and after which I write.
>
> (1654b: 34)

The 'truth', then, does not result from an exact chronological recording of events, but from a combination of memory, expediency, and the repeated narration of those events: these 'write' her narrative for her, and they all depend in some sense on a relationship between her 'self', her material, and her projected readership. Despite presenting herself as no more than a passive medium, an instrument by means of which God communicates his word, her text suggests a rather more earthly concern for the intricacies of the relationship between these elements.

Given the opposition and hostility to which she had been subject, the need for a personal vindication is clear: 'England's rulers and clergy do judge the Lord's handmaid to be mad, and under the administration of evil angels, and a witch' (1654b: 'To the Reader'). Such 'immodest' behaviour as prophesying and preaching implicated Trapnel in all these other areas of immodesty and unnaturalness. And so she offers another, much more worldly, justification for writing:

> I am forced out of my close retired spirit by rulers and clergy who have brought me upon the world's stage of reports and rumours, making me the world's wonder and gazing stock. And as some have said, they thought I had been a monster or some ill-shaped creature before they came and saw, who then said they must change their thoughts, for I was a woman like others that were modest and civil.
>
> (1654b: sig. H)

So, in effect, the report is the plea. Setting the record straight will vindicate not only God's truth but also Trapnel's reputation, will allow her readers to make their own decisions and discover her to be 'modest and civil'.

As well as vindicating herself, Trapnel also seems to delight in herself. The *Report and Plea* is autobiographical, reflective, a political argument, and a drama: some of the courtroom scene included here is even set out like a play. But at the centre, and linking them all, is Trapnel herself. She reports her ripostes and their effect on the judges; she is both innocent and experienced, never before in a courtroom yet outmanoeuvring the judges in their own game of words. What is more, as she reports, this has some effect: those who at her arrival 'mocked and derided' her are now 'loving and careful', convinced that 'this woman is no witch' (p. 84). Whether there was actually such an unequivocal shift of opinion amongst those who witnessed her trial is less important than what it demonstrates about the effect she hopes her actions and writing can have: a successful vindication of God's — and so her own — truth.

Notes

1 The publications attributed to Trapnel (either written by her, or transcriptions of her prophecies) are: *The Cry of a Stone* (1654), *Strange and Wonderful Newes from White-Hall* (1654), *Anna Trapnel's Report and Plea* (1654), *A Legacy for Saints* (1654), and *A Voice for the King of Saints* (1658). There is also a 1000-page folio with a missing title page in the Bodleian Library, Oxford.
2 In Trapnel's account of her spiritual development (1654b: 16–17) she identifies 1 Corinthians 1.27–8, which speaks of the dissolution of the self, as being the text which reconciled her to her public duties. This text also proved to be significant for Anne Wentworth; see p. 185.

Textual note

The copytext is from the Library of the Society of Friends in London, shelf-mark 010 [Qm 1/1]. The page numbering in this edition is somewhat erratic. The first twenty-eight pages are numbered consistently; the next page is then numbered 25, and then this follows through consistently until the end of the text. The extract included here ends on the first page 28.

From: *Anna Trapnel's Report and Plea*

[Trapnel begins her narrative by giving an account of her call from God to go to Cornwall, her temptations by the devil to resist the call and her final decision to go; she then describes the journey down. On her arrival, rumours concerning her activities being rife, many people came to listen to her speak and to witness her trances, 'some out of good-will . . . and others to gaze', and it was not long before warrants were taken out for her arrest for 'aspersing the government'. Awaiting the arrival of the constable at the house of Captain and Mrs Langdon, where many people were still visiting her, Trapnel's 'praying and singing' continued:]

Then the Lord made his rivers flow, which soon broke down the banks of an ordinary capacity, and extraordinarily mounted my spirits into a praying and singing frame,[1] and so they remained till morning light, as I was told, for I was not capable[2] of that. But when I had done, and was a while silent, I came to speak weakly to those about me, saying, 'I must go to bed, for I am very weak'; and the men and women went away, and my friend that tended me, and some other maids,[3] helped me to bed, where I lay till the afternoon, they said, silent. And that time I had a vision of the minister's wife[4] stirring against me; and she was presented to me as one enviously bent against me, calling that falsity which she understood not. And I saw the clergyman and the jurors contriving an indictment against me,[5] and I saw myself stand before them; in a vision I saw this. And I sang with much courage, and told them I feared not them nor their doings, for that I had not deserved such usage.

But while I was singing praises to the Lord for his love to me, the justices sent their constable[6] to fetch me, who came and said he must have me with him. And he pulled, and called me, they said that were by, but I was not capable thereof. They said he was greatly troubled how to have me to his master; they told him he had better obey God than man. And his hand shook, they said, while he was pulling me. Then some went to the justices to tell them I could not come. But they would not be pacified. Some offered to be bound for my appearance next day, if I were in a capacity, but this was refused. They would have me out of my bed, unless some would take their oaths that it would endanger my life to be taken out of my bed, which none could do, without they had loved to take false oaths,[7] like some others in those parts. Then a friend persuaded them to see whether they could put me out of that condition, and told them I was never known to be put out of it; so they came. Justice Launce, now a Parliament-man,[8] was one of them, I was told. These justices that came to fetch me out of my bed, they made a great tumult, them and their followers, in the house, and some came upstairs crying 'A witch! A witch!',[9] making a great stir on the stairs. And a poor honest man rebuking such that said so, he was tumbled downstairs and beaten too, by one of the justices' followers. And the justices made a great noise in putting out of my chamber where I lay many of my friends; and they said if my friends would not take me up, they would have some should take me up. One of my friends told them that they must fetch their silk gowns[10] to do it then, for the poor would not do it. And they threatened much, but the Lord overruled them. They caused my eyelids to be pulled up,[11] for they said I held them fast, because I would deceive the people; they spake to this purpose. One of the justices pinched me by the nose, and caused my pillow to be pulled from under my head, and kept pulling me, and calling me; but I heard none of all this stir and bustle. Neither did I hear Mr Welstead,[12] which I was told called to the rulers,[13] saying, 'a whip will fetch her up'; and he stood at the chamber door talking against me, and said, 'She speaks nonsense.' The women said, 'Hearken, for you cannot hear, there is such a noise'; then he listened, and said, 'Now she hears me speak, she speaks sense.' And this clergyman durst not come till the rulers came, for then, they say, the witches can have no power over them: so that one depends upon another, rulers upon clergy, and clergy upon rulers.

And again, after they had made all the fury appear that the Lord permitted them to vent against me, they then went away, saying, 'She will fall in a trance when we shall at any time call for her.' The Lord kept me this day from their cruelty, which they had a good mind further to have let out against me. And that witch-trier woman of that town, some would fain have had come with her great pin which she used to thrust into witches to try them,[14] but the Lord my God in whom I trust delivered me from their malice, making good that word to me in the Psalms [76.10], 'The rage of man shall turn to thy praise, and the remnant of rages thou wilt restrain.' Then further, to tell you how the Lord carried me in singing and prayer after they were gone two hours, as I was told, and then I came to myself; and being all alone, I blessed God for that quiet still day that I had. And the gentlewoman of the house coming into the chamber, I said, 'Have I lain alone all this day? I have had a sweet day.' She replied, and said, did not I hear the justices there, and the uproar that was in my chamber? I said, 'No.' Then she told me how they dealt by her house, bringing in their followers, and what a noise they made. Then another friend asked me whether I did not hear that stir. I said, 'No.' They wondered, and so did I when I heard the relation, which is much more than I will write, for I don't take delight to stir in such puddles, it's no pleasant work to me. But that truth engageth me to let the world know what men have acted against the pourings-out of the spirit in a dispensation beyond their understanding; they hearkened not to scripture advice, which would not have any judge that they know not.[15]

After that day's tumult, at night many came to catch at my words. And it was very probable that the rulers sent some to watch for what could be had further against me. And there were two women, that they had got their names, who had promised them to swear against me, and of this I shall further speak when I come to it. But now I am

77

telling of what passed that night mentioned: many people spake much to me, asking me questions, the which the Lord helped me to answer. And my friends kept most part of that night in prayer on my behalf. And many watched what they said in prayer, for there were listeners under the window, which fain would have had something to have informed against them. There was great endeavouring to have found a bill of indictment against Captain Langdon,[16] but they could not; they could not vent their spleen, though they to the utmost desired it, the Lord would not let them have their evil desires herein. For though they in this would have brought him into contempt, yet they endeavoured this that so I might want a surety,[17] and then they had had what they desired, which was to have cast me into the gaol. But to leave that, and to tell you that I had the presence of the Lord with me that night abundantly, and my sleep was sweeter than at other times. My sister[18] Langdon lay with me that night, and in the morning she told me that she could not sleep all night for thinking of my going to the sessions[19] that day. She told me she wondered I could sleep so soundly all night. I told her I never had a sweeter night in my life, and as for my going before the rulers, I was no whit afraid or thoughtful, for I had cast my care upon the Lord, which I was persuaded would speak for me. Therefore I was not troubled nor afraid, for the Lord said to me, 'Fear not, be not dismayed, I am thy God, and will stand by thee' [Isaiah 41.10].

Then I rose up, and prepared to go before them at sessions-house; and walking out in the garden before I went, I was thinking what I should say before the justices. But I was taken off from my own thoughts quickly, through the word, 'Take no heed what thou shalt say; being brought before them for the Lord Christ's sake, he will give thee words. Dost thou know what they will ask thee? Therefore look to the Lord, who will give thee answers suitable to what shall be required of thee.' So I was resolved to cast myself upon the Lord and his teaching. And though I had heard how the form of bills run, and of that word 'Not guilty', according to the form of the bill, yet I said, 'I shall not remember to say thus, if the Lord don't bid me say so; and if he bids me, I will say it.' And this I thought, I would be nothing, the Lord should have all the praise, it being his due. So I went, the officer coming for me; and as I went along the street, I had followed me abundance of all manner of people, men and women, boys and girls, which crowded after me. And some pulled me by the arms, and stared me in the face, making wry faces at me, and saying, 'How do you now? How is it with you now?'. And thus they mocked and derided at me as I went to the sessions. But I was never in such a blessed self-denying lamb-like frame of spirit in my life as then; I had such lovely apprehensions of Christ's sufferings, and of that scripture which saith, 'He went as a sheep, dumb before the shearers, he opened not his mouth; and when reviled, he reviled not again' [Isaiah 53.7; 1 Peter 2.23]. The Lord kept me also, so that I went silent to the sessions-house, which was much thronged with people: some said the sessions-house was never so filled since it was a sessions-house. So that I was a gazing-stock for all sorts of people, but I praise the Lord, this did not daunt me, nor a great deal more that I suffered that day, for the eternal grace of Jehovah surrounded me, and kept me from harm. So way was made for me to draw near to the table, which stood lower than the justices; and round the table sat the lawyers and others that attended them, and I with my friends that went with me stood by the lawyers, and the justices leaned over a rail, which railed them in together. Only I espied a clergyman at their elbow, who helped to make up their indictment, so that he could not be absent, though his pulpit wanted him, it being a fast-day, set apart by authority, which he broke without any scruple that so he might keep close to the work of accusation. But though he and the witch-trying woman looked steadfastly in my face, it did no way dismay me, nor the grim fierce looks of the justices did not daunt me, for as soon as I beheld them I remembered a dear friend to Christ, who smiled in the face of a great man that looked fiercely on him, and sat as a judge to condemn him for the testimony of Jesus; but this servant of the Lord looked cheerfully all the time of his accusations charged upon him.[20] So I thinking upon that posture of his before those that acted against him, I begged the same cheerfulness, and I had the same courage to look my accusers in the face, which was no carnal boldness, though they called it so.

And when I came before them, Lobb, being the mouth of the court, as he was foreman of the jury he represented the whole court, and he first demanded my name, and I told him. And he said, 'Anna Trapnel, here is a bill of indictment to be read, for you to give your answer concerning.' Then Justice Lobb said, 'Read the bill', so it was read to me; and Lobb said, 'Are you guilty, or not?' I had no word to say at the present, but the Lord said to me, 'Say "not guilty", according to the form of the bill.' So I spoke it as from the Lord, who knew I was not guilty of such an indictment. Then said Lobb, 'Traverse the bill to the next assizes';[21] so that was done. Then Lobb said I must enter into bond for my appearance at the next assizes, unto which I agreed. Then they demanded sureties, so I desired Captain Langdon and Major Bawden[22] to be my sureties, unto which they were willing. So there were two recognizances drawn, one for my appearance, and the other bound me to the good behaviour; and I was entered into both the recognizances £300,[23] and my sureties as much, to both the recognizances. And this being done, they whispered a while, and I thought they had done with me at that time. So they had, if they had gone according to true law, which was not to have brought their interrogatories[24] then; but the report was that I would discover myself to be a witch when I came before the justices, by having never a word to answer for myself, for it used to be so among the witches, they could not speak before the magistrates, and so they said it would be with me. But the Lord quickly defeated them herein, and caused many to be of another mind. Then Lobb said, 'Tender her the book which was written from something said at Whitehall,'[25] so the book was reached out to me, and Justice Lobb said, 'What say you to that book? Will you own it? Is it yours?'

A. T. 'I am not careful to answer you in that matter.'

Then they said, 'She denies her book.' Then they whispered with those behind them. Then spake Justice Lobb again, and said, 'Read a vision of the horns[26] out of the book', so that was read. Then Justice Lobb said, 'What say you to this? Is this yours?'

A. T. 'I am not careful to answer you in that matter, touching the whole book. As I told you before, so I say again. For what was spoken was at Whitehall, at a place of concourse of people, and near a council I suppose wise enough to call me into question if I offended, and unto them I appeal.' But though it was said I appealed unto Caesar and unto Caesar should I go, yet I have not been brought before him which is called Caesar;[27] so much by the by. Again, I said I supposed they had not power to question me for that which was spoke in another county; they said yea, that they had. Then the book was put by, and they again whispered.

Then Justice Lobb asked me about my coming into that country,[28] how it came to pass that I came into that country.

I answered I came as others did that were minded to go into the country.

Lobb. 'But why did you come into this country?'

A. T. 'Why might not I come here, as well as into another country?'

Lobb. 'But you have no lands, nor livings, nor acquaintance to come to in this country.'

A. T. 'What though I had not? I am a single person, and why may I not be with my friends anywhere?'

Lobb. 'I understand you are not married.'

A. T. 'Then having no hindrance, why may not I go where I please, if the Lord so will?'

Then spoke Justice Launce, 'But did not some desire you to come down?' And this Lobb asked me too, but I told them I would accuse none, I was there to answer as to what they should charge my own particular with.

Launce said, 'Pray, Mistress, tell us what moved you to come such a journey?'

A. T. 'The Lord gave me leave to come, asking of him leave, whitherever I went. I used still to pray for his direction in all I do, and so I suppose ought you,' I said.

Justice Launce. 'But pray tell us, what moved you to come such a journey?'

A. T. 'The Lord moved me, and gave me leave.'

Launce. 'But had you not some extraordinary impulses of spirit[29] that brought you down? Pray tell us what those were.'

A. T. 'When you are capable of extraordinary impulses of spirit, I will tell you; but I suppose you are not in a capacity now,' for I saw how deridingly he spoke. And for answering him thus, he said I was one of a bold spirit, but he soon took me down:[30] so himself said. But some said it took them down, for the Lord carried me so to speak, that they were in a hurry and confusion and sometimes would speak all together, that I was going to say, 'What, are you like women, all speakers and no hearers?' But I said thus, 'What, do you speak all at a time? I cannot answer all, when speaking at once. I appeal to the civillest of you,' and I directed my speech to Justice Lobb, who spake very moderately, and gave me a civil answer, saying, 'You are not acquainted with the manner of the court, which is to give in their sayings.'[31]

A. T. 'But I cannot answer all at once. Indeed I do not know the manner of the court, for I never was before any till now.'

Justice Lobb. 'You prophesy against Truro.'

A. T. 'Indeed I pray against the sins of the people of Truro, and for their souls' welfare. Are you angry for that?'

Lobb. 'But you must not judge authority, but pray for them, and not speak so suspiciously of them,' and more to this purpose he spoke to me.

A. T. 'I will take up your word, in which you said I was not to judge. You said well, for so saith the scripture, "Who art thou that judgest another man's servant? To his own master he standeth or falleth; yea, he shall be holden up, for God is able to make him stand" [Romans 14.4]. But you have judged me, and never heard me speak: you have not dealt so well by me as Agrippa dealt by Paul. Though Agrippa was an heathen, he would have Paul speak before he gave in his judgment concerning him' [Acts 25.21–27; 26].

Justice Tregagle. 'Oh, you are a dreamer!'

A. T. 'So they called Joseph [Genesis 37.5–11], therefore I wonder not that you call me so.'

Justice Selye said, 'You knew we were with you yesterday.'

A. T. 'I did not.'

Justice Selye. 'He which is the major said you will not say so.'

A. T. 'I will speak it, being it's truth.'

He said, 'Call the women that will witness they heard you say you knew we were with you.' And he pulled out a writing, and named their names, calling to some to fetch them.

A. T. 'You may suborn false witnesses against me, for they did so against Christ.' And I said, 'Produce your witnesses.'

Justice Selye. 'We shall have them for you at next assizes.'

They put it off long enough, because one was fallen in a sound[32] before she got out of the house where she dwelt; and the other was come into the sessions-house. And Mrs Grose, a gentlewoman of the town, standing by her that was their false witness, said, 'Wilt thou take an oath thus? Take heed what thou dost, it's a dangerous thing to take a false oath.' And she ran out of the sessions-house; this was credibly reported. And here ended their witnesses that they had procured against me as to that. There was a soldier that smiled to hear how the Lord carried me along in my speech, and Justice Selye called to the jailer to take him away, saying he laughed at the court. He thought him to be one of my friends, and for his cheerful looking the jailer had like to have had him. Then I said, 'Scripture speaks of such who "make a man an offender for a word" [Isaiah 29.21], but you make a man an offender for a look.' They greatly bustled, as if they would have taken him away; but this was quickly squashed, their heat as to this lasted not long. In the mean time, the other, Selye, was talking to Major Bawden, wondering such a man as he, who had been so well reputed for a judicious, sober, understanding man, should hearken to me; many words were used to him to that purpose. I said, 'Why may not he and others try all things, and hold fast that which is best?' But they still cast grim looks on me. And they had a saying to Major Bawden, and to Captain Langdon then, whom they derided in a letter sent from Truro by some of their learned court, which wrote that Captain Langdon and Major Bawden stood up and made a learned defence. They had indeed such learning from the spirit of wisdom and of a sound mind, which the jurors and their companions were not able to contend against, their speech and whole deportment was so humble and self-denying, and so seasoned with the salt of grace [Colossians 4.6], which their flashy unsavoury spirits could not endure. Those that are raised from the dunghill and set on thrones cannot sit there without vaunting and showing their fool's coat of many colours, as envy, and pride, and vainglory; these and other colours they show, which delights not King Jesus nor his followers. Justice Lobb told me I made a disturbance in the town. I asked wherein. He said by drawing so many people after me. I said, 'How did I draw them?' He said I set open my chamber doors and my windows for people to hear.

A. T. 'That's a very unlikely thing, that I should do so, for I prayed the maid to lock my chamber door when I went to bed, and I did not rise in the night sure to open it.' I said, 'Why may not I pray with many people in the room, as well as your professing woman[33] that prays before men and women, she knowing them to be there; but I know not that there is anybody in the room when I pray. And if you indict one for praying, why not another? Why are you so partial in your doings?'

Justice Lobb. 'But you don't pray so, as others.'

A. T. 'I pray in my chamber.'

Justice Trevill. 'Your chamber!'

A. T. 'Yea, that it's my chamber while I am there, through the pleasure of my friends.'

They used more words to me, sometimes slighting and mockingly they spoke, and sometimes seeming to advise me to take heed how I spoke and prayed so again. Many such kind of words Justice Trevill used, and Justice Lobb. And one thing I omitted in telling you when I told you how I answered Justice Launce: I should have told you how I said to him, if he would know what the ordinary[34] impulse of spirit was that I had to bring me into that country, I would tell him. So I related the scriptures, as that in the Psalms, and in the prophet Isaiah, how the presence and spirit of the Lord should be with me, and he would uphold me and strengthen me with the right hand of his righteousness [Psalms 139.7–10; Isaiah 29.21]. He answered such impulse was common, they hoped they had that, they were not ignorant of such impulse of spirit; much to this effect was spoken. I seeing they were very willing to be gone, I said, 'Have you done with me?' Answer was I might now go away. But I said, 'Pray, what is it to break the good behaviour you have bound me over to? I know not what you may make a breaking of it: is it a breaking the good behaviour to pray and sing?' Justice Trevill said no, so[35] I did it at the habitation where I abode. 'It's well,' said I, 'you will give me leave it shall be anywhere.' I said, 'I will leave one word with you, and that is this: a time will come when you and I shall appear before the great judge of the tribunal seat of the most high, and then I think you will hardly be able to give an account for this day's work before the Lord, at that day of true judgment.' Said Tregagle, 'Take you no care for us.' So they were willing to have no more discourse with me.

And as I went in the crowd, many strangers were very loving and careful to help me out of the crowd; and the rude multitude said, 'Sure this woman is no witch, for she speaks many good words, which the witches could not.' And thus the Lord made the rude rabble to justify his appearance. For in all that was said by me, I was nothing, the Lord put all in my mouth, and told me what I should say, and that from the written word, he put it in my memory and mouth; so that I will have nothing ascribed to me, but all honour and praise given to him whose right it is, even to Jehovah, who is the king that lives for ever. I have left out some things that I thought were not so material to be written; and what I have written of this, it's to declare as much as is convenient to take off those falsities and contrary reports that are abroad concerning my sufferings, some making it worse than it was, and some saying it was little or nothing. Now to inform all people's judgments, I have thought it meet to offer this relation to the world's view, and with as much covering as I can of saints'[36] weaknesses herein, praying the Lord to forgive them; and as for the Lord's enemies, that he would confound them; but as for my enemies, I still pray.

(*Anna Trapnel's Report and Plea*, pp. 20–80)

Notes

1 *frame*: mood or state.

2 *capable*: aware.

3 *maids*: young women: not specifically servants.

4 *minister's wife*: Mr Powel, 'a teacher in those parts, came in with his wife' to listen to Trapnel speak (1654b: 16).

5 *an indictment against me*: After Trapnel had spoken in Truro, the clergy, including Mr

Welstead (see note 12), called for her arrest, claiming she was 'an imposter, and a dangerous deceiver'. Subsequently warrants were taken out for her arrest, asserting that she 'went from place to place, aspersing the government': in other words, for sedition (1654b: 18–19).

6 *justices . . . constable*: Justices of the Peace looked after the judicial and administrative government of the county; the constable was a parish officer responsible to them.

7 *false oaths*: Trapnel is condemning as hypocrites those who took oaths of allegiance first to the king and then to the Commonwealth.

8 *Justice Launce, now a Parliament-man* : James Launce became an MP for Cornwall in September 1654. All the justices presiding at Trapnel's hearing were local gentry; most had been county commissioners, and Lobb and Selye, as well as Launce, later became MPs.

9 *A witch! A witch!*: Trapnel's prophetic trances were used as grounds on which to accuse her of witchcraft, a charge also levelled against other sectaries: George Fox was called a witch as early as 1652 (Fox 1948: 94n, 121–2). Moreover, this may have been a particularly sensitive topic in this part of Cornwall, where in 1654 Anne Jefferies's trances resulted in allegations of witchcraft. Justice Tregagle, who ordered her arrest, also sat at Trapnel's hearing (Spooner 1935: 14–15).

10 *silk gowns* : the sumptuary laws dictated that only people of high social rank could dress in silk. Hence this refers to the class of those who would have to arrest her, and aligns her with 'the poor' rather than the upper classes.

11 *they caused my eyelids to be pulled up* : presumably to ascertain whether or not she was simulating a trance.

12 *Mr Welstead* : One of the clergymen who had called for Trapnel's arrest; in 1656 he was involved in the arrest of George Fox in St Ives.

13 *rulers* : those in authority, here referring to local magistrates, MPs, etc.

14 *witch-trier woman . . . her great pin* : the witch-trier gathered evidence against the accused. She (or he) would 'examine the suspect for unusual bodily marks and then . . . test the marks by pricking them to find out whether they were sensible' (Larner 1981: 111). It was thought that the devil consummated a pact with a witch by nipping her, and that the mark that this left was insensible to pain and could not bleed. Such a mark was taken as evidence of a pact.

15 *scripture advice* : possibly referring to 1 Corinthians 4.3–5, Romans 14.13, or John 7.51.

16 *Captain Langdon* : Francis Langdon (c.1600–58) sat in the Barebones Parliament for Cornwall. A Baptist and a Fifth Monarchist sympathiser, he visited Trapnel in London in January 1654. She was staying with him and his wife when she was arrested.

17 *surety* : 'somebody who makes himself [or herself] liable for the default or miscarriage of another; a bail' (OED).

18 *sister* : a fellow believer.

19 *sessions* : a judicial trial or investigation.

20 *a dear friend to Christ* : perhaps a reference to the examination of Vavasor Powell; see p. 73.

21 *traverse the bill to the next assizes* : to traverse a bill was formally to contradict tor deny it, but here it seems to mean 'transfer'. Assizes were the periodic sittings of professional judges.

22 *Major Bawden* : John Bawden was a Fifth Monarchist sympathiser and MP for Cornwall in the Barebones Parliament of 1653.

23 *recognizances £300* : a recognizance is a bond entered into in court, promising the performance of some act or the observation of some condition, such as to appear again before the court when called. It is also a sum of money pledged in surety for such a performance. Langdon and Bawden each pledged £150, a considerable sum of money: Gregory King tells us that in 1688 a military officer had a yearly income of £60 (King 1936: 31).

24 *interrogatories* : 'a question formally put, or drawn up in writing to be put, to an accused person or a witness' (OED).

25 *book . . . from something said at Whitehall* : Trapnel's *The Cry of a Stone* was published in

February 1654. It is a lengthy collection of her prophecies, in prose and verse, made when she fell into a trance at Whitehall in January 1654.

26 *a vision of horns* : Daniel 7.7–8 refers to a vision of horns, and is the reference point for Trapnel's own vision. The four horns were interpreted by Fifth Monarchists as the four great empires of Babylon, Persia, Greece, and Rome, the last still seen as oppressing Europe in the form of the Roman Catholic church and, by extension, the Anglican church.

27 *Caesar* : Trapnel, referring to Cromwell here, is alluding to Acts 25.10.

28 *country* : county, and therefore administrative district.

29 *extraordinary impulses of spirit* : appears in copytext as 'of extraordinary impulses spirit'.

30 *he soon took me down* : he would soon put me in my place.

31 *to give in their sayings* : to speak as and when they wish. It was not until the eighteenth century that court procedures became more formal and strictly regulated.

32 *sound* : a swoon, or fainting fit.

33 *professing woman* : a woman who testifies publicly to her faith.

34 *ordinary* : Trapnel ironically harks back to their earlier exchange; see p. 81 and note 30.

35 *so* : if; as long as.

36 *saints* : God's elect; those predestined to be saved.

4

MARGARET CAVENDISH

A True Relation of my Birth, Breeding and Life
from
*Nature's Pictures drawn by Fancy's Pencil to the Life. Written
by the thrice noble, illustrious and excellent Princess, the Lady
Marchioness of Newcastle.*

*In this volume there are several feigned stories of natural
descriptions, as comical, tragical and tragicomical, poetical,
romantical, philosophical and historical, both in prose and verse,
some mixed, partly prose and partly verse.*

*Also, there are some morals, and some dialogues; but they are as
the advantage loaves of bread to a baker's dozen. And a true story at
the latter end, wherein there is no feignings.*

*London, printed for J. Martin and J. Allestrye, at the Bell in St Paul's
churchyard. 1656.*

Margaret Cavendish, first Duchess of Newcastle (1623–73), has always been
the subject of controversy. She herself admitted taking 'delight in a singularity' (p. 96) in most aspects of her life: she wore distinctive clothes; she was
one of the first women to attend a meeting of the Royal Society; she wrote
prolifically and expected the world to take her writings seriously. When this
individuality led to adverse comments from her contemporaries, she claimed
that she was 'proud' of the 'censures of this age' (1667: sig. (b)^r). In fact, it
seems that those 'censures' were tinged with fascination. 'All the town-talk
is nowadays of her extravagencies', wrote Pepys in 1667: 'the whole story of
this Lady is a romance, and all she doth is romantic' (Pepys 1970–83: VIII,
186, 163). Evelyn commented warmly on her 'fancifull habit' and in addition
noted her 'extraordinary . . . discourse' (Evelyn 1959: 507). It was
Cavendish's own wish to 'be known to the world by my wit, not by my folly'
(1664: 167), and indeed her tombstone in Westminster Abbey honours her
as a 'wise, witty, and learned lady'. However, later generations have not
been so sure that these qualities are present in her autobiographical writing,

if at all. Sir Egerton Brydges, who reprinted *A True Relation of my Birth, Breeding and Life* in 1814, apologized for the fact that in her memoir 'the Duchess was deficient in a cultivated judgment' and 'her powers of fancy and sentiment were more active than her powers of reasoning' (Cavendish ed. Brydges 1814: 1). In 1957, her biographer described the *True Relation* as 'one of the most charming autobiographical sketches of the century' (Grant 1957: 153): praise, certainly, but tinged with a sense of the work as lightweight ('charming') and incomplete ('sketch').

Cavendish knew that by flouting the stereotypes of women's fashions and accomplishment, particularly by writing and publishing, she was inviting controversy: 'true it is, spinning with the fingers is more proper to our sex than studying or writing poetry' (1653: sig. A2ʳ). Typically, having acknowledged this, she pressed on in defiance, first publishing her poems in 1653 though asking that 'all noble and worthy ladies' should refrain from condemning her as a 'dishonour of your sex' (1653: sig. A3ʳ). She anticipated that men would undoubtedly scorn her book, 'because they think thereby women encroach too much upon their prerogatives; for they hold books as their crown, and the sword as their sceptre, by which they rule and govern' (1653: sig. A3ʳ⁻ᵛ). Without inordinate fear of this patriarchal power of pen and sword, Cavendish proceeded over two subsequent decades to write poetry, drama, natural philosophy, biography, orations, letters, science fiction – and autobiography.

Cavendish's *True Relation of my Birth, Breeding and Life*, appended to her collection of stories, *Nature's Pictures* (1656), is striking for its combination of immediacy with sustained self-analysis, and of private modesty with an unashamed and totally secular desire for fame. Her purpose in writing the memoir appears to be both for personal satisfaction and for 'the sake of after-ages' (1656: 367); these motives lead her to produce 'a true story . . . wherein there is no feignings', as the title-page announces. Cavendish's 'truth', however, is expressed with imaginative invention. Her thoughts work 'like silk-worms that spins [sic] out of their own bowels' (p. 95 below) and the writing is vivid in its breathlessness, the restless syntax evoking her vivacious personality. 'My words run stumbling out of my mouth', she claimed (1656: 367), and one of the most impressive moments in the autobiography is a richly metaphoric exploration of her mode of writing (see pp. 93–4). She regarded the female mind as 'fantastical' in its movements (1653: sig. A3ʳ), and her own irregular prose celebrates such variance from a more rational (masculine) norm of self-expression. In order to make Cavendish's complexity accessible to modern readers, this edition has simplified her punctuation and thereby reduced her enormous sentences and paragraphs to manageable lengths. It is to be hoped that her colourful nature – marshalling the troops of her words, emulating Caesar in telling her own life story, hoping Faust-like to stop fortune's wheel when she was at the top – still shines through.

It comes as no surprise that Cavendish, 'singular' though she was in personality and written style, found it impossible to create an image of herself without reference to those masculine forces which, by contradiction, defined her. Not only are her models in the writing of autobiography, Caesar and Ovid, male, but her work is itself framed by men. 'My father was a gentleman' are the opening words of the text (1656: 368), and it concludes by placing her as a daughter and a wife whose history might have otherwise remained unknown; as she pointed out elsewhere, a woman's name 'is lost as to her particular in her marrying' (1664: 183). Though insistent that she had the right to 'write her own life', she nevertheless described her writing as 'scribbling', mere 'words', in comparison with her husband's admired 'wit' (p. 93 below). The memoir was written while Cavendish was in exile from the Commonwealth, and it seems consistent with such a context that she should frequently dwell on her fondness for quiet contemplation, her 'bashful' nature (see pp. 90, 98) and fears for her reputation. The self presented, then, is a shifting image, bold and yet shy, just as the sentences build up through statement and then qualification. Her autobiography fascinatingly encompasses confession and triumph; 'fancy' and 'truth' (p. 99).

Strangely, Cavendish's *True Relation* was only published once in her lifetime. When a second edition of *Nature's Pictures* came out in 1671, after she had written the full-length biography of her husband, her own brief autobiography had been removed. The moment for self-definition had, apparently, passed.

Textual note

The copytext which forms the basis of these modernized extracts is the British Library copy of *Nature's Pictures* (1656), shelfmark G11599. This copy contains marginal corrections in Cavendish's hand which have been incorporated into the text. As mentioned above, Cavendish's punctuation has been substantially altered in accordance with modern conventions.

From: A True Relation of my Birth, Breeding and Life

[Cavendish opens her memoir with an account of her father (Thomas Lucas of Colchester), her older brothers and sisters, and her own upbringing by her mother ('according to my birth, and the nature of my sex', 1656: 369). She then describes, in the following passage, how she went her distinctive, if uncertain, way into court and marriage.]

When the queen was in Oxford,[1] I had a great desire to be one of her maids of honour, hearing the queen had not the same number she was used to have. Whereupon I wooed and won my mother to let me go; for my mother, being fond of all her children, was desirous to please them, which made her consent to my request. But my brothers and sisters seemed not very well pleased, by reason I had never been from home, nor seldom out of their sight. For though they knew I would not behave myself to their, or my own, dishonour, yet they thought I might to my disadvantage, being unexperienced in the world; which indeed I did. For I was so bashful when I was out of my mother's, brothers' and sisters' sight, whose presence used to give me confidence (thinking I could not do amiss whilst any one of them were by, for I knew they would gently reform me if I did). Besides, I was ambitious they should approve of my actions and behaviour, that when I was gone from them I was like one that had no foundation to stand, or guide to direct me; which made me afraid, lest I should wander with ignorance out of the ways of honour, so that I knew not how to behave myself.

Besides, I had heard the world was apt to lay aspersions even on the innocent, for which I durst neither look up with my eyes, nor speak, nor be any way sociable: insomuch as I was thought a natural fool. Indeed I had not much wit, yet I was not an idiot; my wit was according to my years. And though I might have learnt more wit and advanced my understanding by living in a court, yet being dull, fearful and bashful, I neither heeded what was said or practised, but just what belonged to my loyal duty and my own honest reputation. And indeed I was so afraid to dishonour my friends and family by my indiscreet actions, that I rather chose to be accounted a fool, than to be thought rude or wanton. In truth my bashfulness and fears made me repent my going from home to see the world abroad,[2] and much I did desire to return to my mother again; or to my sister Pye,[3] with whom I often lived when she was in London, and loved with a supernatural affection. But my mother advised me there to stay, although I put her to more charges than if she had kept me at home; and the more, by reason she and my brothers were sequestered from their estates and plundered of all their goods.[4] Yet she maintained me so, that I was in a condition rather to lend than to borrow, which courtiers usually are not, being always necessitated by reason of great expenses courts put them to. But my mother said it would be a disgrace for me to return out of the court so soon after I was placed. So I continued almost two years, until such time as I was married from thence.

For my lord the Marquis of Newcastle[5] did approve of those bashful fears which many condemned, and would choose such a wife as he might bring to his own humours;[6] and not such an one as was wedded to self conceit, or one that had been tempered to the humours of another. For which, he wooed me for his wife. And though I did dread marriage and shunned men's companies as much as I could, yet I could not nor had not the power to refuse him, by reason my affections were fixed on him, and he was the only person I ever was in love with. Neither was I ashamed to own it, but gloried therein. For it was not amorous love, I never was infected therewith: it is a disease, or a passion, or both, I only know by relation, not by experience. Neither could title, wealth, power or person entice me to love. But my love was honest and honourable, being placed upon merit; which affection joyed at the fame of his worth, pleased with delight in his wit, proud of the respects he used to me, and triumphing in the affections he professed for me (which affections he hath confirmed to me by a deed of time, sealed by constancy, and assigned by an unalterable decree of his promise). Which makes me happy in despite of fortune's frowns. For though misfortunes may (and do oft) dissolve base, wild, loose and ungrounded affections, yet she has no power of those that are united either by merit, justice, gratitude, duty, fidelity or the like. And though my lord hath lost his estate and banished out of his country for his loyalty to his king and country; yet neither despised poverty nor pinching necessity could make him break the bonds of friendship, or weaken his loyal duty to his king or country.

But not only the family I am linked to is ruined, but the family from which I sprung, by these unhappy wars: which ruin my mother lived to see, and then died having lived a widow many years.[7] For she never forgot my father so as to marry again. Indeed he remained so lively in her memory, and her grief was so lasting, as she never mentioned his name (though she spoke often of him) but[8] love and grief caused tears to flow and tender sighs to rise, mourning in sad complaints. She made her house her cloister, enclosing herself, as it were, therein; for she seldom went abroad, unless to church. But these unhappy wars forced her out, by reason she and her children were loyal to the king. For which they plundered her and my brothers of all their goods, plate, jewels, money, corn, cattle and the like; cut down their woods, pulled down their houses, and sequestered them from their lands and livings.

But in such misfortunes my mother was of an heroic spirit, in suffering patiently where there is no remedy, or to be industrious where she thought she could help. She was of a grave behaviour, and had such a majestic grandeur, as it were continually hung about her, that it would strike a kind of an awe to the beholders, and command respect from the rudest. (I mean the rudest of civilised people; I mean not such barbarous people as plundered her and used her cruelly. For they would have pulled God out of heaven, had they had power, as they did royalty out of his throne.) Also her beauty was beyond the ruin of time, for she had a well-favoured loveliness in her face, a pleasing sweetness in her countenance, and a well-tempered complexion (as neither too red, nor too pale) even to her dying hour, although in years. And by her dying one might think death was enamoured with her, for he embraced her in a sleep, and so gently, as if he were afraid to hurt her. Also she was an affectionate mother, breeding her children with a most industrious care and tender love. And having eight children, three sons and five daughters, there was not any one crooked or any ways deformed. Neither were they dwarfish, or of a giant-like stature, but every ways proportionable; likewise well featured, clear complexions, brown hairs (but some lighter than others), sound teeth, sweet breaths, plain speeches, tuneable voices. I mean not so much to sing as in speaking: as, not stuttering nor wharling[9] in the throat or speaking through the nose, or hoarsely (unless they had a cold) or squeakingly, which impediments many have. Neither were their voices of too low a strain or too high, but their notes and words were tuneable and timely.

I hope this truth will not offend my readers. And lest they should think I am a partial[10] register, I dare not commend my sisters as to say they were handsome (although many would say they were very handsome). But this I dare say: their beauty (if any they had) was not so lasting as my mother's, time making suddenner ruin in their faces than in hers.

(True Relation, pp. 373–7)

[Cavendish follows the eulogy of her mother with further details of her two families and her husband's exile (which she shared except when visiting England to petition on his behalf). In this second (fuller) extract she gives a portrait of the Duke and comments on the pleasures of her life with him, including her writing; after further discussion of her personal disposition, Cavendish concludes the autobiography with defiant self-justification.]

Heaven hitherto hath kept us. And though fortune hath been cross, yet we do submit, and are both content with what is and cannot be mended; and are so prepared, that the worst of fortunes shall not afflict our minds so as to make us unhappy, howsoever it doth pinch our lives with poverty. For if tranquility lives in an honest mind, the mind lives in peace, although the body suffer. But patience hath armed us, and misery hath tried us, and finds us fortune-proof. For the truth is, my lord is a person whose humour is neither extravagantly merry nor unnecessarily sad. His mind is above his fortune, as his generosity is above his purse, his courage above danger, his justice above bribes, his friendship above self-interest, his truth too firm for falsehood, his temperance beyond temptation. His conversation is pleasing and affable; his wit is quick and his judgment is strong, distinguishing clearly without clouds of mistakes, dissecting truth so as it justly admit not of disputes. His discourse is always new upon the occasion, without troubling the hearers with old historical relations, nor stuffed with useless sentences. His behaviour is manly without formality, and free without constraint: and his mind hath the same freedom. His nature is noble, and his disposition sweet. His loyalty is proved by his public service for his king and country, by his often hazarding of his life, by the loss of his estate and the banishment of his person, by his necessitated condition and his constant and patient suffering.

But howsoever our fortunes are, we are both content, spending our time harmlessly. For my lord pleases himself with the management of some few horses, and exercises himself with the use of the sword: which two arts he hath brought by his studious thoughts, rational experience and industrious practice to an absolute perfection. And though he hath taken as much pains in those arts, both by study and practice, as chemists[11] for the philosopher's stone, yet he hath this advantage of them: that he hath found the right and the truth thereof and therein, which chemists never found in their art, and I believe never will.

Also he recreates himself with his pen, writing what his wit dictates to him. But I pass my time rather with scribbling than writing, with words than wit. Not that I speak much, because I am addicted to contemplation, unless I am with my lord; yet then I rather attentively listen to what he says, than impertinently speak. Yet when I am writing any sad feigned stories, or serious humours or melancholy passions, I am forced many times to express them with the tongue before I can write them with the pen; by reason those thoughts that are sad, serious and melancholy are apt to contract and to draw too much back (which oppression doth as it were overpower or smother the conception in the brain). But when some of those thoughts are sent out in words, they give the rest more liberty to place themselves in a more methodical order: marching more regularly with my pen on the ground of white paper. But my letters seem rather as a ragged rout than a well armed body. For the brain being quicker in creating than the hand in writing or the memory in retaining, many fancies are lost, by reason they oft-times outrun the pen. Where I, to keep speed in the race, write so fast as I stay not so long as to write my letters plain: insomuch as some have taken my handwriting for some strange character. And being accustomed so to do, I cannot now write very plain, when I strive to write my best. Indeed my ordinary handwriting is so bad as few can read it, so as to write it fair for the press. But however that little wit I have, it delights me to scribble it out and disperse it about. For I being[12] addicted from my childhood to contemplation rather than conversation, to solitariness rather than society, to melancholy rather than mirth, to write with the pen than to work with a needle, passing my time with harmless fancies (their company being pleasing, their conversation innocent), in which I take such pleasure as I neglect my health. For it is as great a grief to leave their society, as a joy to be in their company. My only trouble is, lest my brain should grow barren,[13] or that the root of my fancies should become insipid, withering into a dull stupidity for want of maturing subjects to write on.

For I being[14] of a lazy nature, and not of an active disposition as some are that love to journey from town to town, from place to place, from house to house, delighting in variety of company, making still one where the greatest number is.[15] Likewise in playing at cards, or any other games: in which I neither have practised, nor have I any skill therein. As for dancing, although it be a graceful art and becometh unmarried persons well, yet for those that are married it is too light an action, disagreeing with the gravity thereof. And for revelling, I am of too dull a nature to make one in a merry society. As for feasting, it would neither agree with my humour or constitution; for my diet is for the most part sparing (as a little boiled chicken or the like), my drink most commonly water. For though I have an indifferent good appetite, yet I do often fast, out of an opinion that [   ][16] if I should eat much and exercise little (which I do, only walking a slow pace in my chamber whilst my thoughts run apace in my brain, so that the motions of my mind hinders the active exercises of my body). For should I dance or run, or walk apace, I should dance my thoughts out of measure, run my fancies out of breath and tread out the feet of my numbers.[17]

But because I would not bury myself quite from the sight of the world, I go sometimes abroad: seldom to visit, but only in my coach about the town[18] or about some of the streets, which we call here a 'tour', where all the chief of the town go to see and to be seen. Likewise all strangers of what quality soever, as all great princes or queens that make any short stay. For this town, being a passage or thoroughfare to most parts, causes many times persons of great quality to be here, though not as inhabitants, yet to lodge for some short time. And all such, as I said, take a delight, or at least go to see the custom thereof, which most cities of note in Europe (for all I can hear) have suchlike recreations for the effeminate sex. Although for my part I had rather sit at home and write, or walk, as I said, in my chamber and contemplate; but I hold necessary sometimes to appear abroad. Besides, I do find that several objects do bring new materials for my thoughts and fancies to build upon. Yet I must say this in the behalf of my thoughts, that I never found them idle. For if the senses brings no work in, they will work of themselves, like silk-worms that spins out of their own bowels. Neither can I say I think the time tedious, when I am alone, so I be[19] near my lord and know he is well.

But now I have declared to my readers my birth, breeding and actions, to this part of my life: I mean the material parts, for should I write every particular, as my childish sports and the like, it would be ridiculous and tedious. But I have been honourably born and nobly matched; I have been bred to elevated thoughts, not to a dejected spirit; my life hath been ruled with honesty, attended by modesty and directed by truth. But since I have writ in general thus far of my life, I think it fit I should speak something of my humour, particular practice and disposition.

As for my humour, I was from my childhood given to contemplation, being more taken or delighted with thoughts than in conversation with a society; insomuch as I would walk two or three hours and never rest, in a musing, considering, contemplating manner, reasoning with myself of everything my senses did present. But when I was in the company of my natural friends, I was very attentive of what they said or did. But for strangers, I regarded not much what they said but many times I did observe their actions; whereupon my reason as judge, and my thoughts as accusers or excusers, or approvers and commenders, did plead, or appeal to accuse, or complain thereto. Also I never took delight in closets[20] or cabinets of toys,[21] but in the variety of fine clothes, and such toys as only were to adorn my person. Likewise I had a natural stupidity towards the learning of any other language than my native tongue. For I could sooner and with more facility understand the sense, than remember the words; and for want of such memory makes me so unlearned in foreign languages as I am.

As for my practice, I was never very active, by reason I was given so much to contemplation. Besides, my brothers and sisters were for the most part serious and staid in their actions, not given to sport nor play nor dance about; whose company I keeping, made me so too. But I observed that although their actions were staid, yet they would be very merry amongst themselves, delighting in each others' company. Also they would in their discourse express the general actions of the world: judging, condemning, approving, commending, as they thought good. And with those that were innocently harmless, they would make themselves merry therewith. As for my study of books, it was little; yet I chose rather to read, than to employ my time in any other work or practice. And when I read what I understood not, I would ask my brother the Lord Lucas[22] (he being learned) the sense or meaning thereof. But my serious study could not be much, by reason I took great delight in attiring, fine dressing and fashions, especially such fashions as I did invent myself, not taking that pleasure in such fashions as was invented by others. Also I did dislike any should follow my fashions, for I always took delight in a singularity, even in accoutrements[23] of habits. But whatsoever I was addicted to, either in fashions of cloths, contemplation of thoughts, actions of life, they were lawful, honest, honourable and modest, of which I can avouch to the world with a great confidence, because it is a pure truth.

As for my disposition, it is more inclining to be melancholy than merry, but not crabbed or peevishly melancholy, but soft, melting, solitary and contemplating melancholy. And I am apt to weep rather than laugh; not that I do often either of them. Also I am tender natured, for it troubles my conscience to kill a fly, and the groans of a dying beast strike my soul. Also, where I place a particular affection I love extraordinarily and constantly, yet not fondly,[24] but soberly and observingly: not to hang about them as a trouble, but to wait upon them as a servant. But this affection will take no root but where I think or find merit, and have leave both from divine and moral laws. Yet I find this passion so troublesome, as it is the only torment to my life, for fear any evil misfortune or accident or sickness or death should come unto them; insomuch as I am never freely at rest. Likewise I am grateful; for I never received a courtesy but I am[25] impatient and troubled until I can return it. Also I am chaste, both by nature and education, insomuch as I do abhor an unchaste thought.

Likewise I am seldom angry, as my servants may witness for me; for I rather choose to suffer some inconveniences than disturb my thoughts, which makes me wink[26] many times at their faults. But when I am angry I am very angry; but yet it is soon over and I am easily pacified, if it be not such an injury as may create a hate. Neither am I apt to be exceptious[27] or jealous; but if I have the least symptom of this passion, I declare it to those it concerns. For I never let it lie smothering in my breast to breed a malignant disease in the mind, which might break out into extravagant passions, or railing speeches, or indiscreet actions. But I examine moderately, reason soberly, and plead gently in my own behalf, through a desire to keep those affections I had, or at least thought to have. And truly I am so vain as to be so self-conceited (or so naturally partial) to think my friends have as much reason to love me as another; since none can love more sincerely than I, and it were an injustice to prefer a fainter affection, or to esteem the body more than the mind. Likewise I am neither spiteful, envious nor malicious; I repine not[28] at the gifts that nature or fortune bestows upon others. Yet I am a great emulator; for though I wish none worse than they are, nor fear any should be better than they are, yet it is lawful for me to wish myself the best and to do my honest endeavour thereunto.

For I think it no crime to wish myself the exactest of nature's works, my thread of life the longest, my chain of destiny the strongest, my mind the peaceablest; my life the pleasantest, my death the easiest, and the greatest saint in heaven. Also[29] to do my endeavour, so far as honour and honesty doth allow of, to be the highest on fortune's wheel, and to hold the wheel from turning if I can. And if it be commendable to wish another's good, it were a sin not to wish my own; for as envy is a vice, so emulation is a virtue. But emulation is in the way to ambition, or indeed it is a noble ambition; but I fear my ambition inclines to vainglory. For I am very ambitious, yet it is neither for beauty, wit, titles, wealth or power, but as they are steps to raise me to fame's tower, which is to live by remembrance in after-ages.

Likewise I am that the vulgar calls proud, not out of a self-conceit or to slight or condemn any, but scorning to do a base or a mean act and disdaining rude or unworthy persons. Insomuch that if I should find any that were rude or too bold, I should be apt to be so passionate as to affront them (if I can), unless discretion should get betwixt my passion and their boldness; which sometimes perchance it might, if discretion should crowd hard for place. For though I am naturally bashful, yet in such a cause my spirits would be all on fire. Otherwise I am so well bred as to be civil to all persons, of all degrees or qualitites. Likewise I am so proud, or rather just, to my lord, as to abate[30] nothing of the quality of his wife. For if honour be the mark of merit and his master's royal favour (who will favour none but those that have merit to deserve), it were a baseness for me to neglect the ceremony thereof.

Also, in some cases I am naturally a coward, and in other cases very valiant. As, for example, if any of my nearest friends were in danger, I should never consider my life in striving to help them (though I were sure to do them no good) and would willingly, nay cheerfully, resign my life for their sakes. Likewise I should not spare my life, if honour bids me die. But in a danger, where my friends or my honour is not concerned or engaged, but only my life to be unprofitably lost, I am the veriest coward in nature: as upon the sea, or any dangerous places, or of thieves or fire, or the like. Nay, the shooting of a gun, although but a pot-gun,[31] will make me start, and stop my hearing; much less have I courage to discharge one. Or if a sword should be held against me, although but in jest, I am afraid. Also as I am not covetous, so I am not prodigal, but of the two I am inclining to be prodigal; yet I cannot say to a vain prodigality, because I imagine it is to a profitable end. For perceiving the world is given or apt to honour the outside more than the inside, worshipping show more than substance; and I am so vain, if it be a vanity, as to endeavour to be worshipped, rather than not to be regarded: yet I shall never be so prodigal as to impoverish my friends, or go beyond the limits or facility of our estate. And though I desire to appear at the best advantage, whilst I live in the view of the public world, yet I could most willingly exclude myself, so as never to see the face of any creature but my lord, as long as I live: enclosing myself like an anchoret, wearing a frieze-gown[32] tied with a cord about my waist.

But I hope my readers will not think me vain for writing my life, since there have been many that have done the like, as Caesar, Ovid and many more, both men and women, and I know no reason I may not do it as well as they. But I verily believe some censuring readers will scornfully say, why hath this lady writ her own life? Since none cares to know whose daughter she was, or whose wife she is, or how she was bred, or what fortunes she had, or how she lived, or what humour or disposition she was of? I answer that it is true, that 'tis no purpose to the readers but it is to the authoress, because I write it for my own sake, not theirs. Neither did I intend this piece for to delight, but to divulge; not to please the fancy, but to tell the truth. Lest after-ages should mistake, in not knowing I was daughter to one Master Lucas of St John's near Colchester in Essex, second wife to the Lord Marquis of Newcastle; for, my lord having had two wives, I might easily have been mistaken, especially if I should die and my lord marry again.

(*True Relation*, pp. 383–91)

Notes

1 *queen . . . Oxford* : Queen Henrietta Maria, wife of Charles 1, set up impromptu court in Oxford in 1643 on account of the civil war.

2 *world abroad* : service to the queen introduced Cavendish not only to the wider English social world but also to foreign parts as the court moved in exile to France and the Netherlands.

3 *my sister Pye* : her favourite sister Catherine, who married Edmond Pye in 1635.

4 *sequestered . . . goods* : the cause of this penury was the civil war, to Cavendish an 'unnatural war' which 'came like a whirlwind' and 'felled down their houses' (1656: 372).

5 *my lord . . . Newcastle* : William Cavendish, first Duke of Newcastle, was a leading royalist and general of the king's army, who left England for Holland after the defeat at Marston Moor and later joined the exiled court in France. He was a patron of the arts, minor poet, and accomplished horseman; when Cavendish met him he was a widower with two sons and three daughters close to Cavendish in age. Their marriage took place in Paris in 1645.

6 *humours* : disposition, frame of mind.

7 *my mother . . . years* : her mother, Elizabeth Lucas (daughter of John Leighton) was widowed in 1625 when Cavendish was two years old. The family home, St John's Abbey, Colchester, was plundered in 1642 on the day that Charles 1 raised his standard at Nottingham in preparation for civil war.

8 *never . . . but* : a common seventeenth-century construction, here meaning 'never . . . without' (weeping).

9 *wharling* : pronouncing the letter 'r' with a gutteral sound.

10 *partial* : biased or inaccurate.

11 *chemists* : alchemists, who sought the 'philosopher's stone' to change base metal into gold.

12 *For I being* : a construction meaning 'For I am'.

13 *brain . . . barren* : in the epistle to her *Poems and Fancies* she admitted 'being so fond of my book as to make it as if it were my child' (1653: sig. A7ᵛ). She herself had no children.

14 See note 12 above.

15 *making . . . greatest number* is : always wanting to be one of a great number.

16 There appears to be a clause missing here, carrying the meaning, 'it would be bad for me'.

17 *dance my thoughts . . . numbers* : 'measure', 'feet', and 'numbers' are all technical poetic terms; Cavendish puns on 'measures' as dance movements, and 'feet' as in walking.

18 *the town* : Antwerp, where the Duke and Duchess lived from 1647 until they returned to England at the Restoration in 1660.

19 *so I be* : so long as I am.
20 *closets* : private repositories (of valuables).
21 *toys* : jewels, trinkets.
22 *my brother . . . Lucas* : her second brother, John, the first legitimate child of the family and therefore the heir to the title; Cavendish described him as 'a great scholar' (1656: 372).
23 *accroutrements* : trappings, clothing.
24 *fondly* : foolishly.
25 *never . . . but I am* : see note 8, above; here the meaning is 'never . . . without being'.
26 *wink* : turn a blind eye.
27 *exceptious* : peevish.
28 *I repine not* : I do not grumble at or resent.
29 *Also* : a condensed version of 'I also think it no crime to . . .' (see opening of paragraph).
30 *abate* : diminish or devalue.
31 *pot-gun* : a small pot-shaped gun.
32 *a frieze-gown* : a homely gown of brushed material, as worn by a nun or hermit.

5

SUSANNA PARR

Susanna's Apology Against the Elders. Or, a vindication of Susanna Parr; one of those two women lately excommunicated by Mr Lewis Stuckley and his church in Exeter. Composed and published by herself, for the clearing of her own innocency, and the satisfaction of all others who desire to know the true reason of their so rigorous proceedings against her.

'Whose hatred is covered by deceit, his wickedness shall be showed before the whole congregation,' Proverbs 26.26. 'They shall put you out of the synagogues, yea the time cometh that whosoever killeth you will think that he doth God service,' John 16.2. 'Let us go forth therefore unto him without the camp, hearing his reproach,' Hebrews 13.13.

Printed in the year 1659.

Susanna Parr wrote and published *Susanna's Apology* in 1659, after she had been excommunicated the previous year by an Independent congregation which, she tells us, she had left some three years before, having found they denied her 'not only the liberty of *speaking* but of *dissenting*'. In the extract printed here she describes her involvement in the early 1650s with the establishment of an Independent Exeter congregation, and their decision to elect Lewis Stuckley as pastor. She also explains in detail the church practices, common among Baptists, of requiring all members, including women, to speak publicly about their religious beliefs and past experiences, and to express opinions and vote on matters of church policy. The account she gives makes it clear that in that congregation at least, women's opinions came to be ignored when they did not agree with a dominant male view: when 'the sisters' refused to 'act by an implicit faith' and approve unspecified undertakings made on their behalf by Stuckley, their vote is disregarded.

Although in this case Parr's position might be seen as more radical or democratic than Stuckley's, in other respects her ideas lie towards the conservative end of the Independent spectrum. Where in the early days of the church Stuckley and the elders seem committed to a complete separation from the national church, and insist on the active participation of all the congregation's members in activities, Parr asserts that her one-time belief in such policies was mistaken. She is also highly critical of the behaviour of 'enthusiasts', the more extreme members of the church. In her dedicatory epistle she denies ever having spoken willingly in church, and affirms: 'Weakness is entailed upon my sex in general, and for myself in particular, I am a depised worm, a woman full of natural and sinful infirmities, the chiefest of sinners, and the least of saints' (sig. A2^{r-v}). She refers to the Savoy Declaration (a document produced by the ministers involved in a recent national meeting of congregational churches), appealing to its rejection of separation from the national church and urging the signatories to 'call Mr Stuckley to an account' (sig. A5). Given her espousal of these conservative positions, it is fitting that she explains her change of heart as originating in matters supposed to be central to the womanly role. When describing the source of her rejection of separation she asserts that the deciding factor had been the death of one of her children: 'When I considered the breach the Lord had made in my family, I beheld how terrible it was to make a breach in his family' (see p. 110). In keeping with traditional notions of femininity, her text, although a vindication, is named by her an 'apology'.

Susanna's Apology was published after Parr had been attacked by Stuckley both in an excommunication sermon (published by Thomas Mall, Stuckley's assistant, as part of his *A True Account*, 1658), and in print, in Stuckley's *Manifest Truth* and *True Account*, 1658. In all these places he criticizes her for speaking in church and asserts 'it is safer in some sense to tolerate an incestuous person than a liar in a church: especially such an one as soweth discord, a discontented liar, as this woman was' (Mall 1658: 10). The wife of a church elder, a Mrs M. Alleine, was also excommunicated at that time, and *Susanna's Apology* includes Parr's defence of her, whom Stuckley has attacked as 'a lawless woman that knoweth no subjection at home or abroad, to her own husband or to the church of God' (Mall 1658: 10). Both women were clearly subjected to prolonged public pressure to change their behaviour and views, and the extract below illustrates how consistently Susanna Parr maintained her position and did as she saw fit.

'Apology' or not, then, Parr's reply to such pressures makes it clear that she does not think much of Stuckley, who 'was so distracted with lawsuits, entangled with the world and money engagements, as that he was seldom with us at our fasts and times of prayer' (see p. 106). This rebuttal of hers, poised between rebellion against the church and affirmation of her understanding of correct Christian behaviour is strongly argumentative, and indicates the independence women could construct, even whilst occupying what seem to be 'conservative' positions.

Note on Exeter Independent churches in the 1650s

The ministers Parr mentions were members of the Devon Association. Formed in 1655, this was an umbrella body co-ordinating between Independent churches, with some responsibility for the ordination of ministers and the discipline of congregations. Lewis Stuckey (d. 1687), who came from a small landowning family, had been minister to various Devon parishes before his appointment at Exeter. Thomas Ford (1598–1674), whose sermons Parr insisted on being allowed to hear in 1654, was a less radical minister than Stuckley. (Calamy (1778) praises his 'wonderful success' against the 'wild notions' of extremists (volume I, p. 362).) He was a preacher at Exeter Cathedral from 1648, and apparently opposed its division into two parts in December 1656, when Stuckley was appointed to preach in the other half of it (Turner 1914). This division of the cathedral took place after the events recorded in the extract below, when Stuckley's congregation was meeting elsewhere in the city. Both men were ejected from their parishes after the Restoration, and I have been unable to find other records of the doctrinal differences between the two men indicated in Parr's text.

Textual note

Copytext is the British Library copy, shelfmark E1784 (2).

From: Susanna's Apology

We were told in the time of the wars that when the Lord did turn our captivity there must be a thorough reformation, everything must be brought to the pattern in the Mount;[1] and by some, that rather no reformation than a partial reformation; and in special, the last war by many was styled a 'sacramental war'.[2]

Considerations of this nature made me willing to engage where was most purity as to the ordinances,[3] and the great affection and good opinion I had of the New England churches made me in liking with the congregational way.[4] Besides, it is well known how much was spoken of a church state, and the privileges thereof (explicit covenant):[5] a greater effusion of the spirit, more purity and holiness, more union and communion, more liberty of conscience and freedom from that yoke of being servants unto men, in this church state, than could be found elsewhere. Many such considerations made me engage in this way, which we did after this manner.

Mr Stuckley[6] being at Torrington and coming often to this city, speaking very much in commendation of Mr Bartlet's[7] church at Bideford and the order therein, and also exhorting me and others to meet together, telling us that we did not live like Christians because we had not communion one with another, and that we must come together so that we might be in a capacity of having the ordinances; we thereupon met very often. The time was spent in praying, and speaking one to another what God had done for our souls. And to this we were enjoined secrecy. The reason was given: because we might be put upon such temptations (if it were known) as we could not resist. This practice we continued once or twice a week for a long time, Mr Stuckley promising to be at our meetings, which he accordingly performed sometimes. At length some of us desired to have the sacrament of the Lord's Supper;[8] and because of that confusion which was among us, in that we wanted[9] abilities for the right managing of our weekly exercises,[10] we desired likewise to have a minister. Mr Hanmer[11] was pitched upon by some, but opposed by others. In the end we agreed to leave it to Mr Bartlet of Bideford, whether Mr Hanmer, or Mr Stuckley was the fittest for us. Hereupon we sent messengers to Mr Bartlet, who, when they came to his house, found Mr Stuckley himself there. Mr Bartlet told the messengers he conceived Mr Stuckley was fittest for the present: but however he would acquaint Mr Hanmer with the business, which he did, but Mr Hanmer refused it. After this Mr Stuckley came to continue in this city, yet not quitting Torrington till the means[12] was settled on him here. And now again some of us (the greater number were very indifferent) renewed our former desires of having the sacrament, and sent about it to Mr Bartlet, who said we were not as yet in a capacity to have that ordinance, that it was necessary we should be first in a gospel order embodied:[13] and said moreover, that then we should see much of God, that the day of our embodying would be such a day as we had never seen. A while after, Mr Bartlet came to the city with his church officers. He himself prayed and preached on Zechariah 6.12[14] in the morning. Afterwards seven or eight persons spake out the experiences they had of the change of their condition,[15] with which I was much affected, and through Mr Stuckley's persuasion did the like. Afterwards there was a confession of faith read, being a copy of that which was composed by Mr Hughes,[16] which copy we had not from the author, but from another. This confession of faith was subscribed by every one of us, and then Mr Bartlet made some proposals unto us by way of query, to this effect as I remember.

1 Whether we would take Christ for our Judge, King and Law-Giver?

2 Whether we would renounce all ways of false worship?

3 Whether we would worship God in all his ordinances?

4 Whether we would give up ourselves to the Lord, and one to another, and would engage ourselves in all duties of Christianity each unto other?

5 Whether we would hold communion with other churches?[17]

6 Whether we would relieve the saints that were in communion,[18] according to our ability?

7 Whether we would not rest in the light that we had received, but would study to know the mind of God, and live up unto it?

This is the substance of our engagement, as I remember. At this time and some while after there was never a woman of the church but myself, and yet at every meeting about church affairs Master Stuckley would send for me. And when I pleaded for my absence (at such times) from the meetings, that of the Apostle, 'Let your women keep silence in the church, for it is not permitted unto them to speak' [I Corinthians 14.34]; he replied he would do nothing without the consent of the whole. And when I was present, he himself would constrain me to speak my opinion of things proposed.

We were (as I said formerly) very desirous of the sacrament, in order to which our first work was to get a minister that might administer it.

Although Master Stuckley was with us, yet the people of Torrington claimed an engagement from him, that town having been visited with the plague, and deprived of their minister's maintenance.[19] Master Stuckley (who was their minister) for those reasons left them, but with a promise of returning so soon as the Lord should remove his hand, and sufficient maintenance[20] for a minister should be procured; both which being at this time effected, we could not choose him to be an officer until he were by them freed from his engagement. In order hereunto much means was used: Master Bartlet was employed to persuade them unto it; but they with one consent refused it, saying that seeing he had promised to return, they expected that he should keep promise with them.

Hereupon we wrote for counsel to some of the congregational

churches in London. Master Feake[21] and Master Harrison[22] (in their answers to our letters) affirmed that Master Stuckley was bound in conscience to go unto Torrington: that it would be dishonourable to the gospel to leave them, unless he could get their consent for his dismission. At length Master Stuckley himself, accompanied with two or three of the church, rode thither: where, having made an agreement with the people, those that rode with him were called in to consent thereunto, which they accordingly did.

At their return Master Stuckley required each one of us to consent likewise unto the agreement they made at Torrington, without declaring what it was; which being done by all the men, he desired the sisters (there being other women now added to the church) to do the like, which myself and some others refused, resolving that we would not act by an implicit faith. Master Stuckley thereupon said that what was done was a church act, because they who went with him consented thereunto; viz, that we were engaged to get a minister for the people of Torrington. Accordingly there was one procured, who continued with them for a time.

This serpentine subtlety of his I took special notice of, and did for it reprove him to his face. We were in the meantime (and so continued for some years) in a bewildered condition, without either of the sacraments: some not having their children baptized in a long time, others did procure some congregational minister to do it; and as for the Lord's Supper, they who would partake of it rode to other places in the country. Most of the people were very indifferent whether we had the ordinances or no, seeking themselves, getting places and offices,[23] designing how they might build their own houses. And as for Master Stuckley himself, he was so distracted with lawsuits, entangled with the world and money engagements, as that he was seldom with us at our fasts and times of prayer.

Hence I began to suspect that they intended nothing but separation,[24] and setting up of themselves and their own interests and designs, which did exceedingly trouble me.

Upon our private fast days when we had done praying, it was our custom (for the help of those that were to pray) to spend a little time in conference, and at such times did I take occasion to speak of the disorders among us, and told them plainly that I feared we did separate from others more godly than ourselves, as Cain, who went out from the presence of the Lord to build cities;[25] that there was little regard had to what we at first pretended, the setting up of pure ordinances. I often told them that I never heard or read in scripture, or other history, that the Lord did make use of a people of such an earthly, luke-warm and indifferent spirit in any public work of reformation; that it was not a party, or confederacy that I looked after, but to have the gospel more discovered in greater light and beauty, and the ordinances to be enjoyed in greater purity; the beauty of God's ornament to be set in majesty, and more purity and self-denial to appear in us, who had separated from all mixtures.[26]

Because I conceived that purity lay only in this way, therefore was I very forward and zealous in it, hoping to leave posterity the ordinances pure, and the name of God glorious in the brightness of the gospel. For this cause did I deal so plainly with them; with which plain and faithful dealing they pretended many times to be much affected, and thereupon would do something more in order to religion than they had formerly.

Master Stuckley (as I said before) being troubled about the things of this world, left us to ourselves very often in our meetings. So that it is not to be wondered at if in them there were much strange fire, both in prayer and exposition of the scriptures, they being mere novices, and in the entrance of Christianity, and many of them scarce well-principled. I feared that the name of God was often taken in vain in prayer. Sure I am that much ignorance, pride and self-confidence, and a Diotrephes spirit[27] strongly working, appeared in many of them.

One of them (N. E.) affirmed that there was no iniquity of the holy things, etc.[28] This being delivered without any caution when the meeting was public, I told him of it in private the same day.

Another (Owen) who had formerly been an Anabaptist, then a Seeker, next (as I was informed) a Papist, or little better, very much addicted to the study of their books, the most conviction that he had (as was reported) was by Jonas Ware, since a Roman Catholic, who went to Rome, and then turning to prelacy and the Book of Common Prayer, and afterward an Independent;[29] the same person was very forward at our meetings, and did often put forth himself in the duty of prayer, which was a great trouble to me to hear how the name of God was taken in vain by him, insomuch as that I earnestly desired Master Stuckley to hinder him from engaging in that duty, till he understood the nature of it better.

I acquainted him likewise of other disorders and miscarriages[30] very frequent at our meetings, declaring how much I was troubled at them; for redress of which I entreated him to be constantly with us. But he endeavoured to quiet me in this, that they were honest, though weak, and further persuaded me to be constant at the meetings, to be faithful unto them in minding them of what was amiss. I told him it was more fit for me to be in private meditation, to be gathering rather than scattering: but he replied that the time was now not to be closet-professors, but to say, 'Come, let us go up to the house of the Lord, to seek the Lord together, with our faces Zionward' [Jeremiah 50.5]. And though I pleaded my sex, my natural and sinful infirmities, which made me unfit to speak unto others, yet he pressed it on me as my duty. And when there was any jarring between them and myself he desired me not to be troubled, though I met with opposition, that one was of a soldierly spirit, another of a dull spirit, that it was mere envy, promising to speak with them about it himself. Yea, when I resolved to be silent at some meetings, Mr Stuckley himself would single me out, and even constrain me to speak.

As concerning my carriage[31] at the admission of members, I shall give a brief account of it, as followeth.

They who desired admission into the society were sometimes desired in a private meeting to speak what experience they had of the work of grace upon their souls. After which we were every one of us, both men and women, to declare our thoughts of what was spoken; it being laid down as a ground, that we must have an account of a change from a natural and legal estate, into an estate of grace and believing,[32] of those whom we admitted into communion with us. I among the rest did according to my weak measure declare myself against that which I thought would not stand for grace. I was so far from delighting in this work as that it was a trouble to me, an employment from which I would willingly have been freed. I conceived it more needful for myself to study the Word, and compare my own heart with the rule, than to be so taken up about the condition of others. But this was our principle: we were to keep the house of God pure, we were set as porters at the door; it was our duty, we were not to be wanting at such times; yea, it was our liberty that we, who were to have communion with those who came to be admitted, should give in our assent or dissent in reference to their admission. I did therefore at such times declare my thoughts as well as the rest, but left the determination to themselves, as it appears in Ganicle, who was admitted though I was at the first against his admission. I mention him because he was brought by Mr Eveleigh[33] as an instance of my censoriousness. I was blamed for disliking him whom they said was one of the most eminent among them, and yet it was not long after before he discovered himself,[34] by renouncing the principles of Christianity and turning Quaker. He, in speaking out his experiences, pretended unto much joy and ravishment of spirit, but (the Lord knows) when he spake of such enjoyments, he spake as a stranger that never intermeddled with this joy, never declaring any powerful effect thereof, but only that which was only but a Balaam's wish.[35] I the rather instance in him because he was the first that kindled the fire of contention, which then brake out in that manner as it is not quenched to this day; here began the quarrel on their part. When I was called by the Elder to give in my thoughts concerning a person proposed, he most disorderly intercepted me, for which there was not the least admonition given him: but not long after, his folly was made manifest by his casting off the very form of godliness. This is one and the chief one of those persons whom I disliked, though approved of by the church. If I be contentious for opposing such a one, let me be contentious still; though none among them will witness for me, yet he doth, he stands to this day as a sad witness between me and them, whether I were contentious in my oppositions, or they infallible in their determinations. Besides, as for some who continue among them, if you look for distinguishing characters they are scarcely visible, much less easy to be discerned.[36]

Thus I did from time to time whilst we were without officers and ordinances, partly through the great desire I had to promote the work of reformation among us, partly through Mr Stuckley's instigation, reprove them for their indifferency of spirit, stir them up to that which I conceived was their duty, for which I always gave them my grounds and reasons. But after the officers were chosen I never meddled (to my remembrance) with church affairs, nor spake in the meetings, after I heard by Mr Stuckley my speaking was disrelished; unless a question was proposed, and I was desired to give my answer unto it.

Not long after the officers were chosen, I, being at Mr Stuckley's house, desired him to resolve me concerning a true church. He then confessed that the churches of New England did acknowledge the churches of Old England, from whence we had separated, to be true churches. I told him thereupon that we could not justify our separation. At length, we falling into discourse of other things, he said my speaking was disrelished by some. I answered that I did not like it myself, and therefore would be from thenceforth silent, though I looked on it as my duty formerly. He told me no, he would have me speak, but it must be by a brother; for a stander-by may see more than he that plays the game; promising, likewise, if I did speak by him, to deliver my words in the same manner as I spake them.

After this it pleased the Lord to exercise me with a smarting affliction, the death of a dear child. The suddenness of the stroke, and some other circumstances, made it a very melting affliction. When my bowels were yearning towards my child, I called to remembrance the Lord's tender bowels towards his children, for whom he had given his only Son; when I considered the breach that the Lord had made in my family, I beheld how terrible it was to make a breach in his family. Then the work I was engaged in, this sin of separation, appeared nakedly unto me to be no other than a wounding of Christ's body, which is his church, the church which he hath purchased with his own blood: I then looked on separation to be a dividing of Christ. Truly I beheld it with terror, this sin of wounding of Christ. It made a wound in my soul, which was kept open in a terrible manner, the Lord bringing to my remembrance his justice and severity and wrath, revealed from heaven on families and nations, yea, on his own people, ever since the beginning of the world. As also his judgments which are in the earth to this day, from Genesis to the Revelation, was brought to my remembrance, and kept hard upon me. Having these impressions on my spirit I was almost overwhelmed, and in mine own apprehension upon the borders of hell, where the Lord made me to behold the execution of his wrath upon sinners: I could then have told what hell was. I felt the flashings of hell-fire in my soul, the wrath of God that lay hard upon me, the effects whereof were very terrible, insomuch as I was even swallowed up, only the Lord was pleased to keep me following after him, resolving to lie at his feet though he should spurn me to hell. Having thus been under a sentence of death with the very terrors of hell in my soul, providence so ordering it, I came (by following the people) where Mr Ford[37] preached. I no sooner came into the congregation but I was so exceedingly troubled as that I vented myself in passionate tears; fearing lest I might be unfit to hear, but in prayer recovered myself. His text was John 16.33, 'Be of good cheer; I have overcome the world.' He instanced in all the enemies of the new creature: the world, the god of this world, sin, death, and hell. The Lord setting it home, every sentence was to me as the rivetting of the nails set on by the great master of assemblies,[38] and in prayer afterward (the Lord so providing), those very particulars which were the burden of my soul were put up unto God. I went out of the congregation with another frame of spirit than when I came in, blessing the Lord for giving his son Jesus Christ, who hath loved us, and washed us from our sins in his own blood, and hath made us kings and priests unto God.[39] But afterwards I began to question whether I had not taken that which did not belong unto me, Christ then speaking comfort to his disciples in reference to that hardship they were to meet with in the world. Among the rest of their sufferings this was one: that they should be put out of the synagogues; yea, the time would come that whosoever killed them would think he did God good service; which things Christ told them that they might not be offended.[40] But yet the sermon being in general of all the enemies of the new creature, I could not put it off. Furthermore, the appearance of God was so remarkable in the change of my spirit, as that I could not but take it home that sins of the right hand and left hand, and separation also, and death and hell, should be cast into the lake that burneth with fire and brimstone [Revelation 21.8]; that in the meantime Christ hath overcome the world [John 16.33], the prince of this world[41] is judged, condemned already, only the execution is deferred till the time appointed by the father. And as for sufferings, that we must look for them, having such provision so remarkably laid in before, I cannot but take notice of it at present. But then I could not conceive how it was likely for me to suffer in that kind, there being then so much love pretended. But now the time is come, and therefore I mention it: Christ sayeth, 'These things have I spoken unto you, that when the time shall come, you may remember that I told you of them' [John 16.4]. Now I can make application of all the sermon, which is food for my faith to live upon, although I suffer as an evildoer. I mention it with admiration,[42] that the Lord even then when he spake peace unto me after my being convinced of separation, should lay also provision against excommunication.

But now, after my conviction of separation, it troubled me very much, because I knew not how to avoid it. My fear was lest I should be constrained to live in it: had I presently[43] come off, I should have made a breach there. They pretended so much love unto me, as I knew not which way to break this bond, which the apostle calls 'the bond of perfectness'.[44] Wherefore I resolved to wait upon the Lord for the opening a way unto me, which he did afterwards in manner following.

(*Susanna's Apology*, pp. 1–17)

[She begins attending Ford's services regularly, to the fury of Stuckley and his congregation. Messengers are sent to dissuade her, and a fast day called.

111

She thinks things over, and decides that Stuckley's church, far from representing 'liberty of conscience', is characterized by 'greater bondage than
ever', requiring total obedience to church officers. On 24 March 1654, New
Year's Eve, by the old way of calculating the calendar, she tells Eveleigh she
is leaving their church, and her resolve is not swayed by a meeting with
Stuckley and others that she is summoned to.]

Some days after, Mr Eveleigh and Mr Slade, officers,[45] and a member
with them, came unto me and (as they said) expected Mr Stuckley's
coming likewise, but he came not.

I then complained of their carriage towards me, telling them how
much I was troubled at it, and desired them also to show me from the
Word what they could expect,[46] and then I should submit.

One of them replied, 'You must return, and do otherwise.'

I answered that I had too much to do with separation already, and
therefore should not return.

'Then,' said one of them, 'Then they will never be satisfied.'

As for Mr Eveleigh, he told me that my going away should cost me
dearer than my coming in; and that they would proceed according to
the order of the churches. This was heard by another.

I answered, whatever I suffered by them could not be so much as
had suffered for them.

After this, others came to me. I told them I did expect to speak
with Mr Stuckley that I might know what he had against me, and
that I was ready to submit to the Word; that they should convince me
thereby how I ought to be affected.

Mrs Roles[47] also came unto me in way of a visit, who desired me to
consider what a dishonour it would be unto the church if I left them.

'And as for what you have at any time spoke unto them,' said she,
'I believe it was in the uprightness of your heart, and so doth my
husband.'

I told her that I did not justify myself in every particular as to the
manner of it. Said she, 'You spoil all in saying you will leave them.
And if you do so, what will they say of my cousin Stuckley? And what
will they say of us? Consider, we are rising, and more will come into
us continually.'

And after this Mrs Stoneham[48] came unto me, asking, with tears
in her eyes, whether I would not return, and whether she was the
cause of my going away.

I demanded of her whether Mr Stoneham knew of her coming?
She answered that she did not see him at her coming away. I then
told her that it was reported by some of them that they could not

partake with me in ordinances now.

'For my part,' said she, 'I was never of that mind, neither do I know any who are, but on the contrary we are all much troubled that you will leave us.'

About two months after, Ezekiel Pace[49] was sent from Mr Eveleigh to tell me that I was suspended by the church.

I told him that I had left their society, and that I had no communion with them.

He answered, they conceived that they could not otherwise discharge their duty unto me, and as for what they had done, it was in order to my return.

I replied that my purpose was never to return unto them.

After I had made my address to the ministers of the city desiring to be admitted into fellowship and communion with them in ordinances, Mr Stuckley understanding thereof sent Mr Eveleigh unto Mr John Bartlet,[50] minister, to give him notice that they had several things against me. Upon which it was by Mr Bartlet desired that they would produce their charge, which they promised to do. Although it was long first, yet at length (after often desiring of it) a meeting was appointed at Mr Ford's house, the minister, between Mr Ford and Mr Bartlet on the one side, and Mr Stuckley and Mr Eveleigh on the other. At which meeting I was present. There they did declare what they had against me concerning Mrs Eveleigh and Babylon,[51] where they charged me with an untruth. And the result of this conference was this: the articles wherewith they charged me, being after serious examination by all the ministers of the city found partly doubtful and proofless, and partly frivolous, I was shortly after (according as I desired) received into communion with them; and so continued near three years, till Mr Stuckley's cursing began to make a noise in the world, which was near three years after I deserted them.

(*Susanna's Apology*, pp. 37–40)

Notes

1 *the pattern in the Mount* : the radical sects commonly interpreted the Sermon on the Mount (Matthew 24) as a promise that a truly Christian pattern of life would be established on earth after Christ's second coming.

2 *sacramental war* : the Parliamentary side in the civil war asserted that their struggle against kingly power was demanded by God.

3 *ordinances* : rituals of the Church, especially Holy Communion and baptism.

4 *congregational way* : Congregationalists argued for less radical independence from the national church than that aspired to by Separatists (see Introduction, pp. 13–16).

5 *church state . . . explicit covenant* : These terms are confusing to the modern eye. By 'church

state' is meant a state in which the church is joined by making an explicit avowal of faith ('explicit covenant'); unlike entry to the Church of England, which (after baptism) was an automatic consequence of being English. Later in her narrative, Parr explains she was wrong to believe in the need for an explicit covenant.

6 *Mr Stuckley* : see pp. 101–2 and note on Exeter congregations, p. 103.

7 *Mr Bartlet* : William Bartlet (d. 1682), minister of Bideford until his ejection after the Restoration.

8 *Lord's Supper* : Holy Communion.

9 *wanted* : lacked.

10 *exercises* : worship.

11 *Mr Hanmer* : Jonathon Hanmer (c. 1605–87), minister at Bishops Tawton and then Barnstaple until his ejection in 1662.

12 *means* : money.

13 *in a gospel order embodied* : made into a congregation modelled on those described in the gospels.

14 *Zechariah 6.12* : God tells Zechariah to go to Josiah 'And speak unto him, saying, Thus speaketh the Lord of hosts, saying, Behold the man whose name is the Branch; and he shall grow up out of his place, and he shall build the temple of the Lord.' This passage was commonly interpreted as prophesying Christ's coming.

15 *persons spake out . . . condition* : people wishing to join Baptist and some other radical churches were admitted by a vote of members after they had described some experience that could be taken as a sign that God had chosen them.

16 *Mr Hughes* : probably George Hughes (1603–67), minister of Plymouth till his ejection in 1662.

17 *Whether . . . other churches* : the congregation saw itself as part of a network of similar Independent congregations.

18 *Whether . . . in communion* : Whether we would give financial support to members of the congregation (and perhaps to related congregations: see McGregor 1984).

19 *maintenance* : aid, support.

20 *maintenance* : financial support. Parr's punning on the meaning of the word implicitly criticizes Stuckley.

21 *Master Feake* : Christopher Feake, Leveller and Fifth Monarchist. From 1649 minister of Christ Church, Newgate, and lecturer at St Anne's, Blackfriars.

22 *Master Harrison* : Thomas Harrison, a soldier and prominent Fifth Monarchist, member of the Council of State.

23 *seeking . . . offices* : looking after their own interests, trying for official or government appointment.

24 *separation* : leaving the national church and establishing an autonomous congregation.

25 *Cain . . . cities* : in Genesis 4.17 Cain, having been banished by God for killing his brother Abel, builds a city. *Annotations 1657*, interprets this: 'he built the City for society and security to himself and his progeny, and . . . that he might be more able to exercise rapine and tyranny upon others.' Parr's criticism is therefore a strong one.

26 *I often . . . mixtures* : Separatist congregations believed the elect must separate themselves from 'the dross'. Where some Separatists, like those consulted by Stuckley, were Fifth Monarchists who advocated the use of force to establish God's kingdom, Parr is arguing for a purely spiritual interpretation of the difference between the elect and others.

27 *a Diotrephes spirit* : 3 John 9, 10: John says that Diotrephes has been 'prating against us with malicious words', and ejecting people from the church.

28 *no iniquity of the holy things* : the idea that no act of the elect could be seen as sinful was a position commonly ascribed by their opponents to the most radical sectaries.

29 *Anabaptist* : Baptist; *Seeker* : unaffiliated sectary; *Papist* : Catholic; *Prelacy* : Presbyterianism; *Independent* : member of an Independent congregation. Owen experimented with most contemporary religious positions.

114

30 *miscarriages* : misbehaviour.

31 *carriage* : behaviour.

32 *change from . . . believing* : describe an experience that demonstrated that they were one of God's elect, in a 'state of grace' rather than blindly following the ten commandments.

33 *Mr Eveleigh* : Nicholas Eveleigh, well-to-do church elder.

34 *discovered himself* : revealed his true nature.

35 *Balaam's wish* : In Numbers 22–3 Balaam is asked by King Moab to curse the Israelites to ensure he beats them in battle, but God commands him not to. When Balaam speaks, he instead blesses them. Parr interprets the phrase loosely, in the sense of saying one thing and meaning another.

36 *Besides . . . discerned* : Separatists believed that their experiences of God's grace made them clearly distinguishable from other people, making it possible to judge who should join their congregations.

37 *Mr Ford* : see note on Exeter congregations, p. 103.

38 *rivetting . . . assemblies* : echoing Ecclesiastes 11.11, where 'the words of the wise are as goads, and as nails fastened by the masters of assemblies', causing sinners to repent.

39 *and washed . . . unto God* : quoting Revelation 1.5, 6.

40 *offended* : displeased, vexed. The word is used in this sense in John 16.1, and the rest of Parr's sentence is a bare paraphrase of the preceding verses in John.

41 *the prince of this world* : the Devil, John 12.31.

42 *admiration* : wonder.

43 *presently* : immediately.

44 *the bond of perfectness* : in Colossians 3.14 Paul names charity (love) as the 'bond of perfectness', but he uses the term with approbation, not ironically.

45 *officers* : church officials.

46 *show me . . . expect* : show me a biblical source for their right to make these demands of me.

47 *Mrs Roles* : earlier in her *Apology* Parr describes how Mrs Roles's husband had acted as a peacemaker during a confrontation with Stuckley.

48 *Mrs Stoneham* : perhaps the wife of Benjamin Stoneham, author of several Baptist doctrinal works. A Mr Stoneham, a church officer, was active in early attempts to change Parr's opinions about the church.

49 *Ezekiel Pace* : despite the lack of courtesy title, not a poor man. He appears in the 1662 Hearth Tax records for Exeter as occupying a house with six hearths.

50 *John Bartlet* : prominent Baptist minister (brother of William Bartlet), one-time minister of St Thomas's, Exeter, then in 1657 of St Mary More, Exeter. Ejected at the Restoration, d. 1680 (Turner n.d., a).

51 *concerning Mrs Eveleigh and Babylon* : on pp. 33–4 and 62–3 of *Susanna's Apology* Parr explains that she had originally objected when Dorothy Eveleigh (late wife of Nicholas Eveleigh, see note 33) applied to join the church, because of her continued communion with Presbyterians. Since in other respects she approved of Dorothy Eveleigh, she had later helped gain her admission. In Parr's own confession of faith on joining the church she had described Presbyterianism as 'Babylon', a position she subsequently discarded as she came to argue for reform of the Presbyterian church rather than separation from it. These two opinions of hers were central to the complaints brought against her by Stuckley, since they demonstrated her inconsistency over matters of doctrine.

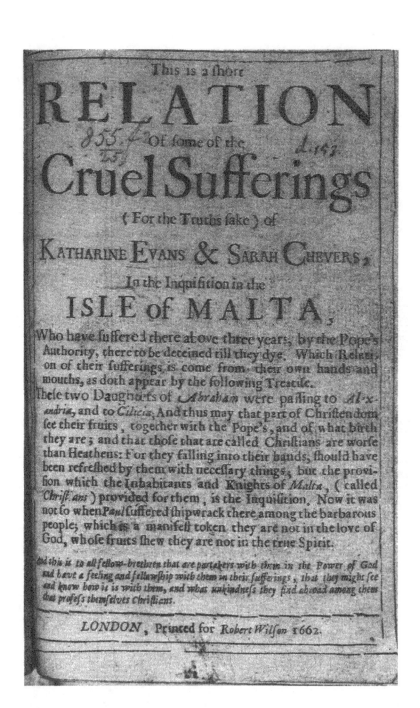

This is a short

RELATION

Of some of the

Cruel Sufferings

(For the Truths sake) of

KATHARINE EVANS & SARAH CHEVERS,

In the Inquisition in the

ISLE of MALTA,

Who have suffered there above three years, by the Pope's Authority, there to be deteined till they dye. Which Relation of their sufferings is come from their own hands and mouths, as doth appear by the following Treatise.

These two Daughters of *Abraham* were passing to *Alexandria*, and to *Cilicia*. And thus may that part of Christendom see their fruits, together with the Pope's, and of what birth they are; and that those that are called Christians are worse than Heathens: For they falling into their hands, should have been refreshed by them with necessary things, but the provision which the Inhabitants and Knights of *Malta*, (called *Christians*) provided for them, is the Inquisition. Now it was not so when *Paul* suffered shipwrack there among the barbarous people; which is a manifest token they are not in the love of God, whose fruits shew they are not in the true Spirit.

And this is to all fellow-brethren that are partakers with them in the Power of God and have a feeling and fellowship with them in their sufferings, that they might see and know how it is with them, and what unkindness they find abroad among them that profess themselves Christians.

LONDON, Printed for *Robert Wilson* 1662.

Title pages often served as advertisements for books, giving considerable detail of their contents.

6

KATHARINE EVANS AND
SARAH CHEEVERS

This is a Short Relation of Some of the Cruel Sufferings, for the Truth's Sake, of Katharine Evans and Sarah Cheevers, in the Inquisition in the Isle of Malta.

Who have suffered there above three years, by the Pope's authority, there to be detained till they die. Which relation of their sufferings is come from their own hands and mouths, as doth appear by the following treatise.

These two daughters of Abraham were passing to Alexandria and to Cicilia[1] and thus may that part of Christendom see their fruits, together with the Pope's, and of what birth they are, and that those that are called Christians are worse than heathens. For they, falling into their hands, should have been refreshed by them with necessary things, but the provision which the inhabitants and Knights of Malta[2] (called Christians) provided for them is the Inquisition. Now it was not so when Paul suffered shipwreck there among the barbarous people, which is a manifest token they are not in the love of God, whose fruits show they are not in the true Spirit.

And this is to all fellow-brethren that are partakers with them in the power of God and have a feeling and fellowship with them in their sufferings, that they might see and know how it is with them, and what unkindness they find abroad among them that profess themselves Christians.

London, printed for Robert Wilson, 1662.

A Short Relation of Cruel Sufferings was originally edited and published by Daniel Baker, a fellow Quaker and friend of Evans and Cheevers, while they were still in the Inquisition. Baker also tried to persuade the Inquisition to release the women and accept him as a prisoner in their place. His request was rejected, but eventually, after the women had been imprisoned for three and a half years, one of the most prominent Quakers, George Fox, made pleas on their behalf to the Queen's Roman Catholic almoner, Lord d'Aubigny, canon of Notre Dame, and they were released at his intervention in late 1662 (see Fox 1973: II, 3; II, 374–5). Their experiences in Malta did not daunt these women, however. They preached and distributed writings in Tunisia on their return journey and, after their return to England, almost immediately set off again on evangelical missions to Scotland, then Wales and Ireland. Sarah Cheevers died two years later and Katharine Evans lived on to 1692. Both women had husbands and children and each of them published doctrinal tracts, two of which survive (Cheevers 1663; Evans 1663), as well as their joint autobiographical account of imprisonment in the Inquisition in Malta.

This account is, above all, a record of resistance – and an act of resistance in itself. But their resistance was not simply of a reactive sort: it involved taking-on and challenging authority after authority. Evans and Cheevers were radicals whose beliefs and passionate activism came out of the early phase of Quakerism (see Introduction, p. 14), one of the later manifestations of 'aggressive radicalism'[3] in the revolutionary years of the Interregnum. They had been active members of the Quaker ministry throughout the 1650s, travelling and preaching together in Scotland, the Isle of Man, Ireland, and parts of England. They had already experienced imprisonment and humiliating punishments (Katharine Evans had been stripped and publicly whipped in Salisbury market-place) before they set out for Alexandria in late 1658 or early 1659, to follow the footsteps of the apostle Paul, on the journey that was to be interrupted by their imprisonment in Malta. Throughout their travels they preached, distributed Quaker writings, testified to their own belief, and sought to convert. It was on account of activities such as these that they came into confrontation with the authorities of the Roman Catholic church in Malta.

The Inquisition in Malta was part of the Italian Inquisition, reconstituted in 1542 on the model of the older Spanish Inquisition. It was part of the counter-Reformation's attempt to revitalize Roman Catholicism and to stop the spread of Protestantism.[4] Conversion was as much an aim of the Inquisition as punishment, as we see in Evans and Cheevers's account of the constant attempts made by the friars to persuade them they would be much respected as religious women if they became Catholics. Characteristically bold, Evans and Cheevers do not just hold fast against persuasion and punishment. Although they are physically powerless, they match the Inquisitors in an urge to convert: they argue with the friars, laugh at them, and even pity them for the errors of their beliefs and ways.

In all of this Evans and Cheevers were given courage to act and an astonishing capacity for endurance by their belief that the inner light of God was guiding them (see Introduction, p. 14). Yet although much of the impetus to act and their survival of their conditions of imprisonment can be linked to the nature of their belief, the text makes it clear that other factors were equally important in allowing them to sustain their faith and their senses of identity which were under attack. Countering the central oppositional relationship between the women and the friars is a series of affirmative relationships. *A Short Relation of Cruel Sufferings* is addressed to the 'wise reader' (p. 122). By writing, they not only made their situation known to the outside world, but they sought confirmation of themselves in the recognitions of a reader who shared their understanding of the meaning of their experience. And it is also evident from the text that human relationships were just as important as spiritual certainty. Included in the original edition, along with the account of imprisonment, are passionate letters to their husbands, children, and other Friends, full of a sense of the emotional and spiritual affinity between them all. *A Short Relation of Cruel Sufferings* is as much a text of love as of resistance. And most important of all the affirmative bonds revealed in it is the closeness and love between the women themselves. As they sustained each other with tenderness, practical help, and spiritual support, their mutuality (which they speak of in terms of marriage) confirmed and generated the emotional and spiritual strength which, along with their belief, allowed them to endure physical suffering and spiritual attack. (The friars, of course, derided the relationship and tried to separate them.)

Evans and Cheevers are revealed by this text as extraordinary women: they had a capacity for dogged rational debate and rhapsodic prophecy. They were ecstatic and common-sensical, practical as well as passionate, full of love and full of anger. Above all, they were immensely courageous.

Notes

1 *Cicilia*: Sicily.
2 *Knights of Malta*: Malta was under Sicilian rule until 1530 when Emperor Charles V handed it over to The Order of the Hospital of St John of Jerusalem (the Knight Hospitallers or Knights of St John) a military and religious order of the Roman Catholic church.
3 The phrase is from Morton 1970: 18–19 who writes, however, of the loss of 'aggressive radicalism' in Quakers. Reay (1985c: 32) disputes this in relation to pre-Restoration Quakers.
4 On the Inquisition see Henningsen and Tedeschi, 1986; Haliczer, 1987; and Grendler, 1977.

Textual note

The copytext used is held in the British Library and is part of a collection of

Quaker testimonies and papers edited by Daniel Baker (shelfmark 855 f2 (25)) which includes letters and documents relating to Evans and Cheevers's imprisonment, as well as their narrative. On the title page Sarah Cheevers is referred to as Sarah Chevers; she was also sometimes known as Sarah Chivers. The spelling 'Cheevers' has been used here, however, since this is how it most often appears in her published writings and in contemporary references. An expanded edition of the text, describing their release and return journey, was published in 1663 and several editions were published in the early eighteenth century.

From: A Short Relation of Cruel Sufferings

[Evans and Cheevers's narrative opens with two versions of their arrival in Malta, where, after distributing Quaker writings and preaching, they were taken to the house of the English Consul and then imprisoned in the Inquisition. This extract follows the description of their initial interrogation there.]

They said it was impossible we could live long in that hot room. So, the next weekday they sat in council. But oh, how the swelling sea did rage and the proud waves did foam even unto the clouds of heaven and proclamation was made at the prison-gate. We did not know the words, but the fire of the Lord flamed against it. (Katharine): My life was smitten and I was in a very great agony, so that sweat was as drops of blood, and the righteous one was laid into a sepulchre, and a great stone was rolled to the door, but the prophecy was that he should arise again the third day, which was fulfilled.[1] But the next day they came to sit upon judgment again (but I say in the true judgment they sat not, but upon it they got up unjustly above the righteous, and upon the same they sat; a child of wisdom may understand). And they brought many propositions written in a paper, but the friar would suffer the magistrate to propound but few to us, for fear the Light[2] would break forth. But they asked how many Friends of ours were gone forth in the ministry and into what parts. We told them what we did know. They said all that came where the Pope had anything to do, should never go back again. We said the Lord was as sufficient for us, as he was for the children in the fiery furnace,[3] and our trust was in God. They said we were but few and had been but a little while, and they were many countries and had stood many hundred years and wrought many miracles, and we had none. We said we had thousands at our meetings, but none of us dare speak a word but as they are eternally moved of the Lord, and we had miracles: the blind receive their sight, the deaf do hear and the dumb do speak, the poor do receive the gospel, the lame do walk and the dead are raised.[4] He asked why I looked so: whether my spirit was weak? I said nay; my body was weak, because I ate no meat (it was in their Lent). He offered me a licence to eat flesh. I said I could not eat anything at all.

The terrors of death were strongly upon me, but three nights after, the Lord said unto me, about the eleventh hour, 'Arise, and put on your clothes.'

I said, 'When wilt thou come, Lord?'

He said, 'Whether at midnight or at cock-crow, do thou watch.'[5]

My friend and I arose and the Lord said, 'Go stand at the door.' And we stood at the door, in the power of the Lord. I did scarce know whether I was in the body or out of the body. And about the twelfth hour there came many to the prison-gate. We heard the keys and looked when they would come in. They ran to and fro till the fourth hour. The Lord said he had smote them with blindness, they could not find the way. And we went to bed, there I lay night and day for twelve days together, fasting and sweating that my bed was wet, and great was our affliction.

The tenth day of my fast, there came two friars, the Chancellor, the man with the Black Rod and a physician and the Keeper.[6] And the friar commanded my dear friend to go out of the room and he came and pulled my hand out of the bed and said, 'Is the Devil so great in you that you cannot speak?'

I said, 'Depart from me, thou worker of iniquity, I know thee not. The power of the Lord is upon me, and thou call'st him Devil.'

He took his crucifix to strike me in the mouth and I said, 'Look here!' And I asked him whether it were that cross which crucified Paul to the world and the world unto him. And he said it was. I denied him and said the Lord had made me a witness for himself against all workers of iniquity. He bid me be obedient and went to strike me. I said, 'Wilt thou strike me?'

He said he would.

I said, 'Thou art out of the apostles' doctrine; they were no strikers. I deny thee to be any of them who went in the name of the Lord.'

He said he had brought me a physician, in charity. I said the Lord was my physician and my saving-health. He said I should be whipped and quartered and burned that night in Malta, and my mate, too. Wherefore did we come to teach them? I told him I did not fear; the Lord was on our side. And he had no power but what he had received and if he did not use it to the same end the Lord gave it him, the Lord would judge him. And they were all smitten as dead men and went away.

And as soon as they were gone, the Lord said unto me, 'The last enemy that shall be destroyed is death.'[7]

And the life arose over death and I glorified God. The friar went to my friend and told her I called him 'worker of iniquity'.

'Did she?' said Sarah. 'Art thou without sin?'

He said he was.

'Then she hath wronged thee.' (But I say the wise reader may judge.)

For between the eighth and ninth hour in the evening, he sent a drum to proclaim at the prison-gate. We knew not what it was, but the fire of the Lord consumed it. And about the fourth hour in the morning, they were coming with a drum and guns and the Lord said unto me, 'Arise out of thy grave-clothes.'[8]

And we arose and they came up to the gate to devour us in a moment. But the Lord lifted up his standard with his own spirit of might and made them to retreat and they fled as dust before the wind. Praises and honour be given to our God forever. I went to bed again and the Lord said unto me, 'Herod will seek the young child's life to destroy it yet again.'[9] And great was my affliction, so that my dear fellow and labourer in the work of God did look every hour when I should depart the body, for many days together. And we did look every hour when we should be brought to the stake, day and night for several weeks, and Isaac was freely offered up. But the Lord said he had provided a ram in the bush.[10] Afterwards, the friar came again with his physician. I told him that I could not take anything, unless I was moved of the Lord. He said we must never come forth of that room while we lived and we might thank God and him it was no worse, for it was like to be worse. We said if we had died, we had died as innocent as ever did servants of the Lord. He said it was well we were innocent. They did also look still when I would die.

The friar bid my friend take notice what torment I would be in at the hour of death: thousands of devils, he said, would fetch my soul to hell. She said she did not fear any such thing.

And he asked if I did not think it expedient for the elders of the church to pray over the sick? I said yea: such as were eternally moved of the spirit of the Lord. He fell down on his knees and did howl and wish bitter wishes upon himself if he had not the true faith, but we denied him. The physician was in a great rage at Sarah, because she could not bow to him, but to God only.[11]

The last day of my fast, I began to be a-hungry, but was afraid to eat, the enemy was so strong. But the Lord said unto me, 'If thine enemy hunger, feed him; if he thirst, give him drink: in so doing thou shalt heap coals of fire upon his head. Be not overcome of evil, but overcome evil with good' [Romans 12.20–1]. I did eat and was refreshed and glorified God. And in the midst of our extremity, the Lord sent his holy angels to comfort us, so that we rejoiced and magnified God. And in the time of our great trial, the sun and earth did mourn visibly three days, and the horror of death and pains of hell was upon me. The sun was darkened, the moon was turned into blood and the stars did fall from heaven and there was great tribulation ten days, such as never was from the beginning of the world [Revelation 6.12–13].[12] And then did I see the Son of Man coming in the clouds with power and great glory, triumphing over his enemies. The heavens were on fire and the elements did melt with fervent heat and the trumpet sounded out of Sion and an alarum was struck up in Jerusalem and all the enemies of God were called to the great day of battle of the Lord. And I saw a great wonder in heaven; the woman clothed with the sun and had the moon under her feet and a crown of twelve stars upon her head and she travailed in pain, ready to be delivered of a man-child. And there was a great dragon stood ready to devour the man-child as soon as it was born. And there was given to the woman two wings of a great eagle to carry her into the desert, where she should be nourished for a time, times, and half a time. And the dragon cast a flood out of his mouth, etc. [Revelation 12]. And I saw war in heaven, Michael and his angels against the dragon and his angels. And the Lamb and his army did overcome them. And there was a trumpet sounded in heaven and I heard a voice saying to me, 'The city is divided into three parts' [Revelation 16.19]. And I heard another trumpet sounding and I looked and saw an angel go down into a great pool of water and I heard a voice saying unto me, 'Whosoever goeth down next after the troubling of the waters, shall be healed of whatsoever disease he hath' [John 5.4]. And I heard another trumpet sounding and I heard a voice saying, 'Babylon is fallen, is fallen, Babylon the great is fallen' [Revelation 18.2]. And I looked and saw the smoke of her torment, how it did ascend. And I heard another trumpet sounding and I heard a voice saying, 'Rejoice, and be exceeding glad: for great is your reward in heaven [Matthew 5.12]. For he that is mighty hath magnified you and holy is his name. And from henceforth all generations shall call you blessed.'[13] And I heard another trumpet sounding in heaven, and I heard a voice saying unto me, 'Behold!' and I looked and I saw Pharoah and his host pursuing the children of Israel, and he and his host were drowned in the sea [Psalms 136.14–15; Exodus 14.28].

Dear Friends and people, whatsoever I have written, it is not because it is recorded in the scripture, or that I have heard of such things. But in obedience to the Lord I have written the things which I did hear, see, tasted and handled of the good word of God, to the praise of his name for ever.

And all this time, my dear sister in Christ Jesus was in as great affliction as I, in a manner, to see my strong travail night and day. Yet she was kept in the patience and would willingly have given me up to death, that I might have been at rest. Yet she would have been left in as great danger, woe and misery as ever was any poor captive for the Lord's truth. For they did work night and day with their divinations, enchantments and temptations, thinking thereby to bring us under their power. But the Lord prevented them every way, so that great was their rage, and they came often with their physician and said it was in charity. I asked them whether they did keep us in that hot room to kill us, and bring us a physician to make us alive.

The friar said the Inquisitor would lose his head if he should take us thence and it was better to keep us there than to kill us.

The room was so hot and so close that we were fain to rise often out of our bed and lie down at a chink of their door for air, to fetch breath. And with the fire within, and the heat without, our skin was like sheep's leather and the hair did fall off our heads and we did fail often. Our afflictions and burdens were so great that when it was day we wished for night, and when it was night we wished for day. We sought death, but could not find it. We desired to die, but death fled from us. We did eat our bread weeping, and mingled our drink with our tears. We did write to the Inquisitor, and laid before him our innocency and our faithfulness in giving our testimony for the Lord amongst them. And I told him if it were our blood they did thirst after, they might take it any other way as well as to smother us up in that hot room. So he sent the friar and he took away our inkhorns. (They had our bibles before.) We asked why they took away our goods. They said it was all theirs and our lives, too, if they would. We asked how we had forfeited our lives unto them. They said, 'For bringing books and papers.' We said if there were anything in them that was not true, they might write against it. They said they did scorn to write to fools and asses that did not know true Latin.[14] And they told us the Inquisitor would have us separated because I was weak and I should go into a cooler room, but Sarah should abide there. I took her by the arm and said, 'The Lord hath joined us together,[15] and woe be to them that should part us.' I said I rather choose to die there with my friend than to part from her. He was smitten and went away and came no more in five weeks and the door was not opened in that time. Then they came again to part us, but I was sick and broken out from head to foot. They sent for a doctor and he said we must have air or else we must die. So the Lord compelled them to go to the Inquisitor and he gave order for the door to be set open six hours in a day. They did not part us till ten weeks after. But oh, the dark clouds and the sharp showers the Lord did carry us through! Death itself had been better than to have parted in that place. They said we corrupted each other and that they thought when we were parted we would have bowed to them. But they found we were more stronger afterwards than we were before. The Lord our God did fit us for every condition. They came and brought a scourge of small hemp and asked us if we would have any of it. They said they did whip themselves till the blood did come.[16] We said that could not reach the Devil: he sat upon the heart. They said all the men and women of Malta were for us, if we would be Catholics, for there would be none like unto us. We said the Lord had changed us into that which changed not. They said all their holy women did pray for us, and we should be honoured of all the world if we would turn. We said we were of God, and the whole world did lie in wickedness and we denied the honour of the world and the glory, too. They said we should be honoured of God, too, but now we were hated of all. We said, 'It is an evident token whose servants we are.' The servant is not greater than the lord and that scripture was fulfilled which saith, 'All this will I give thee, if thou wilt fall down and worship me' [Matthew 4.9].

(A *Short Relation*, pp. 8–14)

[Events and the continued attempts of the friars to convert the women during the following eighteen months are described. For part of this period Evans and Cheevers were separated, but managed to stay in touch through laundry arrangements.]

But there was a poor Englishman heard that Sarah was in a room with a window next the street; it was high. He got up and spake a few words to her, and they came violently and hauled him down, and cast him into prison upon life and death. And the friars came to know of us whether he had brought any letters. We said no; I did not see him. They said they did think he would be hanged for it. He was one that they had taken from the Turks and made a Catholic of him. Sarah wrote a few lines to me of it and said she did think the English friars were the chief actors of it. (We had a private way to send to each other.) I wrote to her again, and after my salutation I said whereas[17] she said, the friars were the chief actors: she might be sure of that, for they did hasten to fill up their measures. But I believe the Lord will preserve the poor man for his love. I am made to seek the Lord for him with tears. And I desired she would send him something once a day, if the Keeper would carry it. And I told her of the glorious manifestations of God to my soul, for her comfort: so that I was ravished with love and my Beloved was the chiefest of ten thousands, and how I did not fear the face of any man, though I did feel their arrows, for my Physician is nigh me, and how I was waiting upon the Lord and saw our safe return into England and I was talking with G. F.[18] to my great refreshment. The name of G. F. did prick them to the heart. I said it was much they did not tempt us with money. I bid her take heed: the Light would discover it and many more things, let it come under what cover it would.

And this paper came to the friar's hands, by what means we could never tell. But as the Light did show us, the Lord would have it so. It smote the friar, that he was tormented many days and he translated it into Italian and laid it before their Lord Inquisitor and got the Inquisitor's Lieutenant and came to me with both the papers in his hand and asked me if I could read it.

I said, 'Yea, I writ it.'

'O! did you indeed!' said he. 'And what is it you say of me here?'

'That which is truth,' said I.

Then he said, 'Where is the paper Sarah sent? Bring it, or else I will search the trunk and everywhere else.'

I bid him search where he would.

He said I must tell what man it was that brought me the ink, or else I should be tied with chains presently.

I told him I had done nothing but what was just and right in the sight of God, and what I did suffer would be for truth's sake, and I did not care. I would not meddle nor make with the poor workmen.

He said, 'For God's sake, tell me what Sarah did write.'

I told him a few words and said it was truth.

Said he, 'You say it is much we do not tempt you with money.'

And in few hours they came and tempted us with money, often. So the Lieutenant took my ink and threw it away. And they were smitten as if they would have fallen to the ground and went their way. I saw them no more in three weeks. But the poor man was set free the next morning.

They went to Sarah and told her that I had honestly confessed all, and that she was best to confess, too, and threatened her with a halter and to take away a bed and trunk and her money, to have half of it for me. She answered she might not send to me any more. She asked him whether he was a minister of Christ or a magistrate. If he were a magistrate, he might take her money, but she would not give it him. And they that were with him said no, he should not meddle with anything. He was a bitter, wicked man. He told her she was possessed. She answered and said she was with the power of an endless life.

The Lord was not wanting to us at any time, for power nor words to stop the mouths of gainsayers of his truth, neither in revelations nor visions. Praises be to his name forever. He kept us in[19] our weakest condition, bold for his truth, declaring against all sin and wickedness, so that many were convinced, but did not dare to own it, for fear of faggot and fire. There were none that had anything to say against what we spake, but the friars [who] would have us to join with them. There were none did come into the Inquisition, but the judgments of the Lord would be upon them so that they would cry and foam and send for a physician, many of them. The unclean spirits would cry out as much as ever they did against Jesus and would gnash with their teeth when we were at prayer [Mark 3.11]. There was a friar and other great men; the friar would run as if he had been at his wits' end and call to the Keeper, and he would run for the English friar, and he would go to the Inquisitor for counsel and sometimes they would send them word they should have a remedy: I should be sent to Rome. And sometimes the friars would come, but had not power to say anything to me of it. The Lord did say to us, 'Lift up your voice like the noise of a trumpet, and sound forth my truth like the shout of a king' [Isaiah 58.1]. There was one that Life[20] was arisen in him, but they were upon him as eagles, till they had destroyed him. He did undergo terrible judgments all the time he was in the Inquisition. Our money served us a year and seven weeks. And when it was almost gone, the friars brought the Inquisitor's chamberlain to buy our hats. We said we came not there to sell our clothes, nor anything we had. Then the friar did commend us for that and told us we might have kept our money to serve us otherwise. We said no, we could not keep any money and be chargeable to any. We could trust God. He said he did see we could, but they should have maintained us while they kept us prisoners.

And then the Lord did take away our stomachs.[21] We did eat but little for three or four weeks. And then the Lord called us to fasting for eleven days together, but it was so little that the friars came and said that it was impossible that creatures could live with so little meat as they did see we did, for so long time together, and asked what we would do, and said their Lord Inquisitor said we might have anything we would. We said we must wait to know the mind of God, what he would have us to do. We did not fast in our own wills, but in obedience to the Lord. They were much troubled and sent us meat and said the English Consul sent it. We could not take anything till the Lord's time was come. We were weak, so that Sarah did dress her head as she would lie in her grave, poor lamb. I lay looking for the Lord to put an end to the sad trial, which way it seemed good in his sight. Then I heard a voice saying, 'Ye shall not die.' I believed the Lord and his glory did appear much in our fast. He was very gracious to us and did refresh us with his living presence continually, and we did behold his beauty, to our great joy and comfort. And he was large to us in his promises, so that we were kept quiet and still (the sting of death being taken away). Our souls, hearts and minds were at peace with the Lord, so that they could not tell whether we were dead or alive, but as they did call to us once a day, till the time the Lord had appointed we should eat. And they were made to bring many good things and laid them down by us, so that scripture we witnessed fulfilled: 'Our enemies treated us kindly in a strange land,' said I. But we were afraid to eat and cried to the Lord and said we had rather die than eat anything that is polluted and unclean. The Lord said unto me, 'Thou mayest as freely eat as if thou hadst wrought for it with thy hands. I will sanctify it to thee through the cross.' And he said to Sarah, 'Thou shalt eat the fruit of thy hands and be blessed.' We did eat and were refreshed, to the praise and glory of our God forever. We did eat but little in two months and they did bring us whatever we did speak for, for eight or ten days. And afterward we were so straitened for want of food, it did us more hurt than our fast.[22] Yet the Lord did work as great a miracle by our preservation as he did by raising Lazarus out of the grave [John 11.44]. The friars did say the Lord did keep us alive by his mighty power, because we should be Catholics. We said the Lord would make it manifest to us, then. They should know the Lord had another end in it one day.

(A Short Relation, pp. 21–4)

[The final six pages of narrative in the copytext include an account of the unsuccessful attempt made by the English captain, who had brought them to Malta, to secure their release and a description of their own appearance in court. Other writings published along with the narrative include: letters to Friends in England and Ireland and to their husbands and children, another narrative of imprisonment entitled *A Vision*, papers written to the friars and Lord Inquisitor by the women and a series of prayers and poems entitled 'Victorious Hymns, Songs, Praises, all in verse, the Same Sprung from the Seed of Life, its Perfect Righteousness'.]

Notes

1 *a great stone . . . fulfilled* : a reference to Christ's entombment and resurrection (Matthew 27.57–28.6; Luke 23.50–24.8; Acts 13.29–31). Evans and Cheevers are mindful of the meaning of Christ's persecution and execution and the promise of resurrection, which they implicitly liken to their own suffering and imprisonment and from which they take comfort.

2 *the Light* : the inner light. See p. 14 for an account of Quaker belief in the Light.

3 *the children in the fiery furnace* : a reference to the story told in Daniel 3 where King Nebuchadnezzar imprisoned the Jews he had set to govern Babylon in a fiery furnace because they refused to worship the golden image Nebuchadnezzar had built. The men were unharmed by the furnace, although everyone else who approached it was destroyed by its heat. Nebuchadnezzar was converted to belief in the Jewish God by this miracle. Again, Evans and Cheevers are referring to those who were saved by faith in God when persecuted and imprisoned.

4 *miracles: the blind receive their sight . . . the dead are raised* : many Quakers claimed to have performed miracles, particularly of healing. See Fox 1948 and Reay 1985c: 36–7.

5 *'Whether at midnight . . . do thou watch'* : cf. Mark 13.35. Christ on the Mount of Olives told the disciples of future sufferings and of his second coming. He warned them to be watchful, since nobody knew when this would be.

6 *the Chancellor . . . Keeper* : officers of the Inquisition.

7 *The last enemy that shall be destroyed is death* : 1 Corinthians 15.26. Paul has just explained the meaning of Christ's resurrection: 'For as in Adam all die, so also in Christ shall all be made alive. But each in his own order: Christ the first fruits, then at his coming those who belong to Christ. Then comes the end, when he delivers the kingdom of God the Father after destroying every rule and every authority and power. For he must reign until he has put all his enemies under his feet' (1 Corinthians 15.22–5). The reference, then, points to freedom from political rule and oppressions as well as triumph over death at the time of the apocalypse.

8 *Arise out of thy grave clothes* : Perhaps a reference to the story of Lazarus rising from the grave (John 11.44).

9 *Herod will seek . . . destroy it again* : This alludes to the account of Herod's attempts to kill the infant Jesus in Matthew 2.

10 *Isaac was freely offered up . . . he had provided a ram in the bush* : A reference to Abraham's willingness to sacrifice his son Isaac to God and God's acknowledgment of this in his provision of a ram as a substitute sacrifice (Genesis 22). This, like the preceeding

references, suggests the need to sacrifice oneself or to make sacrifices for God in order to attain spiritual life. The notion of sacrifice combines ideas of submission to death and of suffering at the hands of oppressive political and religious authorities.

11 *she could not bow to him, but to God only* : Quakers did not acknowledge any social hierarchies. They refused to bow to social superiors or to doff hats and used the familiar form of the second person pronoun 'thou' rather than the polite form 'you'.

12 The visions in this section echo passages from Revelation, the gospels, Psalms, and Exodus, which are noted in the text. These mostly describe the turning upside down of the world at the apocalypse, the coming to glory of the righteous, and the end of corruption, symbolized in the fall of Babylon. The Old Testament references are to events which prefigure the end of persecution of the righteous which is achieved at the apocalypse.

13 *from henceforth all generations shall call you blessed* : Luke 1.46–9, the magnificat of Mary.

14 *fools and asses that did not know true Latin* : Latin was the official language of the Roman Catholic church and all theological and doctrinal works were written in Latin. It is unlikely that Evans and Cheevers, women from the middle ranks of society, would ever have learned Latin. They probably spoke to the friars in English. Also, Quakers believed the workings of the Spirit were a more important source of truth than any written work, even the bible. They denied the superior spiritual understanding of a learned elite. The friars' sneer at the women relates, then, to doctrinal conflict as well as being an intellectual, social (and perhaps sexual) put-down.

15 *The Lord hath joined us together* : a reference to the marriage service, indicating the women saw their relationship as a married one. It was, perhaps, a lesbian relationship.

16 *scourge of small hemp . . . blood did come* : self-flagellation and chastisement of the flesh was practiced by some Catholics.

17 *whereas* : 'as' or 'the same as'.

18 *G. F.* : George Fox, a leading Quaker.

19 *in* : throughout.

20 *Life* : i.e. the Spirit.

21 *stomachs* : appetites.

22 *We did eat and were refreshed . . . more hurt than our fast* : eating, when they are weak after a long period of fasting, makes them feel more ill than the fast itself did.

MARY CARLETON

*The Case of Madam Mary Carleton, lately styled 'the German
Princess', truly stated: with an historical relation of her birth,
education and fortunes; in an appeal to his illustrious highness Prince
Rupert. By the said Mary Carleton. Sic sic juvat ire sub umbra.[1]*

*London, printed for Samuel Speed at the Rainbow in Fleet Street,
and Henry Marsh at the Princes Arms in Chancery Lane, 1663.*

When Mary Carleton was arrested and tried for bigamy in 1663 her case
caused quite a stir, and a great many pamphlets were published defending or
attacking her. Her husband and his family claimed that she was no 'foreign
princess' but the daughter of a Canterbury fiddler, and already married to
Thomas Stedman, a cobbler of that town. They also brought charges of theft
against her, and these assertions and their various claims that she had long
made a living from tricking and robbing men were published anonymously
before the trial as *The Lawyer's Clarke Trappan'd by the Crafty Whore of
Canterbury*. After her acquittal Mary Carleton replied to such pamphlets,
and to John Carleton's attacks on her in his *A Replication*, with her own
version of events: *An Historicall Narrative* and, a few weeks later, the fuller
account of *The Case of Madam Mary Carleton*.

In *The Case of Madam Mary Carleton* she repeats the story she had told
her husband John about her origins, describing her birth in Cologne and the
early deaths of her parents. (Her father, she asserts, was Henry van Wolway,
a prominent lawyer active in the peace negotiations that ended the Thirty
Years' War.) Left without a guardian, she says, she was committed to the
care of the church, and grew up in the nunnery of Sancta Clara. Frustrated
by the restrictions of that life she left, and having learned English, French,
and 'more than a smattering' of other European languages (1663a:23–4),
she claims to have sailed to England and rented a room at the Exchange
Tavern in the Poultry, London. In the section of *The Case* printed here she
describes how she was tricked into marriage with the landlady's brother,
John Carleton, believing him to be a Lord; and how her new husband's

Behold my innocence after such disgrace
Dares show an honest and a noble Face
Hence-forth there needs no mark of me be k
For the right Counterfeit is herein shown—

This portrait of Mary Carleton, with its verse asserting her honesty and nobility, forms the frontispiece to *The Case of Madam Mary Carleton, 1663.*

family sought to use a bigamy charge to rid themselves of her when they discovered the trick to be mutual. The final section of *The Case* includes a minimally-reworked version of the account of her trial published as *The Arraignment, Tryal and Examination of Mary Moders* (1663), which records the jury verdict of not guilty and the 'great shout' that went up in the public gallery when this was announced.

For the moment at least it is impossible to know how much truth there was in Carleton's story, or in the counterclaims of her husband's family.[2] We can however deduce how people reacted to them: *The Case of Madam Mary Carleton* is boldly dedicated to Prince Rupert (cousin of Charles II and son of Elizabeth of Bohemia), beseeching his protection; during her imprisonment on the bigamy charge she was visited by many, including Samuel Pepys, who records sending others to see her on 29 May 1663, and ten days later, shortly after her trial, mentions that Lady Batten 'inveighed mightily against the German Princess, and I as high in the defence of her wit and spirit, and glad that she is cleared at the sessions'. These details, and the 'great shout' that went up at the verdict, suggest that many wanted to believe her.

The Case of Madam Mary Carleton indicates how this belief was inspired. Carleton plays with romance fantasies of female grandeur, reflecting in the section printed below: 'So do conceited heights of sudden prosperity and greatness dazzle the eyes and judgment of the most' (p. 140).[3] John Carleton, those who visited her in prison, and her readers are encouraged to want to believe her. At the same time, she prevaricates over her exact social origins, defending herself with philosophical truisms: 'What harm have I done in pretending to great titles? . . . The best things are to be imitated' (1663a: 36–7). The 'self' presented in her writings and to contemporaries who saw or met her is a performance, a dazzling display, and one in which she is sufficiently conscious of her role to mock her lover for going along with it. In the extract printed here she laughs at his passionate intensity, which would have been well suited to a hero of romance, and reflects to the reader, 'I cannot deny but that I could hardly forbear smiling to see how serious these elders and brokers were in this "love-killing" story' (p. 137). It is fitting that, as Pepys again records (diary entry for 15 April 1664) she later acted in a play by Thomas Parker dramatizing the events of her story.

For all Mary Carleton's finely-controlled irony, the issues at the heart of this trial, and of her text, are not funny at all. During her trial the judge reminds the jury, 'You see what the circumstances are, it is penal; if guilty, she must die; a woman hath no clergy, she is to die by the law, if guilty' (1663a: 102–3). Because she was a woman, regardless of her social class no commutation of the death sentence was possible. An awareness of the constrictions of her legal and social position also fills the text in other ways. Although she presents herself as a romance heroine, she also remarks to her women readers that marriage is no simple romantic matter, but 'an affair to which there are more intrigues and perplexities of kin and alliance, and necessary dependence, than to any other thing in the world' (1663a: sig. A7). In youth she had 'blindly wished I were (what my inclinations prompted me to) a man' (1663a: 16), and after her trial she was to learn that she had indeed been foolish to marry: 'When I might have been happy in myself, I must needs transplant my content into a sterile, ungrateful soil, and be miserable by another' (1663a: sig. A7: 'To the Noble Ladies and Gentlewomen of England'). *The Case* ends with her recording her attempts to have her money and jewels returned to her, and the court advising her that her belongings 'were my husband's, and that if any detained them from me, he might have his remedy at law' (1663a: 104). Whilst she could lament the difference between English law and that of her native Germany, where married women could trade and pursue legal cases independently (1663a: 126–7), as an English wife she was trapped. She had to attempt a reconciliation with her husband, despite her contempt for his 'debility and meanness of spirit' (1663a: 130), and in the extract below she asserts her willingness to return to him.

Such a reconciliation was not to be. Whilst Carleton was producing her *Case* her husband John was writing *The Ultimum Vale*, where he bitterly regrets having been 'misled by a soft and candid nature and easy belief, being won thereto by her charming tongue and sycophantic style' (*The Ultimum Vale*, sig. A2). He will have no more of her, leaving her to the study of law and astrology that he tells us she has recently embarked on. Despite these acknowledgements of her education, intelligence, and verbal skill he none the less denies her authorship of *The Case* and *An Historicall Narrative*, claiming the involvement of a hack writer. We cannot know the truth of this matter, but some details in the passage included here, such as her description of the seizing of her washing by 'the gang' from where it was soaking overnight, suggest her close involvement, at least, with the composition. The style and proficiency of her books are also more credibly hers if we reflect that, whether or not all the details of her story are true, she managed to convince many of her contemporaries that they were.

Mary Carleton's story does not end with her legal and astrological studies. In 1673 she was arrested for theft and, having once before been deported for a similar crime, was hanged at Tyburn. Another rash of pamphlets appeared, reiterating the Carletons' earlier descriptions of her career of tricking men, and claiming for her a series of such adventures since her trial in 1663. The longest of these works, Francis Kirkman's *The Counterfeit Lady* (1679), has been heralded as 'a missing chapter in the history of the English novel', and it is clear that Daniel Defoe knew something of her story, since his Roxana compares her story to that of 'the German Princess'.[4] Such literary speculations have an interest, but of more concern to us might be the fact that despite her celebrated 'wit and spirit' Mary Carleton was constrained by the legal limits of her time: once rejected by her husband, 'whom I would willingly exchange for my jewels, and give him liberty to look after another princess where he can find her' (1663a: 120), she found no satisfactory lawful way to make a living. She died on the gallows.

Notes

1 *Sic . . . sub umbra* : So, so I am pleased to go beneath the shades (i.e. to die). These are Dido's dying words in the *Aeneid* IV 660, before she burnt herself to death because of Aeneas' abandonment of her.
2 Lyndal Roper has advised me that the account given is so plausible that she 'would not rule her story out', though she has not found any confirmation of it (private correspondence).
3 There is a good discussion of Carleton's use of romance convention in McKeown 1987.
4 See Bernbaum 1914 and Main 1956, which include a checklist of most of the pamphlets related to Carleton's case; Daniel Defoe, *Roxana* (1724; repub. 1982), Harmondsworth: Penguin, p. 317.

Textual note

The copytext is the British Library copy, shelfmark 1606/1589, compared where relevant to Mary Carleton's earlier *An Historicall Narrative*, on which parts of *The Case* are closely based.

From: *The Case of Madam Mary Carleton*

[Mary Carleton's story begins with an account of her childhood in Germany. The extract below opens after her arrival in England, where she lodges in London at the Exchange Tavern, run by Mr and Mrs King. She presents herself as a wealthy German, and writes, she says, to her steward to have money sent to pay her board. As she had anticipated, these letters are opened and read by Mr King.]

Let the world now judge whether, being prompted by such plain and public signs of a design upon me, to counterplot them, I have done any more than what the rule, and a received principle of justice, directs: 'to deceive the deceiver, is no deceit.'[1]

I knew not, nevertheless, which way their artifices tended, till Master King brought into my acquaintance old Mr Carleton, his father-in-law, and soon after Mr John Carleton, his son. It seems it had been consulted to have preferred[2] George, the elder brother. He, troubled with a simple modesty and a mind no way competent to so

much greatness, was laid aside, and the younger flushed and encouraged to set upon me. By this time they had obtained my name from
me, viz, Maria de Wolway; which passage also hath suffered by
another lewder imposture and allusory sound of 'de vulva':[3] in the
language of which I am better versed than to pick out no civiller and
eleganter impress.[4]

To the addresses of Mr John Carleton I carried myself with so
much indifference (not superciliously refusing his visits, or readily
admitting his suit; not disheartening him with a severe retiredness, or
challenges of his imparity,[5] nor encouraging him with a freedom or
openness of heart, or arrogance of my own condition), that he and
his friends were upon the spur[6] to consummate the match; which yet
I delayed and dissembled with convenient pretences.[7] But herein I
will be more particular in the ensuing pages.

In the meanwhile, to prevent all notice of me, and the disturbance
of their proceedings that might be occasioned thereby, they kept me
close in the nature of a prisoner; which though I perceived, yet I
made no semblance thereof at all, but colluded with them in their
own arts, and pretended some averseness to all company but only[8]
my innamorato, Mr Carleton. Nor was anybody else suffered to come
near me, or to speak with me. Insomuch, as I have been informed,
that they promised to one Sackvil (whom for his advice they had too
forwardly, as they thought, imparted the business), the sum of £200
to be silent,[9] lest that it should be heard at court, and so the estate
and honour which they had already swallowed would be lost from
their son, and seized by some courtier, who should next come to hear
of this great Lady.

After many visits passed betwixt Mr Carleton and myself, old Mr
Carleton and Mr King came to me and very earnestly pressed the
dispatch of the marriage, and that I would be pleased to give my
assent, setting forth with all the qualities and great sufficiencies of
that noble person, as they pleased to style him. I knew what made
them so urgent, for they had now seen the answers I had received by
the post, by which I was certified of the receipt of mine, and that
accordingly some thousands of crowns should be remitted instantly to
London, and coach and horses sent by the next shipping with other
things I had sent for. And to reinforce this their commendamus[10] the
more effectually, they acquainted me that if I did not presently grant
the suit and their request, Mr Carleton was so far in love with me
that he would make away with himself, or presently travel beyond sea
and see England no more.

I cannot deny but that I could hardly forbear smiling to see how serious these elders and brokers were in this 'love-killing' story. But keeping to my business, after some demurs and demands, I seemed not to consent, and then they began passionately urging me with other stories, some of which long repetition I will now insert.

Wednesday 1 April Mrs King made a great feast, where were diverse persons of quality; as she said, amongst the rest, her brother, Mr John Carleton. At which entertainment Mrs King did advise me to call her 'cousin', the which I did. Thursday 2 April Mr John Carleton came in his coach, with two footmen attending on him calling him 'my Lord', and Mrs King did also call him 'my Lord'. With that, I asked Mrs King if it was not the same person that dined with us yesterday? She said, true, it was so, but he was in a disguise then; and withal, that in a humour[11] he would often do so.

'But,' saith she, 'I do assure you, he is a Lord.'

Upon that I replied, 'Then his father must be an Earl, if living.' She affirmed that he was a person of great honour. The same time my Lord presented me with a rich box of sweetmeats: I could do no less than thankfully accept thereof.

My Lord came every day to Mr King's, and by his importunity would carry me abroad[12] in a coach to Holloway and Islington. Mrs King would often ask me what my Lord did say to me. I told her, nothing that I observed, but his Lordship abounded in civility mixed with compliments.

'How!' said she, 'Madam, he loves you.'

'Loves me? For what, Mistress King?' I replied.

She said, 'For your great parts and endowments.'

I asked her how my Lord could tell that I had either. I said,[13] 'My Lord must have very good eyes if he could see within me, or else I must be very transparent.'

After which, I did order the matter so that his access to me was not so easy. Mistress King importuneth me to admit my Lord to visit me; I told her plainly that I did not understand his Lordship's meaning. He provided me a great banquet, at which his Lordship's mother was very fine dressed, who questioned what I was. I told my Lord that I had received civilities from him, and he had the like from me, and that I had no necessity to give any account to any person what I was, for anything that I intended; and that if any design or affair of his required any such thing out of convenience, or otherwise,[14] he might forbear it. His Lordship excused his mother's inquisition by saying she was his mother, and that parents did think themselves concerned in looking after the good of their children.

'But,' said he, 'Madam, waive all this. However, I will marry you tomorrow.'

'What!' said I, 'My Lord, without my consent? My Lord, I desire your Lordship not to come near me any more. I will not lie under such questioning and scrutiny. Your Lordship will be safe in following my advice, in not coming at me any more.'

Upon this his Lordship wept bitterly. I withdrew myself from his presence. He writ a letter of high compliments to me (the which letter was lost in that violent surprise of me and my things, by the force of Mr George Carleton, my husband's father). At the same time I had a gown making upon my own account by Mrs King's tailor in the Strand. I took a coach and went thither. All this while the young Lord, not knowing where I was, remained impatient until my return, where I found him standing at the bar (in a very pensive and melancholy manner, as if he had been arraigned for not paying his reckoning)[15] at the Exchange Tavern, and suddenly clasped about my middle and violently carried me to my chamber. I asked his meaning. He answered that I had forbid him my presence; that it had almost made him mad; that he desired nothing more of me, than but to let him look upon me. Upon that he did, with a very strange gesture, fix his eyes upon me. In compassion to him I asked him what his Lordship meant and intended. He replied, in a kind of discomposed manner, 'I would have you to be my wife.'

I answered him, 'My Lord, I rather think you have courted me for a mistress, than for a wife. I assure you that I will never be a mistress to the greatest of princes; I will rather choose to be a wife to the meanest of men.'

Upon which, he uttered divers asseverations[16] in confirmation of the reality of his intentions, and earnest desire of the honour in making me his wife, without any respect to what I had.

After my Lord had insinuated his affections so far that I began to understand him, and did mix and scatter some suchlike acceptable words, which put him into some confidence of obtaining me; he began like other lovers to set forth the amplitude of his fortunes, and those brave things he would do if I would finish his suit. Among many other finenesses and grandures he would bestow on me, I well remember, he told me that he had given order for a great glass coach of the new fashion to be presently made, against our wedding was over,[17] where eleven or twelve might conveniently sit; and that he would suit it with a set of lackeys and pages, the neatest and handsomest of the town for their liveries and persons, that I might see I had married a person that not only dearly loved me, but would also highly honour me with the most splendid accommodations[18] that England yielded.

At the very same time he had changed, as he told me (and part of it I saw), two hundred pound of silver into two hundred pieces of gold, for the better portableness thereof, that his princess might see nothing of meanness belonging to him; and that as soon as the coach was made and all things fitted to it, he would presently go to court, and carry me with him, and introduce me to the king and queen. His further intention being, which as yet he concealed to me, to get a knighthood, and have something of honour to oppose the envy of men, that so great an estate was conferred on a private person.

And now my Lord spoke nothing but rodomontades[19] of the greatness of his family, of the delights and stateliness of his lands and houses, the game of his parks, the largeness of his stables, and convenience of fish and fowl for furnishing his liberal and open housekeeping, that I should see England afforded more pleasure than any place in the world. But they were (without the host)[20] reckoned and charged beforehand to my account, and to be purchased with my estate, which was his, by a figure of anticipation, when we two should be all one; and therefore he lied not, but only equivocated a little.

But he did not in the least mention any such thing to me, nor made any offer of enquiry what I was; no, not the least semblance or shadow of it. He seemed to take no notice of my fortunes, it was my person he only courted; which having so happily and accidentally seen, he could not live, if I cherished not his affections. Nor did I think it then convenient[21] or civil to question the credit of his words and the report given me of him. His demeanour, I confess, was light; but I imputed that to his youth and the vanity of a gallant: as necessary a quality, and as much admired, as wit in a woman.

The last day of my virgin state, easter eve, the tailor brought me my gown to my lodging. I being dressed and adorned with my jewels, he again renewed his suit to me, with all importunity imaginable. His courteous mother was also now most forward, pressing me to consent by telling me that she should lose her son, and he his wits,[22] he being already impatient with denials and delays; adding, withal, that he was a person hopeful, and might deserve my condescension.[23] I withstood all their solicitation, although they continued it until twelve of the clock that night. The young Lord, at his taking leave of me, told me he would attend me betimes the next morning, and carry me to

St Paul's Church to hear the organs; saying, that there would be very excellent anthems performed by rare voices, the morrow being Sunday 19 April last. In the morning betimes, the young Lord cometh to my chamber door, desiring admittance, which I refused, in regard I was not ready. Yet so soon as my head was dressed, I let him have access. He hastened me, and told me his coach was ready at the door, in which he carried me to his mother's in the Greyfriars, London, where I was assaulted by the young Lord's tears, and others', to give my consent to marry him; telling me that they had a parson and a licence ready, which was a mere falsehood and temporary fallacy to secure the match.

So on Easter morning, with three coaches, in which with the bride and bridegroom were all the kindred that were privy to the business, and a pretended licence,[24] they carried me to Clothfair by Smithfield; and in the church of Great St Bartholomew's, married me by one Mr Smith, who was well paid for his pains. And now they thought themselves possessed of their hopes. But because they would prevent the noise and fame of their good fortune from public discourse, that no sinister accident might intervene before Mr Carleton had bedded me, offence being likely to be taken at court (as they whispered to themselves) that a private subject had married a foreign princess, they had before determined to go to Barnet. And thither immediately after the celebration of the marriage we were driven in the coaches, where we had a handsome treatment, and there we stayed Sunday and Monday, both which nights Mr Carleton lay with me. And on Tuesday morning we were married again, a licence being then obtained to make the match more fast and sure, at their instance,[25] with me to consent to it.

This being done, and their fears over, they resolved to put me in a garb befitting the estate and dignity they fancied I had; and they were so far possessed with a belief of it, that they gave out I was worth no less than £80,000 per annum. And my husband, as I must now style him, published so much in a coffee-house; adding, withal, to the extolling of his good hap, that there was a further estate, but that it was my modesty or design to conceal it; and that he could not attribute his great fortune to anything but the fates, for he had not anything to balance with the least of my estate and merits. So do conceited[26] heights of sudden prosperity and greatness dazzle the eyes and judgment of the most, nor could this young man be much blamed for his vainglorious mistake.

My clothes being made at the charge of my father-in-law, and other fineries of the mode and fashion sent me by some of his kindred and friends (who prided themselves in this happy affinity, and who had an eye upon some advantages also, and therefore gave me this early bribe as testimonies of their early respect), and as for jewels I had of mine own of all sorts, for necklaces, pendants and bracelets, of admirable splendour and brightness; I was in a princelike attire, and a splendid equipage and retinue, accoutred for public view among all the great ladies of the court and the town, on May-day ensuing. At which time in my Lady Bludworth's[27] coach (which the same friends procured for my greater accommodation), and accompanied with the same Lady with footmen and pages, I rode to Hyde Park[28] in open view of that celebrious[29] cavalcade and assembly, much gazed upon by them all, the eximiousness[30] of my fortune drawing their eyes upon me; particularly that that[31] noble Lady gave me precedence, and the right hand, and a neat treatment, after our divertisement of turning up and down the park .

I was altogether ignorant of what estate my husband was, and therefore made no nicety to take those places his friends gave me. And if I be taxed for incivility herein, it was his fault that he instructed me no better in my quality, for I conceited still that he was some landed, honourable and wealthy man.

Things yet went fairly on, the same observances and distances continued, and lodgings befitting a person of quality taken for me in Durham Yard, at one Mr Green's, where my husband and I enjoyed one another with mutual complacency;[32] till the return of the monies out of Germany failing the day and their rich hopes, old Mr Carleton began to suspect he was deceived in his expectation, and that all was not gold that glistered. But to remove such a prejudice from himself, as if he were the author of those scandals that were now prepared against my innocence,[33] a letter is produced and sent from some then unknown hand, which reflected much upon my honour and reputation. And thereupon, on the 5 or 6 May ensuing, I was by a warrant dragged forth of my new lodgings, with all the disgrace and contumely that could be cast upon the vilest offender in the world, at the instigation of old Mr Carleton, who was the prosecutor; and by him and his agents divested and stripped of all my clothes, and plundered of all my jewels and my money, my very bodice and a pair of silk stockings being also pulled from me; and in a strange array carried before a justice.

But because this story hath not yet been fully discovered,[34] I will more manifestly here declare it. That letter abovesaid came from one

Mr John Clay, the younger son of Mr Clay, a drugster[35] at the Bear and Mortar in Lombard Street, a servant[36] and admirer of Mrs King my fine sister-in-law; who, because her husband hath a weak head (though he sat like a Parliament man once in Richard Cromwell's time for three days,[37] as since I have been informed) must have an assistant to carry on the business. The contents of this letter were near to this purpose:

Sir,
I am unknown to you, but hearing that your son Mr John Carleton hath married a woman of a pretended great fortune and high birth, I thought fit to give you timely notice of what I know, and have heard, concerning her: that she is an absolute cheat, hath married several men in our county of Kent, and then run away from them, with what they had. If it be the same woman I mean, she speaks several languages fluently, and hath very high breasts. . . .

I was at the Exchange Tavern, as it was designed, when this letter was brought, and thereupon their countenances were set to a most melancholy look and pale hue, which showed a mixture of fear and anger. Presently I was brought before the inquisition of the family, and examined concerning the said letter, which I constantly, innocently, and disdainfully denied, so that they seemed something satisfied to the contrary; and so my husband and I went home in a coach. But that very same night all the gang, with one Mrs Clark, a neighbour to King, came to my lodging. Where, after most vile language, as 'cheating whore', and the like, they pulled me up and down and kept me stripped upon a bed, not suffering my husband to come near me, though I cried out for him to take my part, and do like a man to save me from that violence; who at a distance excused it, by putting all this barbarity upon his father. In fine, they left me not a rag, rinsing every wet cloth out of the water, and carrying them away.[38] The whole was a most unwomanly and rude action at the best of it, if I had been such as they pretended me to be; and not to be parallelled, but by a story I have lately heard of the six woman shavers in Drury Lane.[39]

See the fickleness and vanity of human things, today embellished and adorned with all the female arts of bravery and gallantry, and courted and attended on by the best rank of my sex, who are jealous observers what honour and respect they give among themselves, to a very punctilio; and now disrobed and disfigured in mis-shapen garments, and almost left naked, and haled and pulled by beadles[40] and suchlike rude and boisterous fellows, before a tribunal, like a lewd criminal.

The justice's name was Mr Godfrey,[41] by whose mittimus,[42] upon an accusation managed by old Mr Carleton that I had married two husbands, both of them in being, I was committed to the gatehouse.[43] Being interrogated by the justice whether or no I had not two husbands as was alleged, I answered: if I had, he was one of them; which I believe incensed him something the more against me. But I did not know the authority and dignity of his place, so much am I a stranger to this kingdom.

There were other things and crimes of a high nature objected against me besides: that I cheated a vintner of sixty pounds, and was for that committed to Newgate (but that lie quickly vanished, for it was made appear that I was never a prisoner there, nor was my name ever recorded in their books); and that I picked a Kentish Lord's pocket, and cheated a French merchant of rings, jewels and other commodities; that I made an escape, when sold and shipped for the Barbados.[44] But these were urged only as surmises, and old Carleton bound over to prosecute only for bigamy, for my having two husbands.

Thus the world may see how industrious mischief is to ruin a poor, helpless and destitute woman, who had neither money, friends nor acquaintance left me. Yet I cannot deny that my husband lovingly came to me at the gatehouse the same day I was committed, and did very passionately complain of his father's usage of me, merely upon the disappointment, as he said, of their expectations; and that he could be contented to love me as well as ever, to live with me and own me as a wife; and used several other expressions of tenderness to me.

Nor have I less affection and kind sentiments for him, whom I own and will own till death dissolve the union; and did acquaint him with so much there, and protested my innocence to him. Nor do I doubt could he have prevailed with his father, but that these things had never happened.[45] If now after my vindication he prove faithless and renege me, his fault will be doubly greater, in that he neither assisted my innocence when endangered, nor cherished it when vindicated by the law.

In this prison of the gatehouse I continued six weeks, in a far better condition than I promised myself, but the greater civilities I owe to the keeper: as I am infinitely beholding to several persons of quality, who came at first, I suppose, out of curiosity to see me, and did thereafter nobly compassionate my calamitous and injurious restraint.[46]

All that troubled me was an abusive pamphlet which went under my husband's name,[47] wherein most pitifully he pleaded his frailty and misfortune, and entitled it to no lesser precedent than Adam; which I suppose was had out of the new ballad of 'your humble servant'.[48] A hint whereof, please the reader to take in this abridgement:

> Reader,
> I shall not give myself the trouble to recollect and declare the several motives and inducements that deceitful, but wise enough woman used to deceive me with. . . . Her wit did more and more engage and charm me. Her qualities deprived me of my own. Her courteous behaviour, her majestic humility to all persons, her emphatical speeches, her kind and loving expressions; and amongst other things, her high detestation of all manner of vice, as lying, etc.; her great pretence to zeal in her religion; her modest confidence and grace in all companies, fearing the knowledge of none; her demeanour, was such, that she left no room for suspicion, not only in my opinion, but also in others', both grave and wise.

And all this is real and not feigned, and more convincingly and apparently true, by this foil of his own setting.[49] As for his undertaking to tell the story of the management of the business betwixt us: he is so far from doing me justice herein, that he wrongeth me and his own soul by lying.

For confutation of which, I refer the reader to the ensuing trial.

(*The Case of Madam Mary Carleton*, pp. 45–70)

Notes

1 *to deceive . . . deceit* : proverbial.

2 *it seems . . . to have preferred* : it seems they had planned to promote.

3 *suffered . . . 'de vulva'* : suffered from a lewd interpretation through a false association with the sound of 'vulva' (vaginal lips).

4 *impress* : characteristic mark.

5 *imparity* : inequality to me.

6 *upon the spur* : in utmost haste.

7 *convenient pretences* : appropriate assertions ('pretences' might carry an implication of deceit, but did not always do so at that time).

8 *but only* : except for.

9 *Insomuch . . . silent* : copytext reads: 'Insomuch, as I have bin informed, that they promised 209 l. to one *Sackvil*, whom for his advice, they had too forwardly, as they thought, imparted the business, the sum of 200 l. to be silent.' The repetition is probably a printer's error, since the related passage in her *An Historicall Narrative* specifies £200 as Sackvil's fee.

10 *commendamus* : recommendation.

11 *in a humour* : on a whim.

12 *abroad* : outside.

13 *I said* : copytext reads 'she said', which is probably a printer's error. The parallel passage in *An Historicall Narrative*, p. 9, reads: 'She said, my Lord could see within me. I answered that my Lord must have very good eyes if he could see within me, or else I must be very transparent.'

14 *or otherwise* : or for some other reason.

15 *as if . . . his reckoning* : as if he had been summonsed for not paying his bill.

16 *asseverations* : emphatic assertions.

17 *against our wedding was over* : by the time our wedding was over.

18 *accommodations* : comforts.

19 *rodomontades* : boasting.

20 *without the host* : 'reckon without one's host': overlook difficulty or opposition.

21 *convenient* : appropriate.

22 *and he his wits* : copytext reads 'and his wits', but the parallel passage in *An Historicall Narrative*, p. 10, has 'he his wits'.

23 *condescension* : consent.

24 *a pretended licence* : copytext reads 'pretended a licence'.

25 *at their instance* : at their request.

26 *conceited* : imagined.

27 *Lady Bludworth* : I have found no record of a woman of this name. Probably 'blood-worth' is meant, and either Carleton is lying about this incident or she is disguising the Lady's name for reasons of etiquette.

28 *Hyde Park* : it was fashionable for the wealthy to ride in Hyde Park.

29 *celebrious* : thronged.

30 *eximiousness* : excellence.

31 *particularly that that noble Lady* : copytext reads 'particularly that noble Lady'.

32 *complacency* : tranquil pleasure.

33 *But . . . innocence* : But to remove the suspicion that he was the author of those untrue scandals that were now prepared against me.

34 *discovered* : revealed.

35 *drugster* : drug seller.

36 *servant* : lover, follower.

37 *sat like . . . for three days* : was an MP for three days in the Parliament called by Richard Cromwell in 1659. Carleton is probably being ironic at the expense of the short life of that Parliament, which was the last one for which elections were held before the Restoration of the Monarchy. Summoned on 27 January in 1659, it was dissolved on 22 April of that year due to pressures from the army, and the Rump Parliament of 1653 recalled. The only Mr King in the Parliament in question was Thomas Kinge, MP for Harwich Borough, who also represented that constituency in the Long Parliament of 1661–79 (*Members of Parliament*, (Part I, *Parliaments of England, 1213–1702*), 1878).

38 *rinsing . . . carrying them away* : they even took with them the dirty clothes she had left soaking overnight.

39 *the six woman shavers in Drury Lane* : 'shaver' is a slang term with several meanings, including 'swindler' (OED). Carleton appears to be alluding to a recent case in which a woman or women were robbed in Drury Lane by six 'shavers'. I have been unable to trace a record of this incident, or to find a ballad in which a fictional case of this kind is recorded.

40 *beadles* : parish officers appointed by the church.

41 *Mr Godfrey* : Edmund Berry Godfrey (1621–78), J.P. for Westminster, knighted 1666 for his public-spiritedness during the plague of 1665. Most remembered for his involvement in the machinations of the so-called Popish Plot, 1678, when he was found dead, presumed murdered, having taken a statement from Titus Oates which asserted the existence of a Jesuit plot to assassinate Charles II.

42 *mittimus* : warrant committing someone to prison.

43 *the gatehouse* : Newgate prison, which held both debtors and felons from London, Middlesex, and sometimes elsewhere. Prisoners who could afford it could buy extra bedding, fires, and food, and patronize the prison tap room (Heppenstall 1981).

44 *Barbados* : Carleton was later deported to Jamaica for theft; see p. 134.

45 *but that . . . happened* : had these things never happened.

46 *several persons of quality* : Pepys was one of those who visited and was impressed by her (see p. 133).

47 *abusive . . . name* : John Carleton, *A Replication* (1663).

48 *ballad*: Vercingetorixa, the new ballad of 'your humble servant': possibly an ironic reference to *Vercingetorixa: or, The Germane Princess Reduc'd to an English Habit*, 1663, which appeared anonymously under the initials F. B.

49 *this foil of his own setting* : his displaying it to advantage (the terminology is from jewel settings).

8

ALICE THORNTON

A Book of Remembrances of all the remarkable deliverances of myself,
husband and children with their births, and other remarks as
concerning myself and family, beginning from the year 1626.
A.W.T.[1]

Alice Thornton first wrote her autobiography, in a tiny notebook, sometime
after her husband's death in 1668. Later, she reworked this first *Book of*
Remembrances into a series of autobiographies, filling three longer, larger
notebooks. There are notable differences between the versions. The later ones
are much more detailed in the context they give to key events. Interestingly, for instance, her own marriage, which she records with brief factuality
in the earlier version – the text anthologized here – is described at length in
the later ones. From these later accounts we learn that she was uncertain
whether her vocation was to marry, since she was 'soe happy in [her]
condition of a single life, that [she] loved it above all, haveing the excelent
company and example of [her] mother' (Thornton 1873: 78). We learn that
Mr Thornton's estate was the lowest of all her suitors', which worried her
and her mother, that Mr Thornton's family were of the 'ridged oppinnion of
the Presbeterians', although he, like her, professed the religion of the 'true
protestant Church of England' (Thornton 1873: 78), that he persuaded her,
despite her reservations, to marry him, convincing her of his sober, religious
character. Her reluctance to marry, in spite of her assertions throughout
both texts of her love for her husband, is most forcibly suggested – to the
modern reader, at least – when she relates how she fainted at her wedding
ceremony. (Neither she nor her mother can explain this, but speculate that it
may have been caused by washing her feet the night before the wedding.)

In the same way, her father's death, omitted from the earlier version, is
described and commented on in the later ones, details of her childbirths,
her brothers' and sisters' deaths are given more fully and there are long
passages declaring her political views, making detailed reference to national
and local events in the civil war, her family's involvement as Royalists and

the losses they sustained in the 1640s and 1650s, both in Ireland where her father, Sir Christopher Wandesford, had been Lord Deputy, and in England. The later versions read throughout as more consciously explanatory texts, particularizing and contextualizing events.

All the texts, however, contain hints of her motivation to write. Tellingly, in the later texts she details the Wandesford family's and her own financial difficulties with precision. It becomes evident that she writes to vindicate herself. She had lost her inheritance from her father's estate in Ireland through mismanagement, shady deals, and financial disputes between members of her family. Her own inheritance from her mother, willed to her in her own right, was used to rescue her husband from the debts and financial bunglings which he seems to have been persistently involved in. It is probable that all versions of the autobiography were intended for manuscript circulation amongst members of her family and immediate circle, and to serve as a record to be handed down to her children and descendants, explaining her financial actions and defending herself against accusations of improvidence, of having lowered the family name and estate, and of dishonest transactions. It is important to her in her writing to make clear not only her actions, but the sincerity of feeling towards her family and towards God which lay behind them. Although in the earlier version there is less direct attention paid to details of financial transactions, distress over her reputation and over financial matters has a crucial subtextual importance.

Clearly, then, the *Book of Remembrances* can be read as a first draft of an autobiography that aims to justify in this way. But it would be a mistake to see it only as this. Thornton's expressed intention is to write as a pious exercise: to record and to remind herself of God's goodness in saving her from losses and grief and in leading her to salvation through suffering. She sets out to recall her deliverances and, quite literal-mindedly, records every loss survived. Ostensibly expressing her gratitude to God, the *Book of Remembrances* becomes, thus, a catalogue of sufferings, both small and intense. It is a work of mourning. Particularly if it was written soon after her husband's death, as would seem likely, her writing must have had a therapeutic purpose, allowing her to articulate her grief and air her sense of injustice at the unhappiness of her life as well as at slanders and misrepresentations of her by friends (see pp. 157–9). The earlier version of her autobiography with its juxtaposition of note-form records of deaths and illnesses with long passages of emotional intensity, expressing fear, loneliness, difficulties in reconciling herself to God's will, and rage at slanderous gossip, has an urgency and complexity that is, perhaps, dulled in the more controlled and evenly structured later version.

It is a text that presents intriguing contradictions. Alice Thornton creates herself in her *Book of Remembrances* as an extreme model of feminine passivity. Her apparently masochistic religiosity, her love of a husband who leads her into debt, her perpetual illness (which we may be tempted to think of as

148

hypochondria), her emotional collapses, all contribute to a picture of her as a submissive woman, who has no outlet except in suffering and in jealously guarding her family name. Her writing might seem to illustrate, in this way, not only the structure of a particular personality, but the extent of the constraints upon a woman of her class and upbringing: powerless to intervene in the property transactions she was dependent upon, constantly engaged in childbearing, excluded from action beyond the domestic, yet affected by the political allegiances of her family. But against this, Alice Thornton's writing also reveals her as a dogged, sometimes self-possessed woman, full of her own sort of fight, emotionally articulate in grief. And, of course, the dangers of childbirth were real enough, infant mortality was high, threats to health were severe, especially during the years of failed harvests in the 1640s and the disruptions of the civil war. Almost everyone who was close to Thornton died, and she suffered a decrease in social and economic status through her marriage and widowhood – she did indeed suffer great losses. (Although all versions of her autobiography end with her husband's death, we know from other records that she, in spite of her illnesses, outlived all her children, except her widowed daughter Alice, and died when she was 81 or 82.) Alice Thornton's story is one of unremitting misery; but it is also a testament to her tenacity and endurance – not least because of her determination to set straight the record of her worldly and spiritual life.

Note

Special thanks to Pam Watts for all her help in deciphering the manuscript and to Philip Lloyd for being ever ready with help and suggestions.

1 A. W. T.: a monograph, which is difficult to decipher, but probably contains the initials A. W. T. (Alice Wandesford Thornton) but may read A. W.

Textual note

Copytext is Yale University Microfilm MISC 326, *Alice Thornton Papers*, a microfilm made in the 1930s of Thornton's first version of her autobiography. The later versions (see p. 147) were edited by C. J. (probably Charles Jackson) as *The Autobiography of Mrs Alice Thornton of East Newton, Co. York*, The Publications of the Surtees Society, vol. LXII, 1873. The notebooks containing both versions of Alice Thornton's autobiography were in the possession of her descendants, members of the Comber family, until the 1930s, but it has not been possible to trace their present whereabouts.

From: A Book of Remembrances

[The manuscript opens with a note of Thornton's birth and baptism, followed by dedicatory prayers, poems, observations, and a description of her first memories of deliverances from childhood illnesses.]

1631

Being removed from Richmond to London by my father's and mother's order, to be with them, I fell into the smallpox,[1] having taken them of my brother Christopher. We were both sent into Kent, with Sarah,[2] to one Mr Baxter's house, where we were being much beloved and taken care for by them. And by the blessing of God I recovered very soon, nor was I very ill at that time in them. I will praise the Lord our God for my preservation and deliverance, that did not suffer that disease to rage and endanger my life, but raised me soon to my parents again. Oh, let me speak good of the name of the Lord, magnify his goodness to myself and my brother.

After this, it pleased the Lord to begin to come into my soul by some beams of his mercy in putting good thoughts into my mind and to consider his great and miraculous power in the creation of the heavens, the earth and all therein contained, upon the reading of my daily psalms for the months, which happened that day to be Psalm 147:4: 'He counteth the stars and calleth them all by their names.' From whence there came a forcible consideration of the incomprehensible power and infinite majesty of almighty God, who made all things in the heavens and the earth, being above all his creatures in the world and knew what was in my heart and thoughts, and knew I was but a child in age and understanding, not able to do any good thing, which caused a deep and great apprehension and fear with awe of his glorious majesty, lest I should offend him at any time by sin against him or my parents, and that he would punish all sins. It also caused in me a love to him my creator, that had made me to serve him and his particular love and grace to me, a little child, in giving me understanding and reason to know there is a God that ruleth in heaven and earth, and to reward them that serves him truly with joy in heaven that should never have end.

1632

There was a great fire in the next house to my father's in St Martin's

Lane in London, which burned a part of our house and had like to
have burned our house, but was prevented through the care of our
servants. This was done at night when my father and mother was at
court, but we were preserved in my Lady Levenstone's house, being
carried by Sarah thither. This fire did seem to me as if the Day of
Judgment was come and caused great fear and trembling, but we were
all delivered from ruin by the fire, although my father had great loss.
But blessed be the Lord my God who gave us not over to this cruel
element of fire, but preserved us from all evil at that time.

It pleased God to give me a safe passage with my mother and her
family into Ireland about the year 1632, my father being there before
and sent for us over.[3] Where I enjoyed great happiness and comfort
during my father's life and had the opportunity of the best education
the kingdom could afford in the sweet and excellent company of my
Lord of Strafford's daughters, the most virtuous Lady Anne
Wentworth and Arabella, learning those qualities with them my
father pleased to order me, as: the French language, writing and
speaking the same, singing, dancing, playing on the lute and
theorbo.[4]

1632, 1633, 1634

Learning also all the other accomplishments of working silks and
sweetmeats and by my dear mother's virtuous provision and care, she
brought me up in all those things suitable to that of quality as my father's
child. But above all these things, I accounted it my chief happiness in
those pious, holy and religious instructions, examples and admon-
itions, teachings, reproofs and godly education, tending to the
eternal happiness and salvation of my poor soul, which I received from
both my honoured father and mother with the chaste and sober
conversation in all things of this world. For all these things and
infinitely more opportunities of good to my well-being than I can
express, I most humbly and heartily acknowledge my bounden duty
of . . . [At this point the manuscript becomes illegible for two pages.]

1641, 1642, 1643, 1644

I got the smallpox at Rosschester[5] of my brother John and was very
near death with them. But blessed be the God of mercies who,
sparing my life at the time, also with my brother John [who] had
them. But a poor boy, F. Kelly,[6] died of them. Then we were

prevented from the siege at York by Mr Danby's advice,[7] being got half-way thither. (1642)

I got a surfeit at Richmond with eating a piece of lobster. That day I had taken physic which had like to have proved my last, being brought exceeding weak through vomiting and purging.[8] (1643) But by the blessing of God, upon Mr Matrum's[9] advice and my mother's and good Aunt Norton's care, I escaped and yet live to render him the glory and praise of all his wonderful deliverances and mercies. Bless the Lord, oh my soul, and all that is within me praise his holy name forever. Amen.

My sister Danby died at Thorpe, September, 1645 of her sixteenth child, being a son named Francis, whom I baptized.[10]

1648

My cousin Edmund Norton married Mr Dudley's daughter and heir of Chopwell, Jane Dudley, 10th February, 1648 at Chopwell.

My cousin Edmund Norton died at York of a pleurisy or stitch[11] in his side, 30th November, 1648.

King Charles I beheaded at Whitehall, London, 30th January, 1649.

My cousin Julian Norton died at St Nicholas.

My cousin Julian Norton died at Richmond Green at her father's, 9th April 1649.

My uncle Sir Edward Osborne died at Kiveton of a surfeit of eating melons, being too cold for him.

1651

My brother George Wandesford was drowned riding over the Swale at Hipswell [as he] wath[12] going to Richmond to my Uncle William Wandesford, 31st March, 1651.

My cousin Mary Norton was married to Mr John Yorke at her father's house on the Green at Richmond, 12th August, 1651.

My brother Christopher Wandesford married Sir John Lowther's eldest daughter, Mrs Eleanor Lowther, 30th September, 1651 at Lowther.

Myself, Alice Wandesford, was married to William Thornton Esq. at my mother's house in Hipswell, 15th December, 1651. Married by Mr Siddall.[13]

1652

I began my great sickness after I came from Burne Park, the first time, about 6th August, 1652 and miscarried of my first child, being a daughter, 27th of the same August, 1652, being Friday, and she was buried at Easby church, near Richmond, the next morning. The effects of my sickness lasted by[14] an ague, fever and jaundice, three-quarters of a year at Hipswell.

Alice Thornton, my second child, was born at Hipswell, 3rd January, 1654 and baptized the 4th of the same. Witnesses: my mother and my uncle, Major Norton and my cousin York, his daughter. She was born on a Tuesday between the hours of 5 and 6 o'clock in the afternoon. Christened by Mr Siddall, 4th.

Elizabeth Thornton, my third child was born at Hipswell 14th February, 1655, being Wednesday, half [an] hour after 12 o'clock in the forenoon, and was baptized 16th February by Mr Antony.[15] Witnesses: my mother, my Aunt Norton and my brother Christopher Wandesford, Mrs Blackburn stood for my mother, being sick then.

1655

My Mother Gates died at Oswaldkirk of the voidance of the blood, 10th May, 1655, and was buried at Stonegrave, 10th May 1655.

My Father Gates[16] died at Hull 18th May 1655 and was buried at Hull, 18th May, 1655.

1656

My brother Richard Thornton died in Dublin, in Ireland, of the flux,[17] [that] country['s] disease, 3rd July, 1656 and [was] buried in St Patrick's church the next day.

Katherine Thornton, my fourth child was born at Hipswell, 12th June 1656, being Thursday, about half an hour after 4 o'clock in the afternoon, and was baptized 14th June by Mr Siddall. Witnesses: my mother, my niece Danby and Mr Thornton.

Elizabeth Thornton, my third child, died 5th September, 1656, betwixt the hours of five and six in the morning, of a cough, gotten at first by an ague and much gone in the rickets caused by ill suck at two nurses.[18] Her age was one year, six months and twenty-one days. Was buried the same day at Catterick church by Mr Siddall.

1657

I got a great fall over the threshold in the hall at Hipswell, being great with child, of my fifth child, wanting but ten weeks before of my time, 14th September, 1657, which cast me into an ill fit of fever and the jaundice. About three weeks very weak, likely to have miscarried, but it pleased God to restore me to strength through the means of Dr Witty[19] who let me blood and I went to my full time. Bless the most high God, possessor of heaven and earth. I was delivered of my fifth child, being a goodly son, upon the 10th December, 1657, between the hours of 2 and 3 o'clock in the morning, upon Thursday, having had very sore travail, in danger of my life from that time in the morning on Wednesday, caused by the child's coming into the world with his feet first, and so caused him to be strangled almost in the birth. He lived about half an hour, so died and was buried in Catterick church the same day by Mr Siddall. He was turned wrong in my womb by the fall I had in September before.

1658

The weakness of my body continued so great and long after my hard childbirth of my son that it brought me almost into a consumption, not expecting for many days together that I should at all recover. And when it was d[one], I was lame almost a quarter of a year of my left knee, that I got in my labour. But this was nothing to that which I have deserved from the hand of God if he, in much mercy, had not spared my life. The Lord make me truly remember his goodness and that I may never forget this above all, his mighty and stretched-out hand of deliverances to me, his poor creature, that I may extol and praise the Lord with all my soul and never let go my hope from the God of my salvation, but live the remainder of the life he gives me to his honour and glory. And that, at the last, [I] may praise him eternally in the heavens. Bless the Lord, oh my soul, and forget not all his benefits. Amen. Amen.

1659

It pleased God to visit my dear and honoured mother, the Lady Wandesford, with her last sickness upon Friday, 17th November, 1659, beginning then with an exceeding great cough, tormenting her body by stitches in her breast and short breathing. These stitches continued about fourteen days with the cough hindering her from almost any sleep, whereupon the use of bags with fried oats, butter and camomile chopped, laid to her sides, the stitches removed and the cough abated as to the extremity thereof. But then she was seized with a more dangerous symptom of a hard lump contracted in her stomach, that laid on her heart with great pain and rising up to her throat almost stopping her breath when she either swallowed anything or laid to sleep. Which lump was conceived to be contracted of phlegm and wind in the stomach, for lack of voidance. She had also an exceeding sore throat and mouth so that she was deprived of the benefit to swallow almost any kind of food, save to a little drop of beer, which was for four days or five the most she took inwardly, and that but with a syringe. The tongue and mouth at first was black, then turned white, so that with the pains my dear mother took in washing and cleansing, the skin came off like a calf's tongue and was raw and red till the blood came. But this continued and in the end grew with a white skin all over.

In this condition of weakness was my dear mother almost quite without food, rest, ease or sleep for about a week, in which time, as in all her sickness, she expressed extraordinary great patience, still saying the Lord had sent it to her and none could take it from her, and if he pleased he could ease her, and that the way to heaven was by the gates of hell. She was an example and pattern of piety, faith and patience in her greatest torment, still with godly instructions, gentle rebukes for sin, a continual praying of psalms, speaking to God in his own phrase and word, saying that we could not speak to him from ourselves in such an acceptable a manner, as by that which was dictated by his own most holy spirit.

When that any did pray for her, she desired they would not pray for her life, but that these should be the heads on which they should petition God for her: that the Lord would be pleased to grant her true and unfeigned repentance for her sins; to give her remission and forgiveness through Jesus Christ her saviour; to grant her faith in him, with the sanctification of his holy spirit; and at last to glorify her in heaven. 'Which petitions,' said she, 'whosoever shall make for me, the Lord hear and grant the same.' She had always a great and unfeigned love for all God's ministers and often desired their prayers, giving great attention to them, having much comfort in her soul after that ordinance.[20] Her desire was to receive the holy sacrament, which she did with comfort that Thursday [which] was seven-night before she departed, from Mr Peter Samways,[21] although it was with great difficulty of swallowing, never tasting dry bread after, for that weakness. Her desire was to Mr Kirton,[22] he would preach her funeral sermon, text to be out of the fourteenth of Revelation, thirteenth verse: 'Blessed are the dead that die in the Lord . . .' and so to the end. This blessed soul had a gift from God as to continue till the last breath her perfect memory, understanding and great wisdom and piety, ever recommending her soul: 'Behold, I desire to be dissolved and so be with Christ' [Philipians 1.23]. And all the Friday night before she died: 'Come, Lord Jesus, come quickly' [Revelation 22.20], she making Dafeny[23] to pray with her that prayer which Dr Smith made in his book for a person at the point to die, and took great notice of each petition, praying the same with zeal and earnestness.

About Thursday, at night, she sent for her children to take her leave, when Mr Thornton and myself came and prayed with her. And we took the saddest leaves of my dear parent as ever child could to part with so great a comfort: she praying for us, our children and all her friends with her blessings for us both.

It pleased God she continued till Saturday, about noon, when she spoke to my uncle Norton and commended her children to his care with much good prayers for him and his, then took her leave of him.

Towards 6 o'clock at night, her speech failed and [but] still she could lift up her hands to God. And Dafeny prayed for that she would give them some sign that she found comfort of God's spirit in her soul with a taste of the joys of heaven, which she immediately did and lift[ed] up both hands unto heaven three times. And closing her eyes herself, that sweet saint fell asleep in the Lord, between the hours of eight and nine o'clock at night, upon Saturday 10th December, 1659, joyous forever.

(A Book of Remembrances, pp. 12–37)

[Thornton describes several more illnesses of her own, her husband's and her children's, some personal accidents, and the Great Fire of London. She gives birth to the last three of her nine children, two of whom die in infancy. She also records her deliverances from financial problems (involving bailiffs) and a period of despair, and she notes the deaths of members of the Wandesford and Norton families. The next extract follows her account of the birth and death of her son Christopher.]

1667

After my child's death, I fell into a great and long-continued weakness, by the swelling of my milk in my left breast which Kitt[24] last sucked and did so nip the head that I was in fear of a gangrene. And the extreme pain cast me into a fever which, together with other griefs and colds and extreme, violent pain of the teeth, did bring me into that weakness that I could neither stand nor go, for four months, but was carried to bed and from bed in a chair. But ever blessed and magnified be the great and glorious name of the Lord most high, which bringeth me down to the gates of death and raiseth me up again, time without number, and might most justly [have] taken me out of this life, but letting me see the follies of this life and many changes we are accident to, that I might prepare more earnestly and long for those lasting joys that never shall have end. Which he, in his good time, will please to bring me to, for my saviour Jesus Christ his sake. Amen.

1668

After the recovery of my health, I was very much in affliction about my dear husband's illness and often relapses into his former palatic fits[25] which fell on him notwithstanding all the many remedies [which] was perpetually used by Dr Witty's order and with good success. So that from the November 1667 till August 1668, he had not missed one fortnight from a relapse,[26] or the degrees of it,[27] insomuch that I never enjoyed any comfort in consideration of and fear of him and his sufferings and lest I should be deprived of my joy and delight in this life, though I bless God he had intermissions which bringeth me down to the gates of death and raiseth me up according to the earliness of the time in beginning them, the fits was longer or shorter in continuance.

About 20th July, 1668 I had a very great and dangerous sickness fell upon me, being in my perfect health and strength, upon the occasion of a sudden grief and terror that I was seized upon in my niece Kitt Danby's[28] chamber at Newton, when her maid, Barbara Tod, did impudently accuse, before my face, my servant Hanna Alleson for telling her from our Mary Breaks of several stories, which were very great lies and falsehoods against myself, of such a nature as did much unbecome any to hear, and not to have acquainted me with at the first. Which my maid did utterly deny and cleared herself and me, upon her oath. But the other woman, having a spleen against her, did carry so brazenly and unchristianly towards me in her bitter aggravation and in false accusing the honour of some of the persons of my family, and before her mistress, that I fell presently into a most great and sad excess of weeping and lamentable sorrow that it had like to have lost me my life, having only God and my own conscience to give me testimonies of comfort, being so foully and abominably abused for my charity in receiving those that came under my roof and to whom I had done no wrong. (And out of whose mouths God making them instruments to my clearing,[29] notwithstanding these maliciousnesses, both in my accusation and their secret plots of concealment, till the other wicked woman was gone from Newton and by that means did spread her lies abroad at Richmond.) And the highest aggravation of injury in those persons, that was done by my bosom's friend[30] that knew my innocency all my days. But why can I not with patience take the bitter cup out of my saviour's hand, and for his love, lay down my life, that suffered many opprobrious scorns and abuses from his enemies? Oh my soul, bless thou the Lord, that he will please to give thee to suffer and go in such steps as he himself has trodden out the path of life in. Has he not preserved thee from the evils of sin and all those enormous crimes the vild[31] world now lies wallowing in? And will thou not show thy gratitude to thy redeemer that gives thee cheer in sufferings and not with the partakers of their wickednesses? Let thy heart rejoice in his salvation and that thy delight was very much desirous to advance his glory, although Satan would blemish those that he has no part in yet. My hope is in God who redeemed thee from all sin and wickedness and gives thee a stay and support in all thy anguish of spirit and preservation from the designs of those who would and cruelly do devour thy honour as much as in them laid.

And lo, when I was yet nearly recovered of my weakness from this grief, and had kept my bed fourteen days, it pleased God, in his infinite and abundant mercy and goodness, to begin to restore that most valued jewel by me (and which was intended to be wronged: my good name) by the coming of my dear aunt over to Newton, who had heard the vild reports blazed abroad by Mary Breaks, and lies against my innocent soul. This woman, full of deep dissembling and hypocrisy, she could not prevail with her design upon the person of Mr Comber[32] to have drawn him for marriage and in the failing of that end perverted her plausible carriage into an inveterate malice and hatred both against him and myself, with having discovered that it was Mr Comber's desire to obtain my daughter Alice in marriage, and that he was made use on to assist us in the drawing of settlements and writings for Mr Thornton's estate on my children, which I had good cause to see done, in regard of Mr Thornton's and my own dying condition.

I say from hence this woman takes occasion to pervert the most innocent actions in the world and such as was most just and honest, for the preservation of my poor family and children from ruin. I finding a daily decay and great weakness of body and mind was very solicitous to get this done before our deaths, which I may well appeal to God, cost me great sorrow and pains and trouble, being of so great concernment, before and in the transaction of all these businesses [giving] this poor gentleman no small pains, trouble and care, till it was finished, which was done with the comfort and knowledge of my husband's brother Denton, a wise and prudent man, assisting us in the prosecution of the designs and has since been a means of mine and his just vindication from any of those wicked untruths forged against us by this Mary Breaks, whose lies, had my niece Danby's charity extended so far to me as [to have] discovered [them] before the woman's going from Newton, I might have turned them on their own head and their mischiefs on their own pate, before Satan's instruments had divulged them to the infinite dishonour of God and his poor, mean servants. But as my intentions was cordially good, so God would not suffer me to perish, but took the matter into his own hand to stop the mouths of my adversaries. And when I wanted relief, in his providence sent my dear aunt to acquaint me, and so gave me such favour in her eyes and the rest of my dear and Christian friends that I have by this opportunity to make a public clearing and vindication of all my innocent actions. And I hope against such belief that the Lord has appeared to stand on my side and therefore I need not care what men can say against me, but will give all possible glory and praise, adoration and thanks, to my glorious God that would not suffer me to depart this life with any blot upon my person, but to approve my continuance in the true faith of the Lord Jesus Christ in which I was brought up, nor give any occasion of blemish to that most noble family from wherein I was descended.

I acknowledge the goodness of my Lord, which hath several times sent me relief, in the company and comfortable assistances, praise and sweet religious advices and supports of my dear friends. I was in deep distresses, all which I take as great encouragement to serve the Lord with all my heart, which never failed his weak and despised handmaid. And I know, oh Lord, that thou canst, and doest me good by this heavy and sad affliction, [which] as well as all ot[hers] and teach me, oh Lord, by this, thy rod and scourge of wicked tongues who seeketh occasion to slay me and root out the remembrance from the earth. And though they curse yet, bless thou and behold the anguish of my soul, for out of the deeps have I called, 'Lord, save me'. I perish, but still put my trust in thee. Oh, strengthen, stablish and settle my heart in thy faith, that neither life nor death shall separate me from the love of God. And blessed be thy holy name, that has preserved my dear husband's love and faithful affection to me all my life long, and that it was not in the power of man nor devil to shake or remove those faithful and conjugal bonds and ties of Christian, dearest and chaste affections betwixt us, making us both abhor the very mention of all such vild abominations as this world was too full of in all places, but where by grace of our own good God whom we serve, night and day, have lived in a holy and chaste bond of wedlock above these sixteen years. Having this to comfort our hearts, that we are undefiled servants intending to follow Christ in the regeneration, that we might reign with him in glory. Oh, that my soul may forever be thankful to the most high God that had regard to his poor and humble handmaid. What am I, oh Lord, that should have this testimony of thy mercy? I will give thee the glory of thy works, mercies and favours for ever, and most humbly beg, on the account of my Christ's intercession, that I may have the grace of perseverance and a truly thankful heart to walk worthy of these unestimable mercies and glorify thee in the midst of all my trials and sufferings that makest me pray to escape. Now praise the Lord, oh my soul, and forget not all his benefits. Amen. Amen.

(A Book of Remembrances, pp. 118–27)

1668

Whilst I am in this vale of tears and shadow of death I must not expect no more comforts than will preserve me from sinking. Nor will I repine at the great Lord of heaven and earth's most infinitely wise disposition, for he knows how to propose and intermix crosses with comforts, smiles with frowns, to his servants here, as shall be the best for them, not as they shall think fit which are but of yesterday, but himself who sees not as man sees, but has all things in his omnipresent and omnipotent power and shall tend most to his own glory. No sooner was my strength in part recruited again after my dear aunt's departure home, and having been so weak that I kept my bed above a week, so beginning to rejoice at my deliverance from the late illness both of the plague of slanderous tongues and the faintings abated something, but the first day that I did arise out of my bed, I had the news of my dear husband's falling sick at Malton brought to me by a letter to my brother Denton, which did so suddenly surprise my spirit that I fell to tremble exceedingly with great grief and fears upon me for his safety and life. Immediately, I sent for Dr Witty to go to Malton, and sent each day to see my dear and my only joy and comfort. But myself so much afflicted that I went presently to bed and continued with the break[33] and that I was in danger of overflow[34] because of my excessive sorrow, only the Lord did support my soul from sinking. On Wednesday I sent my brother Denton and Mr Comber to my joy at Malton, and longing all that day to hear from him, and if I could go without loss of my poor and miserable life, I would have gone to have seen him myself, but my friends would not suffer me to make an adventure thereof. But I stayed till night when word was brought from Mr Witty that I should be of good cheer, for I should have my dear heart home as well to me as ever I had him in my life. So that I did shore up my hopes in God and pour out my tears and prayers in abundance that night, for the life and health of [my] dear husband with me, if it did stand good with the will and pleasure of our God, and got some little slumbers, though with fears and tremblings and sad, dismal dreams. When, in the morning, my brother Denton came home and very discreetly prepared me with good advice and counsel to entertain the Lord's determinate will in all things, with patience and submission, if the worst should fall on me, according to my fears. But withall, God could raise him up again, if he sees fit, although my dear heart was very weak. And at the news I grew very ill, and the Lord pardon my weakness, for it was a reviving of my great sorrows for the being fearful to be deprived of this my sole delight in this world, next under my good God.

So, betwixt hopes and fears I rested till the next messenger came, which was about 4 o'clock on Thursday, in the afternoon, at which time I receiving news of the most terrible loss that ever woman lost in being deprived of my sweet and most exceeding dear husband that any creature could have. Such was my extremity of passion and trouble upon this change that I was almost changed into nothing, and was ready to go into the grave with him whom God had joined me to, almost seventeen years. Great are the sorrows of my heart and many thorns have gone over my soul, but this is the Lord's sharpest arrow that is gone out against me. Now am I left destituted of head-guide, help or support in this world, tossed with all the sorrows that a poor, desolate widow can meet withal. [This] the Lord has broken in upon me, like a mighty water and poured on me his indignation. Great are my calamities; my case is full of complaints, bereft of a most dear and tenderly loving husband that took part with me in all sorrows, comforted me in sadnesses. We walked together as dear friends. His love was mine, in his sickness I was afflicted. Now am I left of him who was my earthly delight, he being gone to his heavenly father and left me to lament his loss from me and my poor fatherless children, weak in body, afflicted in spirit, low in my estate.[35] Losses of my dearest friends and relations, children and other comforts as dear, and now, to consummate my sufferings, my husband withdrawest. Oh, that my sorrows were weighed, and that the Lord would pity my distress! I am still thy creature by creation, redemption, sanctification, preservation from death, hell and the grave. Do not despise thy weak handmaiden, for thou did make me. I am thine. Oh give me understanding and I shall live. Take me not away out of the land of the living, but give me to serve the Lord with a perfect heart and a willing mind, fear the rod and who hath sent it. Is there any evil in a city and the Lord has not done it? Is there not an appointed time for man once to die? Oh that I may die daily and be with God in soul and spirit, loving him with all my soul and a perfect heart. I must be still, and know that it is God that ruleth in heaven and earth. The Lord is his name. And his mercy is unto us, for he did draw my joy to his own self, and fitted him for this dissolution. He remembered the Lord in the days of his youth, and God was found of him.

I do now want those good and pious prayers of him for me and mine which I have enjoyed for many years. What can I say or what can I do: each remembrance brings me a fresh flood of tears. I water my couch and widowed, desolate bed, for myself and my children. Methinks I hear him:

'Joy, weep not for me, but weep for yourselves and children. I was, in the world, tormented with pains and crosses, losses and sicknesses, troubles on every side. But now I am comforted in the bosom of my Father and thy Father, who I had a desire to go to. Now, my sorrows, cannot ye find relief to assuage the violent passion for this sad separation, is there no hope in the later end? What if though, my heart, thou art deprived of his presence and company? Dost thou not believe that he now enjoys the incomprehensible joys of the great God of heaven? Dost thou not think that all his tears is wiped from his eyes, all sorrow is departed from him and he is delivered from this body of sin and death? Oh, my soul, canst thou not consider for some comfort that what he now enjoys, he would not exchange for ten thousand worlds? Thy loss for the present is his gain, and God will assuredly bring thee at the Resurrection to m[eet] him, when we shall appear together, being clothed with immortality, to enjoy those inconceivable joys he now does possess. Although worms consume this body, yet with my eyes shall I see God and behold him face to face, which this day this body of dust cannot, till my vild body be changed and this mortal shall put on immortality.'

Oh that the Lord would now show himself to his weak servant, and give me faith to believe what good things is laid up for them that love and fear him.

(A Book of Remembrances, pp. 135–42)

[Further details of her husband's death, prayers, meditations, and an index to her Book follow.]

Notes

1 *the smallpox* : smallpox or chickenpox.
2 *Sarah* : Sarah Tomlinson, their maid.
3 *Ireland . . . my father being there before and sent for us over* : her father, Sir Christopher Wandesford had accompanied his cousin and patron, Thomas Wentworth, Viscount then Earl of Strafford to Ireland in 1634 and remained as Lord Deputy of Ireland in Wentworth's place when Wentworth returned to London in November 1640 when he was impeached. Sir Christopher Wandesford, who had a reputation as a mild and gentle man, died suddenly, aged 48, after being faced by the Irish Parliament's attacks on Wentworth and news of Wentworth's imprisonment.
4 *theorbo* : a double-necked lute, highly fashionable in the seventeenth century.
5 *Rosschester* : referred to as Weschester and Chester in the later version; probably Chester.
6 *F. Kelly* : Frank Kelly, an orphaned Irish child who had been taken into the Wandesford household and converted to Protestantism.
7 *prevented from the seige at York by Mr Danby's advice* : i.e. they were kept away from the seige at York where the Marquis of Newcastle and his Royalist troops were defeated by Scottish Presbyterian troops and Fairfax's army in 1645. *Mr Danby* : a family friend from Cave, later killed at the Battle of Marston Moor, fighting for the king.
8 *purging* : diarrhoea.
9 *Mr Matrum* : a physician.
10 *My sister Danby . . . whom I baptized* : at the time of the birth of Lady Danby's (Catherine Wandesford's) son (a breech birth), Scottish Presbyterian soldiers were quartered at the Danby's home at Thorpe. A minister could not, therefore, be called to baptize the child, but it was permissible for anyone present to do so, in urgent circumstances.
11 *stitch* : pain, especially sharp pain.
12 *wath* : sic in ms.
13 *Mr Siddall* : Michael Siddall, minister of Kirkington through the patronage of the Thornton family and later vicar of Catterick.
14 *lasted by* : prolonged by, or lasted in the form of.

15 *Mr Antony* : Charles Antony, vicar of Catterick.

16 *My Mother Gates . . . My Father Gates* : her husband's mother who died of bleeding from the stomach, and her husband, William Thornton's stepfather.

17 *flux* : dysentery, probably amoebic dysentery.

18 *an ague . . . ill suck at two nurses* : ague — severe fever; wet-nursing was common practice. Alice Thornton, however, usually nursed her children herself, when she was able.

19 *Dr Witty* : a famous physician and medical writer.

20 *ordinance* : religious service or duty.

21 *Mr Peter Samways* : rector of Bedale and Wath, 1660–93; prebendary of York and Ripon.

22 *Mr Kirton* : John Kirton, rector of Richmond, 1658–64.

23 *Dafeny* : her maid.

24 *Kitt* : Christopher, her ninth child who has just died.

25 *palatic fits* : fits of palsy. Palsy refers to any nervous disease, including forms of epilepsy, paralysis, Parkinson's disease, and motor neurone disorders, whether they were illnesses in themselves or secondary symptoms of other illnesses.

26 *he had not missed . . . relapse* : i.e. a fortnight did not go by without a relapse.

27 *the degrees of it* : stages of it or symptoms of it.

28 *my niece Kitt Danby's* : Katherine Danby, the daughter of her sister, Lady Catherine Danby.

29 *And out of whose mouths . . . clearing* : i.e. God turns this harm to good.

30 *my bosom's friend* : i.e. Mary Breaks.

31 *vild* : an archaic form of vile.

32 *Mr Comber* : Thomas Comber, a high-flying young curate at Stonegrave in the 1660s, later rector of Stonegrave, Dean of Durham, and chaplain to William and Mary. Alice and William Thornton have arranged the secret engagement of their 14-year-old daughter, Alice, to Thomas Comber. They, in fact, marry later in 1668.

33 *the break* : irregularity, disruption, period of illness, collapse.

34 *overflow* : bodily or emotional excess.

35 *low in my estate* : a reference to her status as a widow and her financial situation.

9

SARAH DAVY

*Heaven Realized, or the holy pleasure of daily intimate communion
with God, exemplified in a blessed soul (now in heaven) (Mrs Sarah
Davy), dying about the thirty-second year of her age. Being a part of
the precious relics written with her own hand. (Styled by her) 'the
record of my consolations, and the meditations of my heart'.*
Published by A. P.

'Come and hear all you that fear God, and I will tell you what he
hath done for my soul', Psalm 66.16.

Printed in the year 1670.

Heaven Realized presents a series of dilemmas, since the interpretation of
events that offers itself most readily to the modern reader – that Davy is
writing about her rage at her mother, her guilt over her brother's death, her
falling in love with another woman – is quite different from that understood
by its seventeenth-century editor and, probably, its author and readers.

Sarah Davy wrote within conventions of Baptist conversion narratives
and meditations that required her to examine her experiences for signs that
God had destined her for heaven, and to draw out broader theological
lessons from things that happened to her. The conversion narrative had its
own expected structure of false confidence in the writer's salvation, doubt,
and renewed, true confidence, and certain insights were expected to be
gained: notably that the believer must abandon herself wholly to God, and
accept that there was nothing she could do to save herself. All events in her
life must be examined for signs of God's will, and illness and the death of
loved ones, in particular, interpreted as indications of his wrath over people's
sins. The conventions of this frame, therefore, largely predetermined what
was recorded and the sense that was made of it. The restraining power of the
structure is increased in the case of Sarah Davy's text (as it is in many
conversion narratives of the 1670s) because the published version of *Heaven
Realized* was not selected by herself but by her Baptist minister, who offers

Sarah Davy as an example to '*younger persons* (especially *young gentle-women*)' (sig. A4ᵛ). Even if the author had included material thought unsuitable in such an exemplary text, it would not have survived into print.

None the less, to the modern eye *Heaven Realized* seems to offer an account of Sarah Davy's guilty feelings of responsibility for her baby brother's death; to record her recovery from long-standing illness at the death of her mother; and to recall the end to her years of isolation when she fell in love with the friend who introduced her to her Baptist faith, another woman. In several passages not included in the following extract she also laments the later-revealed unreliability of friends, and her turning instead to the comfort of God's love:

> Satisfaction is not to be had in anything below a Saviour, no not in very friends. They are but *fading comforts*, may leave thee and forsake thee; but then, saith David, 'even then the Lord took me up'. My heavenly Father hath a *greater* love, a pity for me. He hath said, 'In the presence of the Father shall no ill come to thee', the Lord will take thy drooping soul into his banqueting house, and speak peace to thee. By love embraces he will *stay* thee *with* delights. Oh how *sweet* is his *fruit*, eaten under his *shadow*, what comfort is it to a wearied soul to lie down under so *sweet a shade*, to take *rest* from scorching heats, storms and tempests.
>
> (Davy 1670: 127)

Davy's use here of David's words in Psalm 21 is typical of the way the bible features in her writing. *Heaven Realized* is steeped in echoes of David (who found Jonathon's love 'wonderful, passing the love of women'), Job's sufferings before his salvation, and an identification with Cain who, like she believed herself to be, was responsible for his brother's death: 'I must cry out with Cain, "My punishment should be greater than I can bear"'. Although this kind of interweaving of personal experience and bible reference is typical of the writings of the day, the specific meanings Davy gives to such passages is a deeply personal one. To make reference to David or to Cain was far from unusual: to use them in the way she does seems too carefully apposite for chance.

To the modern eye, Sarah Davy's meeting with the initially ungendered 'one that I never saw before, but of a sweet and free disposition' reads like falling in love, and the 'hungerings and thirstings' Davy describes at her separation from her new-found friend seem further to demand such an interpretation. Perhaps to Davy, certainly to her editor, such a reading simply would not occur: these experiences of joy and longing were consistent with expected emotions on discovering a new faith. A similar ambiguity can be found in the description of the death of Davy's mother, the incident that *Heaven Realized* opens with, and to which the narrative loops back. The present-day reader might wonder how much suppressed rage the text contains: it was at her mother's initiative that Sarah Davy failed to go to church the day her brother died. Where Davy attributes the disappearance of her illness on her mother's death to 'the goodness of God', other explanations offer themselves more readily today. The text's fascination lies in these conflicts of meaning.

What little we know about Sarah Davy comes from *Heaven Realized* itself. She was born into a middle-class family of the name of Roane, sent away to school and until December 1660, at least, was unmarried. At the time of her writing she lived in 'this city': perhaps London, in which case her editor A. P. was probably Anthony Palmer (c. 1618–78), minister of the Pinner's Hall congregation from 1662. She was probably well respected by her congregation, since Palmer recommends *Heaven Realized* as edifying for them, and since parts of it, at least, were written as meditations addressed to her fellow Baptists, probably to be read aloud at services. The majority of *Heaven Realized*, which runs to more than 150 pages, in fact consists not of narrative but of meditations, less tempting to the modern eye but significant in their day, since women were not expected to be learned enough to write at such length on such subjects. One of the most striking of these refers to the persecution of dissenters under the returned monarchy, and since homosexuality was also punishable by imprisonment or death at that time, its courage in the face of persecution might stand both for her religious consistency and her daring love for a woman:

> Man says thou shalt not do this, etc., 'tis disobedience to commands of men, and the issue of it will be either *prison, banishment*, or death; but the *spirit* of God says, 'Pay thy vows', though it come in competition with thy very life.
>
> (Davy 1670: 135–6)

Textual note

Copytext is the British Library copy of *Heaven Realized*, shelfmark 4412 f22, extracts collated also with the Congregational Library copy. Italicization of words and phrases in works of this period often indicates the existence of biblical echoes and quotation. Where it has been possible to identify such references in Davy's text, italics have been removed and the relevant passage noted. In other cases I have been unable to identify a source: perhaps she has in mind other doctrinal works or church practices, or perhaps the italics indicate a speaking rhythm appropriate in a text partly written to be read aloud in church. Such italics have been left, despite their strange appearance to the modern eye, since to remove them effaces the message available to the seventeenth-century reader that such echoes existed. I am grateful to Maureen Bell for her help with these decisions.

From: *Heaven Realized*

The Account of Her Early Conversion

Oh my soul, consider the wonderful goodness of God, revealing his free grace and unbounded love towards thee a poor worm. Oh how wonderful is this condescension[1] of his that thou shouldest be made an object of mercy? My soul, forget not his unspeakable love, let it be recorded. Keep in remembrance these choice blessings of a loving Father, bestowed so freely on me in the Lord Jesus Christ the dear Son of his love, who hath borne with thee in many weaknesses, infirmities, and ever seemed to overlook all corruptions, and set thee under his eye of pity and compassion. Oh let this be a means more to incite to a near closer walking with God, that thou mayest be borne up against the wiles of Satan, thy subtle enemy, whose aim is to destroy thee for ever.

In the eleventh year of my age, the Lord was pleased to take away my dear mother. My parents were very dear and tender of me, and did not leave me without instructions of the things of God. At that time the Lord was pleased to carry out my heart to things I then knew not: for as soon as my parents had taught me there was a God, I had an awe upon my heart concerning him. I could then reason with my heart, and said, 'The Lord made me, and he made me to serve him, and I must do it.' So being young, the Lord was pleased in the freeness of his grace to kindle in my heart some *small sparks* of affections to himself. I remember on a time a little brother of mine was sick, and my mother being very tender of her child, one Lord's day would not go to church, which caused me also to stay at home; but wanting employment, out of my mother's sight went to work about my babies.[2] At night the Lord was pleased to take away the child, I standing by the cradle, which brought a fear upon me presently that I had been the cause, by my working that day, of the Lord's anger in taking away my brother.

I also remember that I went out and wept bitterly[3] in the consideration of my day's work, but never let my friends know it. I was much troubled at it, but hoped, such was the ignorance of my heart, that all would be well again by my praying and going to church, which I was careful to do, and fearful to omit one duty which might hinder the means of my salvation, and cause the Lord to be displeased with me.

The ten commandments was much *upon my heart*, making that my only rule to walk by; and was earnest with the Lord that he would help me to the daily observing and fulfilling of them, for I then knew there must be a greater power than my own to enable me to the performance of it. Also my parents taught me *in my catechism* what was my duty towards God and towards my neighbour, and by my continual saying of them the Lord was pleased to work them upon my spirit, and into my affections, and then in mercy to take notice of me, in the freeness of his grace and tender mercy to own me in the Lord Jesus Christ, whom I was ignorant of as to what he had done and undergone for my soul. But now I can't but admire[4] to behold the infinite goodness and tender love of God, who was then pleased *to choose me from amongst my brethren*, and his own self took care of me, *leading me* by many paths of providence, passing over all my corruptions. My weaknesses and my failings caused me to find a tender-hearted Father of a great and holy God. Oh how sweetly hath the Lord been pleased to carry on the work of grace in my poor unworthy soul! How exceedingly doth his glory shine and his goodness appear in that he who is the High and Mighty One, the Great God of Heaven and Earth, the King of Kings and the Lord of Lords should condescend so far as to cast his eye upon a worm, much more *his love* upon a distressed creature. About the same year of my age the Lord was pleased to take away my dear mother, by which I had a great loss; yet knowing it was my duty to trust God at all times I laboured therefore to be content, and the Lord was pleased to bear me up by considerations of his *love*. I was in the time of my mother's life sickly and weak, subject to divers bodily infirmities, which made my mother the more tender of me, hence I was more sensible of my great loss; but such was the goodness of God that he was pleased then wholly to take away my distemper and so heal me that I have, through his mercy, never since been troubled with it.[5] I fell under some other trial, but the Lord was pleased to enlarge my heart to lay open my case before him, and in mercy caused me to see that he did not despise my poor supplications, but was graciously pleased to sweeten my troubles, and by this to comfort me, in that they carried me nearer to the Lord. Sometimes he was pleased to mitigate them, but mostly gave me strength to go through them and patiently to bear them. Thus was the Lord pleased to exercise his loving kindness and tender compassions to my poor soul, carrying of it as a lamb in his arms. But oh, why was my heart so dead that I was so long contented in a state of ignorance, and not more desirous to come to the knowledge of his ways? But thou, oh Lord, art good, and thy ways past finding out; thy tender compassions never fails those whose hearts are upright before thee. Oh blessed is the soul to whom thou imputest no sin,[6] for certainly, oh Lord, shouldest thou have been so just as to mark what was done amiss. Oh Lord, my sins, my corruptions, my daily actings, besides that guilt of original sin brought into the world with me, was enough to have sunk me into the bottomless pit for ever.

I *could not see the need* I had of my troubles, nor the *end* for which they were sent; but blessed be thy name, oh Lord, who in thy righteousness and goodness and tender mercy didst afflict me, thou mightest have spared thy pains and have bestowed those sweet discoveries of thy *love* on such who would have better improved it, and have let me perish to all eternity.

Oh how is my soul bound for ever to extol the riches of thy grace,[7] now I have seen his glory I abhor myself in dust and ashes,[8] oh how *unworthy* am I to appear before thee! But blessed be thy name who have not left me in despair; but in the sight of my unworthiness and the wretchedness of my condition, caused me to see that there was hope concerning this matter, that thou hadst laid help upon one who was mighty[9] to save.

About a year's time I lived very contentedly and in much ease in my outward conditions,[10] but I began to be unmindful of the Lord who had done so much for me. Oh how apt was I to forget the rock of my salvation [Psalm 89.26]; I began to find these things indifferent to me which before I had prosecuted with much zeal. The dishonouring of God's name by others being so common where I was, I did not find myself so affected as before, nor so much troubled at it; till the Lord was pleased by new alarms *to awaken my drowsy soul*, which was so willing to be lulled asleep by Satan in a sinful security. And by afflictions, some outward trouble brought me truly to consider my ways, and to lie low again before the Lord, often spreading my condition before him in private, who was graciously pleased once more to look upon me, and caused me to see the tenderness of his love towards me.

Then did I begin to grieve at their dishonouring God by their profane walkings,[11] and the Lord was pleased to cause an awe upon my spirit concerning him and his ways. I was mighty desirous to receive the Lord's Supper,[12] but I dared not. I wondered at some that made so light a thing of it, when I found it to be of much weight upon my spirit; I found them in their ways very profane and cold to any good duty. I then began to apply my heart unto the scriptures, desiring the

Lord to give me an understanding therein. It was much upon my spirit to desire that the Lord would be pleased to open my heart as he did Lydia's [Acts 16.14,15] that so I might attend unto the things that were of God.

It pleased the Lord, my time being expired at school, to return me home to my father's house. Mr Pierce[13] being then minister, the first sermon I heard from him did much take upon my affections and raise up my desires unto the ways of God, preaching from Canticles 4.7, 8, 'Thou art all fair my love, there is no spot in thee', wherein he opened the beauty of a soul in Christ, and the love the Lord was pleased to honour such a soul withall. This filled me with desires and longings to be such a one, but how to attain unto it I did not know. Then was I full of fears and doubtings, and Satan brought into my mind my evil and unworthy walkings under so much of the love of God as I had been partaker of. This made my soul walk heavily under much dispute a long time, and when the Lord was pleased to come into my heart by a word at any time which did refresh me, it lasted but a little time.

The Devil would be ready to tell me that was not my part, I was too apt to catch at children's bread[14] and think that my own which did not belong to me. Thus did he follow me a long time, robbing me of the comfort of many a sweet sermon, making me walk in such sadness, which was taken notice of by my friends. I would fain have related my condition and declared my doubts, but could not do it; yet in these doubts found some comfort: I found my soul much carried out in love to Christ. I could delight to sit alone and meditate on the love of Christ held forth in the gospel to poor sinners, and in the former testimonies of his love wherewith he had followed me in every outward providence. My soul would be many times carried out to admire the freeness of his love. My soul longed for such a heavenly communion, which put me much at the throne of grace to desire one glimpse of his glory, one testimony of his love in Christ; but Satan's suggestion put me to a loss in my comfort. He would often persuade me I was a hypocrite,[15] and that I was fallen from grace. This was a sad and great burden upon my spirit, and I thought my sins was so great I must cry out with Cain, 'My punishment should be greater than I can bear.'[16] Yet was the Lord in his goodness pleased not long to leave me in this condition, but to incline my heart more, and with much affection to the Word, remembering the deadness of spirit I had been under.

There was few I was acquainted with whom I could in the least have any converse with in the whole town, thus did I labour to keep my troubles to myself. I remember a sentence which did something refresh me, which was, 'He will lead sinners in the right way'; and the Lord was pleased to come into my heart with this truth: 'I never said unto the house of Jacob, seek ye me in vain.'[17] Then did I go unto the Lord and earnestly desire the assistance of his spirit to seek counsel. In this matter I sought over the book of God, and begged of the Lord with tears that he would be pleased to give me a *right understanding* in what I could not well apprehend. So gracious was the Lord at that time to give in answer to my poor request, and caused me to find much sweetness and comfort in reading, which before I never had found. This raised up my heart to praise the Lord for his mercy towards me, and gave me much comfort, in that I hoped the Lord had not forgotten to be gracious, but had in mercy owned himself to be my God hearing prayer; and that, the poor weak prayer of a wretched miserable creature (who was looked upon with the eye of scorn and much despised). This carried up my soul to joy in the Lord with praises to him, in which I found much comfort and encouragement. Then did I in my heart resolve to wait upon the Lord with my poor petitions for strength till he should please to give me a clearer evidence of his love, and the true knowledge of his ways, which I desired to know above all earthly things. Thus was the Lord pleased to come in with a gracious influence of his holy spirit, whereby I received comfort *from every sermon* I heard for about two months' space.

But then how was my sinful and deceitful heart puffed up.[18] What thoughts did I begin to have of myself. How had the Devil changed his note, and told my proud heart my state was now good and my graces were much increased, for which I ought to be much esteemed. How ready I was to do anything which might secretly make me be thought well of by such as knew it. Then did I walk as one that was well-principled in religion and a great professor.[19] Oh wicked wretch, that after so much love should dare to be so careless as to let Satan steal away my heart. Yet the goodness of the Lord, whose mercies endure for ever, would not suffer me to rest in this condition, but was pleased by a sermon to make me behold my condition and search into with a single eye. The subject he preached from was Matthew 25, the parable of the ten virgins, whereby he showed how far a carnal outward professor might be like a *real* Christian, and yet have never a dram of grace; which the Lord was pleased to fasten upon my soul, making me to weigh my actions and the thoughts of my heart with

the pure word of God, where I found much unsoundness and rotten-
ness. Then was my heart cast into its former sadness, then was the
Lord pleased to *humble* my soul under the sense of a *proud disobedient
heart* and made me to be more *watchful* to my ways and apply my
heart to reading and prayer, which before it was much straitened in.

Thus did I look into the ways of some other professors, where the
Lord discovered to me many weaknesses and failings. By comparing
of their ways unto the pure word of God, I saw a shortness of that
gospel spirit the whole gospel so sweetly treats of. This was a stumbling block to my soul. Thus was my trouble greatly increased, wherein
Satan was very busy to destroy the comforts I had formerly had. None
could I find to declare my trouble, so malicious was the Firebrand of
Hell to cause several jealousies in the hearts of people what might be
the cause of my trouble. And as David says, 'My humbling became a
reproach unto me, I cared not for company but most to be alone',[20] in
which I did contemplate the sweetness of his divine mercy; yet
desiring the Lord would ease me of my burden, which I thought to be
very great. Often should I sit and bewail my sad condition, and be
ready with Job to curse the day of my birth. Yet in this my distress the
Lord was pleased to bring me to his feet. Then would I come with
tears and offer up my poor supplications before the Lord, where I
found my heart much enlarged, being affected with the love of God
to sinners, and carried out much upon those words: 'Call upon the
Lord and he will hear thee, he is nigh unto all that call upon him, to
deliver them out of trouble.'[21] And many more sweet and seasonable
scriptures was the Lord pleased graciously to bring into my remembrance the mercies of old as a tender and a loving Father who
often unto the Lord and spread my condition before the throne of his
grace, having much encouragement to hope in his mercy. Thus did I
find much comfort and sweetness in my secret communion with the
Lord, and found much ease in my troubles, which I took as gracious
returns of my poor broken prayers, and was much carried out to trust
in him and to wait upon him. Then could I sit and call to remembrance the mercies of old as a tender and a loving Father who
nourished up my poor soul, which made me exceedingly admire the
infinite riches of his grace and the freeness of his love in Christ Jesus
to my poor soul; which made me often cry out, 'Lord, what am I that
thou shouldest take such notice of a poor creature, that thou
shouldest cast thine eye of love upon me?' (Though the Devil would
yet be busy and often cast into my thoughts doubtful fear: what was
there in me should cause the Lord to pity me?) And indeed, I could

do nothing in myself, which began to increase my trouble. Yet I remembered it was the saying of David, 'When my father and my mother forsook me, then the Lord would look upon me' [Psalm 27.10]. This did at first revive me, but then I considered David was a holy man after God's own heart. How dare I to lay claim to anything belonged to him?

Thus was my base, distrustful heart exercised with variety of temptations by the Devil, as to distrust the goodness of the Lord; and to rob my soul of the comforts, he was pleased many times to come in withall. Many times has the Lord been pleased to come in by a sermon to my soul, and, as it were, spake unto my present condition. But oh how dull have I been to remember, and how did my unworthy walking cause those blessed truths to slip out of my mind. Yet was the Lord in mercy pleased to keep my heart sincere before him, to plead for mercy for the Lord's sake, for whose sake he was graciously pleased to continue his tender and compassionate love unto me.

(*Heaven Realized*, pp. 1–14)

[While away 'at Mrs W. at school' she is cured of her long-standing illness, and realizes anew that she must trust to God to solve all problems. She lives for a while in 'H-shire', and begins to know she must eschew spiritual pride.]

The Longings of her Soul after Church Fellowship, and all the Ordinances[22] of Christ

Then did I long after God, and the enjoyment of him in his own way, and said, 'Lord, thou hast made me, oh lead me in *that way* wherein I may bring most glory to thyself.' I durst not trust my own judgment, but resigned myself unto his will, and continued my petitions at the throne of grace. And at length he was pleased graciously to answer my poor prayer. *Blessed be thy name, oh Lord, oh let my soul be enlarged in thy praises.*

One day the Lord was pleased by a strange providence to cast me into the company of one that I never saw before, but of a sweet and free disposition, and whose discourse savoured so much of the gospel, that I could not but at that instant bless God for his goodness in that providence. It pleased the Lord to carry out our hearts much towards one another at that time, and a little while after the Lord was pleased to bring us together again for the space of three days, in which time it pleased God by our much converse together to establish and confirm me more in the desires I had to *join with the people of God in society,*

174

and *enjoy communion* with them according to the *order of the gospel.*
She was of a society of the congregational way called Independents,[23]
and gave me so clear a demonstration of their ways, that upon
considerations and searching of the scripture (for the understanding
of which I earnestly besought the Lord), I was clearly convinced in
my judgment that this was the way which came nearest to the rule of
the gospel and the commands of Christ. Then were our hearts firmly
united, and I blessed the Lord from my soul for so glorious and visible
an appearance of his love, for I had many sweet refreshments given
me at that time. When she was gone, I was sensible of the great
mercy the Lord had been pleased to show me, but in an instance
snatched it from me again, at which I began to be troubled. But after
a few reflections to this purpose: 'Why do I not patiently submit to
the will of my Father, who knows what is best for me?', my soul was
again filled with hungerings and thirstings after God, for a more clear
and full enjoyment of him, and that in that blessed ordinance
appointed for a seal to *confirm the covenant* he hath graciously made,
through his dear Son, with all believers. This was at a time when the
Lord was pleased as to outward appearance to frown upon his
people.[24] It seemed an hour of darkness to me, my heart was
troubled. Then was I earnest with the Lord further to direct me in the
way that he should choose, and the Lord was pleased to shine in with
some gospel light, and cause me to see a vast disproportion between a
superstitious way of worshipping of God and a spiritual, sincere way,
in which spiritual Christians serve him. Then I said, 'Oh that God
would please to bring me into the fellowship and communion of his
own people, and if he hath appointed them to suffer, oh that I might
be one that he would count worthy to suffer for the name of Christ.
Oh how doth my soul desire to bear part in the affliction of Sion,[25]
much rather than to enjoy the mirth and pleasure of an earthly
kingdom'. Then did I cast myself upon the Lord, and offer up my soul
to him who knows how to frame it according to his own blessed will.
Then I said, 'Lord, hast not thou the hearts of all creatures in thy
hand, and hast power to turn them into what frame soever thou
pleasest? Bring mine into a conformity to thy blessed will, oh do it,
Lord, for thy mercy's sake.' Then I made known my desires unto my
friend by letter to join in society with that congregation whereof my
friend was a member.

For about that time the minister of the parish, intending to give
the sacrament, preached a preparatory sermon from 1 Corinthians
11.27–29;[26] showing the sweet nature of that blessed ordinance, the

danger of unworthy receivers, and how a Christian ought to be qualified before partaking thereof. At the hearing of which I was awakened, and the Lord was pleased to come in with sweet comfort and refreshments, considering the blessed provision God had graciously made for those that prepared to meet him therein; but I was troubled when I considered that very few or none of his communicants were so qualified to appearance, which was my great burden, for I longed much to partake of that ordinance, but dared not to do it in that manner and with such persons.

None could I use freedom with in this matter but those who I feared would make my trouble greater, but thou, oh God, who art ever ready to help in time of need, thou, the wise counsellor, wilt not be far from the soul that truly seeks thee. Then I called upon the Lord, who was graciously pleased to grant an ear to my request, and through the help of my friend to bring to remembrance 1 Corinthians 10. 16, 17,[27] by which I was much established;[28] but more when I saw the number of his communicants whom he had examined and accepted such as was very blind, ignorant, formal[29] creatures. Then I came to a resolution, through the blessing of God, to wait with patience till he should see good to open a way wherein I might enjoy such ordinances in power and purity, and so as I might expect God's presence and blessing; which at last he was graciously pleased to do, making that my friend an instrument thereof.

Oh let my heart be more carried out to God with praises, and put a new song into my mouth, make it my work to glory that thy great name, since thou art thus pleased to own me in thy dear Son.

Of Recording her Experiences

Oh my soul, thou hast found by sweet experiences how good a thing it is to wait upon the Lord. Let not the gracious taste of his love slip out of thy remembrance, but whilst he hath given thee life, improve these mercies and the talent he hath lent thee to his own glory, and let the gracious workings of the Lord as he is pleased to honour thee with incomes of his love, and the sweet breathings of his holy spirit, recount them here in order as the Lord shall give thee leave that they may be *upon record against an evil day, a day of temptation*. For how many precious evidences hast thou lost, for want of *remembering* them? But now, oh Lord, help me to deal faithfully with my soul in declaring thy power and the riches of thy grace in the *daily remembering* of thy mercies. Oh cause me to see the *growth of my soul* in grace and in the *knowledge* of my gracious God, that my soul may only aim at the glory of my redeemer.

The Lord was thus pleased to carry on his gracious work with much power in my poor soul, notwithstanding the Devil's suggestions, many fears, etc.: as that my condition surely was not yet so good as I did hope it to be, and to doubt whether my joy was not mere presumption. But the Lord in his goodness was pleased in a little time to clear it more fully to me, and cause me to see by the workings of his holy spirit, sweet evidences of his tender love; and brought into my meditation many blessed promises which he was pleased to bless unto my *soul, and confirm unto me with much establishment.*[30]

The Lord being thus pleased by his wise counsel and his tender love thus *to guide my unworthy soul*, at length, by his gracious providence, brought me to the place where the church met. Though they were strangers to me, yet was he pleased to cause me to find much love and tenderness, and there I had that blessed opportunity to receive that sweet, refreshing ordinance which my soul had so much longed after. Blessed be his holy name. Oh thou, my soul, since thou hast seen the gracious dealings of the Lord towards thee, be not thou unmindful of his praise.

Improve thy talent to thy Master's use; lay out thy strength for God, and let thy heart be carried out for ever to remember the tender and unspeakable love of thy dear Lord. Unless thou put thy hand to help, my strength is nothing. I am a poor, weak nothing, not able to do anything if thou shouldest once leave me, never so little.

(*Heaven Realized*, pp. 20–7)

[She begins to meditate on salvation and God's love.]

Meditations upon my Saviour's Love

Oh the transcendent and unspeakable love of God to poor souls, whom the Lord Jesus is pleased, out of the rich treasury of his divine love, to reconcile unto God by the blood of the cross. And what hath the Lord required again of us poor worms for all his benefits, *but that we should return him love again.* And this is the love he requires: that we should keep his commandments. Oh blessed Lord! And thy commandments are not grievous, but delightful, to the soul that loves thee. And what is thy commandment, dear Lord?

'This is my commandment (and it is a new commandment), that

177

you should love one another. My commandments are not grievous, it is only love that is required, and that you should manifest it in obedience to my commands; one of which is that you love one another.'[31]

'But how, dear Lord, shall we manifest our love to thee in loving one another? How hast thou required that we should love one another?'

'Have not I set you an example? Did not I first love you? And therefore give you this new commandment: that as I have loved you, so you would love one another, with a sincere, pure, unbounded love; such a love as seeks not your own things, but the good of others; such a love as is inward and not in outward show only, but in *deed*, and in *truth*, in the sincerity of your hearts; such a love as seeks the good and spiritual advantage of one another's souls; to love one another as I have loved you, or to love thy friend as thou lovest thyself, most willing to do that which may be for thy friend's good, although it be to some prejudice to thyself. This is love, and by this you shall know that you are my disciples: if thus you love one another. And by this, men shall know that you are mine, such as I have loved from the beginning.'
Oh dear Lord how art thou pleased thus to plead with poor clods of clay. What sweet argument of thine own matchless goodness.

(Heaven Realized, pp. 36–8)

Notes

1 *condescension* : affability.
2 *my babies* : my mother's babies: elder daughters commonly looked after their mothers' younger children.
3 *wept bitterly* : she compares herself to Peter, who wept bitterly on realizing that he had indeed denied Christ three times (Matthew 26.75, Luke 22.62).
4 *admire* : wonder.
5 *he was pleased . . . with it* : sickness and death were believed to be caused by sin, originating in the fall from grace in the Garden of Eden.
6 *thou imputest no sin* : Psalm 32.2, an important biblical text to Puritans, used to suggest that Christians are saved by faith, not works: that everything, especially the decision over who is saved and who damned, is in God's hands not the hands of the sinner.
7 *riches of thy grace* : phrase used repeatedly in Paul's Letter to Ephesians.
8 *abhor myself in dust and ashes* : she echoes the words of Job's repentance (Job 42: 6). God then blessed him and ended his sufferings.
9 *laid help . . . mighty* : a phrase used repeatedly in *Heaven Realized*, comparing her situation to David's in Psalm 89.19 (see p. 166).
10 *outward conditions* : body (as opposed to soul).
11 *walkings* : conduct.
12 *Lord's Supper* : Holy Communion.

13 *Mr Pierce* : perhaps Edward Pierce, one-time rector of St Michael's, Crooked Lane, London, then vicar of Dunston 1662, rector of Aldwinckle All Saints', and then rector of Cottesbrooke, Northants., 1663. He died at Cottesbrooke in 1694 (*Alumni Oxoniensis*).

14 *children's bread* : Matthew 15.26, Mark 7.27. A woman of Canaan asks Jesus to cure her daughter, and at first he refuses, explaining 'I am not sent but unto the lost sheep of the house of Israel'. (On seeing her faith, he changes his mind and does as she wishes.) The text was used in the 1650s to show that some merited salvation before others: 'the sense is, that the Gentiles must be content to wait until God has refreshed the Israelites with grace and mercy' (*Annotations* 1657).

15 *hypocrite* : falsely convinced of my salvation.

16 *My punishment . . . bear* : Genesis 4.13. Cain was made an outcast for slaying his brother Abel, and Davy considers herself responsible for her own brother's death.

17 *I never said . . . in vain* : interpreted as God's promise to save the elect (Isaiah 45.19).

18 *puffed up* : phrase used by Paul to warn against the arrogance of believing one knows God's will (1 Corinthians 4.6, 18, 19; 5.2; 13.4).

19 *professor* : someone who makes an open assertion of religion without truly practising it.

20 *My humbling . . . alone* : general sentiment of Psalm 69.

21 *Call upon . . . trouble* : echoes Job 13.22 and 14.15; Psalms 41 and 45.

22 *ordinances* : church sacraments, especially Holy Communion.

23 *congregational way called Independents* : both terms were used to describe religious groups who wanted to purify the established church, either from within or by leaving it. Their precise meaning is difficult to establish since they were used in different ways by different writers (see Introduction pp. 12–16). Davy appears to equate 'Independent' with 'Separatist', using 'congregational way' as the generic term referring to reform within or outside the national church.

24 *This was . . . his people* : probably a reference to the Act of Uniformity 1662 which aimed to restrict all positions in the church, schools and universities to Anglicans.

25 *affliction of Sion* : persecution of God's chosen people.

26 *1 Corinthians 11.27–29* : 'Wherefore whosoever shall eat this bread, and drink this cup of the Lord, unworthily, shall be guilty of the body and blood of the Lord. But let a man examine himself, and so let him eat of that bread, and drink of that cup. For he that eateth and drinketh unworthily eateth and drinketh damnation to himself, not discerning the Lord's body.'

27 *1 Corinthians 10.16, 17* : 'The cup of blessing which we bless, is it not the communion of the blood of Christ? The bread which we break, is it not the communion of the body of Christ? For we being many are one bread, and one body; for we are all partakers of that one bread'.

   It is difficult to see why these verses should reassure Davy that she should not take communion in the established church. Perhaps she had in mind 1 Corinthians 10: 20, 21: 'But I say, that the things which the Gentiles sacrifice, they sacrifice to devils, and not to God: and I would not that ye should have fellowship with devils. Ye cannot drink the cup of the Lord, and the cup of devils: ye cannot be partakers of the Lord's table, and of the table of devils'.

28 *established* : given calmness of mind.

29 *formal* : perfunctory, having the form of religion but not its spirit.

30 *with much establishment* : by giving me much calmness of mind.

31 *This is . . . another* : this passage, to the end of the extract, closely echoes John 15 and 1 John 3, 4.

10

ANNE WENTWORTH

*A Vindication of Anne Wentworth, tending to the better preparing of
all people for her larger testimony, which is making ready for public
view. Published according to the will of God and direction of charity.
By Anne Wentworth.*

*'Be still and know that I am God. I will be exalted among the
heathen: I will be exalted in the earth. The Lord of hosts is with us,
the God of Jacob is our refuge.' Psalms 46.10–11.*

*To which is annexed a letter written by an eminent Christian,
concerning the said Anne Wentworth, and directed to the several
congregations of the Anabaptists and their respective pastors.*

*As also a song of triumph by the said Anne Wentworth, a daughter
of Sion newly delivered from the captivity of Babylon, etc.*

*'How should[1] we sing the Lord's song in a strange land?'
Psalms 137.1, 2, 3, 4.*

'Where is God my maker that giveth songs in the night?' Job 35.10.

*'Let the saints be joyful in glory, let them sing upon their beds.'
Psalms 149.5.*

Printed in the year 1677.

The political climate of the 1670s was very different, and for sectaries
much harsher, than that experienced by the radicals of the 1640s and 1650s.
The years since the restoration of Charles II in 1660 had seen the imposition
of the Clarendon Code, a series of four Acts of Parliament between 1661
and 1665, by which Nonconformists were excluded from political life,
municipal administration, and the universities, and which also made them
subject to fines and imprisonment for holding their own religious meetings.
This intensification of the persecution of Nonconformists was reinforced by

the Test Act of 1673, which excluded all dissenters from civil and military office.

For the Baptists, as for the other sects, this change of climate had its effect. Their central, formative tenets remained unchanged: an opposition to infant baptism, believing it should be a matter of active choice rather than an automatic rite of passage; opposition to a national church and to tithes; and, for the Particular Baptists, of whom Wentworth was one, a belief in restricted atonement, an elect already chosen by God for salvation. But in the face of this persecution, their focus of attention and concern shifted from those outside their ranks to those within; their organization tightened, 'and was more and more used to impose social attitudes' (Hill 1972: 375). Whilst this new emphasis affected all the sects, it was particularly significant for Baptist women. Baptists' literal interpretation of the bible has led some to call them the most conservative of the radical Puritan movements, as it bound them to Paul's commands against women preaching or teaching (McGregor 1984: 47). Such generalizations imply a homogeneity that did not really exist, since each congregation established, to some degree, its own ground rules. None the less it is probably accurate to say that the influence women had on their congregations had tended to be informal, rather than sanctioned by the religious and political stance of their organization, and was thus all the more easily eroded in this changing atmosphere. In the 1640s and 1650s, the wider context of women's activities had also been much more dynamic and outward-looking: women were petitioning Parliament, preaching, prophesying, publishing, and travelling the country and beyond, testifying to their beliefs. By the 1660s and 1670s the sects themselves, as well as the wider society, discouraged such manifestations: in 1677, Wentworth's *Vindication*, justifying having left her husband in order to follow God's call to write, is directed as much at her fellow Baptists as at a wider readership. One factor in this contrast is undoubtedly the changed political circumstances: Wentworth is

> an isolated woman, unsupported by a wider social movement as the earlier Quakers and Baptists had been. She cannot call on others to take up arms, as Trapnel and Cary [another Fifth Monarchist] had . . . Her only possible contribution to the great change she sees approaching is to save her own life, and record her message.
>
> (Hobby 1984: 87–8)

The context does not, however, adequately encompass or describe the complexities and power of the text itself. The structure and the argument of the *Vindication* are remarkably skilful, both circular and thus self-sufficient and all-inclusive, and also highly allusive, thereby gaining their authority from the authority of the scriptural texts on which they draw. She gives, for example, five versions of the relationship between herself, her oppressors, and 'madness' (see pp. 189–90); all are valid because of their internal logic, although contradictory in comparison with each other, but the whole argument is held together by a series of allusions and references whose own authority precludes any dissent. The logic is the logic of the Word rather than of consistency.

Such allusiveness does more, however, than just lend resonance and weight to Wentworth's words, for it also allows her to make tacit comparisons and associations that modesty and the necessary tone of self-deprecation would prohibit being made explicitly. Writing of the strength God has given her to do his work in wrestling against 'principalities and powers' as well as 'flesh and blood' (p. 191), she is paraphrasing and quoting St Paul's epistle to the Ephesians (6.11–18). To identify her struggles explicitly with those of Paul would render her immodest and therefore unworthy of serious consideration. Instead, such readings must be elicited by engaging with the network of references, allusions, and juxtapositions which help form the fabric of the text.

In addition, however, the language of the bible gives Wentworth the framework, the terms, and the argument to build up an image of herself separate from her earthly self, an image that is the linchpin of her whole vindication of her actions.

There are two distinct manifestations of Wentworth's 'self' in the text. First, there is the 'self' that God breaks down to prepare her to accept his call. Her earthly self is dissolved to 'a thing that is not', and it is the new self, consequent to this dissolution, which is commanded to do God's work. This new self is both lesser than the old, because it 'is not', and greater, because directly formed by the hand and will of God. And it was the work of this new self – and therefore of God – that Wentworth's husband threatened to destroy. From there, the step to justify her otherwise outrageous actions – leaving her husband, publishing things to his 'prejudice and scandal', her desire to support herself economically – was a small one. God's creation had to protect herself, in order to safeguard his work, and she therefore had to give priority to her 'heavenly bridegroom' above her earthly one. Thus the fraught issues of duty and loyalty to one's husband, the immodesty and vainglory of a woman writing for publication, are turned on their heads, and protecting the self becomes an act of selflessness.

The significance of this is broadened, too, by Wentworth's interpretations of the events she reports, for they have not only a 'private' and 'spiritual' significance, but also a 'public' and 'political' one. She writes that her 'oppressions and deliverance had a public ministry and meaning wrapped up in them', and the fate of her husband would serve as a model for the fate of 'the same spirit throughout the nation' (p. 194): God's wrath would fall on them both. The private both reflects and foreshadows the public. Her battle is not just against 'the man of the earth' (p. 187), but 'against the rulers of the darkness of this world, and against spiritual wickedness in high places' (p. 191). The newly created Wentworth faces challenges and triumphs, and possibly defeats, unimaginable to the old, and her writing articulates these, as well as manifesting an awareness of just how transgressive such a reading of her life will be seen to be.

Textual note

The extract includes the entire prose section of the text; the 'letter' and the 'song of triumph' cited on the title page have been omitted.

Our editorial policy regarding the use of italics differs here slightly from that relating to other texts in this collection. Where italics are used to indicate proper nouns, reported speech or direct quotations from the bible, they have been, as usual, removed. This accounts, however, for the minority of instances in which they appear. They generally indicate either allusions to or paraphrases of scriptural texts, or else suggest the emphases and rhythms of the spoken word, rather than of the written text.[2] As such, they are integral to the text, and there seemed to be no satisfactory way of removing them without losing the richness and nuances that they brought with them. In these instances, therefore, they have been retained. They have also been retained when used for the word 'God', for here it did not seem possible to differentiate between a proper noun, emphasis, and a biblical allusion.

The copytext is from the British Library, shelfmark T 370(2).

Notes

1 'should' appears as 'shall' in the bible. The error, possibly one of memory, might be the printer's, who could have chosen the title page quotations.
2 Thanks to Maureen Bell for her suggestions relating to the use of italics.

From: A Vindication of Anne Wentworth

The great searcher of hearts [1 Chronicles 28.9] has seen, neither is it unknown to several Christians in and about this city of London, or to the consciences of my very enemies, what severe and cruel persecutions I have sustained for the space of eighteen years[1] from the unspeakable tyrannies of an *hard-hearted yoke-fellow*,[2] and since, from the bitter zeal of several eminent professors of religion,[3] commonly called Baptists,[4] who have most unjustly and unchristianlike caused all their pretended church power to wait upon and serve the wrath of my oppressors. And who, not being able truly to charge me with any sin committed against God that called for such a proceeding, have declared me an *heathen* and a *publican*[5] for *matters of conscience* in which I was faithful to the teachings of God, according to the scriptures of truth, and obeyed the voice of the Lord, who called me out from amongst them, that I might not partake of those terrible plagues and dreadful judgments which are coming upon all *formalists,*[6] *hypocrites* and *profane persons,* who are all of them the inhabitants of this earth. And who, however separated from one another *now,* by outward forms and observations, or inward notions and opinions, in that *particular* and *great day* of the Lord[7] which is coming upon this nation, will be found to be in *one spirit* and *principle.*

My *cause* in this respect, being committed to almighty God, the righteous judge of all, unto whom I have *appealed,* and who has accepted my *appeal* and is speedily arising on my behalf, I will say nothing of *it* here, but only acquaint thee, whoever thou art that readest these few lines, that it has pleased my most gracious God and father, *who abounds towards his children in all wisdom and prudence of love* [Ephesians 1.8], to turn all the fierce wrath [2 Chronicles 28.13; 29.10] of man, which has been against me, into his own praise. And to change all the evil mine enemies have thought and done against me into a sweet design for good, making all my *unspeakable sufferings* from man, my *wonderful supports* and *deliverances from God,* a *figure* of his *intended dispensations* towards his *enemies* and *people* in this nation. Revealing to me how Babylon,[8] the mother of fornications, is in her inward principle and spirit, as also in her outward practices and pollutions, spread over the whole face of the Christian world, and everywhere found among the literal and outward churches. How her delusions, sorceries and fornications are *here* most bewitching and dangerous, because she *here* comes forth as the *mystery of iniquity* [2 Thessalonians 2.7], dressing and adorning herself in all the forms and notions of the heavenly things, sitting and showing herself in the *temple of* God. As also revealing to me that the judgments which are determined to come upon her should begin at the *house of God,* the *formal, carnal, notional* Christians, the worshippers in the *outward court.* And that the flood of the divine vengeance having swept away what is to be destroyed *there,* the rod of God's anger should be thrown into unquenchable fire [Matthew 3.12; Luke 3.17], and the indignation of the Lord should end in the utter desolation, ruin and confusion of the *profane world* and *grosser Babylon.* And that these things are at the *very door,* and ready to enter upon us as an *armed man* [Proverbs 6.11; 24.34].

And because the mouth of iniquity is opened against me, and I bear the reproaches of the *mighty ones* wherewith they have reproached the footsteps of the Lord and h.s dealings with me, representing me as a *proud, passionate, revengeful, discontented* and *mad* woman, and as one that has unduly published things to the prejudice and scandal of my husband, and that have wickedly left him, designing (according to the craftiness and subtlety of the old serpent in all ages) by marring my face to darken and disappoint my testimony from the Lord, which I am with all convenient speed making ready for public view.[9] In great tenderness to all people concerned in my testimony, and that they may be the better prepared to receive the same when it shall be laid before them, I do in the presence of the most *holy* and *jealous* God, who is *our God* and yet a *consuming fire* [Deuteronomy 4.24; 9.3; Hebrews 12.29], and in a deep sense of the manifold weaknesses, infirmities and passions I am subject to, hereby *solemnly declare*:

That I am not conscious to myself of any *spiritual pride* in this matter, nor in the least desirous to have any appearance or to make any noise in this world. Nor durst I for ten thousand worlds pretend to come in the name of God, or in the pride and forwardness of my own spirit put myself into this work, without his express command concerning it, and his spirit and presence with me in it, having learnt what unprofitable things the *staff* and *mantle*[10] are without the God of the *prophets*; how dangerous and desperate an attempt it is to put the *commission* and *authority* of God upon the *dreams* and *visions* of my own heart. I am well assured, if spiritual pride, the eagerness of my own spirit, any worldly design or any other delusion whatsoever has engaged me in my present testimony, the holy God will discover me herein, and take open vengeance on all my *inventions*, my *idols* and *strange gods*; and that this matter will prove unto me like the waters of *jealousy* unto the suspected person.[11] And I have also, through the tender mercies of God, the riches of an assurance that my God who has been so many years *emptying* me from vessel to vessel, *breaking* me all to pieces in myself, and making me to become as *nothing* before him, and who has by many and great tribulations been *bowing* my own will and fitting me for his service, and who having taught me to tremble at his *word* has thereby called and commanded me into this work, when I was as a thing that *is not* [1 Corinthians 1.28] in my own eyes, and pleaded with him to be excused, I have, I say, the *riches of an assurance* that this God will be with me. And however the spirit of prophecy in a poor weak woman shall be despised by the wise and prudent [Matthew 11.25; Luke 10.21] of this world, yet *Wisdom is justified of her children* [Matthew

11.19; Luke 7.35]. And that *God* who has commanded me to go forth in his *name* will by a *divine power* go before me, making way for me, and subduing the spirits before me which I am to deal with, and will also by a *divine presence* support me in the midst of all those sufferings his work can bring me into. 'Out of the mouth of babes and sucklings God has ordained strength, because of his enemies, that he might quell the enemy and the avenger,' Psalms 8.2.

And I declare, I have no wrath, discontent or revenge in my spirit against the person of my husband, or any of his abettors, but am taught by the forgiveness of God freely to forgive all the injuries he has done me; and my heart's desire and prayer to God, who can alone change the heart, is that he may be converted and saved. And I bow my soul to the father of lights [James 1.17], that the eyes of all my persecutors may be opened, some of which I judge to be the Lord's people, however acted in this matter by a *zeal without knowledge* [Romans 10.2]. *God is love, and he that dwells in love, dwells in God, and God in him* [1 John 4.16].

And however I am censured and reproached by persons who judge only according to *outward appearance*, but not *righteous judgment*, that I have unduly left my husband, I do for the satisfaction of all plain-hearted ones that may be offended at their reports herein declare, *first*: that it would be very easy for me, from the great law of *self-preservation* to justify my present absence from my earthly husband to all persons who have learnt to judge of *good* and *evil*, not only according to the *outward act*, but the *inward spirit* and *principle*, and who have *tenderness* enough duly to weigh the various tempers of minds, and the different circumstances of bodies. Forasmuch as the natural constitution of my mind and body, being both considered, *he* has in his barbarous actions towards me a many times over done such things as not only in the *spirit* of them will be one day judged a murdering of, but had long since *really* proved so, if God had not wonderfully supported and preserved me. But my natural life, through the springing up of a *better*, not being otherwise considerable, then as it is my duty to preserve it in a subserviency to the will and service of that God whose I am in *spirit, soul* and *body*, I will not urge anything of this nature as my defence upon this occasion, having learnt through the mercy of God not to be afraid of him who can only kill the *body*, but can do no more. I do therefore *secondly*, in the fear of him who can kill both *soul* and *body*, further declare that I was forced to fly to preserve a life more *precious* than this natural one, and that it was necessary to the peace of my soul to absent myself from my earthly husband in obedience to my heavenly bride-groom, who called and commanded me, in a way too terrible, too powerful to be denied, to undertake and finish a work which my earthly husband in a most cruel manner hindered me from perform-ing, seizing and running away with my writings. And however man judges me in this action, yet I am satisfied that I have been obedient to the *heavenly vision* [Acts 26.19] herein, not *consulting with flesh and blood* [Galatians 1.16]. All the clouds of afflictions, troubles, sorrows and deaths upon the outward man are nothing, compared with those of the inward man[12] when the life of our souls is angry, and with-draws himself, cutting off the sweet beams of a spiritual communion between himself and us. This was my case, and I am not afraid or ashamed to say my soul's beloved has abundantly owned me in this matter. And whilst men have done all they can to break my heart, he has bound up my soul in the bundle of *life* [1 Samuel 25.29] and *love*, and he pleads my cause, and takes my part, and has spoken by his word with power and authority from heaven, saying I shall abide with him, and he will abide with me [John 15.4], and come and sup with me [Revelation 3.20], and never leave me, nor forsake me [1 Kings 8.57]. And he bids me take no thought what I shall eat, what I shall drink, or wherewith I shall be clothed, but cast all my care upon him, for he careth for me. And I am enabled in his power to roll myself upon him; and my heart is fixed, trusting in him, and comforted with his word with power and authority from heaven, saying I shall abide with him, and he will abide with me [John 15.4], and come and sup with me [Revelation 3.20], and never leave me, nor forsake me [1 Kings 8.57]. that he knows all my weaknesses and wants, and my willingness to work, so far as he enables me, that my own hands may administer to my necessity, that I may not be burdensome to any. And he has assured me that the man of the earth shall oppress no more;[13] no more shall I return to be under the hands of the hard-hearted persecutors, unless he become a new man, a changed man, a man sensible of the wrong he has done me with his fierce looks, bitter words, sharp tongue and cruel usage. And I do further declare that in the true reason of the case I have not left my husband, but he me. That I do own every *law* and *command* of God in the letter of his word to be *right* and *true*, and do submit to every *rule* given forth by the spirit of God to govern the relation of man and wife *in the Lord*. And that I always stand ready to return to my husband, or to welcome him to me, and have signified so much to him by several Christian friends, provided I may have my *just* and *necessary* liberty to attend a more than ordinary call and command of God to publish the things which concern the *peace of my own soul* and *of the whole nation*. In which work I stand not in my own will, but in the will of him who has *sent* and *sealed* me, as the *day* will very quickly declare, and decide this matter between me and my husband and all his abettors. To which *day* I do here appeal for my justification, not doubting but that God, to whom I have committed my cause, will speedily arise, and cause my *innocency* to break forth as the *noonday* [Psalms 37.6]. For I do hereby declare in the presence of the most holy God that I have no revengeful, worldly or sinister end in this matter, but am against my own natural will obeying God herein. And I do in all tenderness admonish and caution all my enemies, and all persons whatsoever to whom these papers shall come, that they take heed lest they *hurt themselves* in *reproaching me*, and that they do not set themselves to *justify* by the *letter* that *spirit*[14] that is to be *condemned*, or to *condemn* that *spirit* which it owns and allows. And that they take heed lest they urge the *letter* of any command against the *spirit* of it, and so come to condemn *themselves* in the *person* and *case* of another. The *spirit* and the *letter* are nowhere *contrary*, but thou mayst think them so, and by not duly attending upon the *spirit* in the *letter* mayst unnaturally set the *letter* to oppose the *spirit* from whence it comes, to which it testifies, and whither it tends. I beg of you all that read these lines for your *own sakes*, that you will remember still how the Jews did of old vilify, reproach, condemn and execute our saviour, and justified themselves herein by the *letter* of the law of God; with the *breach* of which law they were continually charging *him* throughout his whole life, yet was it exactly according to their own law, and in those very cases about which they were so much offended at him. Nor has it fared otherwise with the *whole seed* of Christ and all the spiritual manifestations of him in all ages. The best of men and principles have still been challenged for their *nonconformity* to the *letter* and *outward rule*, although they have been most agreeable thereunto. As the apostle speaks, 'Not without law to God, but under the law to Christ' [1 Corinthians 9.21].

And I do further declare that the things I have published and written, and which are such an offence to my husband, and indeed the cause of all the persecutions I have suffered from others, were written sorely against my own natural *mind* and *will*; that I often begged of God I might rather die than do it. That I was commanded of God to record them. That my own natural temper was so greatly averse to it that for eleven months together I withstood the Lord, till by an angel from heaven he threatened to *kill me*, and took away my sleep from me: and then the *terrors of the Lord* forced me to obey the command. And indeed, the writings that man was so displeased with were in themselves very warrantable if I had not had any such command of God, for I only wrote the *way* he led me in a wilderness of affliction for 18 years to do me good, and declared my *experiences*, my *great* and *wonderful deliverances*, my many *answers* of prayers in difficult cases from time to time.[15] But most true it is, I did not speak of these things, nor set pen to paper (for several reasons) till the Lord *commanded* and by his word and spirit constrained me so to do at 18 years' end, after I was consumed with grief, sorrow, oppression of heart and long travail in the wilderness, and brought even to the gates of death, and when past the cure of all men was raised up by the immediate and mighty hand of God. And being thus *healed*, I was commanded to write, and give glory to him who had so miraculously raised me up from the grave. And I do further declare, the things I have written are *true*, and *no lie*; and that what is so distasteful in them to man are such things as I could not leave out without *prejudice* to the truth and *disobedience* to God. And whatever censures I now undergo from *man's day* and *judgment* for this plain dealing in matters which concern so near a relation in the flesh, I am well assured my faithfulness to God herein will be owned in the *day* of his *impartial* and *righteous judgment*. And yet I must declare, it would have been much more agreeable to my spirit to have concealed the miscarriages of my husband than to have exposed them, if I had not been under a *command* herein not to be *disputed*. And it was not without great *resistings* that I was at length made *obedient*, *having tasted of that love, which both covers, and teaches us to cover, a multitude of sins* [1 Peter 4.8; James 5.20]. And yet I am fully persuaded that my duty to God in this matter will be found not only most *reasonable* and *necessary* on my part, but *exceeding beautiful in its season*, and to have been managed in some measure of the spirit of that *God* who is still *love* and *in whom* there is *no fury*, however he *marches against, goes through the briars and thorns, and burns them together when they are set against him in battle* [Ezekiel 2.6; Hebrews 6.8]. And whereas my enemies have represented me as one *distracted* and *beside myself*, in answer to such wicked proceedings against not only *me*, but the *truth*, I do for the truth's sake further say, *first*, that I judge my *enemies* who have raised this false report of *me* to be *themselves* most highly concerned that this, their *report*, should be found a *lie*: for as much as if it were otherwise, the *cause* and *occasion* of my distraction might justly be laid at their own doors, for as the *preacher* says, Ecclesiastes 7.[7], 'Oppression makes a wise man mad.' *Secondly*, and yet I also judge it is the *mistaken* and *rotten interest* of my adversaries not only to *report* but to *believe* me a person beside myself: for if I be found in a *right mind*, how *mad* must they be discovered to have been in their blind rage and fury against *me* and *my testimony*. *Thirdly*, I do with great cheerfulness receive the *reproach* of this *report*, and all the *humiliation* that goes along with it, as a further *measure* of my *conformity* to my *saviour*, and *fellowship with him in his sufferings*. For thus has *he* throughout all ages been *blasphemed* in his *prophets*, his *messengers* and in *himself*. Thus when Elisha sent a *young prophet* with instructions to anoint Jehu, his fellow-servants asked him, 'Wherefore came this mad fellow to thee?' 2 Kings 9.[11]. Thus we read in Mark 3.[21] that 'the kindred of our Lord went out to lay hold on him, for they said, he is beside himself.' And again, in John 10.[20], 'Many of the Jews said, he has a devil, and is mad.' *Fourthly*, I do with great pleasure acknowledge that in this great work (*in which I am set for a sign and a wonder* [Isaiah 20.3]) I have *no wit, no wisdom, no understanding, no will* of my own. And if this be to be *mad*, I confess myself to be *beside myself to God*, whose love *constrains me*, and whose spirit has in this matter after an irresistible but sweetest manner *captivated* my proper understanding, will and affections to his divine wisdom and will. And *lastly*, I am well assured that it will *speedily, very speedily*, be known that I am not *mad*, as my enemies have reported, but have *spoken forth the words of truth and soberness* [Acts 26.25]. I have not *run* before I was *sent*, but the word of the Lord is 'Come unto me', and his *spirit is upon me*. And he will perform every *iota* and *title*[16] of his own word, to overthrow Babylon with such an overturning as never was, nor never will be again. The beginnings of this overturning will within a few days be seen upon her more refined parts, and the severity of the wrath shall afterwards come upon her walls. Although man *is so confident I am deceived*, and has loaden me and my testimony with all manner of reproach, yet the God whom I serve and obey, and who has spoken by me, will speedily turn the flood of scorn, contempt, bitter railing, false accusations, scandalous papers and lying pamphlets[17] upon them by whom they have been poured out against me. 'The Lord frustrateth the tokens of liars, and maketh diviners mad; he turneth wise men backwards, and maketh their knowledge foolish: but he confirmeth the word of his servant, and performeth the counsel of his messengers,' Isaiah 44.[25–6].

And now in this *faith* and *assurance* I do shut up this my *vindication* and *preparatory testimony*, *declaring* unto all people whom it may concern that it is the Lord has moved me, and his spirit which has stirred me up. My heavenly bridegroom is come, and has given me courage, with an humble boldness and holy confidence, to speak the truth in all faithfulness, and to fear no man, but God alone, in whose strength I stand to encounter with all discouragements from my own understanding, will, affections, former thoughts and principles within, and with all opposition from difficulties, dangers, temptations of friends and conspiracies of enemies without. I am sensible any of these things would be too strong for me, a worm of no might or strength, but I have renounced myself, and laid down my own wisdom and will in this work, and am given up to all the will of God herein, standing upon my watch, and having in his power *put on the whole armour of God, the shield of faith, the breastplate of righteousness, with my loins girt about with truth, and my feet shod with the preparation of the gospel of peace, having taken the helmet of salvation, and the sword of the spirit, which is the word of God, praying always with all prayer and supplication in the spirit, and watching thereunto with all perseverance, and supplication for all saints* [Ephesians 6.13–18]. In this spiritual warfare and combat, I am called to wrestle not only against *flesh and blood, but against principalities and powers, against the rulers of the darkness of this world, and against spiritual wickedness in high places* [Ephesians 6.12]; and must have no respect of persons because of advantage, but be faithful to God and his word, sparing neither friend nor brother in matter of truth, nor calling *good evil* or *evil good*, nor putting *light* for *darkness* or *darkness* for *light*, but obeying God and not man, loving him above all, keeping his commandments and pleasing him, although the whole world should be displeased. Man has made my cup very bitter and my cross very heavy for obeying God, but my God has sweetened my cup, and caused it to overflow with draughts of love. My God has made my yoke easy and my burden light, because he bears me and them. He draws me, and *binds me with cords to the altar* [Psalms 118.27], *his left hand is under my head, his right hand doth embrace me* [Song of Solomon 8.3], *and his banner over me is love* [Song of Solomon 2.4]. I *must not, I will not* be afraid to make my boast of my God, by whose almighty power I have been hitherto helped and upheld, or else I had perished in my afflictions. When the compassion and bowels of man were shut up [1 John 3.17], the tender mercies of God were opened. When it was come to Mordecai's pinch, Israel's distress, Paul's strait,[18] God appeared. My extremity was his opportunity. He beheld my affliction, the sorrows and agonies of my soul; my groans, my prayers, my cries, my appeals ascended up for a memorial before him, and were had in remembrance with him. And he will arise, and that right speedily, he will make haste and not tarry, but send relief from heaven, and save me and all the poor of his flock who hear the voice of their own shepherd, and follow him, but a stranger they will not follow. He will smite the rocky heart, he will convince the consciences of men, he will bring down all them that glory in appearance, in face, and not in heart. He will make a speedy decision, he will turn the stream and flood of scorn and contempt cast upon me, and his poor despised ones in me. *He will arise to our joy, and they shall be ashamed that have hated us without a cause* [Psalms 35.19; 69.4; John 15.25] *and cast us out for his name's sake*, saying, *Let the Lord be glorified* [Isaiah 66.5]. I have commited my way unto the Lord who judgeth righteously, who will not suffer the guilty always to go undiscovered and unpunished. He will take the cup of trembling out of my hands, and put it into the hands of them who have afflicted me, who have said unto my soul, *Bow down that we may go over* [Isaiah 51.22–3], and he will make their own *tongues to fall upon themselves* [Psalms 64.8], and *will measure out unto them again, the measure they have meted* [Matthew 7.2; Mark 4.24; Luke 6.38]. The Lord has said it, and he will perform it. The Lord will plead my cause, and the cause of all his meek ones, but his anger is kindled against all *formality, hypocrisy, idolatry* and *profaneness*. He knows the secrets of all hearts [Psalms 54.21], we are all open and naked in his sight. There is no dissembling in his sight, no mocking before him; no outward form, no empty opinion can shelter from his wrath. Upon the 13th of the twelfth month 1673, the Lord wonderfully discovered to me the unprofitableness of the best outward forms of religion without the power [2 Timothy 3.5]. And what a great deal of blindness, injustice, false accusations, barbarous usage, bitter and cruel zeal, with all manner of wickedness, has at this day taken sanctuary in the exactest forms according to the letter, which are without the spirit, yea, in enmity against it. It was the time four eminent professors of the people called Baptists did in a most rough and severe manner come to deal with me, to accuse me falsely, and blindly and bitterly to rebuke me, although I was then in a very weak and dangerous condition of body. And I mention it here because it is a time in remembrance with the Lord, and God was in that very season pleased to open my eyes to show me where Babylon was, what spirit she was built upon, and how the Lord would begin to strike at her and throw her down, and then it was he called me out from her, that I might escape the anger I then saw was kindled against her. And however they are now justifying themselves and their proceedings against me, and have condemned the innocent, yet an appeal has been made to God, and accepted by him, and he will search out this matter and make a true and manifest judgment of it, for there is nothing *hid* from him, and this matter is now become a *public figure*. Yes, I am satisfied God will speedily arise and decide this controversy, and he has shown me when I have been thinking his chariot wheels move slowly that then his motion has been swiftest. And that whatever seems to hinder and work against me does indeed help on and work things to a more full and perfect end. And although I should be surrounded and beset on every side, and left alone in the midst of all discouragements from *within* and *without*, yet can I believingly call to all that fear the Lord to come and behold the wonders of the Lord for my deliverance. I cried unto him when there was none to help me, and in a deep sense of my own unworthiness and nothingness my soul was humbled and laid low at his foot, and my heart was lifted up to him. And he raised me from the grave and took fast hold of me at that very time when he so wonderfully healed me, which was the 3rd of the 11th month 1670. Then was the full communion between Christ and my soul, the love knot, the comely bands of marriage. Then did he espouse me unto himself for ever, and enable me to follow him and give up myself as a thank-offering unto him, no more to be my own but the Lord's, subjecting myself to all his will as a chaste virgin, holy in lip and life, pure and undefiled in heart. Then did the Lord my God say unto me, 'I, even I, am he that comforteth thee; who art thou that thou shouldest be afraid of a man that shall die, and of the son of man which shall be made as grass' [Isaiah 51.12]. And again he said he was come to 'judge the fatherless and the oppressed, that the man of the earth may no more oppress' [Psalms 10.18]. And many more precious promises did the Lord make to me when he first called me to write what man has been so offended with. And his word was and is my support, and he has comforted me therewith, assuring me as soon as I had done his will I should receive the promises. And he afterwards revealed to me what I did not then know, that my *oppressions* and *deliverance* had a *public ministry* and *meaning* wrapped up in them, that it must be seven years before I could perfect that writing, and the Lord would bring forth his end in all this, and give an open testimony to the world that he had chosen and called me to write to glorify him. And now I have done his will, my deliverer is come to make good his word, and set me free from the oppression of man, and to bear witness against him that has wounded and oppressed me for 18 years. And more severely is his anger kindled against them who have so deeply wounded me since the time of my healing, and who have made me an heathen and a publican for no other cause but obeying the word of the Lord and following him. And as near as *New Year's Day* is, before that day the Lord will begin to cast a cloud of his anger upon all them that have done me so great wrong, and persecuted me without a cause; and stroke after stroke will follow, until all hypocrisy be discovered and formality thrown down, and whole Babylon sink like a stone, never to rise up any more. And let not the minds of any be lifted up to scorn me because I have said God will begin to appear in my behalf within so short a time: for my God has a many times over made that *season of the year* eminently signal to me in the dispensations of his grace and providence towards me. Then was I entered into my afflictions, then was I in an extraordinary manner healed, and chosen and called to write what has occasioned so many persecutions to me from formal and literal professors. And now it will be completely 7 years since my healing. And the Lord has made known the end of all his dispensations to me, and has revealed to me that I shall now receive the promises, having done his will, and be made partaker of his blessing: for he will fulfil his word *to bind up the broken hearted, and proclaim liberty to the captive, and open the prison doors* [Isaiah 61.1; Luke 4.18]; and I shall no more be under the oppression of man. And he has also revealed to me what wrath shall fall upon the *same spirit* throughout the nation, which everywhere oppresses the true seed as I have been oppressed by it, and the deliverance which is drawing nigh through terrible things in righteousness to all his *poor* and *meek ones*. A more full account of which things, and how the Lord has led me into this ministry and witness, I am with all convenient speed preparing for the press, and had before this been made public, had not my enemies hindered by seizing and destroying my writings. And in the mean time I beg of all persons to whom this paper shall come that they will for their own sakes lay aside all prejudice and try *me, my spirit* and *testimony* according to the word of God, and wait patiently upon the Lord to know his mind in this thing. And in love to themselves take heed how they rashly reproach and condemn me and my witness, lest they should, in so doing, run against that 'hiding of power' the prophet Habakkuk mentions, chapter 3.4, and that they be watchful over themselves that they be not found *despising prophecy* and *quenching the spirit* [1 Thessalonians 5.19–20], because of the contemptibleness of the *messenger* [2 Chronicles 36.16]; always remembering that God *will destroy the wisdom of the wise, and bring to nothing the understanding of the prudent* [1 Corinthians 1.19]; that *he chooses the foolish, the weak, the base* and *despised things of the world,* yea, and *things which are not, to bring to nought things that are* [1 Corinthians 1. 27–8]. In a word, let all persons so far take the alarm as to look well to their own souls, where they stand: whether they are founded upon that rock against which the gates of hell shall not prevail. Whether they are interested in that covenant of grace which is ordered in all things and sure, and which is *all our salvation in a day of desolation.* Whether they be in the number of those that are *eating and drinking with the drunken,* and *beating their fellow servants* [Matthew 24.49; Luke 12.45], or of the family of the *true Noah* who shall be taken into the ark, and preserved in the day of that flood of the divine vengeance which is ready to overflow the inhabitants of the earth.

What I have here published is according to the word of truth which must be fulfilled in its time. It is but a very little while and this matter will be cleared, made manifest and determined. In the meanwhile, I declare to all the world I am at rest in the will of my God, who has not left me without his *witness, presence* and *seal* in this work. And whoever thou art, that canst not yet see a divine character either upon *me* or *it,* my advice to thee is that thou perplex not thyself concerning me, but wait patiently upon God, and quietly expect the discovery which the *day* will make herein.

(A Vindication of Anne Wentworth, pp. 1–14)

Notes

1 *eighteen years* : perhaps significantly, this was also the length of time during which Israel suffered oppression from the Philistines and the children of Ammon (see Judges 10.8), and during which a woman, a 'daughter of Abraham', was bound by Satan before being 'loosed from this bond' by Christ (Luke 13.16).

2 *yoke-fellow* : her husband. Note the use of the expression in the bible at Philippians 4.3: 'And I entreat thee also, true yoke-fellow, help those women which laboured with me in the gospel.'

3 *professors of religion* : those who 'professed' to a certain creed, here her fellow Baptists. Wentworth uses the word negatively, to indicate insincerity, but see also Vokins, note 2, p. 223.

4 *Baptists* : Wentworth was a member of a congregation of Particular Baptists (see Introduction, p. 13). It seems they sided with her husband when this dispute over Wentworth's writing arose.

5 *publican* : in the bible, publicans were tax and tribute collectors, notorious for their extortion and dishonesty, who were thus the most unpopular and despised members of their community. Consequently a term for anyone hated or rejected by their community.

6 *formalists* : those who follow the 'form' or trappings of the faith, whilst ignoring or going against its essence. Her reference to 'literal and outward churches' below extends this theme. See 2 Timothy 3.5, and Wentworth's discussion of the 'spirit' and the 'letter', p. 188.

7 *that particular and great day of the Lord* : the day of judgment.

8 *Babylon* : the mystical city of the apocalypse (see Revelation 17). Applied rhetorically to any unregenerate kingdom, especially, as here, to the Holy Roman Empire and, by extension, the Anglican national church.

9 *my testimony . . . for public view* : Wentworth published *The Revelation of Jesus Christ* in 1679.

10 *staff and mantle* : each was, on occasion, imbued with a particular power by God. See Judges 6.21 and 2 Kings 2.8–14.

11 *the waters of jealousy* : a woman, suspected of sexual infidelity to her husband, had to demonstrate her innocence by drinking the 'water of bitterness', prepared by a priest. If innocent, she remained unharmed by it.

12 *outward man . . . inward man* : used habitually by sectaries to distinguish between the physical being and the spiritual. See 2 Corinthians 4.16: 'though our outward man perish, yet the inward man is renewed day by day.'

13 *the man of the earth shall oppress no more* : a reference to Psalms 10.18. This gives some idea of the anger of Wentworth's *Vindication*, for the whole psalm is an appeal from David to God for vengeance against the wicked.

14 *the letter that spirit* : this discussion concerning the relationship between the 'letter' and the 'spirit' continues the theme of the necessary distinction between the 'form' and the 'power' of religion (see note 6). See also 2 Corinthians 3.6; Romans 2.27 and 29; and 7.6.

15 *my experiences . . . from time to time* : Baptists' need for direct experience of God's grace as proof of their salvation led to a tendency to keep a record of spiritual debits and credits: proofs of conviction, doubts, and temptations.

16 *iota and title* : 'jot and tittle' in the Authorised Version: the smallest part of something.

17 *flood of scorn . . . and lying pamphlets* : suggests that Wentworth's testimony had been condemned and castigated in print, but I have not traced any evidence to confirm this.

18 *Mordecai's pinch, Israel's distress, Paul's strait* : all instances of liberation from oppressive and life-threatening situations. See Esther 2–10; Exodus 13–14; Acts 15–16.

11

HANNAH ALLEN

*Satan his Methods and Malice Baffled. A narrative of God's gracious
dealings with that choice Christian, Mrs Hannah Allen (afterwards
married to Mr Hatt) reciting the great advantages the Devil made of
her deep melancholy, and the triumphant victories, rich and sovereign
graces, God gave her over all his stratagems and devices.*

'O Lord! I am oppressed, undertake for me.' (Isaiah 38.14)

'We are not ignorant of his devices.' (2 Corinthians 2.11)

London, printed by John Wallis, 1683.

The choice of biblical quotations on the title page of *Satan his Methods and
Malice Baffled*, illustrating and supporting the summary of her experience
contained in the title, was probably made by Hannah Allen's editor. But it
immediately gives a sense of the patterns and concerns of her autobiography,
pointing to the highly conventional format she used in structuring her
experience and to the easy recognition of the purpose and significance of
such an autobiography amongst her contemporaries. *Satan his Methods and
Malice Baffled* is formed within the conventions of spiritual conversion
narrative (see headnote to Sarah Davy, p. 165) and takes the shape of an
account, written looking back from a time of happiness and spiritual
certainty to an earlier period of intense suffering. One of the impulses of the
narrative, quite conventionally, is to recapture moments of despair, intense
self-doubt, fear, and pain which are later perceived as part of the devout
believer's progress towards spiritual grace. In Hannah Allen's case, her long
period of despair is later attributed to melancholic illness which made her
vulnerable to the attacks of Satan, whom she, like most of her contemporaries (except for some radicals such as Quakers) believed had a real, physical
presence in the world. The quotation from Isaiah, 'Oh Lord, I am oppressed,
undertake for me', taking the form of a plea, picks up emotional and spiritual
weariness and yearning. Throughout the narrative, the descriptions of her

anxiety and pain suggest her dependency and contain an implicit calling-out for comfort, help, and response. And her prayers, noted down in her journal in the manner prescribed for spiritual self-examination, and later inserted into her narrative, quite explicitly voice her sense of helplessness and desire for support: 'I know not what to say'; 'For Christ's sake pity my case, or else I know not what to do'; 'Lord, I know not what to do'. The emotional charge of such writing captures her sense of fear and desperation. Depressed to the point where her only sense of herself is as irredeemably sinful, excluded from God's grace and from ordinary life in the world (she identifies with biblical sinners, criminals, and social outcasts and sees herself as a bad mother) she has no volition of her own.

The second impulse of the story, emphasized by its retrospective form, is to show a growth to understanding and to physical and spiritual strength. It is this movement that makes Hannah Allen's story an exemplary one – suitable for giving comfort to those who suffer in the same way that she did, but also to serve as a warning to those who cherish a sense of salvation too smugly. The knowing 'We are not ignorant of his devices', quoted on the title page, points to the growth in self-knowledge and the related development of awareness of Satan's methods which enable her to gain spiritual assurance. The final section of her narrative reveals how, through the help of Mr Shorthose, a cousin by marriage, a friend and a minister, she is able to make a series of spiritual or, as it would seem to us, psychological, separations that frees her from the compulsive circle of negative identifications and self-blame in which she has been stuck. She becomes able to make distinctions between what she is responsible for and what she is not: she separates physical illness (melancholy) from spiritual malady, she distinguishes what might properly be considered her thoughts from those stimulated by Satan, allowing her to acknowledge and confess irreligious and blasphemous feelings, but to shed her guilt. These crucial distinctions which bring about her restoration are made possible when she begins to create boundaries between herself and everything else that is external or beyond her control. Making separations releases her from the confusions and doubts about inner/outer oppositions and correspondences which are apparent throughout the narrative and manifest themselves in her anxieties, her fear of hypocrisy, the psychic splittings involved in her almost hallucinatory terrors and her suicide attempts.

The two spiritual impulses, need for comfort and movement towards understanding, coincide when Mr Shorthose intervenes to help her. And it is his relationship with her which instigates her recovery. Earlier, patient attempts by her aunt, mother, friends, and ministers to reassure her had only served to confirm her sense of isolation and sinfulness. Several ministers, in particular, had sought to comfort her by persuading her to join in worship. But, because they talk to her in the terms that represent and cause her fears, this only had the effect of reinforcing her sense of exclusion. Mr Shorthose, however, accepts the condition she makes that 'he would not compel [her] to anything of the worship of God, but what he would do by persuasion' and so enables her to trust him. The close relationship between Hannah Allen and Mr Shorthose might easily be read by a modern reader as involving a sort of therapeutic transference in which Hannah Allen's desire for a trust-worthy masculine figure is allowed a safe and legitimate rehearsal.[1] Such a reading would be confirmed, perhaps, by her allusion to her second (happy) marriage (to Mr Hatt) which follows on and completes her movement towards spiritual equilibrium.

Like all of the texts in this anthology, Hannah Allen's account is open to modern readings that make sense of her recorded experience in ways that differ from her own, or from general ways of constructing meaning that prevailed in the seventeenth century. Key events which seem significant to us are often only briefly mentioned. Her child is referred to only in passing and a crucial series of absences and losses which we might connect with her melancholy, guilt, and anger (her father's death when she was very young, her first husband's absences and death, her brother's busyness in his trade which prevented him from watching over her and fully caring for her) are not dealt with at length. The conventionality of the form and our lack of knowledge about the context of Hannah Allen's publication of her spiritual autobiography present problems of interpretation too. Although the main part of the narrative is clearly Allen's own and she intended it for publi-cation, the Preface presumably is not written by her – we do not know the extent of editorial mediation, nor whether the text was published in her lifetime or after her death. Nor can the structure of meanings constituted by the form of the narrative and by her predestinarian belief (see Introduction, p. 13) be simply seen as an overlay on or a distortion of actual experience, since her sense of herself was articulated within this framework of meanings in both her living of a life and her writing of it. The appeal of this text perhaps lies in these difficulties of interpretation, but it also is created by the sense that even when the experiences recorded are similar to those of other Nonconformist confessors, writing within the same frame, there is an individual voice here, speaking of herself.

Note

1 For a discussion of the role of the minister in relation to women, especially married women, see Lake 1987: 143–65.

Textual Note

The copytext is held in the British Library (shelfmark 1415 a10).

From: *Satan his Methods and Malice Baffled*

I, Hannah Allen, the late wife of Hannibal Allen, merchant, was born of religious parents. My father was Mr John Archer of Snelston in Derbyshire, who took to wife the daughter of Mr William Hart of Uttoxeter Woodland in Staffordshire, who brought me up in the fear of God from my childhood; and about twelve years of age, for my better education, sent me up to London, in the year 1650, to my father's sister, Mrs Ann Wilson, the wife of Mr Samuel Wilson, merchant, then living in Aldermanbury. And after some time spent there and at school, I being not well in health, had a desire to go down for a time to my mother, being a widow (my father dying when I was very young) where I stayed almost two years. In which time, and a little before my going down, it pleased God to work in me earnest breathings after the ways of God. But the enemy of my soul, striving to crush such hopeful beginnings in the bud, cast in horrible, blasphemous thoughts and injections into my mind, insomuch that I was seldom free, day or night, unless when dead sleep was upon me. But I used to argue with myself to this purpose, whether if I had a servant that I knew loved me and desired in all things to please me and yet was so forced against his will to do that which was contrary to my mind, whether I would think ever the worse of him, seeing I knew what he did was to his grief. And by such thoughts as these, it pleased God to give me some support, wherein his goodness did the more appear in casting such thoughts into my mind, I being young and also bearing this burthen alone, not so much as acquainting my mother with it. But by degrees these temptations grew to that height that I was persuaded I had sinned the unpardonable sin.[1] With these dreadful temptations I privately conflicted for some months, not revealing it, as I said, to anyone, thinking with myself that never any was like me, and therefore was loath to make my condition known. I would often, in my thoughts, wish I might change conditions with the vilest persons I could think of, concluding there was hopes for them, though not for me. That scripture in the fifty-seventh [chapter] of Isaiah, the last two verses, did exceedingly terrify me: 'But the wicked are like the troubled sea, when it cannot rest, whose waters cast up mire and dirt. There is no peace to the wicked, saith my God.'

In this sad and perplexed state, upon a sabbath day, my mother having been reading in the family, in one of blessed Mr Bolton's books,[2] and being ready to go with them to church, I thought with myself to what purpose should I go with them to hear the Word, since, as I thought, all means whatsoever for the good of my soul were in vain. But the same time, I, carelessly turning over Mr Bolton's book as it lay on the table, lighted on a place that directly treated on my case, which it pleased God so to bless, that I was so much comforted and strengthened that I recovered for that time from my despairing condition, and so continued for several years, with good hopes of the love of God in Christ towards me, yet still continually assaulted with temptations, but with less violence than before.

After my abode in the country almost two years with my mother, I returned to London to my Uncle and Aunt Wilson, by whom, about a year and four months after, I was disposed of in marriage to Mr Hannibal Allen, but still lived with my Uncle and Aunt Wilson till after my uncle died, and was about this time admitted to the sacrament by Mr Calamy, with good approbation.[3] And in the time of his life, I was frequently exercised with variety of temptations, wherein the Devil had the more advantage, I being much inclined to melancholy, occasioned by the oft absence of my dear and affectionate husband, with whom I lived, present and absent, about eight years. And soon after he went [on] his last voyage, I went into the country to live with my Aunt Wilson, who was now a widow, and [then] returned to live at Snelston with my aged mother, she being married again and living elsewhere. But in a few months, after I heard of the death of my husband (for he died beyond sea) I began to fall into deep melancholy. And no sooner did this black humour begin to darken my soul, but the Devil set on with his former temptations, which at first were with less violence and frequent intermissions, but yet with great strugglings and fightings within me. As I would express it to my aunt, 'I am just as if two were fighting within me, but I trust the Devil will never be able to overcome me.' Then I would repeat several promises suitable to my condition, and read over my former experiences that I had writ down (as is hereafter expressed) and obligations that I had laid upon myself in the presence of God, and would say, 'Aunt, I hope I write not these things in hypocrisy. I never intended any eye should see them, but the Devil suggesteth dreadful things to me against God, and that I am an hypocrite.'[4] At the first, I began to complain that I found not that comfort and refreshment in prayer as I was wont to do, and that God withdrew his comforting and quickening presence from me.

When I had seen the bible I would say, 'Oh, that blessed book that I so delighted in once!' The Devil was strongly assaulting my faith, and I seemed ready to be overcome. I answered the tempter within myself, in the bitterness of my spirit, 'Well, if I perish, God must deny himself.'

See the difference betwixt the voice of faith and the language of despair. At another time, I cannot[5] be saved because God cannot deny himself. The truth is, it had been[6] most of all worth the publishing my expressions in the time of my combating with Satan at the beginning of my affliction, but those passages are most of all forgotten. One hour my hope was firm, and the next hour ready to be overwhelmed.

(*Satan his Methods* pp. 1–10)

[Allen describes how she kept a record of her 'temptations and afflictions' in a journal during this period. She gives extracts from this.]

12th May, 1664. Still my time of great distress and sore trials continues. Sometimes the Devil tempts me woefully to hard and strange thoughts of my dear Lord which, through his mercy, I dread and abhor the assenting to, more than hell itself. In a word, every day, at present, seems a great burthen to me. My earnest prayer is:

> For the Lord's sake, that if it be thy holy will, I might not perish in this great affliction which hath been of so long continuance, and is so great still, notwithstanding means used. However, for the Lord's sake, let it be sanctified to my eternal good, and give me grace suitable to my condition, and strength to bear my burthen, and then do with me what thou wilt. I know not what to say. The Lord pity me in every respect and appear for me, in these my great straits, both of soul and body. I know not what to do. I shall be undone.

This I write to see what God will do with me, whether ever he will deliver me out of such a distress as this, that I may have cause to praise and adore his name in the land of the living.

> Lord, comfort me and support me, and revive me for Christ's sake.

26th May, 1664.

> I desire (which the Lord help me to do) exceedingly to bless and praise thy Majesty, that hath yet, in some measure supported me under these dread-

ful trials and temptations, which do yet continue and have been woeful upon me, for almost four months together. For Christ's sake, pity my case, or else I know not what to do. And do not deny me strength to bear up under my burthen. And for the Lord's sake grant, whatever thou dost with me, that one sin may not be in me, unrepented of or unmortified. Do with me what thou wilt, as to the creature, so[7] thou wilt subdue my sins and only mine eyes are up to thee. The Devil still keeps me under dreadful bondage and in sad distress and woe. But blessed be my God, that he doth not lay upon me all afflictions at once: that my child is so well and that I have many other mercies, which the Lord open my eyes to see, especially that Christ is mine, for the Lord's sake, and then I have enough.

After this I writ no more. But this and much more I writ before my last journey, aforesaid, for by that time I came back, I soon after fell into deep despair, and my language and condition grew sadder than before. Now, little to be heard from me but lamenting my woeful state, in very sad and dreadful expressions, as that I was undone forever, that I was worse than Cain or Judas,[8] that now the Devil had overcome me irrecoverably and this was what he had been aiming at all along. Oh, the Devil hath so deceived me, as never anyone was deceived! He made me believe my condition was good, when I was a cursed hypocrite.

One night, I said there was a great clap of thunder, like the shot of a piece of ordnance,[9] came down directly over my bed, and that the same night, a while after, I heard like the voice of two young men singing in the yard, over against my chamber, which I said were devils in the likeness of men, singing for joy that they had overcome me. And in the morning, as I was going to rise, that scripture in the tenth of Hebrews, and the last words of the twenty-sixth verse was suggested to me from heaven, as I thought: 'there remains no more sacrifice for sin.' And this delusion remained with me as an oracle all along: that by this miracle of the thunder and the voice and the scripture, God revealed to me that I was damned.

When my aunt asked me, 'Do you think God would work a miracle to convince you that you are rejected? It is contrary to the manner of God's proceedings; we do not read of such a thing in all the scripture.'

My answer was, 'Therefore my condition is unparalleled. There was never such an one[10] since God made any creature, either angels or men, nor never will be to the end of the world.'

One night as I was sitting by the fire, all of a sudden I said I should die presently, whereupon my aunt was called, to whom I said, 'Aunt, I am just dying. I cannot live an hour, if there were no more in the world.' In this opinion I continued a great while, every morning saying I should die before night, and every night, before morning. When I was thus in my dying condition, I often begged earnestly of my aunt to bring up my child strictly, that, if it were possible, he might be saved, though he had such a mother.

Many places of scripture I would repeat with much terror, applying them to myself, as Jeremiah 6.29,30: 'The bellows are burnt, the lead is consumed of the fire; the founder melteth in vain . . . Reprobate silver shall men call them, because the Lord hath rejected them';[11] Ezekiel 24.13: 'In thy filthiness is lewdness, because I have purged thee and thou wast not purged, thou shalt not be purged from thy filthiness any more, till I have caused my fury to rest upon thee'; Luke 13.24: 'Strive to enter in at the strait gate, for many, I say unto you, will seek to enter in, and shall not be able.' This last scripture I would express with much passionate weeping, saying, 'This is a dreadful scripture. I sought, but not in a right way, for the Devil blinded mine eyes. I sought to enter, but was not able.'

When both my inward and outward distempers grew to such a height, my aunt acquainted my friends at London with my condition, for at London I had formerly had four loving uncles, my father's brethren, two whereof were then living, and a brother of my own, that was set up in his trade. These advised to send me up to London, there being the best means both for soul and body, in order to which Mrs Wilson sent to entreat my mother to accompany me to London (for at that time she could not leave her family so long) who accordingly came.[12] But she found it a hard work to persuade me to this journey, for I said I should not live to get to the coach, but I must go and die by the way, to please my friends. I went up in the Tamworth coach, so that it was twenty-two miles thither. Tuesday was the day we set forwards on, and on that day in particular, the Devil had suggested to me, the Friday before, that I must die and be with him, and this the more confirmed me in my fear. My aunt went with me that day's journey, which was first to Tamworth on horseback, and from thence nine miles farther in the coach to Nuneaton, which was a long journey for one so weak and ill as I was. My aunt complaining of weariness, 'Ah,' said I, 'but what must I do, that must have no rest to all eternity?'

The next morning I would fain have returned back with my aunt, but there we parted and I went forward with my mother, and a very sad journey my mother had with me, for every morning she had no small trouble to persuade me to rise to go on my journey. I would earnestly argue against it, and say, 'I shall surely die by the way, and had I not better die in bed? Mother, do you think people will like to have a dead corpse in the coach with them?' But still, at last, my mother with much patience and importunity prevailed with me. As I passed along the way, if I saw a church, as soon as I cast mine eyes upon it, it was presently suggested to me, 'That's a hell-house,' with a kind of indignation. And this, I thought, was from myself, and therefore never spoke of it till after my recovery, for I thought if it had been known how vile I was, I must have been put to some horrible death. When I saw any black clouds gather, or the wind rise, as we went along, I presently concluded that some dreadful thing would fall out to show what an one I was.

When I came to London, I went to my brother's house in Swithin's Lane,[13] where my mother stayed with me, about three weeks or a month, in which time I took much physic of one Mr Cocket, a chemist[14] that lived over the way, but still I was, as I thought, always dying, and I yet wearying my mother with such fancies and stories. One evening, my mother said to me, 'Well, if you will believe you shall be saved if you die not this night, I will believe all that you say to be true, if you do die this night.' To this she[15] agreed, and in the night, about one o'clock as we thought, the maid being newly gone out of the chamber to bed, but left a watch-light burning, we both heard like the hand of a giant knock four times together on the chamber door, which made a great noise, the door being wainscot.[16] Then said I, 'You see, mother, though I died not tonight, the Devil came to let you know that I am damned.' My mother answered, 'But you see he had no power to come into the chamber.'

Soon after this, my mother returned home into the country, and left me in my brother's house, who was a young man unmarried, and had only a man and a maid, and he much abroad himself about his occasions. And now my opinion of dying suddenly began to leave me, therefore I concluded that God would not suffer me to die a natural death, but that I should commit some fearful abomination, and so be put to some horrible death. One day, my brother going along with me to Doctor Pridgeon,[17] as we came back, I saw a company of men with halberds.[18] 'Look, brother,' said I, 'you will see such as these, one of these days, carry me to Newgate.'[19] To prevent which, I studied several ways to make away myself, and I being so much alone, and in a large solitary house, had the more liberty to endeavour it. First, I thought of taking opium, that I might die in my sleep, and none know but that I had died naturally (which I desired that my child might not be disgraced by my untimely end)[20] and therefore sent the maid to several apothecaries' shops for it; some said they had none, others said it was dangerous and would not sell it her. Once she had got some and was coming away with it, the master of the shop coming in, asked what she had, and when he knew, took it from her (this the maid told me). When I had sent her up and down several days and saw she could get none, then I got spiders and took one at a time in a pipe with tobacco,[21] but never scarce took it out, for my heart would fail me. But once I thought I had been poisoned. In the night, awaking out of my sleep, I thought I felt death upon me (for I had taken a spider when I went to bed) and called to my brother and told him so, who presently arose and went to his friend, an apothecary, who came and gave me something to expel it. The next day my uncles and brother, considering the inconveniency of that lonesome house, removed me to Mr Peter Walker's house, a hosier at the Three Crowns in Newgate Market, whose wife was my kinswoman, who received me very courteously, though I was at that time but an uncomfortable guest.

In the time I was at my brother's, I had strange apprehensions that the lights that were in neighbouring houses were apparitions of devils, and that those lights were of their making. And if I heard the voice of people talk or read in other houses, I would not be persuaded but that it was devils like men talking of me and mocking at my former reading, because I proved such an hyprocrite.

> Madam,
>
> As for the time I was at my Cousin Walker's, I refer your Ladyship to them, or any friend else that may assist you. Only I have here set down several passages, as they came to my mind, which passed there, which your Ladyship may make use of as you please.[22]

One time, while I lay at my Cousin Walker's, having promised a friend that was very importunate with me to go to a sermon with her, about two or three days after, the Devil began to terrify me for making that promise, and suggested to me that I had much better break it than keep it, for I had enough sermons to answer for already. And sitting in great distress, contriving how I might put off my going, the Devil found me out a place on the top of the house, a hole where some boards were laid, and there I crowded in myself, and laid a long, black scarf upon me and put the boards as well as I could, to hide me from being found, and there intended to lie, till I should starve to death. And all the family and others concluded I had stolen out at the door unknown to them, to go lose myself in some wood, which I much talked of. But when I had lain there almost three days, I was so hungry and cold, it being a very sharp season, that I was forced to call as loud as I could, and so was heard and released from that place.

(*Satan his Methods*, pp.17–36)

[The narrative covers the next two years: Allen's melancholy continues and she makes more suicide attempts. In 1665 she returns to stay with her aunt in Derbyshire.]

Towards winter I grew to eat very little, much less than I did before, so that I was exceeding lean, and at last nothing but skin and bones. (A neighbouring gentlewoman, a very discreet person, that had a great desire to see me, came in at the back door of the house unawares and found me in the kitchen. Who, after she had seen me, said to Mrs Wilson, 'She cannot live; she hath death in her face.') I would say still that every bit I did eat hastened my ruin and that I had it with a dreadful curse, and what I ate increased the fire within me, which would at last burn me up, and I would now willingly live out of hell as long as I could.[23]

Thus sadly I passed that winter and towards spring I began to eat a little better.

This spring, in April 1666, my good friends, Mr Shorthose and his wife, whose company formerly I much delighted in, came over. And when I heard they were come and were at their brother's house, half a mile off, and would come thither the Friday after, 'Ah,' says I, 'that I dread. I cannot endure to see him, nor hear his voice: I have told him so many dreadful lies.' (Meaning what I had formerly told him of my experiences and, as I thought, infallible evidences of the love of God towards me; and now believed myself to be the vilest creature upon earth.) 'I cannot see his face,' and wept tenderly. Wherewith my aunt was much affected and promised that when he came he should not see me. (I would have seen neither of them, but especially my he-cousin.) On the Friday, soon after they came in, they asked for me, but my aunt put them off till after dinner, and then told them she had engaged her word they should not see me, and that if she once broke her promise with me, I would not believe her hereafter. With such persuasions she kept them from seeing me, but not satisfied them, for that night Mr Shorthose was much troubled and told his wife if he had thought they must not have seen me, he would scarce have gone to Snelston. The next day, they supped at Mr Robert Archer's house, Mrs Wilson's brother that then lived in the same town, where my aunt supped with them. At the table, something was said of their not seeing Mrs Allen, but after supper Mr Shorthose and his wife stole away from the company, to Mrs Wilson's where they came in at the back-side of the house, suddenly into the kitchen where I was. But as soon as I saw them, I cried out in a violent manner, several times, 'Ah, Aunt Wilson, hast thou served me so!' and ran into the chimney and took up the tongs.

'No,' said they. 'Your aunt knows not of our coming.'

'What do you do here?' said I.

'We have something to say to you,' said they.

'But I have nothing to say to you,' said I.

Mr Shorthose took me by the hand and said, 'Come, come, lay down those tongs and go with us into the parlour.'

Which I did, and there they discoursed with me till they had brought me to so calm and friendly a temper that when they went I accompanied them to the door and said, 'Methinks I am loath to part with them.'[24]

Mr Shorthose, having so good encouragement, came the next day again, being Sabbath day, after dinner, and prevailed with me to walk with him into an arbour in the orchard, where he had much discourse with me. And amongst the rest he entreated me to go home with him, which after long persuasions both from him and my aunt, I consented to upon this condition: that he promised me he would not compel me to anything of the worship of God, but what he could do by persuasion. And that week I went with them, where I spent that summer. In which time it pleased God, by Mr Shorthose's means, to do me much good both in soul and body. He had some skill in physic himself and also consulted with physicians about me. He kept me to a course of physic most part of the summer, except when the great heat of the weather prevented. I began much to leave my dreadful expressions concerning my condition and was present with them at duty.[25] And at last they prevailed with me to go with them to the public ordinance[26] and to walk with them to visit friends, and was much altered for the better.

A fortnight after Michaelmas, my aunt fetched me home again to Snelston, where I passed that winter much better than formerly, and was pretty conformable and orderly in the family. And the next summer was much after the same manner, but grew still something better, and the next winter likewise still mending, though but slowly, till the spring began and then I changed much from my retiredness and delighted to walk with friends abroad.

And this spring[27] it pleased God to provide a very suitable match for me, one Mr Charles Hatt, a widower living in Warwickshire, with whom I live very comfortably both as to my inward and outward man,[28] my husband being one that truly fears God.

As my melancholy came by degrees, so it wore off by degrees. And as my dark, melancholy, bodily distempers abated, so did my spiritual maladies also. And God convinced me by degrees that all this was from Satan, his delusions and temptations working in those dark and black humours and not from myself. And this God cleared up to me, more and more, and accordingly my love to and delight in religion increased. And it is my desire that, lest this great affliction should be a stumbling-block to any, it may be known (seeing my case is published) that I evidently perceive that God did it in much mercy and faithfulness to my soul, and though for the present it was a bitter cup, yet that it was but what the only wise God saw I had need of, according to that place, 1 Peter 1.6: 'Though now for a season, if need be, ye are in heaviness through manifold temptations.' Which scripture did much comfort me under my former afflictions in my first husband's days.

(Satan his Methods pp. 64–73)

[The account ends with a selection of biblical quotations which Allen found useful in giving her hope during her despair.]

Notes

1 *the unpardonable sin* : many Presbyterians and Baptists feared committing the one sin that could never be forgiven, alluded to in Psalms 19.13: 'Keep back thy servant also from presumptuous sins; let them not have dominion over me: then shall I be upright, and I shall be innocent from the great transgression.' This unpardonable sin or great transgression was also sometimes identified as the sin referred to in Mark 3.29: 'But he that shall blaspheme against the Holy Ghost hath never forgiveness, but is in danger of eternal damnation,' cf. Bunyan 1931: 46–7.

2 *Mr Bolton's books* : theological writings of Robert Bolton, specifically, *Instructions for a Right Comforting Afflicted Consciences* (1631), a Puritan manual describing the conversion experience and giving advice on the spiritual counselling of those in despair.

3 *admitted to the sacrament by Mr Calamy, with good approbation* : she received her first communion and was accepted by the congregation. This indicates she was a Presbyterian. Edmund Calamy was an important and influential Presbyterian preacher, curate of St Mary, Aldermanbury, London from 1639 to 1662 when he was ejected and briefly imprisoned.

4 *hypocrite* : this has a technical sense, referring to someone who had the appearance of being one of the elect and whose experience coincided with that of someone in whom the Spirit was working, but who was in fact one of the reprobate (see Introduction p. 13)

5 *I cannot* : i could not (be saved).

6 *it had been* : it would be.

7 *creature, so* : creature — person or human being; here perhaps with the sense of body and human experience; so — as long as.

8 *Cain or Judas* : she identifies with the worst biblical sinners, Cain the first murderer and Judas who betrayed Christ.

9 *piece of ordnance* : the shot of a large gun.

10 *such an one* : such a one, i.e. anyone comparable.

11 *reprobate silver* : this quotation, like those following, confirms her belief that she is one of the reprobate or damned.

12 *Mrs Wilson sent . . . who accordingly came* : i.e. her aunt, Mrs Wilson, who has remarried, was unable to accompany Hannah Allen to London herself, so she asks Hannah Allen's mother to do so.

13 *Swithin's Lane* : now St Swithin's Lane.

14 *chemist* : alchemist.

15 *she agreed* : more easily understood as 'I agreed' or 'we agreed'.

16 *wainscot* : pannelling, i.e. the door was pannelled.

17 *Doctor Pridgeon* : possibly William Pridgeon, a doctor of physic.

18 *halberds* : military weapons carried by soldiers and guards.

19 *Newgate* : Newgate Prison.

20 *my child . . . my untimely end* : suicides were considered self-murderers who were tried posthumously. If found guilty they had their goods confiscated by the crown and were denied Christian burial (MacDonald 1986:53). Mainstream Puritans and most sectarians believed the Devil instigated temptations to suicide.

21 *spiders . . . tobacco* : spiders were believed to be poisonous. Smoking tobacco was thought by some to be good for health, but was more generally considered decadent, dangerous, and a vice.

22 Nothing in the text allows us to identify the addressee of this letter. Possibly Allen is writing to Lady Baker whom we are told has been interested in her: 'The Lady Baker was pleased to write me several letters which I would not so much as look on' (p. 59 of copytext). This letter indicates that Hannah Allen is writing her account at the request of this Lady.

23 *I would say . . . hell as long as I could* : she is saying that eating feeds the evil and the hell inside her. So, to avoid nourishing this evil inner self and thus ultimately being consumed by internal fire, she avoids eating.

24 *'Methinks I am loath to part with them.'* : in the copytext this is italicized, a conventional indication of both direct and indirect speech. Grammatically, this remark is a mixture of both direct and indirect speech and is, perhaps, more easily read, 'Methinks I am loath to part with you.'

25 *duty* : religious duty and prayer.

26 *public ordinance* : church service.

27 *this spring* : that spring, rather than spring 1681, when she is writing, I think.

28 *inward and outward man* : body and soul or physical and spiritual being.

JOAN VOKINS

God's Mighty Power Magnified: as manifested and revealed in his faithful handmaid Joan Vokins, who departed this life the 22nd of the 5th month, 1690, 'having finished her course, and kept the faith' [2 Timothy 4.7]. Also some account of her exercises, works of faith, labour of love, and great travels in the work of the ministry, for the good of souls.

2 Corinthians 4.7. 'But we have this treasure in earthen vessels, that the excellency of the power may be of God, and not of us.'

2 Corinthians 12.9. 'And he said, my grace is sufficient for thee; for my strength is made perfect in weakness.'

London, printed for Thomas Northcott in George Yard in Lombard Street, 1691.

God's Mighty Power Magnified was published the year after Joan Vokins's death, as a testimony to a life of faith and an example to the reader, who could 'come to receive the comfort that is couched under the words and expressions, and partake of the sweetness of that life' (1691:sig.A2ʳ). Vokins's account of her life takes only thirty-three of the 166 pages, the rest of the text comprising dedicatory epistles, letters she sent to family and fellow Quakers whilst on her travels, and a few pious documents that she had written.

Vokins was, the dedicatory letters suggest, an exemplary woman: her devoutness complemented and enhanced her womanly qualities, and vice versa. She tirelessly served God, 'not sparing her weak body, which in appearance was fitter to keep her chamber than travel as she did' (1691:sig.A3ᵛ). Her work amongst Friends, they suggest, was an extension of her maternal duties: 'Her tender care was great. She was a nursing mother over the young convinced, and in her own family, great was her care and endeavours for her husband and children, that they might partake with her of the everlasting comfort and celestial consolation that is the portion of the righteous' (1691:sig.A2ʳ). This, though, seems something of an effort to contain or dilute the implications of a life of very 'public' activity by interpreting it as having only 'private' or domestic significance. The record of Vokins's travels, however, rather belies this emphasis, for she journeyed extensively in America, the Caribbean, and Ireland, visiting Friends' communities, exhorting them and (by letter) those at home, to stand firm in the faith and resist any temptations the secular world might offer.

These ministrations certainly included her family, but Vokins several times made clear that her concern for them was by no means the central focus of her life's work. She suggests that whatever pleasures or satisfactions she derives from them are inadequate without 'the marriage union with the lamb of God' (see p. 215): 'The feeling of his [Christ's] sweet refreshing life that he communicates to my soul is a hundred-fold better than husband or children, or any other outward mercies that he hath made me partaker of, though very near and dear unto me' (1691:66). 'Outward mercies', then, are no match for the inward ones derived from her faith, which give her satisfaction and scope for activity otherwise unavailable to her. As Cynthia Pomerleau suggests, it 'allowed her to find by turning inward the meaning, mystery, exaltation and ceremony that were lacking outwardly. In effect, she could admit that she was not satisfied with her domestic lot without actually rebelling against it' (Pomerleau 1980:28 –9).

Her faith gave her not only an arena for activity, but also the language to place herself at the centre of those activities without making herself vulnerable to charges of immodesty, vainglory, or egocentricity. By scriptural allusions in her text, she tacitly aligns herself with David, St Paul, and, much more directly, with the children of Israel – God's chosen people – in flight from their persecutors (see p. 216). By identifying herself with Israel and her enemies with 'Pharaoh and his host', she is able to suggest the importance of this time in her own 'heavenly progress', the special nature of her relationship with God, her doubts regarding that relationship, and the magnitude of the opposition she felt she was facing from the state and the Church of England. She thus creates an image of herself of dignity and strength, firmly at the centre of her narrative, but with the sense of the power and importance of her struggle deriving from the imagery rather than from a first-person account.

This imagery contradicts any idea of Vokins as weak in anything other than body, a condition which certainly did not inhibit her in the fulfilment of God's work. In Rhode Island, she tells us, she silenced Thomas Case, 'the grand Ranter, [who] was bawling very loud' (1691:35) and disrupting Friends' meetings. Later, she predicts the destruction of the vessel of a captain who had mistreated her, adding, with some relish, 'accordingly his vessel was split on a rock in a little time after'; and she relates her encounter with a hostile crowd, having been thrown out of church for interrupting the clergyman (see pp. 220 and 222).

These contradictions, of strength and weakness, of the 'nursing mother' leaving her family for extended periods of time, and of the 'modest' writer identifying herself with God's chosen people, are centrally important not only to Vokins's writing, but to that of all sectarian women writers. The challenge they present to dominant definitions of acceptable activities for women is manifested as a part or an extension of those activities; stress is laid on God's call on them to do this work, rather than on the transgressive nature of the work itself. And the contradiction is embedded in the scriptures, in the passages that both justify and anatomize such activities and aspirations. Vokins – or rather her editors – preface her work with two such quotations, which refer to 'treasure in earthen vessels', and God's strength being 'made perfect in weakness' (see title page). But the biblical text most often cited by sectaries locates this contradiction or reversal with the coming of the kingdom of God, when it will become clear that 'God hath chosen the weak things of the world to confound the mighty . . . and things which are not, to confound things which are' (1 Corinthians 1.27–8). This promised reversal of the status quo justified much that would otherwise have been unjustifiable, such as women leaving their families, travelling, and preaching. So although Vokins wrote that she 'chose rather to suffer with the people of God, than to enjoy . . . all the pleasures, or profits, or honour this world can afford' (1691:9), she makes clear that she found these 'pleasures' inadequate. The text, and the context of other sectarian writings and contemporary reactions to them, also demonstrate the near impossibility of her retaining the 'honour' of her community whilst engaging in the kind of activities demanded by God's call, other than in a radical sectarian setting. Although the Quaker doctrine did not offer complete equality, either to women and men or to different races (separate meetings for black and white people were held in Barbados, see p. 221), and despite the movement's greater quietism and conservatism after the Restoration, it did consistently offer a notion of spiritual equality. This, combined with the sense of individual responsibility fostered by the doctrine of the inner light (see Introduction p. 14), enabled women such as Vokins to continue their radical activities into the 1680s, some twenty years after increased state persecution had silenced the vast majority of the women from the other sects.

Textual note

The copytext used here is from the British Library, shelfmark 1419 a28. This was the first edition; another was published in 1871.

From: *God's Mighty Power Magnified*

[The following extract opens Vokins's autobiography. It is preceded by a number of testimonies to her life and character by her family and fellow Friends.]

Some account given forth by Joan Vokins of the great goodness and mercy of the Lord towards her, and of the wonderful works that he hath done for her, conducing to his glory and her great joy and comfort. Written with her own hand a few months before her decease, as followeth.

Something of the tender dealing of the Lord with me ever since my childhood: for (blessed be his name) he preserved me from many evils that youth is often ensnared with; and by his light, that I then had no acquaintance with, showed me the vanity and vain customs of the world when I was very young, and all along my youth his good spirit did strive with me to preserve me from sin and evil. And if I had at any time, through persuasion of others, gone to that they called recreation, I should be so condemned for passing away my precious time that I could have no peace, so that I could take no delight in their pastime, but was still condemned. And many times I cried to the righteous God to reveal his way unto me, and I promised to walk therein whatever I endured. For the snares of the world the Lord was pleased to discover, and in some measure to make known the cross of Jesus that crucifies unto the world. And as I inclined to take it up and follow Jesus through the many tribulations, he endowed me with his almighty power, wherein hath been my help, blessed be his worthy name for ever, for his loving kindness never fails, but his mercies endure for ever. And his great compassion and tender dealing towards my soul, when in darkness and under the region of the shadow of death (Job 10.21; Psalms 107.10, 14) is never to be forgotten, for it hath been largely extended unto me when in deep distress.

When my cry was often, 'Lord, reveal the way unto me, that I may walk therein whatever I undergo', but when I found the way so strait and narrow, I could very willingly have turned aside for ease, for flesh and blood could not bear that which I had then to undergo. But blessed and renowned be the spirit of truth, my comforter, which leads into all truth. For when I was in a dejected condition about reprobation and election,[1] neither priest nor professor[2] could open

214

the mystery of election and reprobation, but the spirit of light and life, which is the spirit of Jesus, opened my understanding, and revealed the mystery of the two seeds, how that the one is forever blessed, and the other cursed.[3] And also what happiness might be received by taking heed to the light that shined in my heart,[4] which makes manifest that the way to the crown of glory is through the daily cross to my own will, and to take Christ's yoke upon that nature that would not be subject. Oh how precious is the counsel of him who said, 'Take my yoke upon you, and learn of me; for my yoke is easy, and my burden is light, and ye shall find rest for your souls' [Matthew 11.29–30]. And that rest I sorely wanted, until I learned of Jesus to be meek and low in heart, and to suffer for well-doing. And then (glory unto his holy name for ever) his blessed reward my soul was daily made a partaker of, though hated by evil-doers, yet loved by the Lord, and that engaged me to give up to his dispose, and to answer his requirings, not accounting myself nor anything he hath give me too much to part with, that the truth may be propagated and my tender God honoured. For (blessed be his worthy name) he hath filled my cup with the sweet salvation (Psalms 116.13) of his son Christ Jesus, the light and saviour of his poor and helpless ones, who have no other to depend upon for help at all times, but wait daily to be furnished upon every occasion to serve him in all faithfulness. For he is worthy, my soul can truly say, for he gave me of his good spirit [Nehemiah 9.20], and it was with me, yet unknown, when I rebelled against it and was not willing to be subject to its leadings, nor observing of its dictates, as I ought to have been. Oh then did I want power, as many do now, not knowing the sufficiency of the engrafted word of God's grace that is able to save [James 1.21]. But when I followed its counsel, I found it sufficient to bring good to me, out of great afflictions, beyond my expectation, and then could I plead no excuse, knowing that unto the Lord Jesus, who had brought great things to pass, I must give my account. For he hath manifested his power, and I have cause to believe it will never fail towards his people if we fail not to obey the manifestation of it; but faithfulness is required to the talent received [Matthew 25.14], for which we must give an account, and then what can stand us in stead, if we have not an increase? This was my concern for many years, and I could not take comfort in husband or children, house or land, or any visibles, for want of the marriage union with the lamb of God, that takes away the sins of the souls of those that cannot be satisfied in them, but are weary of the burden of them, as I was. And God by his spirit showed me he abhorred my self-righteousness, and let me see that in him was righteousness, life and power. And then I was sensible that he is the light of the world, that enlightens everyone that comes into the world,[5] and that it was striving with me from my youth, which was before ever I heard the name Quaker. And then I did believe that there was a people or church over whom Christ Jesus was head, though I could yet not find them, nor be a member of them, yet long sought after it sorrowfully, with many strong and fervent cries and desires. But the Lord in his own due time answered my weary soul, and made known more and more of the way of his truth and people, and at length sent some of his messengers as instruments in his hand for my encouragement and confirmation. Then was I and many desolate ones right glad, whose souls had long languished, for the glad tidings that they brought with them, how that we might inherit substance which we had long sought and been searching for, both in the scriptures and amongst professors of many sorts of profession. For we would fain have filled our souls with the husks [Luke 15.16], but that could not satisfy. We knew not the saving health [Psalms 67.2] of him who said, 'I wisdom lead in the midst of the paths of judgment, to teach them that love and follow me to inherit substance' [Proverbs 8.20–1). Oh this is that which did at first convince us, and tendered our hearts in the beginning. Then what was too near or dear for us to part with in the day of our deep distress, when none could cure our wounded souls? Oh how precious was the heart-searching light when we first knew it to shine upon our tabernacles, to guide us in the narrow way wherein is life [Matthew 7.14] and perfect peace for those whose minds are stayed on the Lord [Isaiah 26.31]. And when I have read that he would keep them in perfect peace whose minds are stayed on him, what would not I have done, that it might have been my condition? But then I could not watch nor wait, but was as a ship without an anchor among the merciless waves. But praises unto the Lord for ever, he caused the living hope to spring that anchored [Hebrews 6.19] in trying times. And I was even as Israel at the Red Sea [Exodus 14], compassed all round on every hand. Great was the strait that I was then in [2 Samuel 24.14], much hardship: the sea before, and the enemy presenting so much impossibility that his proud waves of temptations, buffetings and false accusations had almost sunk me under. Oh then did I cry unto the God of mercy and tender compassion, that I might but stand still and behold his salvation. And he did arise and rebuke the enemy, and made way for me to travel on in my heavenly progress, and overturned the mountains [Job 9.5; 28.9] that were on each hand, and dismayed Pharaoh and his host, which I may compare my relations and the professors unto, for they pursued me and made my suffering great, till they had wearied themselves. And their oppression was so sore that I sometimes was ready to faint, and even to say, 'Surely I shall one day fall.' But living praises unto the almighty, he hath made me a partaker of the sure mercies of David [Isaiah 55.3; Acts 13.34], and hath subdued truth's enemies before him, and kept and preserved me faithful till several of my relations were convinced that God's power was with me. And now when my husband and children and relations are with me in a good meeting, and the powerful presence of the Lord is amongst us, it is a blessed reward for all, for one soul is more worth than all the world, as saith the scripture [Mark 8.36–7]. Therefore faithfulness is very needful, for it doth produce a good effect, whatever we may endure, for the momentary affliction that we meet with here doth produce a further weight of glory hereafter. And in the sense of the same, my head was borne up to endure hardships, when I could willingly have hid or gotten ease; but I considered that I could not hide from the Lord, who brought to my remembrance my promise that I made before his way was revealed to me, and if I broke covenant with the Lord I should never enter into his rest. Oh then a suffering in the flesh and a ceasing from sin [1 Peter 4.1] was the delight of my soul, although the enemy ceased not, but night and day, as a roaring lion [1 Peter 5.8] and a cunning hunter [Genesis 25.27] seeking for the precious life, and chased my poor soul as a partridge on the mountains [1 Samuel 26.20]. But my God had showed me that the way to rest was through many troubles, and that he would be at hand to deliver out of them all by his almighty power, but I could hardly trust it then. But yet, turning to it, I found preservation by it, when the backsliding of some had like to have caused me to stumble. But the unerring spirit of Jesus showed me that if thousands fall on the one hand, and tens of thousands on the other, that should not defile me; and if all the rest were righteous, that should not justify me if I did not obey the truth, now he had made known his covenant of life, which I so deeply engaged to be faithful unto. And then I turned my back on the world and all the friendship and glory of it, that I might obtain the favour of Jesus, who condemned me for my self-righteousness as for my known sins, for I was cautious of sinning against the Lord ever since my youth, and desired after the best religion and company. And when I was very young in years I greatly delighted to go to professors' meetings, and could bring home the text and repeat much of their sermons, but yet that brought no benefit to my poor hungry soul. And when I was in secret, before the all-seeing eye of the Lord, he administered condemnation upon it all, and I had no peace inwardly, although none could condemn me for any misdemeanour as outwardly. But when my own righteousness became loathsome to me, then was I made willing to part with all that had been near and dear unto me, that I might feel and witness the robe of Christ's righteousness [Isaiah 61.10] revealed, and be clothed therewith. And as for my husband and children, my true and tender love was so great that I could have done or suffered much for them. But if I had disobeyed the Lord to please them, I might have provoked him to have withholden his mercies from us all, and to bring his judgments upon us; and then who shall excuse in the day of account?[6] Then if a man, as the scripture says, should give the fruit of his body for the sin of his soul [Micah 6.7], it will not be accepted. Then husbands and wives, and parents and children, and servants shall all receive according to their doings, and none that disobeys the Lord can be excused, no more than Adam was when he said that the woman gave him the forbidden fruit, and he did eat, and so provoked the Lord that the curse came upon himself and could not be excused [Genesis 3]. And although man and wife should be helpful one to another in righteousness, yet too many there are since the fall that hinder and hurt each other, for which an account must be given unavoidably. And this did I consider many a time, and earnestly endeavour to avoid, notwithstanding the false aspersions that might arise. Yet I still endeavoured to keep my conscience clear in the sight of my tender God, and none can lay anything to my charge, except it be for serving the living and true God, though in that way that many may call heresy, yet I do worship him in spirit and in truth. For as Christ Jesus hath said, 'It is come to pass that our heavenly father seeketh such, and always sought such, to worship him in his own spiritual way of worship' [John 4.23–4], which shall stand when all idolatry and invented worships shall fall.

(*God's Mighty Power Magnified*, pp. 15–24)

[Vokins goes on to describe her call to spread God's word overseas, and her travels in New England. The following extract recounts the next stage of her journey, to the Caribbean, and then the events following her return to England.]

And when I was clear[7] of West Jersey and those parts, I returned to

New York in order to take my passage for England. But before I came there, the living God, whom I served with all my heart, further tried me, and laid it weightily upon me to go to Barbados, which was no little cross to my mind. But the overcoming power of the true and living God wrought so strongly with me that I was made willing to take up the cross and follow Jesus [Matthew 16.24; Mark 8.34; 10.21; Luke 9.23] through many tribulations, and he (magnified be his power) most wonderfully supported and conducted me all along. For I took shipping at New York, and as the Lord put it into my heart to visit Friends in the Leeward Islands, so he carried the vessel, let them that sailed do what they could; and they could not steer their course Barbados-road,[8] although they endeavoured it with all their might. And I had good service amongst them in the vessel, and they were made to confess to the almighty power that I testified of. And we laid by Antigua a week before the owner would let me go ashore. But the all-wise God ordered it so that the vessel could not go away till I had been there and performed what service he had appointed for me. And blessed be his name, his reward was precious, for we came ashore on a first day,[9] and I hastened to a Friends' meeting, and when I came in, I found the Lord's power was amongst his people, and I had a precious time with them. There was a little handful of plain-hearted Friends, and our hearts were tendered and our souls comforted, and we rejoiced that the Lord Jesus had visited us, and caused us in his love to visit each other.

So when I returned to the sea again, it came into my heart to visit Friends at Nevis. And when I had taken leave of Friends of Antigua that came aboard with me, and God's heavenly power was with us and sweetly refreshed our souls, as we were aboard the vessel, and remained with us. And we were concerned one for another, not knowing that we should ever see each others' faces more. But see how the Lord ordered it. As we were sailing on the sea, it opened in my heart to visit Friends at Nevis, but the owner of the vessel, being a hypocritical professor, caused my exercise to be the more. But the power of the Lord was manifest, and 'the winds and sea obeyed' [Matthew 8.27; Mark 4.41; Luke 8.25], that we were carried to Nevis against his will. But he would not let me go ashore, for he had heard that those should pay a great fine that carried any Friend thither, and hoisted sail again for Barbados, and said he would weather the point of Guadeloupe.[10] And he laboured three weeks, but could not do it, for the hand of the Lord was against him, else he might have done it in a few days; but he provoked the Lord, and trusted in his vessel and in his own skill. And he locked up the bread, and dealt hardly with his passengers when he saw he should be longer at sea than at first he did expect. And he knew that for three weeks there was stinking water, and we were close by a French island, and they said the French would not let us have any, if we starved: they were papists, and said if we came for water, they would take our ship for a prey and us for captives. And yet this owner of the vessel would not go to any other island, until the merchants that were aboard threatened him very sorely. And then he put in at a mountainous place called Montserrat. And they went all away from me as soon as they were landed, for I was very weakly, being aboard the vessel so long with such bad accommodation: I went aboard with my clothes so wet that I could wring water out of them, and so dried them upon my weakly body, which cast me into such a feverish condition that I was very dry. And I sat down on the shore, and a girl came to fetch fresh water near where I sat, and I drank until I sweat, and then I swooned, and lay some time. But the arising of the life of Jesus set me on my feet again, and in the strength and relief thereof I went to enquire for a passage for Barbados, and heard of none. But I was not clear of Nevis, but hearing of a leaking vessel to go to Antigua, took my passage in that, hoping that way might be made from thence to go to Nevis. And then having got a passage, it being night and rainy, I tried to get me a lodging on the land. And the people were generally Irish papists, but the Lord did so order it that I met with an Englishwoman, and she treated me kindly, but she had neither bread nor drink, but wine and sugar. And I desired half a pint of Madeira wine[11] to be boiled and that served me night and morning, and the Lord blessed it to me, and his holy power accompanied me. And while I stayed for the vessel, I had good service there, though there was no Friend in all the island. They had banished a Friend out of it, as I heard, but a little before, and the people told me they did not dare to have a meeting, yet I published truth in the streets, and they confessed to it. And so I left truth honourably amongst them, and then came aboard the vessel where I last took my passage, and sailed to the other vessel, that I had suffered in, and called for the owner and cleared my conscience to him, and told him the hand of the Lord was against him, and warned him to repent, else he should suddenly feel the stroke of it to be heavy upon him; and in as much as his heart had been too much set on that bark, he should shortly see that the Lord would destroy it. And accordingly his vessel was split on a rock in a little time after. So when I, through tender mercy, came to Antigua again, the Friends told me how they had been concerned for me, and so had Nevis Friends. And there was a passage ready for Nevis, and an honest woman Friend, whose name was Mary Humphery, was very ready to go with me. And Friends there were very joyful of my coming, and we had many good and powerful meetings in that island. And there was a judge and his wife came to meeting, and people of several sorts, and we had some meetings at the houses of them that were no Friends, and Friends were well satisfied and comforted, and the mighty power of God was with us: glory unto it for it is worthy over all, and in us all. Oh that we may have an eye to its glory in our whole lives and conversations,[12] for it is by it we live, move and have our being, and its dealing with us and working for us in that place is worthy to be remembered, for this was the place that the owner of the vessel aforementioned was afraid to carry me to. But the Lord was on my side, and prevented much evil when it was intended. And the governor of that place was so kind that he gave us his letter of recommendation to carry with us. And so I came back with M. Humphery to Antigua and to five islands,[13] and there we and some Friends that went with us visited a poor people that complained of their priest, and said he came to them but once a year, and then it was to take that which they had from them.[14] And we had a precious opportunity to manifest the truth, and they were very kind to us, and seemed to be well satisfied and affected.

And then, I being clear and a passage presented for Barbados, as soon as I was ready I went aboard, and was there sooner than could have been expected. And when I arrived, I met with many Friends at Bridgetown, and there took an account of the monthly meetings, and went to them and other meetings as brief as I could. And most days I had two or three meetings of a day, both among the blacks, and also among the white people. And the power of the Lord Jesus was mightily manifested, so that my soul was often melted therewith, even in the meetings of the negroes or blacks, as well as among Friends.[15] And when I had gone through the island, and was clear, having been well refreshed with Friends, in the feeling of the heavenly power and in the strength of the same, I came aboard the ship for my native land again.

Written aboard the ship coming
from Barbados, in the 3rd
month, 1681.

J.V.

Before I went to sea, I was two weeks in the service of truth in Kent, and then it was showed me, being at Sandwich, that I should bear my testimony for God and his divine spiritual worship in a steeple-house[16] there; and coming home, the heavenly power wrought mightily in my heart. And when I was clear of those countries, I was better in health than I had been for many years. And, as the light of Jesus showed me before I left England, as is afore hinted, so the power thereof ordered me when I came back, and it was so weightily on me before I came ashore that I thought it long ere I came to Kent to clear my conscience, and the God of sea and land brought me safely thither, and I hastened to Sandwich. And on a first day, being the 5th of the 4th month, 1681, I went to the steeple-house, as it was before me and had been of a long time, and in the strength of the almighty power I delivered that message which I received of the Lord Jesus, saying, 'The day is come, spoken of and foretold by the prophet, of the pouring forth of God's spirit upon all flesh, sons and daughters,' etc. [Acts 2.18–19]. And I exhorted them, both priest and people, to take heed to a measure or manifestation thereof in their own hearts, and leave off their idolatry, and come to be true spiritual worshippers. And I laid before them the danger of the one and the benefit of the other, till the priest caused me to be haled out. And when I came forth, many of his hearers followed me, and I had a good opportunity with them, and cleared myself to them, and left them. And as I was going away I felt the arising of that power that is worthy to be obeyed, and it was with me to go to them again. And when they came from their worship I met them, first the mayor and his company, then the lawyer and his, and after that the priest, with many more.[17] And I invited all to come to our spiritual worship, and I would engage that if any of them, young or old, male or female, had a message from the Lord to deliver there, that they should have liberty, and not be abused as the priest caused me to be, for the man that haled me out hurt my arm, so that it was swelled some time after. And I told the priest that he was not of the primitive faith and church of Christ testified of in scripture: for there, if anything was revealed to the standers-by or hearers, they might speak one by one, the first holding his peace.[18] And he was silent before I spoke, and he said I should not have spoken in the church. And I asked him what church that was, for I had spoken in the true church many times amongst God's people and they did not hinder me. And he said Paul spoke against a woman's speaking in the church [1 Corinthians 14.34]. I asked him what woman that was and what church that was, that she should not speak in. And he did not answer me, but went away. And a woman Friend that was with me took hold of him and said, 'My friend, answer the woman's question,' and the Dutch people were coming from their worship the while,[19] but the priest put off his hat to us and bustled away, and afterwards endeavoured to send me to prison. But the God of power, who preserved me when much evil hath been intended, prevented him, that he could not prevail with the mayor; but he endeavoured to harm the Friends of that place after that I was gone. And after the first day meeting was over, I went the beginning of the week to some other meetings, and came again a fourth day, and God's power was over all, and Friends had no harm, and we had another heavenly meeting. And so I came away and left Friends peaceable, and all was well, blessed be the Lord, and magnified be his preserving power over all for evermore. Amen saith my soul.

J.V.

I was informed that the priest above specified did do his endeavour to stir up persecution against Friends, and put the mayor to some trouble for not punishing me. But therein he did, nor could do, no more than manifest his own malice and what birth he was of. The Lord had set his bounds.

(God's Mighty Power Magnified, pp. 38–46)

Notes

1 *reprobation and election* : reprobation is preordination to eternal damnation for the sinner, and thus the opposite to election which is preordination to salvation for God's chosen people or 'elect'.

2 *professor* : someone who 'professes' to a faith. Often used derogatively to refer to those that profess a faith but whose actions belie this profession. Both a neutral and a negative meaning can be substantiated by reference to the scriptures: see 1 Timothy 6.12, Titus 1.16 and Romans 1.22.

3 *the two seeds . . . the other cursed* : Vokins comes to understand the mysteries of 'election and reprobation', the division between the 'blessed' and the 'cursed', through direct revelation, not through the explanations offered by priests and 'professors'.

4 *the light that shined in my heart* : the Quakers believed that the 'inner light' of God, within every believer, was the ultimate guide and source of authority.

5 *enlightens everyone that comes into the world* : reference to John 8.12. Interestingly, Vokins writes of the light of the world enlightening 'everyone', which John does not; this illustrates the Quaker belief in the inner light as present in everyone, if only they choose to recognize it.

6 *day of account* : day of judgment. See Matthew 12.36: 'But I say unto you, that every idle word that men shall speak, they shall give account thereof in the day of judgment.'

7 *when I was clear of* : when my conscience was clear, having done my duty.

8 *Barbados-road* : towards Barbados.

9 *first day* : Sunday. Quakers did not use the names of days or months because of their unchristian origins.

10 *point of Guadeloupe* : appears as 'point of Cordilopa' in the copytext; context and geography suggest that the reference is to Guadeloupe.

11 *Madeira wine* : 'madary wine' in copytext. A rich, sherry-like wine.

12 *conversations* : behaviour.

13 *five islands* : presumably Anguilla, Montserrat, Nevis, St Kitts, and Barbuda, which lie close to each other and were all administered by Britain.

14 *to take that which they had from them* : probably a reference to tithes, by which people had to give a proportion of their income to support the clergy, a practice vigorously opposed by the Quakers and other sects.

15 *the meetings of the negroes or blacks . . . Friends* : not all Quakers show such surprise that Christ's power should be manifested in meetings attended by black people: Alice Curwen, another Quaker travelling and preaching in the Caribbean, admonished a woman she had met in Barbados in these words: 'as for thy servants, whom thou callst thy slaves, I tell thee plainly, thou hast no right to reign over their conscience in matters of worship of the living God; for thou thyself confessedst that they had souls to save as well as we. Therefore, for time to come let them have their liberty' (Curwen 1680:17–18); she was, though, only referring to spiritual liberty.

16 *steeple-house* : church.

17 *the mayor . . . the lawyer . . . the priest* : representatives of the civil state, the legal system, and the national church, all institutions from which Friends had experienced opposition or persecution.

18 *the primitive faith . . . holding his peace* : Paul detailed those who were authorised to speak in church, and when. Vokins is here referring to the words 'if anything be revealed to another that sitteth by, let the first hold his peace' (1 Corinthians 14.30).

19 *the Dutch people* : a community of some 400 Dutch Protestant refugees had been established at Sandwich in the reign of Elizabeth; they used the church of St Clements. Quakers had strong links with Dutch Protestants, so perhaps with the appearance of numbers of potential sympathisers with Vokins the priest felt outnumbered, and hence 'bustled away'.

BIBLIOGRAPHY

Seventeenth-century publications

Unless otherwise stated, the place of publication is London.

Allen, Hannah (1683) *Satan his Methods and Malice Baffled. A Narrative of God's Gracious Dealings with that Choice Christian Mrs Hannah Allen, (Afterwards Married to Mr Hatt)*, printed by John Wallis.

[Anon] (1657) *Annotations Upon all the Books of the Old and New Testaments*, third edition.

—— (1663) *The Arraignment, Tryal and Examination of Mary Moders, Otherwise Stedman, now Carleton*, for N. Brook.

—— (1663) *The Great Tryall and Arraignment of the late Distressed Lady, Otherwise called the late German Princess*, printed for W. Gilbertson.

—— (1663) *The Lawyer's Clarke Trappan'd by the Crafty Whore of Canterbury*, for J. Johnson.

—— (1663) *A True Account of the Tryal of Mrs Mary Carleton*, for Charles Moulton.

—— (1663) *A Vindication of a Distressed Lady* [no printer].

—— (1673) *An Elegie On the Famous and Renowned Lady, for Eloquence and Wit, Madam Mary Carlton*, for Sam. Speed.

—— (1673) *The Memoires of Mary Carleton*, for Nath. Brooke.

—— (1673) *Memories of the Life of the Famous Madam Charlton*, for Phillip Brooksby.

Baxter, Richard (1673) *A Christian Directory*, R. White for N. Simmons.

Bell, Susannah (1673) *The Legacy Of A Dying Mother*, sold by John Hancock, senior and junior.

Biddle, Hester (1682) *The Trumpet Of the Lord* [no printer].

Blackborow, Sarah (1660) *The Just and Equal Balance Discovered*, for M. W.

Blaithwaite, Mary (1654) *The Complaint of Mary Blaithwaite*, [no printer].

Bourgeois, Louise (1656) 'Advice to her daughter', in T. C. et al. (eds) *The Compleat Midwifes Practice*, printed for Nathaniel Brooke.

Brown, David (1652) *The Naked Woman*, printed for E. Blackmore.

Carleton, John (1663) *The Ultimum Vale*, printed for J. Jones.

Carleton, Mary (1663a) *The Case of Madam Mary Carleton*, printed for Sam Speed and Henry Marsh.

225

—— (1663b) *An Historicall Narrative*, for Charles Moulton.

Cary, Mary (1651) *The Little Horns Doom and Downfall*, followed by *A new and more Exact Mappe or Description of New Ierusalems Glory*, [no printer].

Cavendish, Margaret (1653) *Poems, and Fancies*, T. R. for J. Martin and J. Allestrye.

—— (1656) *Natures Pictures drawn by Fancy's Pencil to the Life*, for J. Martin and J. Allestrye.

—— (1664) *Philosophical Letters*, [no printer].

—— (1667) *The Life of the thrice noble . . . William Cavendish*, London: printed by A. Maxwell.

Cellier, Elizabeth (1680) *Malice Defeated*, printed for Elizabeth Cellier and are to be sold at her house.

Cheevers, Sarah (1663) 'To All People', in Evans, Katharine and Cheevers, Sarah, *A Brief Discovery* (1663).

Clifford, Anne (1616) *Diary*, ms. Sackville of Knole U269/F48, Maidstone: Kent County Archives.

Collins, An (1653) *Divine Songs and Meditacions*, printed by R. Bishop.

Curwen, Alice (1680) *A Relation Of The Labour, Travail and Suffering of that faithful Servant of the Lord Alice Curwen*, [no printer].

Davy, Sarah (1670) *Heaven Realiz'd*, [no printer, sold by Elizabeth Calvert].

E. T. (1632) *The Lawes Resolutions of Womens Rights*, printed by the assignes of Iohn More; to be sold by Iohn Grove.

Evans, Katharine (1663) *A Brief Discovery of Gods Eternal Truth*, for R. Wilson.

Evans, Katharine and Cheevers, Sarah (1662) *This is a short Relation of some of the Cruel Sufferings (For the Truths sake) of Katharine Evans and Sarah Chevers*, printed for Robert Wilson.

Forster, Mary (1659) *These several Papers was sent to the Parliament the twentieth day of the fifth month, 1659*, printed for Mary Westwood [Quaker women's petition against tithes].

Gouge, William (1622) *Of Domesticall Duties*, John Haviland, for William Bladen.

Kirkman, Francis (1679) *The Counterfeit Lady Unveiled*, P. Parker.

Lanyer, Aemilia (1611) *Salve Deus Rex Judaeorum*, V. Simmes for R. Bonian.

Mall, Thomas (1658) *A True Account*, R. W. for Matthew Keinton.

Moore, Elizabeth (1657) 'Evidences for Heaven', in Edmund Calamy, *The Godly Man's Ark*, for John Hancock and Thomas Parkhurst.

Parr, Susanna (1659) *Susannas Apologie against the Elders*, Oxford [no printer].

Porter, Thomas (1663) *A Witty Combat*.

Rainbowe, Edward (1677) *Sermon Preached at the funeral of Anne, Countess of Pembroke*, F. Royston and H. Broom.

Rogers, John (1653) *Ohel or Beth-shemesh*, printed for R. I. and G. and H. Eversden, sold at the Grey-Hound.

Shaw, Hester (1654a) *Mrs Shaw's Innocency Restored*, printed by T. M. for G. A.

—— (1654b) *A Plaine Relation of my Sufferings* [no printer].

Simpson, Mary (1649) *Faith and Experience or, A short narration of the holy Life and Death of Mary Simpson*, for Richard Tomlins.

Stuckley, Lewis (1667; another ed. 1670) *A Gospel-Glasse*.

Trapnel, Anna (1654a) *The Cry of a Stone: or a relation of Something Spoken in Whitehall, by Anna Trapnel, being in the Visions of God*, [no printer].

—— (1654b) *Anna Trapnel's Report and Plea, or, A Narrative of her Journey from*

London into Cornwal, for Thomas Brewster.

Trye, Mary (1675) *Medicatrix, Or. The Woman-Physician.*

Turner, Jane (1653) *Choice Experiences of the Kind dealings of God before, in, and after Conversion*, printed by H. Hils, sold at the Black-spread Eagle and the Three Bibles.

Vokins, Joan (1691) *God's Mighty Power Magnified; as Manifested and Revealed in his Faithful Handmaid Joan Vokins*, for Thomas Northcott.

Walker, Henry (1652) *Spiritual Experiences of Sundry Believers.*

Waugh, Dorothy (1656) 'A relation concerning Dorothy Waughs cruell usage by the Mayor of Carlile', in *The Lambs Defence Against Lyes*, printed for Giles Calvert.

Wentworth, Anne (1677) *A Vindication of Anne Wentworth*, [no printer].

—— (1679) *The Revelation Of Jesus Christ*, [no printer].

Whateley, William (1619) 2nd edn, *A Bride Bush: Or, A Direction for Married Persons*, [no printer].

White, Elizabeth (1696) *The Experiences*, Glasgow: printed by Robert Sanders.

Volley, Hannah (1674) *A Supplement To The Queen-like Closet*, by T. R. for Richard Lownds.

Modern publications of seventeenth-century texts

Baxter, Richard, ed. N. H. Keeble (1931,1974) *The Autobiography of Richard Baxter*, London: Everyman Series, Dent.

Behn, Aphra, ed. P. Lyons (1989) *Aphra Behn: Plays, Poems and Other Writings*, Oxford: Blackwell.

Bunyan, John, ed. G. B. Harrison (1931, 1976) *Grace Abounding to the Chief of Sinners*, London: Everyman Series, Dent.

Cavendish, Margaret, ed. Sir Egerton Brydges (1814) *The Memoirs of Margaret, Duchess of Newcastle, written by herself*, Kent: Lee Priory.

Cavendish, William, ed. Douglas Grant (1965) *The Phanseys of William Cavendish Marquis of Newcastle addressed to Margaret Lucas and her Letters in Reply*, London: Nonesuch Press.

Clifford, Anne, ed. Vita Sackville-West (1923) *The Diary of the Lady Anne Clifford*, London: William Heinemann.

Collins, An, ed. Stanley Stewart (1961) *Divine Songs and Meditations, (1653)*, Los Angeles: Clark Library.

Evans, Katherine and Cheevers, Sarah (1715) *A Brief History of the Voyage of Katherine Evans and Sarah Cheevers.*

Evelyn, John, ed. E. S. de Beer (1959) *Diary*, London: Oxford University Press.

Fanshawe, Ann, and Halkett, Anne, ed. John Loftis (1979) *The Memoirs of Anne, Lady Halkett and Ann, Lady Fanshawe*, Oxford: Clarendon Press.

Fowler, Constance, et al., ed. Arthur Clifford (1815) *Tixall Letters; Or the correspondence of the Aston Family and their Friends, During the Seventeenth Century*, 2 volumes, London.

Fox, George, ed. Norman Penney (1911) *Journal*, 2 volumes, Cambridge: Cambridge University Press.

Fox, George, ed. Henry J. Cadbury (1948) *George Fox's 'Book of Miracles'*, Cambridge: Cambridge University Press.

King, Gregory, ed. George E. Barnett (1936) *Two Tracts: a) Natural and Political*

Observations and Conclusions upon the State and Condition of England; b) Of the Naval Trade of England A⁰ 1688 and the national Profit then arising thereby (1696), Baltimore: Johns Hopkins Press.

Knatchbull, Lady Lucy, ed. David Knowles (1931) *The Life of Lady Lucy Knatchbull*, London: Sheed & Ward.

Milton, John, ed. John Carey and Alastair Fowler (1968) *The Poems of John Milton*, London: Longman.

Mordaunt, Elizabeth, (1856) *The Private Diaries of Elizabeth Viscountess Mordaunt*, Duncairn.

Osborne, Dorothy, ed. Kenneth Parker (1987) *Letters to William Temple*, Harmondsworth: Penguin.

Penington, Mary, (1821) *Some Account of the Circumstance of the Life of Mary Penington, from her Manuscript, Left for her Family*, London: Harvey & Darton.

Pepys, Samuel, ed. Robert Latham and William Matthews (1970–83) *Diary*, 11 volumes, London: Bell & Hyman.

Rich, Mary, Countess of Warwick (1847) *Diary*, published by the Religious Tract Society.

Rich, Mary, Countess of Warwick, ed. T. C. Croker (1848) *Autobiography*, London.

Sidney, Dorothy, Countess of Sunderland (1819) 'Letters to George Saville, Earl of Halifax, in 1680', in *Some Account of the Life of Rachel Wriothesley, Lady Russell, by the editor of Madam du Deffard's Letters*, London: Longman, Hurst, Rees, Orme, and Brown.

Thornton, Alice (1873) *The Autobiography of Mrs Alice Thornton of East Newton, Co. York*, Yorkshire: Surtees Society, Vol.62.

Whateley, William (1975; first published 1617) *A Bride Bush or A Wedding Sermon*, Amsterdam, Norwood, NJ: Walter J. Johnson Inc.

Wriothesley, Rachel, Lady Russell (1853) *Letters of Rachel, Lady Russell*, 2 volumes, London: Longman.

Secondary sources

Anderson, Linda (1986) 'At the threshold of the self: women and autobiography', in Moira Monteith (ed.) *Women's Writing: A Challenge to Theory*, Brighton: Harvester.

Aylmer, G. E. (ed.) (1972) *The Interregnum: The Quest for Settlement 1646–1660*, London: Macmillan.

Baker, J. H. (1971) *An Introduction to English Legal History*, London: Butterworth.

Bauman, Richard (1983) *Let Your Words Be Few: Symbolism of Speaking and Silence Among Seventeenth-Century Quakers*, Cambridge: Cambridge University Press.

Beer, Gillian (1970) *The Romance*, London: Methuen.

Belsey, Catherine (1985) *The Subject of Tragedy: Identity and Difference in Renaissance Drama*, London and New York: Methuen.

Bernbaum, Ernest (1914) *The Mary Carleton Narratives 1663–1673: A Missing Chapter in the History of the English Novel*, Cambridge, Mass.: Harvard University Press.

Bottrall, Margaret (1958) *Every Man A Phoenix*, London: John Murray.

Bowerbank, Sylvia (1984) 'The spider's delight: Margaret Cavendish and the "female" imagination', *English Literary Renaissance* 14(3):392–408.

Brailsford, Mabel Richmond (1915) *Quaker Women 1650–1690*, London: Duckworth.

Braithwaite, W. C. (1919) *The Second Period of Quakerism*, London: Macmillan.

Burn, J. S. (1846) *The History of the French, Walloon, Dutch and other Protestant Refugees Settled in England*, London: Macmillan.

Burr, Anna (1909) *The Autobiography: A Critical and Comparative Study*, Boston and New York: Houghton Mifflin Co.

Burrage, Champlin (1911) 'Anna Trapnel's prophecies', *English Historical Review* 25:526–35.

Butler, Richard (1968) *The Difficult Art of Autobiography*, Oxford: Clarendon Press.

Calamy, Edmund (1778) *Nonconformist Memorials*, 2 vols.

Caldwell, Patricia (1983) *The Puritan Conversion Narrative. The Beginnings of American Expression*, Cambridge: Cambridge University Press.

Cameron, Deborah (1986) 'What is the nature of women's oppression in language?', *Oxford Literary Review* 8(1–2):79–87.

Capp, B. S. (1972) *The Fifth Monarchy Men: A Study in Seventeenth Century English Millenarianism*, London: Faber.

—— (1984) 'The Fifth Monarchists and popular millenarianism', in J. F. McGregor and B. Reay (eds) *Radical Religion in the English Revolution*, Oxford: Oxford University Press.

Cavaliero, Glen (1985) 'Autobiography and fiction', *Prose Studies* 8(2):156–71.

Clark, Alice (1919; republished 1982) *The Working Life of Women in the Seventeenth Century*, London: Routledge & Kegan Paul.

Clifford, H. (1911) *Early History of Nonconformity in Bourton-on-the-Water, Gloucestershire*, London: J. H. Alden.

Coate, Mary (1933) *Cornwall in the Great Civil War and Interregnum*, Oxford: Oxford University Press.

Cook, Chris and Wroughton, John (1980) *English Historical Facts (1603–1688)*, London: Macmillan.

Collinson, Patrick (1984) 'The religion of Protestants: the church in English society 1559–1625', in J. F. McGregor and B. Reay (eds) *Radical Religion in the English Revolution*, Oxford: Oxford University Press.

Cranfield, Geoffrey (1978) *The Press and Society from Caxton to Northcliffe*, London: Longman.

Crawford, Patricia (1985) 'Women's published writings 1600–1700', in Mary Prior (ed.) *Women in English Society 1500–1800*, London: Methuen.

Cressy, David (1980) *Literacy and the Social Order: Reading and Writing in Tudor and Stuart England*, Cambridge: Cambridge University Press.

Cross, Claire (1976) *Church and People 1450–1660*, London, Fontana.

Cruden, Alexander, ed. C. H. Irwin and A. D. Adams (1930; 1977 edition) *Cruden's Complete Concordance to the Bible*, Cambridge: Lutterworth Press.

Culler, Jonathon (1974) 'Introduction' to F. de Saussure, *Course in General Linguistics*, London: Fontana/Collins.

Davies, K. M. (1977) 'The sacred condition of equality', *Social History* 5:563–80.

Davis, Natalie Zemon (1975a) 'Women on top', in *Society and Culture in Early Modern France*, London: Duckworth.

—— (1975b) 'The reasons of misrule', in *Society and Culture in Early Modern France*, London: Duckworth.

Delany, Paul (1969) *British Autobiography in the Seventeenth Century*, London: Routledge & Kegan Paul.

Dodd, Philip (1985) 'Criticism and the autobiographical tradition', *Prose Studies* 8 (2: special issue: 'Modern selves: essays on modern British and American autobiography'):1–13.

—— (1987) 'Literature, fictiveness and the dilemma of nonfiction', *Prose Studies* 10(1):5–8.

Ebner, Dean (1971) *Autobiography in Seventeenth-Century England: Theology and the Self*, The Hague: Mouton.

Edkins, Carol (1980) 'Quest for community: spiritual autobiographies of eighteenth century Quaker and Puritan women in America', in Estelle C. Jelinek (ed.) *Women's Autobiography: Essays in Criticism*, Bloomington and London: Indiana University Press.

Ferguson, Moira (ed.) (1985) *First Feminists: British Women Writers, 1578–1799*, Bloomington, Old Westbury NY: Indiana University Press, Feminist Press.

Findley, Sandra and Hobby, Elaine (1981) 'Seventeenth century women's autobiography', in Francis Barker, Jay Bernstein, John Coombes, Peter Hulme, Jennifer Stone, Jon Stratton (eds) *1642: Literature and Power in the Seventeenth Century. Proceedings of the Essex conference on the Sociology of Literature, July 1980*, Colchester: University of Essex Press.

Fraser, Antonia (1984) *The Weaker Vessel: Woman's Lot in Seventeenth-century England*, London: Weidenfeld & Nicolson.

Gilbert, Davies (1838) *The Parochial History of Cornwall*, 4 volumes, London.

Gillespie, J. T. (1943?) 'Presbyterianism in Devon and Cornwall in the seventeenth century', unpublished MA thesis, University of Durham.

Graff, Harvey J. (ed.) (1981) *Literacy and Social Development in the West: A Reader*, Cambridge: Cambridge University Press.

Grant, Douglas (1957) *Margaret the First: A Biography of Margaret Cavendish Duchess of Newcastle 1623–1673*, London: Rupert Hart-Davis.

Greaves, Richard L. and Zaller, Robert (1982–4) *Biographical Directory of British Radicals in the Seventeenth Century*, 3 volumes, Brighton: Harvester.

Greer, Germaine, Medoff, Jeslyn, Sansone, Melinda and Hastings, Susan (eds) (1988) *Kissing the Rod: An Anthology of Seventeenth-Century Women's Verse*, London: Virago.

Grendler, Paul I. (1977) *The Roman Inquisition and the Venetian Press*, Princeton, New Jersey: Princeton University Press.

Hageman, Elizabeth H. (1988) 'Recent studies in women writers of the English seventeenth century (1604–1674)', *English Literary Renaissance* 18(1):138–67.

Haliczer, Stephen ed. and trans. (1987) *Inquisition and Society in Early-Modern Europe*, London: Croom Helm.

Haller, William and Malleville (1941–2) 'The Puritan Art of Love', *Huntington Library Quarterly* 5:235–72.

Hannay, Margaret P. (ed.) (1985) *Silent But for the Word: Tudor Women as Patrons, Translators, and Writers of Religious Works*, Kent, Ohio: Kent State University Press.

Hartmann, Heinz (1964) 'Comments on the psychoanalytical theory of the ego' in his *Essays on Ego Psychology*, New York: International Universities Press.

Heilbrun, Carolyn G. (1985) 'Women's autobiographical writings: new forms', *Prose Studies* 8(2):14–28.

Henderson, Katherine Usher and McManus, Barbara F. (1985) *Half Humankind: Contexts and Texts of the Controversy about Women in England, 1540–1640*, Urbana and Chicago: University of Illinois Press.

Henning, Basil Duke (1983) *The History of Parliament: The House of Commons 1660–1690*, London: Secker & Warburg.

Henningsen, Gustav and Tedeschi, John, with C. Amiel (1986) *The Inquisition in Early-Modern Europe: Studies on Sources and Methods*, Decalb, Illinois: Northern Illinois University Press.

Heppenstall, Rayner (1981) *Tales from the Newgate Calendar*, London: Constable.

Higgins, Patricia (1973) 'The reactions of women, with special reference to women petitioners', in Brian Manning (ed.) *Politics, Religion and the English Civil War*, London: Edward Arnold.

Hill, Christopher (1961; republished 1980) *The Century of Revolution 1603–1714*, Walton on Thames: Nelson.

—— (1972; republished 1975) *The World Turned Upside Down: Radical Ideas during the English Revolution*, Harmondworth: Penguin.

Hobby, Elaine (1984) 'English women's writing 1649–1688', unpub. Ph.D. thesis, University of Birmingham.

—— (1988) *Virtue of Necessity: English Women's Writing 1649–1688*, London: Virago.

Holmes, Martin (1975) *Proud Northern Lady: Lady Anne Clifford 1590–1676*, London: Phillimore.

Ingram, Martin (1985) 'The reform of popular culture? Sex and marriage in Early Modern England', in B. Reay (ed.) *Popular Culture in Early Modern England*, London: Croom Helm.

Jacobson, Edith (1964) *The Self and the Object World*, New York: International Universities Press.

Jelinek, Estelle C. (1980) *Women's Autobiography: Essays in Criticism*, Bloomington and London: Indiana University Press.

Jones, Ann Rosalind (1986) 'Surprising fame: Renaissance gender ideologies and women's lyric', in Nancy K. Miller (ed.) *The Poetics of Gender*, New York and Guildford, Surrey: Columbia University Press.

Keeble, N. H. (1986) 'The autobiographer as apologist: *Reliquiae Baxterianae* (1696)', *Prose Studies* 9(2):105–19.

Kohut, Heinz (1971) *The Analysis of the Self*, New York: International Universities Press.

—— (1977) *The Restoration of the Self*, New York: International Universities Press.

Kristeva, Julia (1974) ed. Leon S. Roudiez (1984) *Revolution in Poetic Language*, New York: Columbia University Press.

Kristeva, Julia (1987) 'The pain of sorrow in the modern world: the works of Marguerite Duras', translated by Katharine A. Jensen, *PMLA* 102:138–52. Translation of (1987) 'La maladie de la douleur: Duras', in *Soleil noir: mélancolie et dépression*, Paris: Gallimard.

Lacan, Jacques (1951) trans. and ed. Anthony Wilden (1968) *The Language of the*

Self: the Function of Language in Psychoanalysis, Baltimore and London: John Hopkins University Press.

―――― (1966) *Ecrits*, Paris: Editions de Seuil.

Lake, Peter (1987) 'Feminine piety and personal potency: the "emancipation" of Mrs Jane Ratcliffe', *The Seventeenth Century* 2(2):143–65.

Larner, Christina (1981) *Enemies of God: The Witchhunt in Scotland*, London: Chatto & Windus.

Layton, Lynne and Schapiro, Barbara Ann, (eds) (1986) *Narcissism and the Text: Studies in Literature and the Psychology of the Self*, New York and London: New York University Press.

Louvre, Alf (1987) 'Signs of the Times', *Literature and History*, 13.

McArthur, E. A. (1909) 'Women petitioners and the Long Parliament', *English Historical Review* 24:698–709.

Macdonald, Michael (1986) 'The secularisation of suicide in England 1660–1800, *Past and Present* 111:50–97.

McFarlane, Alan (1986) *Marriage and Love in England: Modes of Reproduction 1300–1840*, Oxford and New York: Basil Blackwell.

McGregor, J. F. (1984) 'The Baptists: fount of all heresy', in J. F. McGregor and B. Reay (eds) *Radical Religion and the English Revolution*, Oxford: Oxford University Press.

McKeown, Michael (1987) *The Origins of the English Novel 1660–1740*, Baltimore and London: Johns Hopkins University Press.

Main, C. F. 'The German Princess: or, Mary Carleton in fact and fiction', *Harvard Library Bulletin* 10.

de Man, Paul (1983) *Blindness and Insight*, London: Methuen.

Marcus, Laura (1987) 'Coming out in print: woman's autobiographical writing revisited', *Prose Studies* 10(1):102–07.

Mason, Mary (1980) 'The other voice: autobiographies of women writers', in James Olney (ed.) *Autobiography: Essays Theoretical and Critical*, Princeton and Guildford, Surrey: Princeton University Press.

Matthews, William (1955) *British Autobiography: An Annotated Bibliography of British Autobiographies Published or Written Before 1951*, New York: Archon Books.

Mehlman, J. (1974) *A Structural Study of Autobiography: Proust, Leiris, Sartre and Levi-Strauss*, Ithaca, New York: Cornell University Press.

Mendelson, Sara (1985) 'Stuart women's diaries and occasional memoirs', in Mary Prior (ed.) *Women in English Society 1500–1800*, London: Methuen.

Milsom, S. F. C. (1969) *Historical Foundations of the Canon Law*, London: Butterworth.

Morgan, Fidelis (1981) *The Female Wits: Women Playwrights on the London Stage 1660–1720*, London: Virago.

Morton, Arthur (1970) *The World of the Ranters*, London: Lawrence and Wishart.

Olney, James (1980) *Autobiography: Essays Theoretical and Critical*, Princeton and Guildford, Surrey: Princeton University Press.

Plant, Marjorie (1965) *The English Book Trade: An Economic History of the Making and Sale of Books*, London: Allen & Unwin.

Pollock, Linda (1983) *Forgotten Children: Parent–Child Relations from 1500–1900*, Cambridge, New York, New Rochelle, Melbourne, Sidney: Cambridge University Press.

—— (1987) *A Lasting Relationship: Parents and Children over Three Centuries*, London: Fourth Estate.

Polsue, Joseph (1867–73), *A Complete Parochial History of the County of Cornwall*, 4 volumes, London and Truro: John Camden Hotten and W. Lake.

Pomerleau, Cynthia S. (1980) 'The emergence of women's autobiography in England', in Estelle C. Jelinek (ed.) *Women's Autobiography*, Bloomington and London: Indiana University Press.

Powell, Chilton (1917) *English Domestic Relations 1487–1653*, New York: Columbia University Press.

Prior, Mary (ed.) (1985) *Women in English Society 1500–1800*, London: Methuen.

Reay, Barry (1984a) 'Radicalism and religion in the English revolution: an introduction', in J. F. McGregor and B. Reay (eds) *Radical Religion in the English Revolution*, Oxford: Oxford University Press.

—— (1984b) 'Quakerism and society', in J. F. McGregor and B. Reay (eds) *Radical Religion in the English Revolution*, Oxford: Oxford University Press.

—— (1985a) 'Introduction: popular culture in Early Modern England', in B. Reay (ed.) *Popular Culture in Seventeenth Century England*, London: Croom Helm.

—— (1985b) 'Popular religion', in B. Reay (ed.) *Popular Culture in Seventeenth-Century England*, London: Croom Helm.

—— (1985c) *The Quakers and the English Revolution*, London: Temple Smith.

Rose, Mary Beth (1986) 'Gender, genre, and history: seventeenth-century English women and the art of autobiography', in Mary Beth Rose (ed.), *Women in the Middle Ages and the Renaissance: Literary and Historical Perspectives*, Syracuse, NY: Syracuse University Press.

Ross, Isabel (1949) *Margaret Fell: Mother of Quakerism*, London, New York, Toronto: Longman, Green & Co.

Sanders, Valerie (1986) '"Absolutely an act of duty": choice of profession in autobiographies by Victorian women', *Prose Studies* 9(3):54–70.

Sharpe, James (1985) 'The people and the law', in B. Reay (ed.) *Popular Culture in Seventeenth Century England*, London: Croom Helm.

Shepherd, Simon (ed.) (1985) *The Women's Sharp Revenge: Five Women's Pamphlets from the Renaissance*, London: Fourth Estate.

Shumaker, Wayne (1954) *English Autobiography: Its Emergence, Materials and Form*, California: University of California Press.

Siebert, Frederick (1952) *Freedom of the Press in England 1476–1776*, Urbana: University of Illinois Press.

Spencer, Jane (1986) *The Rise of the Woman Novelist: From Aphra Behn to Jane Austen*, Oxford: Basil Blackwell.

Spengemann, William C. (1980) *The Forms of Autobiography: Episodes in the History of a Literary Genre*, New Haven and London: Yale University Press.

Spooner, Barbara C. (1935) *John Tregagle of Trevorder, Man and Ghost*, Truro: A. W. Jordan.

Spufford, Margaret (1979) 'First steps in literacy: the reading and writing experiences of the humblest seventeenth century spiritual autobiographers', *Social History* 4(3):407–35. Reprinted in Harvey J. Graff (ed.) (1981) *Literacy and Social Development in the West: A Reader*, Cambridge: Cambridge University Press.

—— (1981) *Small Books and Pleasant Histories*, London: Methuen.

Stanley, Liz (1988) 'Writing Feminist Auto/biography', unpub. paper read to the

Manchester Feminist Research Seminar.

Stanley, Liz and Scott, Sue, (eds) (1986-8) *Writing Feminist Biography*, Manchester: SSP, Sociology Department, University of Manchester.

Stanton, Domna C. (ed.) (1987) *The Female Autograph*, Chicago and London: University of Chicago Press. Originally published (1984) 'The female autograph' in *The New York Literary Forum* 12–13.

Stauffer, Donald (1930) *English Biography Before 1700*, Cambridge, Mass: Harvard University Press.

Steedman, Carolyn (1988) 'Life Studies: Women's biography and autobiography', in *My Guy to Sci-Fi*, ICA tape of talk given, ICA, London.

Stewart, Louise and Wilcox, Helen (1989) '"Why hath this lady writ her own life?": studying early female autobiography', in Ann Thompson and Helen Wilcox (eds) *Teaching Women: Feminism and English Studies*, Manchester: Manchester University Press.

Stone, Albert E. (ed.) (1981) *The American Autobiography: A Collection of Critical Essays*, Englewood Cliff, New Jersey: Prentice-Hall.

Thomas, Keith (1958) 'Women and the civil war sects', *Past and Present* 13:42–62.

Thompson, John B. (1984) *Studies in the Theory of Ideology*, Cambridge: Polity Press.

Thompson, Roger (1974) *Women in Stuart England and America: A Comparative Study*, London: Routledge & Kegan Paul.

Thomson, John A. F. (1965) *The Later Lollards 1414–1520*, London: Oxford University Press.

Tilley, M. P. (1950) *Dictionary of the Proverbs in England in the Sixteenth and Seventeenth Centuries*, Ann Arbor: University of Michigan Press.

Towgood, Micarah (n.d.) 'An imperfect Account of the Succession of Ministers in the Several Dissenting Congregations in the County of Devonshire', Dr Williams's Library ms. 24.60.

Turner, G. L. (1914) *Original Records of Early Nonconformity Under Persecution and Indulgence*, 3 volumes, London: T. Fisher Unwin.

—— (n.d.,a.) 'Extracts from the Common Council Minute Books' c.1632–85, Dr Williams's Library ms. 89.14.

—— (n.d.,b) 'The first ten years of Nonconformity in London', Dr Williams's Library ms. 89.9.

Underwood, A. C. (1947) *A History of the English Baptists*, London: The Baptist Union Publication Dept (Kingsgate Press).

Venn, J. and Venn, J. A. (1922–27) *Alumni Cantabrigiensis*, 4 vols, Cambridge: University of Cambridge Press.

Vivien, J. L. (ed.) (1887) *The Visitation of Cornwall, comprising the Heralds' Visitations of 1530, 1573 and 1620*, Exeter: William Pollard and Co.

Watkins, Owen (1972) *The Puritan Experience: Studies in Spiritual Autobiography*, London: Routledge & Kegan Paul.

Watson, Foster (ed.) (1912) *Vives and the Renascence Education of Women*, London: Edward Arnold.

Watt, Ian (1957) *The Rise of the Novel. Studies in Defoe, Richardson and Fielding*, London: Chatto & Windus.

Watts, Michael (1978) *The Dissenters, Volume 1: From the Reformation to the French Revolution*, Oxford: Clarendon Press.

Webber, Joan (1968) *The Eloquent 'I': Style and Self in Seventeenth Century Prose*,

Madison, WI and London: University of Wisconsin Press.

Weintraub, Karl J. (1978) *The Value of the Individual: Self and Circumstance in Autobiography*, Chicago and London: University of Chicago Press.

White, B. R. ((1983) *The English Baptists of the Seventeenth Century*, London: Baptists Historical Society.

Whiting, C. E. (1931) *Studies in English Puritanism from the Restoration to the Revolution 1660–1680*, London: Macmillan, for The Society for the Promoting of Christian Knowledge.

Wilden, Anthony (1972) *System and Structure: Essays in Communication and Exchange*, London: Tavistock.

Williams, Raymond (1977) *Marxism and Literature*, Oxford: Oxford University Press.

Williamson, G. C. (1967) *Lady Anne Clifford Countess of Dorset, Pembroke and Montgomery 1590–1676: Her Life, Letters and Work*, Wakefield: SR Publishers (reissue of 1922 edition, Kendal: Titus Wilson and Son).

Wilson, Walter (1808) *The History and Antiquities of Dissenting Churches and Meeting Houses in London, Westminster and Southwark; including the Lives of their Ministers, from the Rise of Nonconformity to the Present Time*, 2 volumes, London.

Woodbridge, Linda (1984) *Women and the English Renaissance: Literature and the Nature of Womanhood, 1540–1620*, Brighton: Harvester.

Woolrych, Austin (1982) *Commonwealth to Protectorate*, Oxford: Clarendon Press.

Wright, Louis B. (1935) *Middle Class Culture in Elizabethan England*, Chapel Hill: University of North Carolina Press.

Yeo, Stephen (1988) 'Difference, autobiography and history', *Literature and History* 14(1).

INDEX

THEIR GUILTY PLEASURES

June Tate

severn
House

This first world edition published 2011
in Great Britain and in the USA by
SEVERN HOUSE PUBLISHERS LTD of
9–15 High Street, Sutton, Surrey, England, SM1 1DF.
Trade paperback edition first published
in Great Britain and the USA 2012 by
SEVERN HOUSE PUBLISHERS LTD

British Library Cataloguing in Publication Data

Tate, June.
  Their guilty pleasures.
  1. World War, 1939-1945–Women–Great Britain–Fiction.
  2. World War, 1939-1945–Social aspects–Great Britain–
  Fiction. 3. Americans–Great Britain–Fiction.
  4. Prisoners of war–Germany–Fiction. 5. Prisoners of
  war–Great Britain–Fiction. 6. Love stories.
  I. Title
  823.9'14–dc22

ISBN-13: 978-0-7278-8077-2 (cased)
ISBN-13: 978-1-84751-375-5 (trade paper)

All Severn House titles are printed on acid-free paper.

Severn House Publishers support The Forest Stewardship Council [FSC],
the leading international forest certification organisation. All our titles that
are printed on Greenpeace-approved FSC-certified paper carry the FSC logo.

Typeset by Palimpsest Book Produ
Falkirk, Stirlingshire, Scotland.
Printed and bound in Great Britai
MPG Books Ltd., Bodmin, Cornv

THEIR GUILTY PLEASURES

A Selection of Titles by June Tate

RICHES OF THE HEART
NO ONE PROMISED ME TOMORROW
FOR THE LOVE OF A SOLDIER
BETTER DAYS
NOTHING IS FOREVER
FOR LOVE OR MONEY
EVERY TIME YOU SAY GOODBYE
TO BE A LADY
WHEN SOMEBODY LOVES YOU
THE TALK OF THE TOWN
A FAMILY AFFAIR
THE RELUCTANT SINNER
BORN TO DANCE
THEIR GUILTY PLEASURES

For my elder daughter Beverley, who survived a horrendous car crash with such bravery and courage. Whose mental attitude in the months that followed was incredible, and who never lost her sense of humour.

Amazing!

Acknowledgements

To Janet and Richard Cartwright in Stafford, who proved their friendship far beyond the call of duty. Ronnie, Beverley and I could not have managed without you. My grateful thanks.

Prologue

Southampton, June 1940

Jenny Procter stood at the French windows of her drawing room, looking out over the large garden before her. The rhododendron bushes were in full bloom, the horse chestnut trees full of leaf, and there was the promise of a bumper crop of fruit. Beyond one of the large lawns, the gardener was digging the earth and planting vegetables which had been started in the greenhouse. It was a peaceful scene, yet in Europe the Germans had swept through France. The phoney war was over and the nation stood ready to defend its coastline.

Adam Procter was to leave his prestigious post as bank manager at the National Provincial Bank and join the Hampshire Regiment. As an officer in the Territorial Army, it was to be expected, and Jenny stood wondering just how it would feel when his presence was no longer part of her daily life.

Her husband of fifteen years was heavy maintenance. Extremely fastidious about his appearance, demanding perfection in the ironing of his clothes, the upkeep of the home and the constant entertaining of his most wealthy clients, which with wartime rationing, was a headache for any housewife.

Jenny let out a deep sigh. She was tired. She had spent the previous days laundering, packing underwear and shirts – which, of course, had been meticulously ironed – and, in the odd moment, she felt it would be a relief when Adam was gone . . . and immediately was overcome with a sense of guilt. After all, he would be transferred to France to fight the enemy. She gave a wry smile. It would have to be a brave man that had to face her husband. She knew that the staff at the bank tried their best to please their boss, rather than face his wrath. His quick temper would be another thing that she wouldn't miss either, concluded the lovely Mrs Procter as she made her way to the kitchen.

★   ★   ★

Adam Procter was in his office at the end of the days banking, sipping a gin and tonic, bidding farewell to some of the senior members of the staff, introducing them to the man who would take his place. He had mixed emotions as he chatted, making polite conversation, anxious to get away, now the time had come. He had enjoyed his prestigious position in the bank and his standing in the upper echelon of society in the town and knew he would miss it, but he felt the rank of captain would offer some sort of compensation. He eventually took his leave, calling a taxi to take him home.

As the vehicle made its way along the Avenue towards Chilworth, he gave a soft smile of satisfaction. He had done well, achieved much in his life. Had reached a good position in business, had been able to afford a large house in a high-class neighbourhood and was married to a woman who was not only beautiful, but who also had been able to grow with him as he climbed the ladder of success. Yes, he had really made it, and when the war was over he would return to the bank and take his place in society once more. After all, the war couldn't last that long. It would be, in many ways, an adventure.

As a natural-born leader, he mused, he had enjoyed the military side and had thrived on the training – being in command. In one way, he was looking forward to the change. He liked a challenge, indeed he thrived on it!

Jenny heard the front door open. 'Is that you, darling?' she called.

Adam walked into the drawing room and taking off his jacket hung it carefully round the back of a chair. He loosened his tie as he walked towards his wife and gave her a brief kiss.

'How did today go?' she asked.

Adam walked over to the sideboard and poured two drinks. 'It was fine. Everyone was very kind; you know, lots of good wishes, lots of hand shaking, a few drinks. The new man seemed all right, but a bit weak I thought. Too nice by far! You need to have a firm grip at the top to keep your staff in control. But of course he's older – that, and the fact that he has bad eyesight, has kept him out of the forces.'

Jenny secretly thought how the staff would appreciate a man

who wasn't so controlling and, irritated by Adam's attitude, said: 'Of course, he's had more years in banking than you. With so much experience, he must know what he's doing, otherwise the bank wouldn't have kept him on.'

'Who knows!' With that Adam changed the subject. 'Is everything ready for tomorrow?'

'Yes, everything is packed, uniform pressed, shoes cleaned. All you have to do is pack your toiletries just before you go. I can't believe we have only twenty-four hours left and then you'll be on your way.'

He heard the note of uncertainty in her voice and saw the look of concern in her eyes. It suddenly hit him as to how much he was leaving behind. Until this moment there had been so much to do at the bank to prepare for the handover that he'd had little time to think. Suddenly, the reality of it all was painfully apparent.

He took Jenny into his arms and kissed her, wanting to feel the closeness of her, the comfort of her warm body. His kiss became more insistent as he felt her respond. He took her by the hand and led her upstairs to the bedroom.

Once there, he undressed her slowly, caressing her, kissing her, telling her how much he would miss her, until the two of them lay on the bed, their bodies entwined.

As Adam thrust himself inside her, Jenny sensed the desperation in his love-making. Unexpectedly, her husband had shown a certain vulnerability – but only for a moment. Knowing him as she did, she knew that he would soon be in control of his emotions once again. She opened her eyes and saw the relief on his face as, above her, he reached his climax. Yes, things were back to normal.

The following afternoon, a military car arrived at the house to take Adam, immaculately dressed in his uniform, to join his regiment; he handed his baggage to the driver and turned towards his wife.

'I'll call you when I know what's happening of course, but I'll be busy for the next couple of days, so don't worry if you don't hear from me. Take care.' He leaned forward and kissed her goodbye. There was no warmth or affection in his lips. It was a duty performed; his mind was now elsewhere.

Jenny watched the car drive away. She felt as if a weight had been lifted from her shoulders, and with a sense of relief, she walked back into the house. She was determined to fill her time and do something useful with her new-found freedom, but at the same time she was mindful of the dangers that lay ahead for her husband and prayed he would be safe.

One

It was almost three years to the day since Adam had left to join the army, Jenny mused as she opened a letter from him. So much had happened during the intervening years. Southampton had been decimated by the Blitz in 1940, and since then the war had escalated in Europe. Many children had been evacuated to other parts of the country, and a few were even taken abroad – some to the United States of America, others to Canada. This summer, the town had been invaded by American troops who would be using the docks to receive and send supplies – and their troops to the battlefields. Jenny was now on a committee set up to help them integrate into the British way of life, during their stay.

She read the letter. It was brief and to the point. Aware that censorship was essential, Adam, unable to say where he was, kept the details succinct. He was fine, the regiment was doing well, there had been some fighting, but he was unscathed. He hoped she was in good health, and he was happy that she was doing her bit for the war effort. There were no words of love or affection, except at the end he told her that he missed her. But it seemed a perfunctory remark – without meaning.

With a sigh, Jenny put the letter in a drawer with the others. She'd answer it tonight, but now she was off to a meeting where she was to liaise with an officer in charge of the welfare of the American troops that had been arriving by the truckload. It had been decided to hold a dance at the Guildhall, to introduce the troops to the locals. Jenny herself was not at all sure this was a good idea, but realized that sooner or later the local dances would be full of the visiting troops anyway. She foresaw a certain amount of friction between the British boys – both the troops and the local boys who were yet to be called up – and the gregarious Yanks, with their superior uniforms and pockets full of money. The red-light district was doing a roaring trade, according to the police, which put even more pressure on them as they dealt with drunken brawls to try and keep the peace and entente cordial with the Americans.

Jenny made her way to the headquarters of the 14th Port and was taken to the office of Captain Brad Jackson. The soldier accompanying her tapped on the door and, being told to enter, announced her.

'Mrs Procter, sir.'

A tall man, with mid-brown hair and blue eyes, stood up and offered her his hand. 'Mrs Procter, how nice to meet you. Please sit down.'

His voice had a soft accent and was cultured, she noticed, not as loud and brash as some she'd heard on the High Street as the troops investigated their new surroundings and eyed up the local talent.

'Would you like some coffee?' he offered. 'Or would you prefer tea?'

Jenny chuckled. 'I'd prefer coffee, thank you, Captain Jackson. I'm led to believe the Americans are unable to make a decent cup of tea as yet.'

He started to laugh and his eyes twinkled. 'Just give us time, Mrs Procter, just give us time.'

During the following hour, they discussed how they could show the troops the British way of life. Ideas such as inviting some of them into local households on a Sunday, and putting on baseball matches, to show the Brits American sports, were talked about. During this time, they exchanged a few personal details. Jenny told him about Adam, and his having to leave his position in the bank. She asked the American what he did in civilian life. He told her he was a doctor.

Jenny wondered if this charming man had left a wife and children behind, but didn't feel able to question him too closely after such a brief introduction, but when he confessed to having a couple of horses at home, and told her how much he missed riding them, she was delighted. It had been the one thing that had kept her spirits up during these hard times. Near to her home was a riding stable where at weekends she would go and help muck out the horses, as many of the staff were now in the forces, and she would ride out whenever she could, to keep the horses exercised.

'Do you have any free time this coming Sunday, Captain Jackson?' she asked.

He looked a little surprised. 'As a matter of fact I have. Why do you ask?'

'How would you like to go riding?'

He beamed at her. 'Are you serious?'

'Absolutely!' Then she explained. 'You will have to do a bit of mucking out first though. Would you mind that?'

'I can't think of a better way to spend my time! Somehow, around horses I can relax completely.'

'I know just what you mean!' she exclaimed. 'I feel exactly the same. It's like gardening, totally therapeutic.' She then gave him her address and directions. 'Can you be there at nine thirty in the morning?'

He said that he could, and they parted company.

As she walked back through the town, Jenny thought what a nice man Captain Jackson appeared to be. For her part she would welcome his company. She didn't mind riding alone, but with him she could show him the surroundings, familiar to her but for the American it would be a new experience and she would review it again – but through his eyes, which would be interesting.

Rusty Dobbs reluctantly pushed back her bedcovers and moaned as she got to her feet. She was seriously hung over! She staggered into the kitchen, poured herself a glass of water and drank thirstily. Her mouth felt like the bottom of a birdcage. She peered into the mirror and grimaced. If this war continued for much longer she would be old before her time. My God these Yanks could drink! Not that there was a great deal of spirits to be had these days in any of the bars, but all the GIs that had shared her bed had always seemed to be able to produce a half bottle of bourbon from their back pockets. She didn't enjoy the sweetness of the liquor – she preferred a drop of gin – but with the shortages, you took what was on hand and didn't complain.

Walking back to the bedroom, she sat on the bed, opened a drawer in the small bedside table and counted her money. It had been a good night! But she was tired. *This is a hell of a way to earn a living*, she thought as she washed her face and cleaned her teeth. But she'd been on the game these past four years, ever since she'd had a row with her mother and stormed out of the house. She'd never returned. Her father had walked out a couple of years before she had, unable to live with his harridan of a wife. He'd signed on with one of the shipping lines just before the war and had jumped ship in Australia. He had written to her and told her what he'd done and advised her to make her own way in life as soon as she was able.

Rusty loved her father and knew he would be horrified if he knew how she made a living. But life on the streets had hardened her. It could be dangerous dealing with strange men who were prepared to pay for sex. The majority were just lonely and wanted a woman, but there were those who had frightened her as soon as they had closed the door to the bedroom, trapping her inside. She had a few scars to show for those times and some very bad memories, which sometimes caused her to have nightmares.

She could have got a job in a factory, at least that was safe, but life would have been so dull. She was a gregarious young woman and loved to party. The war had made many lose their inhibitions, knowing that their life expectancy could be curtailed, and there was a certain air of jollity in people, determined to enjoy themselves whilst they could . . . and she was one of them.

Rusty took a hairbrush to her long tresses. The light auburn hair really was her crowning glory. She wore it long and loose, knowing this was how most men liked it. Not for her the victory roll, the most fashionable hairstyle these days. Her clients loved to run their fingers through her locks. Many said her hair reminded them of Rita Hayworth, the glamorous American movie star, which always delighted her.

Once her hair was neat, she decided to take a walk. A look at the shops, and a stroll in the park afterwards, would do her good. She felt she needed to fill her lungs with fresh air before facing the evening and smoky bar rooms, but tonight she wouldn't drink quite so much.

Southampton's town centre had been decimated during the blitz, and one-storey shops had been quickly erected on the bombed sites. The windows were full of utility clothes, so called because all pleats, frills and any kind of frippery had been removed to save on material. Furniture was much the same. Plain with no frills.

Rusty gave a cursory glance at the goods on view, but she didn't really need anything at the moment – and anyway, she didn't have many clothing coupons left, which were needed when purchasing clothing. Hats were not on coupons, though, and she took a little time trying on the latest models before making her way to the park.

Although all the park railings had been taken down to help with the war effort, the local council still maintained the flower beds, which were always a pleasure to see, and now as Rusty walked through, she gazed at the flower display with great delight. At least some things still stayed the same.

She stopped and sat on a park bench, and taking out a packet of Craven A cigarettes she lit one. She drew on the nicotine and blew out the smoke with great satisfaction. She had often been given Camel and Lucky Strike cigarettes by her American clients, but found them much too strong.

'So this is what you get up to during the day.'

Rusty looked up at a GI she knew, who frequented her local pub and was one of her clients. 'Hello, Hank, how are you, and what are you doing here?'

He sat beside her. 'I've got a twenty-four-hour pass, but decided not to go to London this time, so I've been taking in the local sights, like the old walls and the Bargate. They tell me it's a medieval gate that was the entrance to the town many years ago.'

Rusty shrugged. 'Don't know about that, Hank, but it is old.'

'I'm going to find a place and have an English cup of tea as I've yet to discover a decent cup of coffee in the town. Wanna come too?'

'Why not. If we can find a scone too, you'll be having a proper English tea.'

'A what?'

She sighed. Wasn't it enough that she had to service these men without having to educate them too? 'Never mind, I'll explain later,' she said and led the American away.

Two

It was seven thirty when Rusty wandered towards The Grapes pub in Southampton's cosmopolitan Oxford Street. As usual, a mixture of troops from different nationalities walked around, killing time, exchanging stories and dirty jokes, and chatting up the girls, whose gas masks were slung over their arms and who were giving most of their attention to the GIs – looking for Nylon stockings, chewing gum or candy, as the Yanks called chocolate or sweets. A free night out and a good time was on their agenda.

Rusty ignored the many flirtatious remarks sent her way. She wasn't ready to work just yet. She wanted a quiet drink and chat with some of her friends before business began.

'What'll it be tonight, darling?' asked Maudie, the buxom barmaid, as she hooked up the strap of her bra.

'Just a half of bitter, please. I'm thirsty.'

'Not surprised after what you had last night! Bloody hell! You were well on your way when you came in here, then you left to go on somewhere else.'

'Oh, I know, you should have had my head when I woke up this morning.' She grinned broadly. 'But I wasn't so far gone I didn't remember to take the money first!'

Both women laughed raucously. Maudie knew the score. She'd been on the street years before. 'That's my girl!' she said and moved away to serve another customer.

Rusty took her drink and sat away from everyone in a quiet corner and surveyed the scene before her. As yet none of her contemporaries had arrived. At the bar stood a couple of British soldiers deep in conversation, and further along were two French sailors with the ubiquitous red pompoms on their berets, chattering away in their native language – and four American servicemen, laughing loudly.

Rusty watched them with some amusement. She never ceased to be amazed at the exuberance of the Americans. They mostly appeared to have no reticence at all, unlike the British with their emotions bottled up inside – or 'reserve', as it was normally referred to. But, in her line of work, Rusty had long since discovered that beneath that reserve was often a seething lava of emotion. Some of it good – some of it bad.

A couple of her friends arrived and joined her. They exchanged tales of what had happened to them all the night before.

'One of my punters last night was one of them darkies,' said one. 'Nice gentle bloke, kind of shy. He told me if he'd fucked a white woman in the South where he came from, he'd have been lynched!'

The others were horrified. 'Was he serious?' asked Rusty.

'Oh yes, he wasn't kidding.' She giggled. 'I suppose you could say it was a new experience for both of us. Christ, you should have seen the size of him! It frightened me to death.'

'Did you manage?' 'Just about, but blimey, I was knackered afterwards. I took the rest of the night off!'

They continued to chat for a while, then departed to start work.

It was Sunday morning, and Jenny Procter sat drinking a cup of tea, dressed in jodhpurs, ready for her trip to the stables. Through the open window, she heard the sound of an engine and walked to the front door. As she stepped outside, Captain Brad Jackson, driving a jeep, pulled up in front of her.

'Good morning, Mrs Procter, I hope I'm not late?'

She waited for him to get out of the vehicle. 'No, Captain Jackson, you're right on time. Would you like a cup of tea?'

'Do you have any coffee?' He followed her into the kitchen.

'I had an idea you would say that, and I have a percolator ready.'

With a chuckle he said, 'I can see you are a woman who is organized and ready for any eventuality.'

She handed him a cup. 'I do my best.'

Jenny had warned the owner, Beth Harris, a friend of hers, that she was bringing the American and had been told that an extra pair of hands was always welcome. So it was no surprise when they arrived together.

Beth came over to greet them, and Jenny introduced her to Brad.

'Jenny told me she was bringing you. We are always pleased to have an extra man around, as most of ours have been called up.' She held out her hand.

As he shook it, Brad smiled. 'I can't thank you enough, Mrs Harris. I get lonesome for my horses, and I sure miss riding them. Today will be a great treat for me. What can I do for you in return?'

He and Jenny were set the task of mucking out a couple of stables and filling the feed bags after trundling the muck over to an outside field to add to a pile already there.

'Beth sells this off as fertilizer to those who have gardens in the area and to the local farmers,' Jenny informed Brad. 'Nothing is wasted in war time, as I suppose you realize?'

'Well, I've certainly found that out since I arrived,' he said. 'But you must realize, back in the States we don't have the short-ages that you do.'

'Ah well.' She laughed. 'America *is* the land of plenty we're told!'

'Mrs Procter, I do believe you are teasing me.'

'Jenny, please – and yes I am!'

'Please call me Brad, and I guess I'll get used to the British sense of humour in time!'

Eventually, their chores finished, they saddled up two of the mounts and rode out of the stable yard into the quiet of their surroundings. It became quickly apparent that Brad was an excellent rider.

It was the best of mornings, Jenny thought as they rode through a wood. The bluebells were almost over, but the wild aquilegias were blooming, bobbing their heads on their long stems in a gentle breeze, alongside the poppies.

As for Brad, he was at peace with the world. The feel of the animal between his knees made him nostalgic for his home in Denver, Colorado. There, of course, the vegetation was different. Situated at the base of the Rocky Mountains, the terrain was more arid than the pleasant lush green of the English countryside. There were no mountains to be seen here, only the stretch of fields beyond the wood.

'Look!' Jenny called and pointed in the distance.

Following her gaze, Brad saw wild rabbits playing, until a sudden shot from a gun frightened all but one away.

Jenny looked crestfallen. 'Oh, what a shame!' Then she shrugged. 'I know they have to be culled or we would be overrun, but I don't enjoy seeing it happen.'

'You wouldn't approve of my deer hunting then?'

She looked at him aghast. 'How could you?'

'For the same reason. Venison is great to eat, and I imagine you've eaten rabbit before now?'

She started to laugh. 'That's unfair!'

'But true,' he said.

They rode on in silence. Both lost in their own thoughts, enjoying the moment, until eventually they returned to the stables.

Once the horses had been unsaddled and watered, Jenny turned to Brad. 'If you are still free, would you like to come back to my place for lunch?'

'That's really kind; I would love to, thanks.'

They drove back to the house, and Brad helped Jenny alight and then delved into the back of the jeep and took out a cardboard box, following her inside to the kitchen. He placed the box down on the table.

'I thought you could make good use of these few things,' he said, unpacking the contents. There was a packet of coffee beans, tins of fruit, a pack of butter and a dozen eggs. Plus a bottle of wine.

'Oh my goodness!' she exclaimed. 'It looks as if Christmas has come early. How wonderful, thank you so much.'

'My pleasure. The PX stores here are well stocked; we're very lucky.'

'Uncle Sam looks after you well,' she said as she started to put the things away.

He chuckled. 'Nylon stockings seem to be the favourite purchase of my soldiers.'

She smiled at him. 'I wonder why?'

'I think we both know the answer to that. Fraternizing is OK but it brings its own hazards. You know, venereal disease, pregnancies, family problems. It happens during any war. Here in Southampton, in my job, it becomes my problem too.'

She was immediately sympathetic. 'That can't be easy.'

They sat at the table drinking their coffee, discussing the problem.

'You know how it is, Jenny. Men are away from home, knowing they are going into battle, wondering if they will survive a bullet. They are going to enjoy every moment they can.'

'That I can understand – to a point,' she said. 'But no one thinks about the consequences for the woman.'

He leaned back in the chair. 'That's not entirely fair. The women come on to the men, encouraging them. They must be aware of the risks they take.'

'Some of them do, I'm sure, but what about the girl who genuinely falls in love with a GI? What happens to her?'

'That's the biggest problem of all. Some of the guys are already married or are engaged to a girl back home. That can lead to heartbreak.' He looked at her and smiled. 'Anyway, let's forget about that for today. How about I open the wine?'

Jenny rose from her seat. 'What a good idea. I'll start the lunch. Do you like salmon?'

'Indeed I do.'

'Good. Someone gave me two fillets yesterday. We'll have them with some new potatoes and vegetables from the garden.'

They ate their lunch, walked around the garden, and then sat and drank tea beneath the trees before Brad told her he had to go. They walked to the jeep together.

'Thank you, Jenny, for a delightful day. It was the best time I've had since I arrived here. Will you let me take you out to dinner one evening to return the compliment?'

'Thank you, Brad, that's really nice of you. I'd love to.'

'I'll call you,' he said as he got into the vehicle.

Jenny watched him drive away. For her too it had been a really good day and she looked forward to talking again to this charming and intelligent man. She didn't envy him his job. She was sure he had many more difficulties to deal with than he had told her. Welfare, in any shape or form, was never easy.

The following morning, Brad was sitting in his office, preparing for the first problem of the day. A company of Negro soldiers had been posted to Southampton, and this had not been without its issues. For the Negros, many who had come from the southern states where integration was either frowned upon or illegal, the freedom to mix with the local girls, to use any bar, eat in any restaurant of their choosing, was really something, and most of them had eagerly taken advantage of the situation. This, of course, had caused problems with the local inhabitants of the town, but even more so with the white American soldiers – in particular with any who came from the south.

Now Brad had to punish two of his troop. One white, the other black. The two men had been fighting in the camp, cheered on by their contemporaries, until the fight had been broken up by the military police.

The duty sergeant marched the two men into the office. Both showed bruises and black eyes from the confrontation. But they stood to attention before Brad, upright and seething with resentment.

He looked coldly at them. 'We are here to fight the Germans, not each other! I will *not* tolerate such behaviour from my soldiers – do you understand?'

'Yes sir,' they answered in unison.

He looked at the white soldier and glanced down at the paper before him. 'You, Private Franklin, are no longer on your home ground in Alabama. You are a soldier in the United States Army, and as such you have a duty to perform. One of which is to uphold the good name of the country for which you serve! Every single one of us will have to face the enemy in the future, and I suggest you keep your anger for that moment. It could mean the difference between life or death.'

He continued: 'Every member of the American forces is pivotal to their company, whatever their colour and creed. Black or white, when you bleed, your blood looks the same. On the battlefield, you may both have to watch each other's back. There is no place, then, to harbour such feelings.'

Then he looked at the Negro soldier. 'And you, Private Nichols, you must think you've died and gone to heaven, here in the United Kingdom. You are no longer restricted by your colour. But that doesn't mean you can behave without decorum, in the town – or here in the camp.'

Brad assigned the soldiers extra duties as a punishment. 'Give me any more trouble and I'll throw the book at you!' Brad warned them. 'Dismiss!'

He was not without understanding for the problems both men faced. Slavery had long been abolished, but in the Southern states, the Negro population still had to sit in the back of the bus – and if it was full, they had to give up their seats to white people. Schools were segregated. For the men brought up all their lives with such rules, the sudden freedom they were given in this country was unbelievable, and Brad could well understand things could get out of hand.

For those white soldiers brought up in the south, to see a Negro walking along the street with a white girl on his arm was intolerable, and the military police had a difficult task, keeping the lid on the situation. There were separate Red Cross clubs for both groups of soldiers, but there were no such restrictions else-where in the town.

Brad leaned back in the chair and longed for the tranquillity of the previous day, riding out in the countryside with the delightful Jenny Procter. How civilized that had been, how very enjoyable. What a lucky man her husband was.

Brad himself was unmarried. There had been a girl, but despite his hopes of settling down with her, it had not materialized. When he had been called up, she had backed off, not wanting to be tied down. Now when he thought about it, it had probably been for the best. He picked up a sheaf of papers, ready for the next case.

Three

Sarah Biggs walked through Mayflower Park every morning on her way to work. It was here that German prisoners were kept in an improvised pen. They were a subject of great curiosity to the locals, who would walk by slowly to get a closer look at the enemy.

The first time Sarah had seen them she'd been surprised. Quite what she'd expected, she didn't know, but when she'd looked at the men peering out from behind the wire, they hadn't seemed that different. Apart from their uniforms, of course. Some had glared balefully at her, muttering in German to each other; some had called out; others had taken no notice of her at all.

But one tall young man, with blonde hair and piercing blue eyes, had caught her eye. They'd gazed at one another, and the German had smiled shyly at her. There had been something about him that had intrigued her, and now every morning she looked for him. He always stood in the same place, slightly apart from the others, and he always smiled at her. Sarah would slow her pace and smile at him in return.

One morning he spoke. 'Hello, Fräulein.'

She was startled but secretly pleased. 'Hello,' she replied and kept walking.

The following morning she stopped beside him. 'Hello, are you all right? Are they looking after you?'

He looked delighted. 'Thank you, yes. What is your name?'

'Sarah. What's yours?'

'Gunter Reinhardt. I come from Hamburg.'

And every morning after that they exchanged a few words, until one day he asked if she ever walked in the Park in the evenings.

'Why?' she asked.

'Then we would have time to talk for longer. We are here from six o'clock for an hour before we are taken to our quarters.'

'How long will you be held here?'

He shrugged. 'I don't know, but I would like to get to know you better before we are moved to another camp.'

And so their strange courtship began.

Gunter told her he was about to study law when he was called up. His father was a lawyer, but he, too, was now in the army, though Gunter didn't know where. He was a quiet young man and Sarah assumed a studious one, from the way he spoke. He had a serious side to his nature, but his smile was warm and she loved the way his eyes seemed to light up when he saw her.

She, at seventeen, was a typist. She told him about her work, her family – her father was also in the army, somewhere in France.

They exchanged their plans for the future, though he was some-what reticent about what lay ahead for him.

'It depends on who wins the war,' he said.

Sarah was certain that Britain would be victorious, but it didn't seem right to say so. They held hands through the wire . . . and fell in love.

But when her mother, Dora, found out eventually how her daughter was spending her evenings, she went ballistic.

'Mr James next door told me he's seen you talking to a German prisoner every evening when he comes home through the park. Sarah, how could you?'

'Gunter is a charming young man!' Sarah protested.

'Gunter! Gunter is it? Just how friendly have you got with this man?'

'He's nineteen, not much older than me, and he was called up, just like Dad. It isn't his fault he's in the army. He wants to be a lawyer like his father before him.'

'He's the bloody enemy! Think about it, if he and your father met on a battlefield he would shoot your father without a second thought.'

'And Dad would do the same. It's war, Mother – that's what happens!'

Dora calmed down. 'Yes, you're right, but Sarah, there is no future in it, don't you see? You get too friendly and then he's sent to a prison camp and you'll never see him again. Then how will you feel?'

'Devastated! I love him, you see.'

Her mother was speechless for a moment. 'Don't be ridiculous, you are far too young to be thinking that way. Infatuated, maybe, but love . . . That's preposterous.'

Sarah stood up. 'I don't expect you to understand – I hardly understand myself – but you can't tell me how I feel. Gunter and I are in love, German or not.' She ran upstairs to her bedroom.

The next morning she told Gunter what had happened. He reached through the wire and took her hand. 'I can understand how your mother feels, *liebling*. Mine would probably say the same. But no matter what happens, who wins the war, we'll be together. Now off you go or you'll be late for work. I'll see you this evening.' He raised her hand to his lips and kissed it.

He watched her walk away, ignoring the coarse remarks from his fellow prisoners about his friendship with the girl. He hated the war, saw no reason for it. So many people dying – and for what? To satisfy the Führer? A demented man, overcome with a power complex. He had no time for Adolf Hitler, and neither did his father, but now both of them were in the German Army, fighting for a cause they didn't believe in. It angered him that this madman could cause such mayhem and bring death to thousands, just to satisfy his ego.

The only thing that lifted his spirits was Sarah. He counted every minute of every day until he could see her. He dreaded being moved away and wondered if he would be allowed any mail if it came to pass. He wanted to be able to keep in touch with the girl with whom he'd fallen in love. How could they be together in the future? He felt saddened by what seemed to be an impossible dream.

The month passed quickly, and despite the shortages and difficulties that such times can bring, life in the town went on. Jenny and Brad continued to meet at the stables whenever they were free and occasionally met for dinner. Their friendship grew and they slipped into an easy relationship, both learning about one another and appreciating each other. Finally Jenny received a letter from Adam, telling her he was coming home on leave.

As she sat in the garden reading his letter, she had mixed emotions. She was, of course, delighted that he was safe, but during the long time he'd been absent, she'd built a life for herself. She was no longer Jenny Procter, wife of a prominent citizen of the town. She was now Jenny Procter, busy woman, on several committees, doing what she hoped was useful to the war effort. Her work with the American soldiers, she felt, helped both the Americans and the locals to appreciate one another, therefore also helping to keep the peace between them.

Brad Jackson was pivotal in this, of course, and because of their shared responsibility, they had a common interest. Now Adam was coming home on leave for three weeks. Her routine would be upset because he would demand her total attention and would have little patience with anything less. And how would he feel about her spending time with a male friend? Well, he would have to understand that the work she was doing was important, and although she would try and give him as much of her time as possible, he would have to make allowances – like it or not!

Two days later, Jenny waited for her husband to arrive. She was unbelievably nervous. How ridiculous this was, she chided herself as she sipped a gin and tonic to calm her nerves. After all she had been married to the man for eighteen years, although she'd not seen him for the past three. She heard a car toot outside and, taking a deep breath, walked to the front door.

Adam Procter climbed out of the military vehicle and walked towards her.

He had changed, was her first thought. He looked older, care-worn and tired.

'Hello, Jenny.' Adam kissed her briefly on the cheek and entered the house; his driver walked behind him, carrying his luggage. 'Just put those down there, Corporal.' Turning back to Jenny, he said: 'I could do with a drink!'

The corporal left, and the two of them walked into the drawing room. Jenny poured Adam a stiff gin and tonic. As she turned towards him she saw that he was looking round the room, eyeing every item of furniture, the drapes at the window, and eventually he walked over to the French doors and looked at the garden.

Jenny joined him and handed him his drink.

'You have no idea how many times I've closed my eyes and tried to picture this room, this view . . . and you.'

She was at a loss for words. This was so unlike the man who had left three years ago, and she didn't know what to say.

He turned towards her. 'You look wonderful. How are you?'

Taken aback by a compliment from the man who in the past had seldom noticed what she wore, she said, 'I'm fine, but how are you? Were things really bad over there?'

He crossed to the settee and sat down. 'It was dreadful! I lost a lot of my men during the fighting, which was hard, because in wartime your company becomes your family, so it's like losing a relation. The Germans were better equipped than we were led to believe, so it was a nightmare.'

She sat beside him. 'I am so sorry, but in these three weeks you will be able to rest and recharge your batteries.'

He smiled wearily. 'It's good to be home, not to have to listen to the sound of guns and the whistle of bullets. It all seems very strange . . . but wonderful.' He drank deeply. 'My God, that feels good. Now I want to sit in a hot bath and relax.'

This was not the time to remind Adam that he was only allowed a certain depth of bathwater, Jenny decided. She felt he had earned the right to a decent soak.

'You finish your drink and I'll run a bath for you,' she said and left him sitting quietly getting used to his surroundings.

'Darling,' he called, 'would you put out some comfortable civilian clothes for me to change into? I want to get out of this damned uniform.'

So it had started, she thought as she turned on the taps. Why he couldn't sort his own clothes she didn't know, but then, of course, in the past, she had always laid out his clothes for the day, every morning, as he had washed and shaved. So not a lot had changed, really.

Jenny was in their bedroom when Adam climbed out of the bath, and he entered the room with just a bath towel wrapped round his torso. He stood behind her and gathered her into his arms, kissing the back of her neck, caressing her breasts. Breathing heavily.

She shut her eyes and tried not to tense. It had been a long time, and she wasn't sure she was ready for such intimacy. But Adam was.

He removed her clothes with almost indecent haste and pushed her on to the bed. His kisses were demanding, almost brutal in their intensity. She struggled to try and calm him down but he was hell bent on sexual relief.

There was no tenderness in his love-making, and when it was eventually over, Jenny felt as if she'd been used like a whore, rather than as a wife, and she was angry.

She got off the bed, dressed hurriedly and left the room.

Downstairs, she fumed. She would not be used like that again. Only the fact that Adam had just got home, after obviously having been through a great deal, stopped her from venting her anger. She opened the French doors and strode into the garden, walked around it until her anger subsided, then sat on the bench beneath the trees and lit a cigarette. This was where she and Brad often sat after they had been riding, and she couldn't help but compare the two men. Her friend Brad, with his quiet manner and sharp humour, his gentleness and understanding that was no doubt helped by the fact that he was a doctor . . . and Adam. She didn't know what to make of him after the scene in the bedroom. There had been no gentleness there. No concern for her and her needs. It had been all about him . . . as usual.

She needed to get away. Creeping upstairs, Jenny peeped round the bedroom door and saw that Adam was in a deep sleep. She took her jodhpurs from the wardrobe, changed in another bedroom and went downstairs.

Climbing on her bicycle she rode to the stables and, with Beth's permission, saddled a horse and rode out to the wood. Here among the trees, surrounded by nature, she began to relax.

As she rode, she tried to make allowances for her husband, attempting in her own mind to picture what he might have been through. It was impossible, of course. She had no idea at all what it was like to be on the field of battle, to see men killed, to feel the fear coursing through you in case you were the next man to stop a bullet.

As she headed back to the stables, she told herself she had to show a little more understanding . . . but then so would Adam. After all, she had certain responsibilities, and they were all to do with the war effort. Her way of fighting the enemy, if you like.

Four

The first few days of her husband's leave seemed to be nothing but a whirl of social activity, Jenny thought. Adam, resplendent in his uniform, calling on old and influential friends – re-establishing his place in society.

On the Wednesday, Jenny had promised to meet Brad at the stables to give Beth a hand, and she told Adam she would be out all day.

'That's fine,' he said. 'I'm going to play golf at Stoneham, and after that I'll have some lunch at the golf club with friends. I'll see you back here in time for dinner.'

Jenny arrived at Beth's house and put her bicycle up against the wall. She saw Brad's parked jeep and wandered over to the stable yard, but to her surprise, the American talking to Beth was a stranger.

'Jenny! Captain Jackson can't make it today but he's sent this gentleman in his place. Wasn't that kind of him?'

The tall, fair-haired soldier smiled at Jenny. 'Corporal Chad Maxwell at your service, ma'am!'

At that moment there was a terrible racket coming from inside one of the stalls. A clattering and a banging, followed by the sound of a horse neighing in fright, filled the air. As they rushed over to see what was happening, one of the grooms hurtled out of the stable, slamming the bottom half of the door shut behind her. The girl was white, and her hands shook.

Beth and Jenny ran over to help her, but the corporal walked over to the stable door, talking softly, trying to calm the terrified animal. Eventually the horse stopped rearing and kicking its hooves against the wall. The three women watched in astonishment as the American opened the door slowly, still talking softly – and entered.

'Is he mad?' asked Beth in horror. 'The PDSA – you know, that veterinary charity – asked me to take the animal, but he's dangerous. I'm going to ask them to take it away or one of my staff could be seriously injured.'

The sudden quiet from inside the stall fuelled their curiosity, and they approached warily. Inside stood Chad Maxwell, stroking the nose of the animal, speaking continuously in his quiet voice. The women watched in fascination as he patted the horse's flanks, then picked up a curry comb and started grooming it.

The steed snorted every now and then, shook its neck and pawed at the ground, but Chad didn't flinch. Eventually, after stroking its nose and nuzzling its neck, he left the stall, closing the door, leaning over the open half – and waited. After a few moments, the horse ambled over to him, snorting softly.

'I know, I know,' said Chad, stroking its neck. 'But things will get better.' He picked up a carrot from a basket nearby, fed it to the animal, then walked slowly away.

Beth followed him. 'I've never seen anything like that in my entire life!' she exclaimed.

'That poor beast has been traumatized,' he told her, 'but I think I can sort him out if you'll let me. I have a forty-eight-hour pass, which would give me enough time to work with him.'

'Of course! What do you need?'

'A place to sleep and the use of your practice ring without too many people around.'

'You've got it!' She looked at Jenny. 'Why don't you take Corporal Maxwell into the kitchen and give him some coffee? That's the least we can do for him.'

Once the two of them were settled at the table with their drinks, Jenny asked the question that was intriguing her: 'Where did you learn how to handle horses in such a manner?'

'I was brought up in Wyoming, and I've been around horses all my life. My dad was a rodeo rider – he used to break horses for a living, and he taught me how to do so at a very early age.'

'But that wasn't just breaking an animal. That was far more!'

He looked bemused. 'When I was fourteen, I discovered this . . . gift, if you like. It was like I was able to read their minds, knew what made them tick, what it was that turned them maverick. It just started there and kinda developed. At home they call me a horse whisperer.'

'Amazing!' she said. 'Can I come and watch you work tomorrow?'

'Sure, as long as you don't spook the animal.'

'I promise. When we've finished our coffee, would you like to help me exercise two of the horses? I ride out whenever I can to help Beth.'

'That would be great,' Chad said with a broad grin. 'When this war is over – if I survive, of course – I'm going to buy a small ranch back home and break horses for a living.' He looked wistful. 'I long for the open range, dinner round a camp fire, the peace of the countryside . . . How about you?'

Jenny sat and thought about her life. Was she content? She had been a bank clerk, which was how she met Adam. Had it been her dream job? No, it was what was on offer at the time and what she'd felt capable of doing. Then had come marriage, and eventually the big house, but no children, which was a great disappointment. She'd never really had a dream. *How sad is that?* she thought.

'I've never lived in a big city, only Southampton. I suppose I'm satisfied with my life as it is.'

He looked intently at her, as if reading her mind. 'I don't think that's true,' he said quietly. 'I think deep down you want *much* more.'

She didn't like to ask him what he meant, but it unsettled her.

As they rode out Jenny discovered that Chad was good company. He made her laugh with tales of the army, his life on the range and his musings on how strange an English saddle was, as opposed to a Western one.

'You ride well, Mrs Procter, but you need to relax into the saddle more . . . like this.'

She did as she was told and immediately felt better. She smiled her thanks.

'There you go,' he said. 'Come on, I'll race you across the field!'

Chad flew ahead of her, and she could see he was at one with his mount and envied his natural talent.

Breathless, she reined in beside him. 'I had no chance!' she protested.

'Of course you didn't, I knew that, but it was fun wasn't it? You should come out to Wyoming after the war – you'd love it. You would feel free; it would be good for your soul. You would blossom, be able to give rein to all those hidden dreams.' He stared at her and smiled. 'You have no idea what I'm talking about, have you?'

Jenny shook her head.

'You will – in time.'

Whilst Jenny prepared the dinner that evening, she couldn't help but relive the extraordinary experience of the day. She'd never seen anything like it. Chad Maxwell was amazing, but also an enigma. The way he'd handled the frightened animal was unbelievable, and then when they rode out together, his insight into her personal feelings was extraordinary. It started her soul-searching. Was she as happy with her life as she thought she was? She realized that indeed she was not. Her marriage was all right; it certainly wasn't perfect, but that was life. After eighteen years with one man, the excitement had long died. She and Adam just went through the motions. Was it enough to sustain her in the years to come? With a sudden realization, she knew that it was not.

At that moment, Adam walked into the kitchen. As he leaned forward to kiss her cheek, she could smell the alcohol on his breath and turned her head away. He hardly noticed as he put his arms around her.

'Hello, darling, did you have a good day?' he asked as he nuzzled her neck.

Oh no, she thought, remembering how he'd used her in bed the previous night . . . not again. She eased herself from his hold and moved away, pretending she needed something from the other side of the kitchen.

'Go and freshen up,' she told him. 'Dinner will be ready in fifteen minutes.'

He looked at her through bleary eyes. 'Can't it wait?'

'No, Adam, it can't! It's hard enough to find decent food these days, and I'm certainly not going to spoil it.' She glared at him. 'Fifteen minutes!'

He did not look pleased. 'For Christ's sake, Jenny, I've been away a long time.'

All her thoughts of trying to be understanding flew out of the window. 'I'm well aware of that,' she retorted, 'but that's no excuse to treat me like a whore when you take me to bed.' There, she'd said it.

He was outraged. 'A whore? Whatever do you mean?'

'You didn't make love to me, Adam, you used me. That was the first time and the last. If it's a whore you want, go into town and pay for one!'

His shocked look almost made her smile. She couldn't remember the last time she'd stood up to her husband, and it gave her a good feeling. In three years, she'd changed. Now she was not just his wife, but her own person, and she knew that nothing was ever going to be the same again.

★   ★   ★

With a feeling of excitement, Jenny cycled to the stables early the next morning to watch Chad work with the maverick horse. He was leading the animal out of the stall when she arrived. The horse was frisky – rearing, snorting and prancing – but Chad just kept talking to it as he led it to the practice ring. With Beth and the female groom, she waited and watched.

Once inside the ring, the American removed the lead rein and let the horse go. It raced around, tossing its mane, rearing and neighing. Chad stood in the centre and watched it. Eventually the animal slowed to a stop, pawing the ground, a wild look in its eyes, ears pricked. Chad sat down and waited.

Beth and Jenny exchanged puzzled glances. What would happen now?

The animal, it seemed, was just as mystified. It pranced and trotted about, then stopped, looked around, neighed loudly, and slowly walked the perimeter of the practice ring, casting the odd glance at the quiet figure in the centre, until it finally stopped still.

Chad rose slowly to his feet. The horse immediately tossed its head and backed up. Staying in the centre of the ring, Chad took a few steps to one side, and after some time the horse moved towards him. Chad retraced his steps, and the animal immediately moved back.

This strange procedure continued until Chad had the animal moving in any direction he required. Progressively the horse calmed down and seemed to be enjoying this strange ritual; it was only then that Chad slowly approached it and stroked its neck, talking softly the whole time. After some time, he walked away, and the animal followed him. When he turned and walked in a different direction, so did the horse. Chad kept this up for half an hour and then finally stopped, his back towards the horse. The animal came slowly closer until it placed its head over Chad's shoulder, snorting softly.

Chad stroked its nose, talking softly as he did so. Then he walked over to the fence and picked up a saddle. He walked slowly towards the horse, talking softly all the time, and very slowly placed the saddle over its back, which unsettled it a little, but Chad just kept talking as he tightened the girth. Then, gathering the reins together, he placed one foot into the stirrup and hauled himself into the saddle.

All those who were watching held their breaths. Chad gave a little pressure with his heels and the horse moved forward. Chad rode him round the ring several times, then he stopped him and changed direction; the animal answered every demand of the rider.

Chad trotted him, put him into a canter, then a gallop and finally a walk, bringing the horse to a standstill. He climbed out of the saddle, stroked the long neck, talking all the time. Then he caught hold of the horse's mane and, twisting it and the neck, eased the horse down on two knees and, ultimately, on its side.

The onlookers were astonished when Chad then sat on the prostrate animal. He continued stroking it, murmuring all the time, until he got off, and he let the animal stand for a moment before leading him – calm, docile and obedient – back to the stall. It was as if he were a different horse entirely.

The three women followed, awed by what they had seen.

When Beth and the groom went about their work, Jenny spoke to Chad. 'That was amazing!'

He smiled at her. 'Not really. An animal is very much like a woman. It thrives on attention, consideration, a firm hand – but above all love.'

Jenny didn't know what to say.

Chad caught hold of her hand. 'All the things that are lacking in your life, I believe, Mrs Procter.'

She gazed into his eyes, eyes that showed no guile, and wondered just what it was about this man that seemed to give him the right to look into her soul.

She removed her hand. 'And if you are correct . . . and I do say *if* . . . what's to be done about it?'

'That would be entirely up to you. Go away and think about it. We'll talk some more tomorrow. You will be here, won't you?'

'Yes, I'll be here,' she said, then left the stables, somewhat mystified.

When, eventually, Jenny returned home and walked into the kitchen, Adam appeared at the door. 'Where the hell have you been?'

'I beg your pardon?' Jenny's hackles rose at the dictatorial tone in his voice.

'When I woke up you were nowhere to be seen. No note, no nothing!'

'You were fast asleep, and I left early. I expected to be back long before now.'

'Where were you, anyway?'

'I was at the stables watching a man break in a horse.'

His look of astonishment was almost comical. 'You thought that was more important than being with your husband, who has been away for three years?'

Jenny stared at the outraged man before her and thought: *how on earth have we stayed together so long?* Chad's words echoed in her head. 'As a matter of fact . . . yes! This man at the stables is extraordinary, and I will probably never see the way he works ever again. It was an experience not to be missed. In fact, I shall be going back tomorrow morning to see him finish his work!'

Adam, for once, was speechless. He stomped around the kitchen, then stopped and looked at Jenny. 'I don't know what's got into you. Ever since I've been home, you've been different. You've changed beyond recognition.'

'Well, I can't say the same for you, Adam! Apart from looking older and a bit more careworn – which is not surprising, under the circumstances – as soon as you settled in you became the same overbearing man who left here three years ago, but now I'm not prepared to put up with it.' Seeing the anger and bewilderment on his face, she did feel some sympathy for him. After all, he had been involved in a war, and he didn't need another one in his own home.

'Sit down,' she said. To her surprise he did so. 'Look, Adam, three years is a long time. I've had to make a life for myself. I belong to lots of committees, I help Beth whenever I can, I *am* a different person.'

'Undoubtedly!'

She ignored this. 'Yes, I am still your wife, and of course I want to spend time with you, but I can't stop all the other things I have to do because you are here.'

He didn't like this one bit. 'A woman's place is with her husband, looking after his needs.'

'I am your wife, not a damned servant!' Now Jenny was angry. 'I have seen to your every need for years – with little reward, I might add! You took me for granted – Jenny do this, Jenny I want that – but now you will have to consider my needs for once!' Having vented her spleen, she capitulated. 'Adam, I am so very happy that you're home, and I do want to spend time with you, of course I do, but we both are leading different lives. That's what a war does to people. We just have to compromise, that's all.'

She gave a half smile. 'In all honesty, I find it strange having you around again. Three years is a long time for us to be apart, you must realize this?'

He suddenly looked weary and, rubbing his forehead, said, 'Of course I understand. As I was driven back here, I wondered how it would be between us. I just wanted everything to be as I remembered, that's all.'

She then realized that he, too, had been unsettled, but in his usual way had hidden his feelings. 'Come on, I'll pour us a couple of stiff drinks, cook the dinner, and then we can sit and listen to the wireless. Have a quiet evening on our own.'

Later, when they were in bed, Adam gently took her into his arms and kissed her. Jenny really wasn't in the mood for sex, but after their argument, and because of the fact that he would not be home for long, she responded, even feigning an orgasm to please him. But she was relieved when he kissed her goodnight, turned over and fell asleep.

Five

Gunter Reinhardt was pacing the ground with excitement when Sarah went to meet him that evening. He rushed to the barbed wire fence when he saw her approach and reached out for her hands, gripping them firmly.

'*Liebling*! I have some good news.'

'Whatever is it?' she asked, hearing the urgency in his voice.

'Some of us are being allowed to work outside the encampment. If we are very careful, we'll be able to spend some time together.' He looked at her with longing. 'I want so much to be able to hold you in my arms and kiss you.'

She blushed and lowered her gaze with embarrassment.

'Don't you want that too?'

'Of course I do, but how will it be possible?'

'We are to work in the public park where there is a rock garden. I think it's East Park.'

'Yes, I know where you mean. When do you start?'

'Tomorrow morning. We'll be there all day, I'm told.'

She beamed at him. 'Tomorrow is my half day! I finish at one o'clock. I'll come looking for you.'

'Be careful, *liebling*, there will be sentries on duty, but hopefully by the afternoon they will have relaxed a bit more and forgotten we are the enemy.'

She hated him referring to himself that way. Squeezing his hand she whispered, 'You are not *my* enemy.'

The next afternoon, Sarah strolled along to the rockery area of the park and in the distance saw the men at work. There were only six of them and two British soldiers who were sitting chatting, occasionally casting an eye towards the prisoners of war. She saw Gunter working slightly away from the others and managed to walk in his direction without causing any bother.

He looked up and smiled when he saw her. He glanced over at the sentries, then motioned to Sarah to walk over towards a huge shrub which would shield them from the others. She did and waited, heart pounding, scared of being seen.

A few minutes later, Gunter sauntered round and, with a quick glance over his shoulder, stepped forward and took her into his arms. His urgent kisses took her breath away.

'I have longed to hold you, *liebling*,' he said and kissed her again. 'You feel so good,' he whispered as he held her close and buried his head into her hair. 'You smell so fresh.' His arms held her even closer. 'How wonderful to be able to feel you without any barbed wire between us. But I must go. If they see me, I may never have such a chance again.' He kissed her long and hard, caressed her face, then walked away.

Sarah stood for a moment, catching her breath, her hands shaking. The nearness of Gunter, and the feel of his arms about her and his hot mouth on hers, had been sudden and all encompassing. She walked shakily away and sat on a park bench where she could watch him, longing to be in his arms once more. She would see him again this evening, though the barbed wire would be between them, but at least they could hold hands.

Rusty Dobbs had managed to get hold of an invitation to a dance given by the American GIs at a local hall. She thought she deserved a break and enjoyed getting dressed for an evening's entertainment strictly for herself. She wore an emerald green summer dress covered in white daisies. The green went well with her auburn hair. She wore a pair of silver shoes, hoping to dance the night away.

As she approached the hall she could hear the band playing. Inside, she presented her invitation to the soldier on the door. He looked at her and smiled.

'Good evening, ma'am. Have yourself a good time, you hear?'

'Thanks, I intend to,' she said, laughing.

Brad Jackson saw her arrive. The long auburn tresses first caught his eye, and he watched as two soldiers approached her at the same time. It was obvious to Brad that the men had both asked her to dance, and there was friendly banter being exchanged, with Rusty watching with much amusement. He walked over to them.

'Good evening, ma'am, allow me to settle this argument . . . Would you care to dance?'

Laughing, she looked at the handsome officer. 'Thanks, I'd love to.'

The two soldiers protested. 'That's not fair, sir.'

Brad grinned at them, patted the bar on his shoulder ostentatiously, and led Rusty to the floor. The band was playing Glenn Miller's 'String of Pearls' as he took her into his arms.

Rusty loved to dance, and fortunately for her the officer was very accomplished – she was delighted. As the music finished, Brad asked her if she would like a drink.

'Thank you, a gin and tonic please.'

He led her to a table and went to the bar. She watched him and liked what she saw. It was such a treat to be treated like a lady instead of as a sex object, like some of her punters did. Some were polite, others shy, but a few tried to treat her like a piece of dirt beneath their feet, until she put them in their place. She would never let any man disrespect her. If they continued to do so, she returned their money and refused their business. It had caused her a couple of black eyes in the past, but she figured she would have suffered much more had she let them continue. But tonight she was a different woman. Tonight was for her.

She and Brad chatted easily together. She asked how he was settling in England and in the army.

'England is quaint,' he told her. 'You folks are so different, so reserved. We Americans must be a shock to you all. I'm sure we must appear brash and very loud.'

'Believe me, it's a wonderful change,' she assured him. 'I would love everybody to be so open, it's so much fun! You say reserved, I would say stuffy!'

He thought this highly amusing. 'Well, Miss . . .?'

'Rusty, all my friends call me Rusty.'

'Well, Rusty, you don't appear to be at all stuffy.'

She burst out laughing. 'Dear God, no! Life's too short, Captain. Life is for living, and I don't want to go to my maker without enjoying every moment that I have.'

'Brad, please. Well, Rusty, let's take to the floor again before it gets too crowded.'

Eventually, the band played their last number, and Brad held her close as they waltzed around the floor. As the final notes died, he offered to walk her home.

Rusty hesitated. It wasn't that she didn't still want to be with him, but she didn't want him to see where she lived. She had a small bedsit near Canal Walk, which was by no means a salubrious part of the town. He had treated her like a lady, and she didn't want anything to spoil this illusion. 'Thank you, Brad, but I'll be fine. Honestly.'

He looked concerned. 'At least let me pay for a taxi. It's late, and no young woman should walk these streets alone at this time of night.'

If only he knew how at home she was on these streets at night, she thought. 'Thank you, that would be kind of you,' she demurred.

'How about I take you out to dinner? I'm free on Monday evening. It will be my way of thanking you for tonight.'

'I'd like that very much.'

'Shall I come and pick you up?'

'No, I'll meet you outside the Red Cross club at the Bargate. How about seven thirty?'

'I'll be there,' he said and smiled, then leaned forward and kissed her on the cheek. 'It will give us time to get to know one another better.' He called a taxi, gave the driver some money after Rusty had told him her destination and, with a wave, watched her being driven away.

As she sat in the back of the vehicle, Rusty frowned. This lovely American had no idea that she was a prostitute. How on earth was she to spend an evening with him without revealing too much about her life? He was such a gentleman, well educated, that much was obvious. He had told her he was a doctor in private life, so he probably came from a good background. She was playing with fire, but she told herself that this was war time and people only passed through – nothing was permanent. She dearly wanted to see him again, so she would just have to invent a life that he would find acceptable, she decided. Yes, that's what she'd do, and then she'd enjoy his company until it was time for him to move on. She sat back with a feeling of contentment. Rusty Dobbs, a lady – that's what she would be.

It was Sunday, and Rusty decided to take the day off. She wandered along to the Hoglands where usually the cricket matches were held for local clubs, but today the Americans were playing what to her appeared to be a glorified game of rounders. They called it baseball.

An American GI sat beside her and explained the rules to her as the game progressed. She thoroughly enjoyed the afternoon, as did many of the local children, drawn there primarily in their search for gum and sweets. The soldiers were only too happy to oblige. It was all part of the plan to integrate with the locals, and for all concerned it was a pleasant way to spend an afternoon. Tomorrow, she'd see the handsome captain and enjoy being spoilt yet again.

As arranged, Rusty met Brad outside the Red Cross club by the Bargate. The medieval gateway was a relic of a bygone day which straddled the street and was a constant interest to the foreign soldiers, especially the Americans who had nothing ancient in their country.

Brad suggested they dine at the Polgon Hotel, so they walked past the shops in Above Bar, window gazing. He was astonished when she explained that to purchase any clothes displayed in the window meant that a woman or a man would have to part with clothing coupons also and that there was a limited amount of these.

'You would just love New York, Rusty. You could shop until you dropped with exhaustion. The Big Apple is a woman's dream.'

'I've seen it in American films,' she said. 'It certainly looks exciting, but dangerous.'

'Then you would maybe prefer my hometown in Denver, Colorado.' As they walked he described his hometown and the way of life there. It all sounded so very different to anything she'd ever known. And then they reached their destination.

They sat in the cocktail bar with their drinks, and Brad turned to her. 'So tell me about your life, Rusty.'

She told one lie after another. 'My parents emigrated to Australia before the war, but I didn't want to go, so I got a job as a clerk in an office.'

'Don't you miss them?'

'Of course, but Dad had an offer of a job there and it was an opportunity not to be missed.' And so it went on.

During dinner, Brad listened intently to what she had to say. He thought Rusty was vibrant, beautiful and intelligent, and for the first time in an age he was really interested in a woman. She appeared so confident, so happy in her own skin. She seemed to have no hang ups at all . . . and that was refreshing – and she made him laugh.

As they walked back through the town, Brad asked her if she'd like to go to the Red Cross club, but she declined saying it was getting late and she had to get some sleep. But, truthfully, she was fearful that inside the club she might meet one of the GIs who had been a punter and that would have been horrendous.

'Are you sure?' he asked. 'Only, I have to pick up some stuff they have for me.'

'You carry on, Brad,' she insisted. 'I'll go on home.'

'I can't let you do that!'

She touched his arm. 'Of course you can. You'd only have to walk back, and that's crazy.'

'When can I see you again?' he asked.

Rusty was thrilled. She liked this man. 'How about Thursday evening?'

'That's great. What would you like to do?'

'There's a good film on at the Forum cinema I would like to see. I could meet you outside at seven.'

'It'll be my pleasure, Rusty.' He drew her close and kissed her softly. 'Thanks for a great evening.'

'I enjoyed it too,' she told him, then she left.

Just after, she encountered two GIs who were among her regulars.

'Hi, Rusty, what are you doing here? Why aren't you doing your bit for the war effort tonight?'

She laughed. 'Well, boys, I've taken the night off.'

'See you soon,' they said and carried on their way.

She quietly looked up and whispered, 'Thank you God!' How awful it would have been had the two soldiers seen her with Brad! If she continued to see him, life would be fraught with the danger of being found out . . . but she was prepared to take the risk. Especially after he'd kissed her. She made a rule that she never allowed her punters to kiss her, it was much too personal. But when she'd felt Brad's mouth on hers, she'd known she wanted more. She wanted to be bedded by a man who was attracted to her, who thought of her as a woman and not a business transaction. But would she be able to fool him that long without being found out? She certainly hoped so.

The next morning, Brad drove to the stables to make his apologies for not turning up the previous Wednesday, but Beth brushed his words aside.

'Please, I can't thank you enough for sending Corporal Maxwell along.' She then told him what had taken place and how the soldier had tamed the maverick horse.

'He was here for forty-eight hours working with the animal, and he came back today to continue. Come with me,' she said. 'Chad has the animal in the practice ring now.'

He followed her, curious to see what was happening. He saw Jenny and walked over to her. 'What's going on?'

'Just watch,' she whispered. 'It's amazing!'

Once again, Chad moved around the ring making the horse turn in any direction he chose. He saddled up and rode the horse around the ring until once again he had the animal laying on its side, where he sat on it. Then, to everyone's surprise, he called the groom into the ring.

The girl looked nervous as she slowly walked towards him.

Chad held out his hand to her and in a quiet, calm voice told her to sit beside him, nearer the neck of the animal. She did so. The horse just raised its head to see what was happening, then lay back down on the ground.

'Stroke him and speak softly to him,' she was told by the American.

The girl leaned forward and stroked the mane, talking all the time. After a while he told her to stand up, and he got the horse to its feet. Chad took a carrot from his pocket and gave it to the girl. 'Feed him,' he said, 'then stroke him, talking to him all the time so he'll get used to your voice.'

Whilst she was doing so, Chad walked over to the fence and picked up a saddle, then walking back he gently put it across the back of the animal, which pricked up his ears, but remained still.

He tightened the girth and told the girl to return to the safety of the fence, then he put his foot into the stirrup and pulled himself on to the back of the animal, talking all the time.

The maverick animal tensed and pawed at the ground, but Chad pulled gently on its mane, then stroked its neck. Gathering the reins, he put pressure on his heels into the side of the horse, and it moved forward and trotted around the ring.

Everyone watched with baited breath as he urged the animal into a gallop, circling the ring several times, before stopping and beckoning to the groom.

He slipped out of the saddle and held the reins whilst the groom put her foot into the stirrup and mounted, then he handed her the reins.

'Now do what I did. Walk him, then take him into a trot, then a gallop. Try and relax or he'll feel your tension, and don't worry, he won't throw you – not now.'

He stood in the centre of the ring as the girl followed his orders.

The animal responded to her every move. The girl flew around the ring, grinning broadly as she gained in confidence. It was a joy to watch the two of them.

At Chad's signal, she slowed down to a walk and eventually came to a halt. She leaned forward, stroking the horse's neck. 'You good boy!' she said, then she slipped out of the saddle, walked to the front of the animal and stroked its nose.

'You can walk him back to his stall now and unsaddle him,' Chad told her. 'He won't give you any more trouble.' Then he walked over to Beth. 'There you are, ma'am! He'll be fine now.'

'How can I ever thank you?' she said, looking delighted and amazed.

'Well, you can let me come out here when I have a pass!'

With a smile she told him, 'You are welcome at any time.'

Brad looked at Chad. 'Well, Corporal, I had no idea you had such a talent. Well done.'

'Thank you, sir. It was my pleasure, it was like being at home . . . Well, almost.'

'Come into the kitchen, all of you. I'll make us some coffee.' With this, Beth led the way.

Shortly after, Brad took his leave. 'Sorry, but I have to get back to the office. Good to see you, Jenny. How's your husband enjoying his leave?'

'Very much, thank you.'

'That's great. I'll get back when I can,' Brad told Beth, and turning to the Corporal he said: 'I'll see you back at camp.'

Beth too made her excuses, leaving Chad and Jenny alone.

'You were amazing!' Jenny told the American.

He smiled lazily. 'No I wasn't, Mrs Procter.'

'Jenny, please.'

'I was just doing what comes naturally to me, that's all, Jenny.' He looked at her with his penetrating gaze which she found so unsettling. 'And how are you finding things with your husband home? Are you enjoying his leave too?'

She hesitated just a fraction. 'Of course.'

'No, you're not! You are not enjoying it one bit.'

'What makes you say that?'

'Because you're not happy. You're tense, your back is tight, and there is a certain sadness in your eyes.'

She was speechless.

'Come on,' he said and took her by the hand. 'Let's go for a drive. You need a change of scenery.'

Six

Jenny sat in the jeep beside Chad as he drove to Botley, where he stopped and parked the vehicle. They had travelled in a comfortable silence, despite Jenny wondering why she had agreed to come. She should have returned home by now – although Adam had said he was meeting friends at lunchtime, so he wouldn't be waiting for her, breathing fire at her absence.

She and Chad walked along the peaceful river bank. Apart from a few ducks and a couple of swans, they had the place to themselves. They stopped and sat beneath a tree overlooking the water.

'There are two miracles of nature that bring peace to a person's soul,' he proclaimed.

'And what are those?'

'Water and mountains. Back in Wyoming we have the glorious Rocky Mountains, and lakes of course, but you have no idea what a mountain range can do for your soul. Among them, you can forget everything – except the wonder of nature.'

'You truly are a man of the outdoors, aren't you? I don't think I've ever met anyone like you, Chad.'

His laughter echoed. 'That's because I'm an American!'

'No, it's much more than that. You have an inner peace which is most unusual. You're not in the least egotistical, as most men are.'

He turned his gaze on her. 'Like your husband, you mean.'

It was Jenny's turn to laugh. 'Oh yes. Adam has a huge ego.'

'How long have you been married, Jenny?'

'Eighteen years, although Adam has been away for that last three.'

'That's a long time. People change. You've probably changed more than he has.'

'What makes you say that?'

'Well, it makes sense. Without a man to care for you would have found other things to fill your time. With him away, you were free . . . at last.' He continued: 'Within you is a free spirit, Jenny, but sadly it has been smothered during your marriage. Now, having tasted freedom for the first time, you find it difficult to return to your marriage ties.'

'You have an uncanny way of getting into people's minds as well as those of horses. It is very unsettling!'

He found this highly amusing. 'Sorry, I usually keep such thoughts to myself, but I would love to take you to Wyoming because there you could be that free spirit. You could really live the life you want.' He stood up. 'Come on, I think it's time to go home.'

He drove her back to the stables where she could collect her bicycle.

'Would you like me to drive you home? We could put the bike in the back of the jeep,' Chad said.

'No, thank you. I need the exercise. Will I see you again?'

'Oh, yeah, I'll be around here whenever I'm free. You take care, you hear?'

Chuckling, Jenny said, 'You have no need to worry about me, I can take care of myself.'

'I bet you can . . . given the opportunity!'

As she rode home, Jenny pondered over the American's words and his uncanny understanding of the human spirit. It was fascinating, but at the same time, somewhat unnerving. She could imagine him back in Wyoming, riding the range, dealing with maverick horses. Well, she wasn't a maverick woman!

The remainder of Adam's leave seemed to fly by. Jenny was busy with committee meetings and keeping her husband entertained, which left no time to visit the stables, and now Adam was returning to his regiment after lunch.

The two of them sat at the table in the kitchen, neither of them feeling at ease with the other now the time had come to part once again. Jenny was wondering when Adam would have his next leave; would he even come through the war alive? She quickly pushed this thought to the back of her head.

Adam sat wondering if the fighting would be as bad as it had been in the past and how many of his men would fall in battle. He gazed across the table at his wife. She had an air of independence about her these days which he found hard to cope with and for a moment he wondered if his marriage would survive this separation. But he immediately thought that once he was home for good things would return to normal, because he would once again be in control and Jenny would no longer belong to so many of the things which these days seemed to occupy most of her time.

He drained his coffee cup, lit a cigarette and suggested they take one last walk around the garden. They eventually sat on the bench beneath the trees. He gazed around the area. 'This is so typically English,' he said. 'I'll carry this scene with me when I get back to France.'

Jenny took his hand. 'You take great care. I want you back in one piece.'

He looked at her with a quizzical expression. 'Are you sure you want me back at all?'

His question shook her. 'Whatever do you mean?'

He shrugged. 'I don't know. It's just that I feel we have drifted so far apart. I seem to have come home to a very different woman from the one that I married.'

What could she say? She was different. She felt different. She also knew that although she loved Adam, she was no longer in love with him. She didn't want to return to the old days, to be at his beck and call. As Chad had said, she wanted much more, and that didn't include her husband . . . but she couldn't tell him that, not today of all days.

'It's the war, Adam. Things change, people change, the world changes. When it's all over then everything changes yet again.'

He looked at his watch. 'My driver will be here any moment now.' As he said this, they could hear the sound of a car's engine. They walked into the house and collected Adam's suitcase. At the front door, the driver saluted and picking up the case took it to the car.

Adam put his arms around his wife and kissed her. 'Take care, darling. I'll write when I can.' He hesitated, as if he was going to say more, then he smiled at her and walked to the car.

She watched until the vehicle was driven on to the road. Jenny felt sad. After all, she'd spent so many years with this man, but during the three weeks he'd been home it had been a strain. She'd found it hard to tolerate his dictatorial ways, yet for many years it had been a way of life. She felt confused. What was the future to hold for them, she wondered. Could she continue in this marriage when Adam eventually returned home for good? She didn't think that she could.

Rusty Dobbs was weary. It seemed to her that the troops of all nationalities, waiting to be shipped abroad, had only one thing on their minds – and that was to get laid! During the past two weeks she'd catered for the Americans, the French and a couple of Poles. Language had no barrier when it came to sex. It was: take the money, get your clothes off and get fucked! It was as cold-blooded as that. But Rusty was used to that by now. She knew that to become involved further with a punter was a dead loss. A couple of her mates had done so, and the men concerned then wanted their services exclusively – and for free. That was not for her; she was on the game strictly to make as much money as she could, and when the war was over she'd retire from prostitution.

But also during these past two weeks she'd been able to meet with Brad Jackson a few of times. They'd been to the cinema, out to lunch and dinner, and they'd once driven to the New Forest to a local pub for a drink. She felt completely at ease with him and enjoyed his company; thankfully, he reciprocated these feelings. They just seemed so well matched, although they came from such different backgrounds. With the exception of having to lie about her family and job, she was able to be herself with him. Apart from liking him as a man, she found him physically very attractive, which was not usual for her, and she was delighted when his kisses became increasingly ardent. The last time they'd met, Brad had told her he had a weekend pass – and would she like to spend it with him in Bournemouth?

He had been so sweet when he'd asked her; he had taken her into his arms. 'At home if I met a girl, I would court her, bring her flowers, candy, spend time getting to know her, but Rusty, in wartime that's not possible. I could be shipped out tomorrow, so I'm being very forward – would you like to spend the weekend with me? I have a weekend pass and would love to take you with me to a nice hotel in Bournemouth. What do you say?'

She smiled as she thought of the concerned expression on his face. He'd been worried that she'd be outraged at such a proposal. 'Why, Captain Jackson,' she had teased, 'are you trying to seduce me?'

'I guess I am. Does that offend you?'

'Not one bit! I told you when first we met, life is for living. I'd love to come with you.'

He looked delighted. 'We'll have to take the train, I'm afraid.'

'That's fine! Let me know which train and I'll meet you at the station.'

Rusty packed her prettiest underwear and a frilly nightgown with growing excitement. She was going to be made love to by a man she desired and who desired her for herself and not as a prostitute. How marvellous! And to be staying in a hotel, where she would be waited on and cosseted. She could hardly wait.

They managed to sit together, although the trains were busy, not only with civilian passengers but also with so many troops. They chatted away as they passed through the stations, with Brad holding her hand. Rusty didn't give a hoot for the odd glance cast her way by the civilian passengers, who seeing the American uniform were obviously making judgements about her. Whenever she caught one such glance she would smile at the person concerned, who would then look quickly away.

They arrived and took a taxi to a large hotel near the front. Brad signed the register and was given the key to their room on the first floor. In the lift he put his arm around her. 'Hello, Mrs Jackson.'

She grinned broadly at him. 'I am going to enjoy my wifely duties, I think.'

Brad roared with laughter. 'Rusty, you are outrageous.'

The lift stopped, and stepping out, they found their room. It was spacious, and walking over to the window, Rusty looked out to the sea. Opening the French windows, she cried, 'Brad, we have a balcony!'

He stood behind her, looking at the view, then, putting his arms round her waist, nuzzled her neck. 'About these wifely duties . . . Now or later?'

She turned within his embrace and gently ran her finger across his mouth. 'Now – *and* later,' she said as she kissed him.

Brad picked her up in his arms and carried her over to the bed. He put her down and removed his jacket and tie, then he lay beside her, took her into his arms and kissed her, gently exploring her mouth.

Rusty returned his kisses, running her fingers through his hair, then she unbuttoned his shirt. 'You are wearing far too many clothes, Captain.'

They undressed one another and made love. For Rusty it was like a rebirth. Brad was gentle and thoughtful . . . and accomplished. She lay in his arms and for once let her senses run free. She was with a man of her choosing for all the right reasons. Her need for him grew as he explored her body until she cried out for him to take her. He paused only to take precautions, and then he entered her.

Rusty lay back against the pillows, at peace with the world. Her orgasm took her by surprise. She had wondered, as she lay in Brad's arms, if it was possible after so long. She had never done so with a punter and had wondered if she would ever have another. Well, today she had – and it was wonderful.

Brad leaned across her and fondled her breast. 'Let's get dressed and go and find a place to eat. I'm ravenous.'

'Do we have to?' she pleaded, putting an arm round his neck and kissing him.

He looked at her, his eyes twinkling. 'Yes, I think we do, unless you want to wear me out.'

'That's the last thing I want to do.' She chuckled softly. 'I want you to be fit and able to make love to me again and again before we have to go home.'

'You are an insatiable woman!'

'Are you complaining?'

He ruffled her hair. 'Are you kidding!'

★　　★　　★

They walked along the promenade, went window shopping, and then found a cosy restaurant to have lunch. They chatted and laughed together, both enjoying the secrecy of their new intimacy. It was like being on a honeymoon, Rusty thought. She gazed into the eyes of her new lover and remembered how he looked when he was making love to her, his naked body thrusting himself inside her, murmuring to her, telling her how beautiful she was and how much he wanted her. She reached out to touch him and felt the sexual urgency once again coursing through her veins. As they finished their coffee, she reached out and took his hand. 'Let's go back to our room,' she said softly.

Brad smiled at her, asked for the bill, paid it, then said quietly, 'Let's go.'

The weekend was the happiest that Rusty could ever remember. Brad was a perfect companion as well as a lover. They shared the same sense of humour. They swam, they went dancing, and they walked, talking and laughing together the whole time. Not a moment was wasted.

As they sat in the train on the way home, Brad glanced at the woman beside him, staring out of the window. How lovely she was, he thought. He sat picturing every curve of her body that he'd explored, remembering her little cries of pleasure as he made love to her. But he could also see her cooking his breakfast, being a permanent part of his life, and that made him happy . . . but with the war, he'd have to wait before making plans.

As she watched the passing scenery, Rusty knew that when the time came for Brad to be posted, she would be broken-hearted. This man was very special, and she felt so lucky to have been a small part of his life. If only things had been different. She felt she could spend the rest of her life with Brad Jackson and be the happiest woman alive. Meantime, she would just relish every moment they spent together and try not to think too far into the future.

Seven

The latest news of the war filtered through the camp housing the German prisoners, and they didn't like what they heard. In August, the Americans bombed the Messerschmitt works at Regensburg, causing untold damage. For those dyed-in-the-wool Germans who believed in Hitler, it was devastating news; for young Gunter, it was further proof that the war was useless. He now believed that Germany would lose, but he kept those thoughts to himself.

It had been decided by the authorities that if they had to house these men and feed them, then they should earn their keep. Besides, such men with time on their hands could be trouble. With so many Englishmen called to serve in the armed forces, manpower was limited in many areas. Some of the prisoners were escorted to local farmers, who used them to work in the fields. Fields which had been turned into grounds for growing vegetables and corn, to help with the rationing. Others were helping to clear bomb sites – places which had been devastated during the blitz. It soon became the norm to see Germans working for their keep, watched over by armed soldiers.

Gunter had been lucky. He was sent to a small farm, to help the farmer with his cows and pigs, and was allowed to stay with the farmer's family, on the understanding that if he tried to escape, the consequences would be dire.

He was only too happy to comply; anything to get out of the camp. He was able to tell Sarah where he was going, and when he confessed to Mrs Brown, the farmer's wife, that he was in love with an English girl, she allowed Sarah to visit at weekends.

Mr and Mrs Brown took to Gunter, realizing that he was an educated man and not a Nazi. He worked well and was polite and soon became part of the family.

For Sarah, it was a perfect situation. If there was work to be done when she visited, she stepped in and helped too, which endeared her to the farmers, who were getting on in years. Their son, who would eventually inherit the farm, was away in the army.

Over a meal one Sunday, Mr Brown chuckled. 'If Tim, our boy, knew we had a German working for us, he'd have a bloody fit!'

'Not if he really knew Gunter,' Sarah chipped in.

Mrs Brown looked fondly at her. 'I can only hope that when this war is over, you and Gunter can meet under better circumstances.' It worried the older woman that these two young people, who were so obviously in love, could face great heartache in the future. She wondered just what Sarah's mother thought about the situation.

But Sarah hadn't confided in her mother, knowing how hostile she had been about her daughter consorting with the enemy. Instead, she made excuses when she went to the farm, saying she was with a friend.

During Sunday evenings when all work was finished, Gunter and Sarah would climb into the loft of one of the barns so they could be alone. It was there one evening that Sarah lost her virginity. Being together without restraints of any kind had brought their love affair into the open, and they were able to kiss and cuddle without fear of reprisals, and eventually, their need for each other overcame constraint – and they made love.

As Gunter held her during their love-making, he spoke quietly to her in his own tongue – which didn't bother Sarah, because the tone of his voice was so soft and full of love and passion – and she gave herself to him, willingly.

After, as she lay in Gunter's arms, Sarah knew she wanted to spend the rest of her life with this man and was determined that, no matter what, she would fight for the right.

Brad Jackson had been busy at headquarters and had only been to visit the stables a couple of times in the last few weeks, but he asked Beth if he could bring a young lady over the next weekend. She had immediately agreed, so he mentioned it to Rusty, warning her that they would have to work at the stables, mucking out, but after, they could go for a ride.

'What, on a horse?' she exclaimed. Horrified at the idea.

'Of course on a horse.' He looked at her scared expression. 'Don't worry, I'll give you a lesson first. You'll be safe with me, I promise – oh, and wear a pair of slacks.'

She hadn't been really convinced, but Rusty being Rusty, she never turned a new adventure down, and so on the following Sunday morning she drove to the stables with her captain.

Jenny and Chad were already working when they arrived. Brad introduced Rusty to them, and the four stopped for a chat. Rusty told them that she was decidedly nervous.

'You'll be fine,' said Chad. 'Captain Jackson knows what he's doing.'

During the next hour, they cleaned several stables, put down new straw and filled water buckets, and then Brad saddled one of the quieter horses and helped Rusty to mount.

Once on the animal's back, she looked down and said, 'The ground is a hell of a long way away from up here, Brad.'

He put a lead rein on and, trying not to laugh, led the steed away to the practice ring. There he walked the horse around until Rusty began to relax, showing her how to grip with her knees, relax in the saddle and how to hold the reins. After a while she began to enjoy it.

He then told her to gently kick the animal with her heels. She did so and let out a scream as it broke into a trot. 'Oh my God!' she cried. 'How do I stop it?'

'Just relax! I'm on the other end of the rein. Enjoy it, Rusty.'

And eventually she did.

The workforce broke for a snack lunch and gathered beneath the trees. Brad took the horse back to the stable, and then he and Rusty joined them. He'd bought some decent white bread with him and, to everyone's delight, some fresh cheese.

Jenny watched Rusty and Brad chatting away and immediately realized that there was something between them from the intimate looks they exchanged as they talked. She was pleased for Brad; their friendship had grown through their shared work, and she liked the quiet American.

Chad, sitting beside her, also took note. 'It seems as if the captain has found himself a girl,' he remarked. 'That's how two people look at each other when they're in love.'

Gazing at them, Jenny had to agree. 'How marvellous, but what happens when Brad is shipped away, what then?' She turned to Chad. 'War breaks so many hearts one way or another.'

He took her hand. 'Not necessarily so. It can also bring great happiness.'

She gazed at the man beside her and recognized the same expression in his eyes as in Brad's. It confused her considerably. During the times she'd met Chad and seen his work she had at first been filled with admiration and awe, but as she grew to know him better, there had been an affinity with him and a physical attraction, which she'd tried to ignore. For one thing he must be at least ten years her junior – and she was married! She told herself that in any case he didn't feel the same, but looking at him now, she knew that he did.

'Come on, let's saddle up a couple of horses and go for a ride, somewhere where we can be alone.' He held out his hand to her, and she took it and stood up.

'We're going to exercise the horses,' Chad told the others, and they walked away.

They rode for quite a while until they arrived deep inside a wood, where Chad reined in his horse, dismounted and tied the reins to a tree. He walked over to Jenny and did the same with her reins, then he waited.

She climbed down from her mount. Chad took a step towards her and took her into his arms. 'I've been wanting to do this from the moment we met,' he said . . . and he kissed her.

Jenny lost all her inhibitions when she felt his mouth on hers, demanding her complicity, which she willingly gave. Never had she felt this way, not even when Adam first took her into his arms, and as Chad led her to a clearing and pulled her down beside him, she gave vent to all the frustration that had built up inside her, surprised at the wanton feelings that flooded her being.

'Oh, Jenny, Jenny,' he murmured as he kissed her. 'You are a wonderful woman, you have so much love in you that has been smothered for far too long.'

She scarcely heard him as she returned his ardour.

They made love beneath the trees in the quiet of the wood, surrounded by the nature that Chad held so dear to him. It seemed a fitting place for her to give herself to this extraordinary man, which she did with great abandon. Never before had she felt free, able to let go of her inhibitions − but with Chad, she was a different person. It was almost like being reborn, and she relished every moment.

After, they lay replete in each other's arms.

Chad gently caught hold of her face and turned it towards him until she was looking at him. 'What are you thinking right this minute?'

'I'm thinking that we have made a lot of trouble for ourselves,' she said quietly, 'but I don't regret a minute of it.'

'Things have a way of working out, honey,' he said. 'We just have to live for the moment − the future will take care of itself. Come along, we best get back before they send out the posse.'

Brad was called away to another camp for a few days, and Rusty returned to her way of life. After all, she had to make a living, and in her mind her world and her love affair with the handsome officer were two separate entities. As long as he didn't find out how she earned her living everything would be fine.

She was sitting in the Horse and Groom in East Street with one of her friends, a place she didn't often frequent as it was the roughest pub in Southampton with a history to match. Most Saturday evenings there was a fight and the police would be called. There'd even been a stabbing and a fatality in recent months, but her friend, another prostitute, worked out of this bar.

It was early in the evening and the bar was quiet, which gave the girls time to chat. They looked up as two GIs walked in. The men strolled to the bar, looked round and seeing the girls asked them if they would like a drink. Before Rusty could say a word, her friend had invited them over.

The soldiers were good company and plied the girls with drink before they got down to business. Rusty eyed the one she would be taking home. Joe was a well-built man, quieter than his friend, but he seemed pleasant enough as they walked down Canal Walk to her bedsit.

Once inside her room he looked around and then at her. 'At least it's clean,' he said and started to undress.

Rusty stopped him. 'Money first, Joe.' She told him how much, and he pulled out his wallet and paid her. As she took her clothes off, Rusty started chatting to him, but he wasn't interested in the niceties.

'I didn't come here to talk!' he snapped. 'That's not what I paid for. Lie down!'

Rusty felt her blood run cold, and warning bells started ringing inside her head, but before she could say a word, the American pulled her on to the bed and held her down. Everything he did was brutal. He held her by the throat, and he pawed at her body, clasping her breast in a vice-like grip which made her cry out with pain. When she complained, he hit her. She struggled against his brute force, to no avail. He hit her again, and she lay still.

The next thirty minutes she thought would be her last as he violated her body. During this time he was silent, which in itself was menacing and terrifying. He took her in various positions, turning her this way and that like a rag doll, until eventually he was satisfied. He then got off the bed, got dressed and, with only a look of disdain cast in her direction, he walked out of the door.

Rusty was unable to move for a while. It seemed to her that every part of her body hurt. She moaned as she tried to get up. She tasted blood from her lip where he'd hit her. As she put her hand to her mouth she could feel the swelling. Tears of anger trickled down her cheeks. 'Bastard!' she cried as she crawled off the bed.

She walked over to the sink in the corner and ran the cold tap, looking at her reflection in the mirror. Her face was now beginning to swell, and she soaked a flannel in the cold water and held it over her face to try and stem the swelling. Putting a dressing gown on she took her toiletries and staggered to the bathroom down the hall, which was shared by the other tenants, and ran a bath. She tried to scrub away every vestige of the brute who had used her so cruelly. As she soaked in the water, she began to cry.

Eight

Rusty felt like hell the next morning. Her face was less swollen, but she was covered in bruises. She silently thanked God that Brad was away because there was no way she would let him see her in this state – how could she have explained? They usually communicated by phone. He told her when to call his office, and that way they were able to keep in touch as she had been careful to keep her address from him and her supposed place of work. Had he been in Southampton at this time, she would have had to make excuses, until her body and face had healed.

Brad had booked them a room in a hotel in Lymington for the following weekend, and Rusty prayed that by then she would be back to normal. She cursed the American who had done this to her and later that day, wearing dark glasses, she met up with her friend from the previous evening, to warn her about him.

'Bloody hell, Rusty, you look as if you've been in the ring with a prize fighter!' said Dorothy when Rusty had lifted her glasses for a moment.

'That bastard took me by surprise. I thought I was a goner, honestly I did. He frightened me to death. I want you to warn all the other girls. That man is dangerous.'

'You should report him to the army; no man should get away with that.'

'What are they going to say? As a prostitute, it's a risk you take. They wouldn't want to know.' Although what she said was true, Rusty knew that if she had made a complaint, Captain Brad Jackson would be the officer to deal with her, so that *wasn't* going to happen, but she didn't share this fact. She'd kept her relationship with Brad a secret from everyone.

Joe Kowalski was not a popular man in his company. He mainly kept himself to himself, but he was known for his vicious temper. A brooding, silent character, he took offence at the smallest thing and had lost many days' pay as a consequence of the fights he'd been involved in. But he was an arrogant man. Today he was having breakfast with the soldier that he'd been with in the Horse and Groom the previous night.

'How did you make out last night, Joe? My girl was great; she gave me a real good time. Worth every nickel.'

Joe swigged down his coffee. 'Mine wanted to talk; I soon put a stop to that.'

'What do you mean?' asked the other warily.

'She was there to service me. That's what I paid good money for, and I let her know it.'

'What did you do?'

'I had to slap her around a bit; she didn't like the feel of my hands on her sweet body. Said I was hurting her.'

The other GI looked worried. 'You didn't do anything stupid, did you?'

'Nah! But I fucked her good and hard, that's what she was there for. I just made her earn her dough, that's all.'

His companion made excuses and left him. He didn't want to get mixed up with anything bad, and he had a feeling that one day there would be a price to pay if he stuck around with this guy.

Joe wasn't bothered by being deserted. He was basically a loner, always had been. He'd been a steel worker in Pennsylvania, like his father. You had to be tough to survive there, and Joe was a survivor. When America came into the war after Pearl Harbour, Joe had seen a way out of his mundane life and signed up. He wanted to see the world, widen his horizons. And now he was in England; next would be France and the fighting. Well, he was used to fighting, and now trained by the army he was a fighting man with a gun and the authority to use it. That suited him just fine.

Rusty rang Brad's office on Friday evening as planned and was told that he had the use of a jeep for the weekend. She arranged to meet him outside the bombed Holy Rood Church at nine thirty on Saturday morning.

'I've really missed you Rusty,' Brad told her, 'I can't wait to see you again.'

'I've missed you too, Captain,' she laughed. 'See you in the morning.'

Saturday dawned, and they set off in bright sunshine with a cool breeze and drove through the picturesque New Forest. Rusty had applied her make-up carefully, as the bruises on her face had faded to yellow, but she still felt sore; however, she laughed and joked with her lover as they journeyed.

When they arrived in Lymington, they checked in to the hotel; but their room wasn't ready so, leaving their bags with the receptionist, they walked down to the harbour and sat on a seat.

Brad took her into his arms and kissed her hungrily. 'God, you taste so good.' And he kissed her again.

'I've missed you too, darling. How did your trip go?'

He sighed. 'War does crazy things to people. The police wanted to take two of the men to court, but I told them the army would deal with them and they would be punished. They caused a hell of a fracas in a pub, and there was no end of damage. They assaulted a couple of the local men. It was a mess. We covered the costs of the repairs, which will come out of the soldiers' pay. They will serve some time in the glasshouse for their trouble.' He smiled tenderly at her. 'What have you been up to in my absence?'

'Nothing much, work and sleep, that's about it.'

He pulled her close. 'Never mind, we have two days to enjoy ourselves. Come on, let's find a place that will make a decent cup of coffee, then we'll take a walk, have some lunch. By then our room should be ready.'

Rusty longed to be in Brad's arms again, but she was worried that in the daylight he would see the bruises on her body that had not entirely faded. 'Wouldn't you rather drive around and see the countryside first?' she suggested, thinking if they made love in the dark, she would be safe from prying eyes.

He looked surprised. 'If that's what you really want to do.'

There was such a note of disappointment in his voice, she gave in. 'No, of course not. I want to be close to you, of course I do.'

'You had me worried for a moment, Rusty darling. I wondered if you had found yourself another man.'

She caressed his cheek. 'Don't be so silly. Why on earth would I want anyone but you?'

They made their way to a nearby cafe, walked along the harbour, had a satisfying meal with several glasses of wine and, after paying the bill, walked back to their hotel.

Once in the bedroom, Brad reached for her. 'Come here, I need to hold you. I feel as if I've been away for an age.'

They eventually climbed into bed, Rusty keeping her underwear on until she was safely beneath the sheets to hide what was left of her bruises. But Brad, caressing her, kissing her, exploring her body, soon discovered them. He looked at her with more than a little concern.

'What the hell has happened to you since I've been away? You're covered in bruises, which by their coloration look to me to be days old.' He waited for her reply.

'I fell over,' she said hastily.

He frowned and stared at her. 'Rusty, you forget I'm a doctor. These bruises are far more than you would have from a fall. To me you look as if you've been manhandled.' He touched her face, which by now had lost the covering of make-up. 'You have the remains of a bruise here too . . . Rusty?'

She closed her eyes, thinking rapidly, then opening them she said, 'I wasn't going to tell you because I didn't want to worry you, but a drunken soldier attacked me as I was going home from the cinema one night.'

'You reported this to the police, of course.'

'What was the point? I didn't see what he looked like, so what could they have done?'

He cursed beneath his breath. 'Was the soldier British or American?'

'He was a GI. I could tell that much by his uniform.'

Brad looked down at her bare breasts. 'These look like fingermarks!' His jaw tightened and he asked, 'Rusty, were you raped?'

What could she say? No longer could she deny the telltale marks, and in a way she *had* been raped. 'Yes,' she whispered.

He looked appalled, and seeing the tears brimming in her eyes, he held her gently. 'Oh my darling, I am so sorry.' Wiping a tear from her cheek he said, 'What a dreadful thing to happen to you. It must have been terrifying.' He kissed her forehead and tried to comfort her, then he said, 'There is one thing you must do as soon as we go home – you need to go to your doctor and be examined.'

'What for? It's over and done with.'

He spoke very softly. 'You don't know your attacker, but you need to be sure that he hasn't infected you.'

She felt a chill run down her spine. She'd handed Joe a condom when he paid his money, and in the mayhem that followed, she couldn't remember if he'd used it. 'Oh my God!' she cried, now filled with horror.

'It's all right. If by any chance you are, these things can be treated with antibiotics. Trust me.'

Suddenly, her world fell apart, and she broke down and sobbed. 'How can you bear to touch me now?'

He held her tightly. 'Don't be a goose. I love you, I want to take care of you. You couldn't help what happened. Now, Rusty, stop crying, we'll get through this together.'

But of course they didn't make love, and wouldn't until Rusty had been tested, which made her feel dirty. Despite Brad's continued affection and support, their weekend had been ruined.

When on Sunday evening Brad dropped Rusty back outside the church, he drew her into his arms. 'Listen, darling, make an appointment to see your doctor, don't leave it, promise?'

'I promise.'

'Call me in a couple of days. I have to clear a mountain of paperwork, then we'll go out for a meal somewhere.' He saw the uncertainty in her eyes. 'Please don't worry; just remember that I love you.' He drove away.

She walked home, her mind in a whirl. She had always been so careful about her punters using protection, knowing the dangers of her occupation, but now . . . now she was frantic. She wouldn't go to the doctor as there was a special clinic set up in the town. She would make an appointment there. All she could do now was pray.

As Brad drove back to headquarters, he fumed inwardly. If he could only get his hands on the man who had defiled his girl, he would throw the book at him! He pictured her bruised body and tried to shut out the images of what she must have endured. He remembered the fear in her eyes when he suggested she be examined, but he had no choice. As a doctor it was his duty, and as her lover he wanted to ensure her physical being. This girl was very dear to him, and he really couldn't envisage leaving her behind after the war, but these thoughts he'd kept to himself. At some time in the future he was sure to be shipped across the channel into the thick of the fighting, and it didn't do to make too many future plans until the war was over. He would have time then to make his thoughts known.

It was a lot to expect of a woman to leave her country and step into a world that was so different, but he hoped that Rusty loved him enough to do so. In his job, he knew all the difficulties such a move entailed. It wouldn't be easy, but that was life. He could offer her a comfortable existence, a nice home, and he couldn't see why they couldn't be really happy together as long as she was willing to make the move. He chuckled to himself. Rusty's vitality and sense of fun would certainly be a surprise to his family, but he was sure they'd grow to love her as he did.

He visualized her in their home, with guests, friends and colleagues of his, and smiled as he pictured her outspoken ways and imagined how she would see the American way of life. She would find things very different, but he hoped she would come to enjoy them. It would be quite an experience for both of them.

He found the English and their ways quaint, yet there was a certain dignity about the way of life, their reticence, which was rather endearing. It would be something that Rusty, as his wife, could teach to any children they might have.

Nine

Captain Adam Procter sat beneath a tree in the shade, wiping the perspiration from his neck. Sicily was hot! The race for Messina had finally been won by the allies. On August 17th, Messina fell. The allies had captured huge amounts of weapons, fuel and ammunition, but the civilians who emerged from cellars and other hiding places, to see their beloved town flattened, were too distressed to welcome the troops. There were no flowers or wine to greet the conquerors; by now nobody cared.

There were a few cafes and wine bars open, which looked as tired as the local inhabitants – those who had survived the bombings. But the cost to the American, Canadian and English troops had been high, so they too were weary.

Adam sat and removed the last letter he'd received from his wife. It was now weeks old. Jenny had written to him about her daily life, had seemed to be cheerful, yet he noticed a certain reticence in her writing. It was almost as if she was writing to a friend, not her husband. He couldn't quite put his finger on it, but then she'd changed so much. He put the letter away; he'd write to her this evening when hopefully they would all get some rest.

He sat back and drank his wine as he sat outside the taverna, thankful for the canopy of the huge tree, grateful for the break. How long would it be, he wondered, before the damned war was over and he could return to normal life? War hadn't been quite the adventure he had envisaged. He supposed, like many men, he'd gone into it without realizing what would be asked of him. He'd certainly not been prepared for the carnage he'd seen, the men who'd died, some right beside him. To know he'd been inches from death more than once was a shock to the system.

Jenny, in fact, was enjoying life. Her affair with Chad filled her every moment. Fortunately, he worked for Brad Jackson and was therefore more or less stationary for the moment. When they weren't at the stables, Chad came to the house, and when he had a pass, he stayed the night. The two of them slept together in a guest room, because it didn't seem right to Jenny to take her lover to the same bed she normally shared with her husband.

The difference in their ages only came up once when Jenny mentioned it one evening as they sat curled up together on the large settee. Chad had been dismissive.

'Age is all in the mind, honey. Some people are born old. What to me is more amazing is that a lovely lady like you, from such an illustrious background, could be interested in me, a simple cowboy from Wyoming.'

She had laughed. 'You, Chad, are far from being a simple cowboy!'

His eyes twinkled mischievously. 'If you were to see me on the back of a horse wearing chaps and a Stetson you wouldn't say that.'

'Do you look like Gary Cooper?'

'Hell no, I'm much better looking!'

The situation had not been mentioned since. She just relished the affection that he gave her, the feel of his arms around her at night. The future would sort itself out, and she would enjoy what was on offer from this extraordinary man, for as long as it lasted.

Jenny took the opportunity to show Chad the surrounding countryside and the English way of life, which he found interesting and amusing. They went to Buckler's Hard, where old Elizabethan ships used to be built; to the New Forest, where they both were involved in rounding up the New Forest ponies. This, of course, delighted him.

'Gee, honey, it's almost like being back on the range!' he cried as he whooped his way behind numerous horses being corralled. He was such fun to be with, and Jenny felt free of any encumbrance when she was with him. It was like leading an entirely different life, and she thrived on it . . . and it showed.

Beth remarked on it one day when Jenny went along to the stables to help out. After the morning's work had been done and the two women had ridden out for an hour, they returned to the house to eat. They sat in the kitchen chatting about the day.

Beth gazed at her friend with affection. 'Being in love suits you,' she said.

Jenny nearly choked on her coffee, and then she laughed. 'Is it that obvious?'

'Oh yes! You are absolutely glowing, my dear, and you look younger. I'm happy for you; Chad is a lovely man.'

'At first I was filled with guilt,' Jenny confessed. 'I even had dreams of Adam coming home and finding out about us, but as time passed I didn't care any more.' She frowned. 'I just want to be with Chad. Is that so wrong, Beth?'

'You forget, I know Adam and his controlling ways. Over the years he's smothered every bit of spirit in you; now, you are full of life. Grab it with both hands, is my advice!'

'It can't last though; eventually, it all has to come to an end. I can't bear to think about it, to be honest.'

'Then don't! War changes everything, it's inevitable. For you, it's made you happy for the first time in years, and that is worth anything that follows. Come on, there's more work to do.'

Rusty had not been working. She had been to the clinic and undergone the necessary examinations, which made her feel soiled.

The doctor involved was brief and to the point when he was able to give her the results. 'You are lucky, Miss Dobbs. You are free of any infection, but I do advise you to take precautions in the future.' His face was expressionless as he gazed at her. 'It would be a pity if you had to endure this again.'

She felt her hackles rise. 'Do you think I'm an idiot? Believe me, to come here was humiliating enough, and it certainly wasn't my fault that I had to do so!'

His eyes narrowed. 'If you were raped, Miss Dobbs, I hope you reported this to the authorities.'

She picked up her handbag and rose from the chair. 'Thank you for your time, Doctor, you will not see me in here ever again!'

Once outside she leaned against the wall with relief. She didn't dare think of the consequences if the news had been different. Yes, Brad said it could be treated, but she would never have felt the same again. The stigma of having had a sexually transmitted disease would have been for ever carved on her soul. Even now, she wondered if it would affect her relationship with the lovely captain. How did he feel about her being raped . . . as he thought? Would he feel differently about her, knowing she'd had sex with another man? Men were strange creatures. They could have sex with anyone they liked, it meant nothing, but if their woman did, well . . . that was an entirely different matter. If he ever discovered her profession, that certainly would be the end.

Brad and Rusty sat at a table in the Cowherds Inn and ordered from the menu. It was the first time they'd been together since she'd been tested at the clinic. Brad had picked her up, chatted cheerfully about inconsequential things until they were settled. He leaned across the table and took her hand.

'It's good to see you, darling. You look well. I like your dress.'

'You don't have to be polite, you know!' Rusty was feeling edgy.

'Woah! What brought that on?' he asked with surprise.

'Well, I've been tested; don't you want to know the results?'

He paused and studied her for a moment. Then he said, quietly, 'Yes, eventually, but why are you so angry?'

She closed her eyes and took a deep breath. 'Because I feel humiliated. I'm angry that some bastard used me – and because I'm afraid you won't want me any more!'

Brad stared at her, then, getting to his feet, he said, 'Wait there and don't you dare move!'

The sharpness of his tone so surprised her that she did as she was told.

Five minutes later, he returned, took her by the arm and said, 'Come on, we're getting out of here.'

'But what about the dinner we ordered?'

'I've cancelled it; now get into the jeep.'

He drove down the Avenue into the town, past the Bargate and into the car park of the Dolphin Hotel, where he parked the vehicle, opened the passenger door and said, 'Come on.'

Rusty was so stunned by this turn of events, she went along with him. At the desk, he paused. 'I'm Captain Jackson, I called five minutes ago.'

The receptionist gave him a key.

Taking Rusty by the arm, he led her to the lift and pressed the button for the first floor.

'Brad?'

He ignored her and, when the lift stopped, walked her to a room, unlocked it and gently pushed her inside. 'Come here!'

He took her into his arms and kissed her longingly until she could hardly breathe. 'You don't think I want you any more? Well, my darling, I'm about to prove to you just how much I do.'

To Rusty, the world suddenly looked a much brighter place, and she started to laugh. 'Oh, bloody hell! I've got my own Rhett Butler.'

Brad grinned at her. 'But unlike him, my dear, I *do* give a damn!'

Sarah Biggs and Gunter sat in the garden at the farm at the end of a Sunday, talking about their future. Wondering how much longer the war would take before it was over and the German prisoners of war were repatriated.

'I've not heard from my family, of course,' he said. 'No doubt they have been informed that I am a prisoner, and I have no idea if we still have a home or if it's been bombed during the air raids.' He frowned. 'In fact, I have no idea if my parents are still alive.'

'Oh Gunter, don't say that!' Sarah was horrified by such a thought.

He shrugged. 'I have to prepare myself for this. Both countries were bombed so badly, and there were so many casualties.' He brightened for a moment. 'Maybe if it was bad they might have gone to my grandmother's in the country. Let's hope so. Whatever, *liebling*, we will be together eventually.'

Sarah loved to talk about their future – it was like a dream come true – but the reality of it ever happening was always in doubt. For one thing, her parents would be against it, she knew that for certain. To her mother, the only good German was a dead one! Hadn't she said that often enough? And her father was fighting them somewhere in Europe; she couldn't imagine he would relish a German for a son-in-law. That was only one of the problems that would face them, but at least they were able to be together now; the future would have to wait.

Mrs Dora Biggs had long been suspicious about her daughter's weekends and the fact that she'd stopped meeting the German behind the barbed wire in the park. She knew because her neighbour had told her he no longer saw Sarah there. He'd also informed her that many of the men were now employed on farmlands. Maybe that was the reason, she thought. She decided to find out one way or another. And so the next Sunday, she followed her daughter.

She watched Sarah queue for a bus and take a seat upstairs. Dora quickly climbed on the lower deck and sat down. Not knowing Sarah's destination, she bought a ticket which took her to the last stop. As they neared the outskirts of the town, Sarah alighted and walked away, and just before the conductor rang the bell, her mother also got off, keeping her distance, making sure she wasn't seen. She had to keep hiding in the hedgerows as there were hardly any people around.

She was surprised when Sarah walked in through the gates of a farmhouse. Dora stopped, wondering what to do. She walked along a bit further where, peering over a hedge, she could see the cow sheds, and to her surprise saw a man in German uniform walk forward and embrace her daughter.

Dora Briggs was horrified and furious. Now she had discovered her daughter's duplicity, she was fuming. *Cunning little bitch!* she thought, Well she wasn't having it. In any case, how could it be possible for an enemy of the country to be allowed such freedom? There didn't seem to be any sentries around. She walked back to the bus stop and waited.

She would go to the council. This wasn't right. Her Sarah was in moral danger; God knows what was going on. It had to be stopped before it got completely out of hand.

Unaware of all this, Gunter and Sarah worked together for the rest of the morning. He tried to show her how to milk a cow, with hysterical results. The cow moved suddenly, and Sarah ended up off the milking stool, on her backside, the pail of milk spilt over her feet.

'Bloody good job you ain't marrying a farmer, lass!' said Mr Brown, who walked into the barn at that moment. 'You'd be hopeless!'

Getting up and trying to wipe away the milk and hay, she had to agree with him.

Ten

Two weeks later when Sarah arrived at the farm on the usual Sunday morning she was met by Ethel Brown, the farmer's wife. 'Come in, my dear,' she said.

The kindly woman looked so worried that Sarah wondered if something bad had happened to her husband. 'Is something wrong?' she asked.

'Sit down, my lass, I'll make us a cup of tea.'

Sarah waited with growing concern.

Mrs Brown eventually sat at the table with her. 'I'm afraid I've some bad news. Gunter has been moved.'

This was the last thing Sarah expected, and she felt as if the wind had been knocked out of her. 'Where is he . . .? When did this happen . . .? Do you have an address for him?' The questions poured forth.

Shaking her head, Ethel said, 'I have no idea where he is. Some soldiers came one day, had a few brief words with him, bundled him upstairs to get his things and drove him away.' She paused for breath. 'My husband questioned them, of course, but they gave no explanation, and what's more we won't be having another to take his place.'

Sarah was stunned. 'Did he leave me a message?'

'He didn't even have time to say goodbye; he was as surprised as we were. I can't imagine why they've done this. To me, it's a complete mystery.'

The young girl sat, stunned. How on earth was she to find out where he was? She couldn't sit and do nothing. Gunter and she were going to spend their lives together after the war. They loved one another! Tears filled her eyes. 'Oh Mrs Brown, what am I to do?'

'Well, my dear, all I can suggest is that you go to the military authorities and enquire. I can't think of anything else. You can leave me your address, and then if I do hear anything, I'll let you know. Come on now, have a nice strong cup of tea, it's good for shock.'

★   ★   ★

Sarah sat on the bus on the way home, absolutely devastated. Gunter hadn't done anything wrong, he'd worked hard, and the Browns had been more than satisfied with his work, so why? Perhaps all the prisoners were to be moved. She had to find out, but she'd have to wait until tomorrow as she doubted the necessary office would be open on a Sunday. But she would take the following morning off and try and discover what had happened. She needed to be able to write to Gunter. He'd be so worried, and he didn't have her address to write to, anyway. The whole thing was a complete mess! She couldn't go straight home or her mother would wonder why she was home so early and start to question her, so she stopped off at Hoglands Park to kill time and watch the Americans playing baseball.

Lots of the GIs were there, and many of the locals who had become interested, even if they didn't understand the rules – and, of course, many young women of the town on the lookout for a free pair of nylons, plus a host of children asking for gum.

Joe Kowalski was also watching, interested in both the game and the girls. He'd caught the eye of one young woman and was chatting to her, teaching her the rules, flirting with her, but when, towards the end of the game, he asked her to go out with him, she refused.

'What do you mean, no?' He was angry because he was sure that he'd scored.

She looked surprised by his response. 'I said no. Besides, I already have a boyfriend.'

'Then what the hell are you doing talking to me?' he demanded.

She retaliated: 'You were telling me the rules of the game, that's all. You bloody Yanks, you're all the same, you think every woman is easy pickings!'

He grabbed her by the arm. 'Now you listen to me, bitch!'

'What's going on here? Let go of the girl, soldier.'

The note of authority in the voice made Kowalski turn. He looked into the face of Captain Brad Jackson.

'Are you all right, young lady?' asked Brad.

The girl wrenched her arm free. 'Now I am, thanks to you.' She glared at Joe. 'You need to teach him some manners!'

As the girl walked away, Brad turned to the GI. 'I want you

in my office at oh nine hundred hours tomorrow, soldier – and don't be late!'

'Sir!' Kowalski saluted and turned away, fuming. 'Friggin' women,' he grumbled. 'They give you the come on, then shut you out!'

He was heckled by one or two other soldiers, which didn't help his temper, and he gave them a lot of abuse before he stormed away. He walked to the Horse and Groom, which had just opened, and ordered a beer.

The place soon started to fill up, and he sat at a table watching until he saw a couple of the regular prostitutes enter. The girls stood at the bar and looked around for likely punters whilst they waited to be served. Dorothy, Rusty's friend, was one of the girls, and she immediately recognized the American and quickly whispered to her friend, who cast a glance at the soldier over her shoulder.

Kowalski eyed them both before deciding that he preferred the blonde. He rose from his seat and walked over to the bar. 'Can I get you girls a drink?' he asked.

'No, thank you,' said Dorothy very quickly.

'That's not very friendly,' he said, his eyes narrowing.

'We've just come in for a quiet drink and a chat,' said the other. 'Sorry.' She picked up their two half-pint glasses and the girls left him standing – feeling a fool. This was turning out to be a really bad day, he thought angrily as he returned to his seat.

It didn't get any better. He got into an argument with two British soldiers, who baited him about America not wanting to be involved in the war, happy to let the Europeans take the brunt of the fighting, until they were bombed at Pearl Harbour.

'And now look at you Yanks!' stated one. 'You strut around flashing your money, your nylons, your Camel cigarettes and your gum, thinking you're the answer to every woman's prayer. You can't even march in step!'

The argument became so heated that the landlord came over. 'That's enough! You want to argue? Take it outside or I'll bar the lot of you!'

With a lot of mumbling, the British soldiers moved to another part of the bar and to Kowalski's great annoyance started talking to the two girls he had approached earlier. When, a little later, they all left together, he was furious. He sat until closing time, slowly getting drunk.

When the pub closed for the afternoon, he staggered to the park, curled up under a tree and slept. Three hours later he woke with a raging thirst and made his way to a cafe and had a meal followed by several cups of coffee, waiting for the pubs to open again.

Meantime, Sarah had left the baseball game and walked home. She hardly spoke to her mother as she made a cup of tea before sitting down to read the Sunday papers. But even though she looked at the pages of the newspaper, she didn't read a word. She was thinking of Gunter and wondering how on earth she could find out where he was.

Dora Biggs watched her daughter and saw the unhappiness etched on her face. She guessed that she was the cause of it but had no regrets. She had to save Sarah from making a fool of herself, it was a mother's duty. One day in the future, Sarah would thank her for her intervention.

Joe Kowalski went on a pub crawl that evening, and with the amount of alcohol he'd consumed earlier that day, he was soon in an alcoholic haze. Joe was never a happy drunk, and already in a bad mood, his consumption only fuelled his temper. He was thrown out of the Lord Roberts, in Canal Walk, and staggered down to the Grapes in Oxford Street, where he ordered a beer at the bar.

'Sorry, soldier, you've had more than enough. I suggest you return to your barracks,' said the landlord.

'Gimme a beer, and less of your mouth!'

'This is my pub, Yank, and you won't get served here. Now leave, or I'll put you out myself!'

The American was enraged. He grabbed an empty beer bottle off the bar and smashed it, pointing the jagged edges at the landlord. 'Come on then. Let's see what you're made of, Limey!'

It was bad timing because, unknown to Joe, two military police had walked into the bar and seen the commotion. They walked up behind him and one of them, using his truncheon, knocked the bottle out of Kowalski's hand. Before he knew what had happened he was handcuffed and bundled into a jeep, cursing loudly.

The next morning, Joe stood before Brad Jackson. He stood to attention, flanked by two military policemen. His head ached, and he felt like hell.

Brad read the report before him; then, looking up, he spoke. 'Kowalski, you are a pain in the butt! You have the makings of a good soldier if it wasn't for your mean disposition and your temper. Being in the army means you must be a team member, but you are a loner. You don't mix with the other men, and when you go out on the town, you make trouble. I saw that for myself yesterday – and now this! God alone knows what you'd be like on the field of battle. My one concern is that you would be out for your own skin instead of helping your fellow soldier, and that worries me. I'm not at all sure I want you in my troop or any other. You are a liability.'

Kowalski's heart sank. Being in the army was a way out from his mundane life. If he was court-martialled he'd have to return to Pennsylvania and the steel works. It was the last thing he wanted. 'Permission to speak, sir?'

'Permission granted.'

'I know I've made a fool of myself, sir, and I apologize. I love the army; in fact, after the war, I'd thought of signing on as a regular. Just give me another chance and I promise I'll be a better soldier and obey the rules.' It cost him a great deal to plead, it was not in his nature to kowtow to anyone, but he *had* to stay in the army – the alternative was too much to contemplate.

Brad saw the genuine concern in Kowalski's face. 'You, soldier, can serve fourteen days in the glasshouse whilst I consider your future. Dismiss!'

Sarah Biggs sat in the waiting room of the local army headquarters the next morning, gripping her hands nervously. She had no idea how she would be received, especially as she would be enquiring about a prisoner of war, but she was determined.

Soon she was ushered into an office and invited to take a seat by the officer sitting behind the desk. 'What can I do for you, Miss Biggs?'

She took a deep breath. 'I am enquiring as to the whereabouts of Gunter Reinhardt, a prisoner of war who was working for Mr Brown at Cherry Tree Farm in Hedge End, but who has now been removed from there.'

The officer looked surprised. 'Why are you interested in this man, miss?'

With a defiant look she said, 'Because Gunter and I plan to marry after the war.'

'Aren't you a little young to be thinking about marriage? And to a German!'

'Gunter and I are in love. It doesn't matter to me that he is German!'

The officer rose to his feet and walked over to a filing cabinet. He admired the young girl's spirit, but personally felt she was wasting her time. During a war, many young women fell for service personnel. It was a known fact, and with heartbreaking consequences mostly, but he would do what he could for her. He sorted through the files and pulled out one, which he took to his desk and read.

Sarah saw the officer frown. 'Is something wrong?'

He sighed. 'It would appear, Miss Biggs, that your mother complained to the authorities about your relationship with this young man.' He read on and looked up from the papers. 'It seems that you have been visiting Gunter Reinhardt at the farm – is that right?'

'Yes, it was the only way we could meet, but I'm sure my mother didn't know about it.'

He raised his eyebrows. 'According to this report, she did, and she demanded that we put a stop to it. That's why he was moved.'

Sarah was furious. 'How dare she interfere!'

The young man looked at her kindly. 'I'm sure she thought it was for the best.'

'Where is Gunter now?' Sarah demanded.

'I am sorry, miss, but after reading this, I'm not at liberty to disclose that information.'

No pleading from Sarah could make him change his mind, and she left the office in tears. Tears that changed to anger as she made her way home. By the time she walked into the kitchen to face her mother, she was enraged. 'How dare you interfere with my life!'

For a moment, Dora Biggs was startled, then she realized that her daughter had discovered her intervention. 'I had no choice!' she retorted. 'I couldn't stand by and see you get involved any further with this German. Who knows where it would have ended?'

'We were going to get married after the war,' Sarah cried. 'That's where it would have ended, Mother . . . in marriage.'

Dora was incandescent with rage. 'Marriage? Marriage to a bloody German . . .? Over my dead body!'

'That's as far as you can see, isn't it? The fact that he is German, not that he is educated, a gentleman who hated the war. He'll be a lawyer in civilian life, a noble profession, but no, to you he's a German and that's that! Well, let me tell you, I'll move heaven and earth to find him, and you won't stop me!' She stormed out of the house.

Sarah walked to the enclosure were she'd first met Gunter and began to ask the other prisoners if they knew where he was. She had a mixed reception. Some of the men were rude to her, others ignored her, but her pleading reached the ears of one of Gunter's friends. He walked over towards her. 'Are you Sarah, Gunter's girlfriend?'

'Yes, yes, I am! Do you know where he is?'

He walked down the side, away from the others, and she followed on the other side of the barbed wire. 'Can you help me?' she begged.

'I only saw him briefly whilst he waited for transport. He asked me to give you a message if I saw you.'

'Yes?' She waited eagerly.

'He said that when he knew where he was being moved to, he'd write to Mrs Brown and tell her, then she could pass on the address to you.'

'Oh, thank you, thank you so much.' She beamed at him with relief.

'I know that you're both in love and plan to be together after the war. Gunter is a fine man, I hope you make it.' With that, he strolled away.

Sarah was delighted. She'd write to Mrs Brown and tell her the news; then she'd have to wait until the farmer's wife wrote to her with the address. She'd be on pins until she heard, but at least now she had something to cling to. When she knew where he was, she'd go and visit him, but she wouldn't tell her mother. She would never trust her ever again.

Eleven

Brad Jackson drove out to Chilworth for a meeting with Jenny to discuss a forthcoming children's Christmas party to be given by the Americans. Many of the troops were saving candy from their rations towards this end, and Brad wanted to confirm the arrangements.

Jenny opened the door and invited him in. 'It's good to see you, Brad, it's been some time.' She thought for a moment. 'The last time was when you brought your girlfriend over to the stables. How's she doing, by the way?'

'Oh, Rusty's fine. Full of life. She keeps me on my toes!'

They sat in the large kitchen and chatted about the party over several cups of coffee.

'The boys are really looking forward to this shindig,' he said. 'You know how it is, Christmas is a family time, a time for children, and the men feel this even more when they're away from home, so they've put a lot of effort into getting things done.'

She was delighted. 'The children will be thrilled.' A look of disappointment crossed her features. 'I wanted children but it just didn't happen.'

'Did you go to your doctor about it?'

'*I* did, but Adam refused. As far as I was concerned the doctor could find nothing wrong, and when I told Adam this, we had a fearful row. He accused me of thinking he wasn't a man.' She sighed. 'Oh well.'

'Have you heard from your husband?'

'Off and on, not that he ever has a great deal to say – though you know, with censorship, it's difficult.'

'And what about your relationship with Chad?' he asked softly.

Jenny looked at him for a moment before replying. 'Chad is my guilty pleasure.'

'Your what?'

'You know, when you are doing something you know is wrong but you're enjoying it immensely anyway. That's a guilty pleasure.'

Brad chuckled. 'Well, I've never heard it put into those words before.'

Jenny gazed at the captain. They had become firm friends during the previous months, and she felt she could talk to him. 'Of course, there's always a price to pay, isn't there?'

'What are you trying to tell me, Jenny?'

'I suppose I'm trying to say that, foolishly, I've fallen in love with Chad.'

He frowned. 'Does he feel the same?'

'Yes.' She closed her eyes for a moment, then opening them she looked at Brad and asked, 'What *am* I going to do about it?'

'What do you want to do about it?'

'Oh, that's easy! I want to run away after the war and go with him to Wyoming, ride with him, camp out, sleep beneath the stars, because he makes it sound so wonderful. He makes me feel like a different woman, Brad. I want to change my life . . . but I'm married to Adam.'

'Do you still love Adam?'

She shook her head. 'I still love him, but I'm not *in* love with him. Does that make any sense?'

'Oh yes, a great deal. Chad is an unusual man; he's come into your life when you are most vulnerable. Adam's away, you're alone. He's opened up strange vistas, a different way of life. It sounds exciting and probably is – but you'd have to give up a great deal. Are you prepared to do so?'

'I'm damned if I know! The more I try and think about it, the more of a mess it seems to be. Anyway, let's get back to business; sorry to use you as a sounding board, that wasn't fair of me.'

'Don't be ridiculous. I'm your friend, and as a doctor I'm used to listening.'

'You have a great bedside manner, Brad, I'll say that for you!'

'I just don't want to have to treat you as a patient, that's all.' He paused. 'It's possible that in the near future we'll all be shipped out; you should prepare yourself mentally for that.'

Brad knew that plans were in progress for an invasion. There was no way he could tell Jenny about it, of course – it was top secret – but he could warn her of the consequences.

'Wars are dreadful!' she cried. 'Not only do they cost so many lives, but they also mess up the lives of so many of the folk that are left behind.' She rose from her chair. 'I'll make some more coffee.' And the subject was closed.

As he drove back to headquarters, Brad thought about Jenny and her predicament, knowing that many couples would be asking the same questions. For him it wasn't so bad – he was a single man, and Rusty was also free. If they wanted to spend their lives together, at least their problems were halved. He had been careful not to speak of the future when he was with Rusty – he didn't think it right to do so with a war still raging – but deep down he knew that in the end he would ask her to be his wife. He loved everything about her. Her personality, her sense of fun – her honesty. He wanted this lovely vibrant woman to share his life, but he would bide his time until things settled down, when he was sure he *had* a future. In war there was always the uncertainty that you could become a casualty – or worse.

Gunter Reinhardt was now settled in a prisoner of war camp at Bishop's Waltham and was not a happy man. It had all happened so quickly. He'd been taken by surprise when he'd been removed from Cherry Tree Farm, and until he'd been taken before the military he had no idea why. Then he was told by the officer in charge – a man not entirely unsympathetic, who realized that Gunter was an educated man who had been drawn into the war against his better judgement.

'It has been brought to my attention that you have been fraternizing with a young English girl, Reinhardt. Her mother is demanding that I put a stop to this.'

So that was what it was all about, thought the German.

'What do you have to say for yourself?'

'It's true, sir. Sarah and I started talking one day when I was being held in Southampton, and when I was moved, she came to the farm on a Sunday. This is far more than fraternizing, sir. We love each other, and after the war we plan to marry.'

The officer looked surprised. 'Well, I can tell you now, that her mother will certainly be against such a liaison. She hasn't a good word to say about you Germans! And I believe that her daughter is a teenager.'

'She's seventeen. I do realize that we have many difficulties to overcome, but we truly want to be together after the war.'

'That's fortunately not my problem,' said the officer. 'You will remain at Bishop's Waltham for the time being – and no visitors are allowed. Dismiss!'

The prisoners were allowed to write letters, and Gunter had quickly written to Mrs Brown and given her his address, asking her to tell Sarah where he was. If he couldn't see her, then at least they could keep in touch.

The postman posted a letter through the door of Sarah's house just as she was leaving for work. When she saw her name on the envelope, she quickly pushed it into her pocket and stepped into the street. Once outside she opened it and was delighted to see it was from Mrs Brown.

Dear Sarah, I've received a letter from Gunter who is now at a camp at Bishop's Waltham. Unfortunately he isn't allowed visitors but can receive mail. He asked me to let you know. I have written the address for you. Love, Ethel Brown.

Sarah breathed a sigh of relief. Gunter still wanted her! She was afraid, despite all his endearments, that once they were apart, he would change his mind about them, and she desperately needed him as she was in a great deal of trouble. Her period was late, and she was afraid she was pregnant. Now more than ever she needed his assurance that they did have a future together because when her mother discovered her condition, Sarah was fearful of the consequences. She would write to him tonight.

Later, Sarah, alone in her bedroom, was filled with trepidation as she penned her letter. What would she do if Gunter, on learning her news, then wanted nothing more to do with her? Whatever his reaction, she would certainly keep the baby, there would be no backstreet abortion for her. She wanted his child, someone to love other than Gunter. There had been little affection in her own childhood. Her parents looked after her well and cared about her, but neither was demonstrative. There had never been any cuddles when she was small, and she'd never seen her father and mother embrace each other. This need for affection had been fulfilled by Gunter, who was gentle and caring. She knew they could be happy together, given the chance. If he still wanted her after hearing her news, she wouldn't let anything stand in her way!

Gunter Reinhardt was handed the letter two days later, after roll call. He walked to a quiet corner of the camp and opened it. After reading the contents, he frowned. My God! What a predicament for Sarah. Her mother was bound to discover that her daughter was pregnant eventually – a woman could only disguise the fact for so long – and then there would be trouble. What on earth could he do to help? He paced up and down, feeling absolutely helpless. There was no one he could turn to for assistance. He lit a cigarette and tried to gather his thoughts . . . then he stopped his pacing. Of course there *was* one person he could rely on. He walked to his quarters and sat down to write.

On Friday morning, Sarah saw the envelope on the front doormat and picked it up, her heart racing when she recognized Ethel Brown's writing. She'd heard from Gunter, the farmer's wife wrote, and she had a letter for her. If Sarah would come to the farm on Sunday, she could collect it and stay for lunch.

Sarah could hardly wait. What would her lover have to say about the baby? What if he said he wasn't interested? A million thoughts raced through her mind. If he wanted it and her, how long would he have to wait before they could all be together – and how would she manage in the meantime to keep the child in food and clothes? Her mother wouldn't help, she was sure of that. She was near to tears as she wrestled mentally with all these questions.

Eventually Sunday arrived, and Sarah caught the bus to Hedge End and Cherry Tree Farm. As she walked up the path to the farmhouse, she felt nauseous. Would the letter contain good or bad news? She knocked on the door.

'Come in, love,' said Mrs Brown, and on seeing how pale the young girl looked, she led her to a chair, handed her the letter and said: 'Here you are, Sarah, you read that whilst I make a pot of tea.'

With trembling fingers, Sarah tore the envelope open.

Liebling, it began, *I was so thrilled to hear from you. I had been so worried after I was moved from the farm without being able to let you know what had happened. I love you, Sarah, and although I know the fact that you may be carrying my child will cause you many problems, please know that I am thrilled that we made a baby together.* Sarah let out a muffled cry as she read his words. *I feel so helpless as I am unable at this time to be of any assistance to you, but I have written to Mrs Brown – she knows what is happening and has told me that if she can help you in any way, to ask. I love you, and one day we will be together, I promise. Gunter xx*

With tears of relief trickling down her cheeks, Sarah looked up at Ethel Brown. The woman, seeing her distress, rushed over to her and held her. 'There, there, love, now don't you worry. It'll all be all right in the end, you'll see.'

The two of them sat at the table and, over several cups of tea, Sarah told Ethel she was worried as to how her parents would react when they discovered her condition.

'Are you sure about the baby?'

'I've missed a couple of periods and I'm as regular as clockwork usually,' Sarah told her. 'And another thing, my breasts are tender.'

'Well, sometimes that happens just before you come on,' Mrs Brown remarked. 'However, my dear, I've been thinking after I received Gunter's letter, and I've discussed this with my husband.' She paused to pour more tea. 'Just supposing your mother goes bananas and you want a place to stay, you can have Gunter's old room.'

Sarah's eyes widened with surprise. 'You would do that for me?'

'You and Gunter, yes. Look, love, he was a lovely young man, not the usual soldier. He is a man with a good background, a profession. We grew very fond of him when he was here, and he loves you dearly. He used to talk to Mr Brown and me about his plans for both of you. He had the future all worked out, and he did realize that it wouldn't be easy, knowing how your mum feels.' She sighed. 'Not all Germans are bad, and not all Englishmen are good.'

'If only Mum thought that way, my life would be so easy.'

'If you really are pregnant, when will you tell her?'

Sarah pulled a face. 'Not until I have to, that's for sure!'

'But if you are, you'll have to see a doctor. You must look after yourself and the baby.'

'Yes, I suppose I must.' She frowned. 'To be honest, the only thing I could think about was how Gunter would react when he knew. I hadn't thought further than that.'

Ethel smiled her understanding. 'That's natural. So many young women in wartime are left in the lurch by soldiers who have promised them the earth to get them into bed, but Gunter's different. For that we must all be thankful.'

Arthur Brown joined them for lunch. He was kind to Sarah, as always, but he made no comment about the reason for her being there, except to say how good it was to see her and how they had missed her.

As she left to go home, Ethel Brown said, 'I've suggested that Gunter send his letters for you to the farm only – they are marked with a military stamp, and if your mother saw that, the cat would be out of the bag.'

Sarah hugged her. 'What would I do without you!'

'Ah well, my dear, I'm a sucker for a real love story.' And she kissed her on the cheek. 'See you next week. You take care now.'

As she walked back through the farmyard, Sarah remembered just how happy she and Gunter had been spending their time together here; it had been a great start to their relationship. Being part of a family had seemed so normal. They'd been able to forget the differences between them that the war had only emphasized.

Sitting on the bus heading for home, Sarah felt as if a load had been lifted from her shoulders. Gunter still loved her, and Mrs and Mrs Brown had pledged their support. What a lucky girl she was, but she knew that ahead of her was a very rocky road.

Twelve

It was mid December and the day of the Christmas party for the children, held at the Red Cross Club in the High Street. The room was decorated with paper chains and Chinese lanterns. Inside was a spread of food that made the eyes of the invited youngsters widen with surprise. There were spam sandwiches, and hot dogs in fresh bread rolls, baked in the camp. There were sausage rolls, hamburgers, jellies, blancmanges, and small cakes with icing. A twelve foot high Christmas tree, decorated with coloured lights and baubles and lots of tinsel, stood proudly at one end of the room. Three hundred children gazed in wonder at all that was placed before them.

There was a conjuror, a ventriloquist, and a singer who also danced, who had all been hired to entertain the children, and everything would end with community singing. But the highlight of the afternoon, of course, was the arrival of Father Christmas from a specially built fireplace. The children were each presented with a packet of candy, a packet of cookies and some fruit, all given by the Americans from their rations. The children, filled with excitement, didn't realize his: 'Ho, ho, ho,' and chat with each child was in an American accent.

Both Jenny and Rusty had been invited to help out with the children, and they too were carried away with the excitement of it all.

'Just look at that child's face,' said Rusty as a small boy licked his ice cream, clutching an apple at the same time.

'And look at the faces of the men; they are getting as much out of this as the little ones.'

It was true. Several GIs were playing games and entertaining the children, grinning happily as they did so, having a really good time, their efforts well rewarded by the joy on every child's face.

Chad was there too, down on his knees, giving several children piggyback rides. Jenny smiled to herself. Even now he couldn't get away from horses.

Brad walked over to the two women and putting an arm around Rusty said, 'Thanks, girls, you were a great help. I think this party has been a success, don't you?'

'These children will remember today for a very long time,' Rusty remarked. 'In fact, so will I. I've never had a hot dog before!'

Laughing, he said, 'It's part of the American way of life, honey.'

When it was all over and the children taken home, the girls were exhausted. 'Come back to my quarters and we'll all have a drink together,' suggested Brad. He called Chad over to join them.

But as they entered the corridor leading to Brad's quarters, Joe Kowalski, now back on duty, saw them and recognized Rusty and her auburn hair from the night he had paid for her services. He was more than a little surprised to see her being looked after so attentively by his captain, who was followed by the corporal and another classy looking lady.

'Well,' he murmured, 'who would have thought it? Captain Jackson with a hooker!'

As Christmas approached, Sarah was getting increasingly nervous. She was now three months pregnant and was beginning to find it difficult to hide her condition. She knew that it was only a matter of time until her parents were aware of it too. Already, her mother had remarked that her face was fuller and she was gaining weight. Sarah had passed it off as being the result of their wartime diet. So far, her mother had accepted this.

Ethel Brown had loaned Sarah one or two items of her clothing, which were a size larger, to help Sarah disguise her condition, but the farmer's wife was concerned about the future for this girl, of whom she'd grown fond. She'd discussed her fears with her husband: 'Sarah's mother will hit the roof when she finds out that her daughter's pregnant!'

'Well, love, that's understandable, after all.'

'I know, but now is the time that she needs her family behind her. I can't see that happening at all.'

They were soon to find out.

Sarah stepped out of the bath and dried herself. She'd washed her hair too, which had got soaked from the rain that had fallen all day. Just as she put aside the towel and turned to pick up her clothes to get dressed, her mother walked in, as Sarah had forgotten to lock the door.

'Oops, sorry,' Dora began, but as she turned to leave, she saw the telltale swelling of her daughter's stomach and she looked at Sarah in dismay. 'You're *pregnant!*'

Sarah felt the blood drain from her body. She clutched at the bath to steady herself, then she looked up defiantly. 'Yes, I am. I'm carrying Gunter's child, Mother.'

For a moment Dora was speechless, then she began her tirade. 'You cheap hussy! You stand there and tell me you are carrying that German's child – and you have no shame?'

'It's not how I would have planned it, but no, I'm not ashamed. We love one another. He's going to marry me after the war.'

'Ha!' Dora was derisive. 'That's what they all say. You stupid little fool for believing such a thing. You gave yourself to him on an empty promise; well, you'll have to pay the price. What will people say, do you think, when they see you on the street with your bastard in a pram?'

The cruel words cut deep.

Sarah picked up the towel and wrapped it around her. 'It's no one's business but mine and Gunter's. When we get married the baby will be legitimate.'

'You were brought up to be a decent girl, but instead you behave like a tart!' Dora looked at her with disgust. 'You have brought shame on this family. God knows what your father will have to say about this.'

Sarah found her courage. 'I'll get dressed and come downstairs, then we'll find out!'

Whilst she dressed in her bedroom, Sarah could hear the raised voices echoing from below and her heart was thudding. Now she was really scared. She took a picture of Gunter out of her handbag and held it to her. Then, taking a deep breath, she headed for the stairs.

That evening, Ethel Brown was surprised to hear a knock at her door. She frowned and looked at the clock. Who on earth would be calling now? She walked to the door.

Standing outside, wet and bedraggled from the rain, was Sarah, clutching a suitcase.

Without hesitation, Ethel ushered her inside. 'My goodness, you're soaked. Now sit by the fire, I'll go and get a dressing gown for you, then you must get out of those wet clothes. It's not good for you or the baby.' And she rushed out of the room. She returned and helped Sarah shed her clothes, gave her a towel and wrapped her in a dressing gown, and then sped into the kitchen to make a pot of tea.

When she returned with it all on a tray, Sarah looked at her in amazement. 'You are an extraordinary woman. Not once have you asked me why I'm here!'

Ethel poured the tea. 'It's fairly obvious, love. I imagine that your family have kicked you out once they discovered you were pregnant.' She looked up at Sarah. 'I'm right, aren't I?'

'Sadly, you are.'

'To be honest, Sarah, it's no more than I expected. I'm just so sorry that I was correct. Here, drink this tea, it'll warm you.' Ethel didn't question her, knowing that once Sarah had settled, she'd tell her what had happened.

After a while, she sat and listened to the sad story and was inwardly furious with Sarah's parents for their heartless attitude towards their daughter. She could see that the young girl was upset.

'Now, you listen to me. Gunter's room is all ready. This is your home for as long as you like. Until you leave to get married, if that's how it works out.'

'You believe that Gunter will keep his word?'

'Of course I do. Don't you?'

'Yes, but after listening to my mother, I couldn't help wondering if she was right about him and I was wrong.' She was fighting back the tears.

Ethel leaned forward and took her hand. 'That man idolizes you, and don't you ever doubt him – not for a minute!'

At that moment Arthur Brown walked in. He looked at Sarah and his wife and knew instinctively what had happened. 'Hello, Sarah dear. Moving in, are you?'

'If that's all right with you, Mr Brown?'

'You are more than welcome, girl. Now, how about a cup of

tea? It's bloody miserable out there, and I've just delivered a calf.' He grinned at Sarah. 'If when it's your time you get caught out, don't you worry, I'll deliver your calf too!'

It was Christmas Day, and Jenny had invited Brad and Rusty to join her and Chad. The two Americans had both given Jenny food from the PX stores to help with the Christmas dinner, plus some champagne and wine.

The day was dry and crisp with a hoar frost in the morning. Jenny lit a fire in the drawing room, with a stack of logs at the ready which Chad had chopped a few days earlier. He arrived early to help her prepare.

As Jenny stood at the kitchen sink, washing the vegetables, he came behind her and encircled her waist with his arms. The scent of his aftershave drifted over her shoulder.

'How's my girl?' he whispered.

She turned within his hold and put her arms around his neck. 'I'm fine now that you're here.'

He gave her a long lingering kiss. 'Mmm, that's nice,' he said and kissed her again.

She reluctantly broke free. 'Now stop that!' she chided. 'Or we'll never be ready when the others arrive.'

'We have lots of time, honey. What's the rush?' he teased.

'Chad, behave yourself! Here, you can peel the carrots and parsnips.' She handed him a knife.

He pulled a face at her. 'Slave-driver!'

The aroma from the turkey cooking in the oven filled the room. 'That smells real good,' he said as he worked away. 'Thank goodness I've found a woman who can cook.'

'And if I couldn't?'

'I'd have to look elsewhere. After all, I need a woman who can cook when I'm out working the range.' He smiled softly to himself and said, 'I'll have to teach you how to use a rifle, just in case some marauding Indians arrive at the ranch when I'm out working.'

Jenny looked at him with horror. 'Indians?'

He laughed until his sides ached. 'I'm only kidding! They're all on reservations these days, but you should have seen the look on your face!'

At that moment the front doorbell went, and Jenny left him still laughing. As she let Brad and Rusty in she said, 'You're just in time to save Chad from being murdered.'

'Oh my God, why?' asked Rusty.

'He's been teasing me unmercifully.' And she explained.

The day was one of the happiest either woman could remember. For Jenny, it was being without the constant demands from Adam and the stress of entertaining a room full of people she neither knew nor liked. Of now being held in the arms of the man she loved whilst they all sat enjoying the festivities, eating, and listening to records, and then dancing.

For Rusty, it was being in a nice home, away from the seedy side of Southampton, the pubs and the half-drunken men who were alone and would want to buy her body as a means of bringing some form of comfort to celebrate Christmas. Instead of such a sordid day, she was with a man who loved her for herself. She still lived in fear of being found out, so enjoyed every second she could, with her captain. The man she now knew she loved back and who would break her heart when he left these shores.

At Cherry Tree Farm, Sarah settled down to Christmas dinner with the Browns. It was good to see Arthur Brown sitting enjoying himself, thought Sarah, knowing how long his day was normally. A farmer's life was not easy, but these two lovely people seemed to thrive on it, and Sarah admired their tenacity and enthusiasm.

In her pocket was a long letter from Gunter. He now knew that she was living there permanently. He'd written to say how sorry he was that he was the cause of the break-up of her family, but he'd told her to just think of the family they were starting, together.

I love you with all my heart, liebling. Just think of our future together and of our baby. I just wish I could be with you, but one day we will all be together.

These words would sustain her in the days ahead.

Thirteen

Winter had passed, and the spring of 1944 was upon them. Jenny wondered how the time could have gone so quickly. She heard infrequently from Adam, but so far he was fine. Like so many serving men, all he prayed for was the war to be over so he could return home to normality.

But life was far from normal. Troops and tanks poured into Southampton in preparation for the invasion of Normandy. Code name Overlord. June the sixth the designated day. Men, landing craft and war machines filled every available space. Bulldozers cleared bombed sites to make way for the ever increasing armoury.

Brad was busy, keeping the welfare of the troops in check. Not an easy task, as by now they all felt that something big would happen soon, and they were determined to have a last wild fling whenever they could. Fights broke out in bars between men fuelled with alcohol, wondering if soon they would be dead – and once again, Joe Kowalski, with three other GIs, was up before the Captain. They had been involved in a fracas in a pub with some British soldiers, ending when one of the Brits was thrown through a window.

First up was Kowalski, marched in by Chad and a military policeman.

Brad glowered at the GI. 'I'd hoped I'd seen the last of you, soldier! I see the time in the glasshouse didn't teach you a thing.'

Joe didn't answer, but stared defiantly at the captain. He hated being disciplined; he'd had enough of that in Pennsylvania from his father.

'For Gods sake, Kowalski, you'll be facing the enemy soon enough, why the hell can't you wait until then?'

Joe straightened his stance. 'I wasn't going to take that crap from no Limey! He was calling us all cowards for not coming into the war before Pearl Harbour. He said we were a shower of layabouts, without discipline, only interested in booze and women.'

Brad raised his eyebrows and couldn't help but agree, as far as some of the men were concerned, but he wouldn't give this man the satisfaction of knowing. 'Are you telling me that women were also involved in the argument?' Brad asked, hoping that there were no female casualties as well.

'There were a couple of whores, yes, sir. They wanted to be with us, and the British soldiers didn't like it.' With a sly smile he added, 'You know what it's like, sir. The broads love us Americans, just like your dame. Now *she's* really hot – and very popular.'

Brad froze. 'What are you implying, Kowalski?'

The GI suddenly realized that the captain was unaware that Rusty was a prostitute – this man who'd put him in the glasshouse. What a perfect opportunity to get back at him. 'You mean you get her services for free, when I had to pay? But then you being an officer and all, I expect she gets paid in other ways.'

Chad saw Brad's knuckles clench until they showed white as he fought to keep control.

'Get him out of here until I decide what to do with him!'

As the men marched out of the room, escorted by Chad, Brad took a cigarette out of a pack and lit it. Kowalski must be lying, surely? He couldn't conceive that he was speaking the truth. Not his Rusty . . . and yet, there had been a certain ring of truth in the man's voice.

Chad returned to the room. 'Are you ready for the next man, sir?'

'Give me ten minutes, Corporal, then bring him in.'

Outside, Chad took a deep breath. Jesus, he thought, if that GI was right . . . But he couldn't quite get his head around the fact. He liked Rusty. Could she really be a prostitute? He knew that she and the Captain were real close, he had seen the way they had looked at each other. Whatever would Brad do? He couldn't let the matter rest there; he'd have to find the truth.

How he got through the day, Brad didn't know. He was a professional, so he kept it together, but all the time in the back of his mind was the awful question: was the GI right?

Was Rusty a whore? Had Kowalski paid her for sex? The very idea sickened him. If the man was speaking the truth, how many other men had shared her bed, stroked her body and caressed her – as he had done, but with so much love. This was the woman he'd hoped to spend the rest of his life with if he was spared. Had she lied to him about being a typist? Had *everything* she'd told him been a lie? Surely not! It was driving him crazy. Well, this evening he was taking her out to dinner; tonight he'd search for the truth.

Unaware of the situation, Rusty dressed in readiness for her date. She hummed a tune as she did so. She was deliriously happy. She loved Brad, and he said he loved her too. Never had she thought she'd be lucky enough to meet such a man, and although war was a dreadful time, without it she'd never have met the good-looking captain. Secretly, she wondered if perhaps after the war she and Brad could be together. He had hinted as much without actually committing himself. As he had said, war was full of uncertainties; until it was over it would be foolish to make plans. She lived in hope, almost too scared to believe it was a possibility. After all, he came from a different class than her, he was a doctor, had been well educated, but happily that didn't seem to make a difference when they were together.

Brad waited for Rusty outside the restaurant where he'd booked a table. His shoulders and neck ached, he was so tense. He lit a cigarette and drew deeply on it to try and bring some kind of relief. He *had* to find out if Kowalski was speaking the truth, but how on earth was he going to broach the subject? He could hardly ask outright: 'Are you a whore?' Besides, he didn't really believe it, not his Rusty . . . but he couldn't rid himself of that vague feeling of doubt.

He saw her approaching, saw her face light up as she spied him waiting.

She ran into his arms and kissed him. 'Hello, darling, I'm so happy to see you. Have you had a busy day?'

He answered briefly and ushered her into the restaurant.

As they sat reading the menu, Rusty looked at Brad. She couldn't quite put her finger on it, but something was different. Brad wasn't smiling, he looked so serious. Perhaps something had happened during his working day. She knew that sometimes he had to make decisions that caused him great concern. That was probably it.

They ordered from the menu, and Brad asked the waiter to bring the wine and pour it whilst they waited.

When he had done so, Rusty picked up her glass. 'To us, darling.'

Brad clinked his glass with hers and drank. 'How was your day?' he asked.

She shrugged. 'Same old same old. Letters to be typed, files to be filed.'

'Just where is your office?' he asked. 'You've never told me.'

This took her by surprise. 'Down by the docks,' she said.

'What sort of firm is it that you work for?'

She had to think quickly. 'One of the shipping lines.' She quickly changed the subject. 'How was your day?'

Brad paused for a moment as the waiter served the first course. 'To be honest it was a hell of a day one way and another! Some of my men were involved in a fight at a pub, and one of the British soldiers was thrown through a window.'

'Oh my God! Is he all right?'

'He'll be fine, though he had a few cuts from the glass. He's in hospital with a few stitches. He was lucky. Unfortunately, one of the men involved is always in trouble. A big guy called Kowalski.' He looked at her, waiting to see her reaction. There was none.

Rusty only knew the GI as Joe, so his surname didn't mean a thing.

Brad began to relax. 'The men are all under a great deal of stress, knowing that they'll soon be in the fighting line. All they want is to get drunk and get laid. Business is good for the whores of the town. They must be making a fortune.'

Rusty choked on her food.

Brad stood up and thumped her hard on her back, and then handed her a glass of water. 'Here, drink this.'

She did so, then with some difficulty said, 'It went down the wrong way.' And took another drink of water.

Brad just watched her as she recovered. Was it guilt that had made her choke? He still didn't want to believe that she had been lying to him all this time. He couldn't bring himself to question her further, but neither could he behave normally. His suspicions made conversation stilted, no matter how he tried to be himself . . . and Rusty couldn't help but feel the tension between them.

After the meal, Brad made an excuse that he had to return to camp and catch up with some paperwork. He kissed her briefly, put her into a taxi and told her he'd be tied up for the rest of the week so she should call him on Friday evening – and then he went to the nearest pub for a beer.

As she sat in the taxi, Rusty tried to understand Brad's mood during the evening. Yes, he'd had a bad day, but there was more to it than that – his attitude towards her was different. She'd been with him before when his day had been difficult, but he'd always treated her with the same tenderness that had grown between them. Tonight, that warmth had been missing. It was almost like being with a stranger, not a lover. And why all the questions about her work? He'd never been bothered about that before. She just couldn't understand it.

The next morning Brad called Chad into the office. Although they met socially at the stables and at Jenny's, when they were in the office, before other ranks, they maintained a professional outward appearance. Now, however, Chad was the only person who Brad could trust to help him.

'Sit down,' said Brad. 'You heard what Kowalski said yesterday about Rusty?'

'Yes, I did.' Chad wondered what was coming next.

'I want you to find out where he goes usually, what pubs he uses, his general movements when he's on the town.'

Now Chad knew what was wanted of him and why. 'Are you really sure you want to go down this road?' he asked softly.

With a deep sigh, Brad said, 'I have no option. I have to find out the truth or I'll be wondering all the time I'm with Rusty.'

'Look, Brad, you love the girl, it's obvious to everyone when you're together. What if Kowalski is right? How will you feel about Rusty then? The girl is crazy about you, surely you know that?'

'Frankly, at this moment I'm not even sure of my own name!' He shook his head. 'This has thrown me completely. Yes, I do love Rusty; in fact, I had hoped that after the war she'd marry me and move to the States.'

'And now?'

'And now, I'm going crazy.' He looked at the other man, his face grim with worry. 'Could it possibly be true?'

Chad was filled with sympathy. What if it was true, he wondered. It would be terrible. His captain had been so happy with the vibrant woman, and she with him. They looked so right together, and he was filled with trepidation about the task in front of him. 'OK, if that's what you really want, I'll do what I can. But be very sure, because once I leave the room, you'll have started something you may live to regret.'

'No, do it! I won't be able to rest until I know, one way or another.'

Chad rose from the chair. 'Very well. I'll start tonight.'

But, once sitting at his own desk, Chad prayed that Kowalski was wrong. Could he have mistaken Rusty for another woman? No, she was very distinct, with her hair and her exuberance. He couldn't shake the feeling that the GI had sounded genuine. He wasn't just being a smart Alec, and when Brad had queried his comment about Rusty, the soldier had looked surprised. Chad had a bad feeling about what he was about to do. But there was no way he could get out of it. Brad was his friend and had asked a favour of him, so he'd have to do as he was asked. No matter what.

Fourteen

Sarah had just another month to go before the birth of her baby. By now she was feeling heavy and had difficulty sleeping, as the baby seemed to be a night owl and kicked her as she lay in bed. Mrs Brown had advised her to give up work, and when Sarah had said she needed to earn money, the farmer's wife had dismissed her concerns.

'Rubbish! You've been saving, and the baby has a layette all ready. Your stay here and your food doesn't require money; no, lass, you take it easy during these final weeks. The baby will surely benefit, and so will you. You need the rest now, because after you've given birth, you'll be up during the night feeding your child. Anyway, I'll be glad of the company, and you can do little jobs for me in the house.'

To be truthful, Sarah was relieved. She was so tired at the end of a working day, and by now she felt part of the family, which was a great comfort as her own family had disowned her. The Browns had been so good to her, and she welcomed the fact that she could be of some use to Ethel, whose working day seemed long and arduous, so she agreed.

She kept in constant touch with Gunter by mail. They exchanged letters frequently, and last week she'd sent him a snap showing her ever-increasing girth. On the back she'd written: *Your first view of your baby.*

When Gunter received the letter and photo, he took it off to a quiet corner to read and to study the picture. He smiled softly as he looked at the happy face of the mother of his forthcoming child. He ran his finger over her swollen stomach, wondering if he'd fathered a boy or a girl. Then a frown creased his forehead as he realized he might not see his offspring for some time. The future was full of uncertainties. The war was still raging, he was still a prisoner and when eventually hostilities ceased, he would be repatriated to Germany. Would he be allowed to see the mother and child before he left? And when he was home, what would he find there? Would he still have a home – were his parents alive, would he be able to work? If he had a wife and child, he wouldn't be able to afford to continue his legal studies; he'd have to earn a wage to keep them. He let out a deep sigh. Oh, why was life so complicated and so full of problems?

Captain Brad Jackson was thinking much the same as he waited for Chad to report back to him. When, on Friday, Rusty had phoned as he had requested, he made an excuse, said he was snowed under with work and to call again at the end of the following week. He knew from the tone of her voice that she was disappointed, but at this moment in time, he felt he couldn't face her. He was so wound up about Kowalski's slur on her that he wouldn't have been able to behave naturally, and that would have caused Rusty to question him . . . and how the hell could he have explained? No, it was easier this away.

For Chad, too, his task was problematical. He hated what he was having to do. Most of all he dreaded finding out that the GI had been speaking the truth and having to tell Brad, a man whom he admired greatly. It was giving him sleepless nights, and as he tossed and turned one night in the bed he occasionally shared with Jenny, she asked him what was wrong. So he told her.

'Oh my God! I can't believe that of Rusty.'

'I don't want to, but there was something in Kowalski's voice that made me think he was speaking the truth, and that worries me.'

'Oh, Chad, wouldn't it be terrible if it was true? I don't mean so much about Rusty being a prostitute, I mean for Brad finding out. He adores her.'

'And she loves him; it's obvious when you see them together. But I have a bad feeling about this. I wish Brad hadn't asked me to look into it, I really do.'

'If it is true, will you tell him?'

'I don't have a choice, honey. Let's hope I don't have to.'

But a week later, when he had followed Kowalski into The Grapes pub in Oxford Street, Chad's worst fears were realized. He bought a beer and kept himself in the background of the crowded bar, out of Kowalski's sight, and watched. Shortly after, Rusty came into the bar with another woman, and Chad waited to see what would happen.

Kowalski didn't bother them, he was talking to a couple of GIs, but in time, two other soldiers joined the girls, and after a few drinks, they all left together. Chad followed at a distance.

Rusty was laughing and chatting to the American with her, and then they parted from the other couple. Chad followed at a distance and saw Rusty take the soldier into a small house. When he walked up to the door, he could see Rusty's name alongside one of the four doorbells. It was obviously where she lived. That surprised him, as seedy Canal Walk was not the sort of place where a young, respectable typist would live. He waited. An hour later, the soldier came out alone.

Chad walked up to him. 'Gotta light, pal?'

The fellow American stopped and took out a lighter from his uniform and handed it to him.

Handing it back, Chad looked at the man. 'Was she worth the money?' he asked with a forced chuckle.

The soldier grinned broadly. 'I'll say. You want a good lay, buddy, you couldn't do better!' And he walked off.

Chad walked slowly away. He felt sad that in the morning he would have to impart such news to Brad, and he wondered what the consequence would be.

Alone in her room, Rusty put the money she'd earned away in the drawer. She sat on the side of the bed, still in her underwear, and thought: *I can't do this any more.* Every time she took a punter, she felt she was being unfaithful to Brad. She hated it when men pawed at her. Before, it was part of the job, but now it seemed obscene. She walked over to the mirror and looked at her reflection. She ran her fingers through her auburn tresses.

'You need a proper job, girl,' she said. Tomorrow she'd look for something. That American had been her last punter, she decided. From now on she'd be respectable; she owed it to the man she loved.

Chad waited for Brad to arrive in the office the following morning, filled with trepidation. As the captain walked through the door, he stepped forward. 'Can I have a word, sir, before you start the day?'

Brad looked at him and saw the expression on his face, and his heart sank. 'Yes, Corporal, come in.' They walked into his office and closed the door.

Chad stood in front of the desk. He hesitated. 'You asked me to check on Rusty, and I've done so.' He stopped there, hardly knowing how he could carry on.

Brad held his gaze and, with a grim face, asked, 'And?'

Chad gave him all the details; he had no choice. Had he lied, and Brad had discovered the truth later, it would have been worse for the captain.

Brad looked devastated as he listened. 'Thank you, Chad,' he said quietly. 'I know this wasn't easy for you, and I appreciate what you've done. Hold my calls for a while, will you?'

'Yes, I will. I'm real sorry.' He turned and left the office.

Brad sat staring into space, not wanting to believe what he'd heard. How could he have been so easily fooled? How could

Rusty declare her love for him when all the time she was taking other men to her bed . . . for money! She had lied about her work; had she lied too about loving him? All his hopes for the future died at that moment. And yet . . . he still loved her. In his mind he saw her face, heard her laughter, remembered how her soft skin felt as they made love. He got up and walked over to the window, looked out beyond his office, saw people going about their business – and cursed the war.

There was a knock on his door. 'Come in.'

Chad entered and, closing the door behind him, said, 'We don't have anything major to deal with today, so why don't you get out of here? Get some fresh air – it helps to clear the mind. I can cope with anything that comes in.'

Brad looked at him gratefully. 'Thanks, Chad, that's a great idea.'

'No sweat, I'll see you in the morning.'

Brad drove out to the stables and asked Beth if he could take out one of her mounts. She was pleased to see him; she told him which one needed exercising and left him to it.

As he rode out of the stables, he breathed a sigh of relief. Riding, for him, was totally therapeutic; it was just what he needed. He dug his heels into the horse and trotted away towards the woods, trying to clear his mind of the tortuous thoughts that invaded it.

An hour later, he found himself near Jenny's house and rode up the path. He saw her deadheading the roses in the front garden.

Jenny was surprised when she saw him, and knowing from the phone call she'd had from her lover that his worse fears had been confirmed, she wondered just what Brad was doing here. She waited for him to dismount.

'This is a nice surprise,' she said as she walked towards him. 'Here, tether the horse to this garden post. I'll fetch some water for him,' and she disappeared into the house, emerging soon after with a bucket, filled to the brim.

After the horse had satisfied his thirst she turned to her friend. 'Coffee?'

'Thanks, that'd be great.'

They sat in the kitchen by the window, looking out over the

back garden. 'It's so peaceful here,' he said as he sipped his drink and lit a cigarette. 'It's just what I need right now.'

She didn't press him, figuring if he wanted to tell her anything, he would do so in his own time. 'I so enjoy the summer in the garden,' she said, 'because when autumn does come, although it's also a beautiful season, it's a sad one. You know, everything coming to an end before the winter sets in.'

He gazed at her and said, 'I feel pretty autumnal myself right now.'

She waited, and then he began to tell her what had happened. She was silent as she listened, but when he said that the hardest thing to accept was Rusty's lies, she spoke. 'Rusty, for whatever reason, lives a precarious life, and I for one won't judge her, Brad, but one thing I am certain of is that she loves you. That was not a lie; I'd stake my life on it.'

'I'd like to think you're right, but what am I going to do, Jenny?'

She thought deeply as she knew this matter was of the utmost importance; the future of both of them hung on a very thin thread. 'That depends on how deeply you love her and if you can forget the way she earns her money.'

'I find that very hard to do. The thought of other men . . .'

'You have to talk to her, Brad.'

'And say what?'

'That all depends on you. I can't help you there, I wish I could. But you can't leave things up in the air. You have to sort it, one way or another.'

'Yes, I guess you're right.' He finished his coffee. 'I'd best get back to the stables or Beth will think I've stolen her horse.'

Jenny put a comforting arm through his as they left the house. As he mounted the horse, she looked up at him. 'Good luck, Brad.'

He smiled. 'I guess Rusty was *my* guilty pleasure,' he said. And he rode away.

That evening, Chad drove over to Jenny's house, and they discussed what had happened. She felt so sorry for the doctor who had become such a friend to her. 'Is there anything we can do?' she asked.

Chad shook his head. 'No, honey, Brad will have to work this out for himself. If I was in his shoes, I'm damned if I know how I would react. I feel for Rusty too. OK, she might be a whore, but she's a terrific woman and she's crazy about him . . . What a mess!'

'I told him that he should see her and get it sorted, but however it turns out, two people are going to be deeply hurt.'

When, on Friday, Rusty rang Brad as arranged, he said he'd be free at seven thirty and he'd pick her up outside Holy Rood Church. He spoke abruptly, which was unlike him. Usually, his voice was full of warmth when he spoke to her, but not now.

'Are you all right, darling?' she asked.

'Yes, fine, just rushed off my feet. I'll see you later.'

As she put down the receiver, she felt her stomach tighten. Something was very wrong. Was he going to tell her he was being shipped out, was that it? It was obvious to all the towns-people that something big was going to happen – you couldn't move for troops queuing alongside the quay and the docks. Armoured tanks were lined up, and the huge Mulberry Harbours being built were now finished. That had to be it, he was leaving!

At seven thirty, Rusty waited outside the church, her heart beating so hard that she almost felt faint. When Brad pulled up in front of her and told her to get into the jeep, she did so.

'Rusty, we need to talk,' he said as they drove off.

Fifteen

They drove in silence. Rusty glanced across at Brad and saw his grim expression, the tightness of his jaw, and she was scared. This man she loved as much as life itself was leaving. By now she was sure this was the reason. What if he was killed in action? She didn't think she could survive such a loss.

Brad headed out through Bitterne and turned off the road towards Hamble, where he eventually parked the vehicle, overlooking Southampton Water. He switched off the engine and turned to her.

'Whatever is it, Brad?' she asked. But the answer she received shocked her to the core.

'You lied to me, Rusty. You told me that you were a typist with one of the shipping lines, when all the time you were "entertaining the troops"!'

She felt the blood drain from her body. 'Oh my God!' The words escaped her lips before she was aware of them.

'Is that all you have to say to me?' Brad's voice was like ice.

She was stunned into silence. With trembling fingers, she reached into her handbag for a cigarette and lit it, trying to think what she could say. Taking a deep drag on the cigarette, she blew out the smoke and then stared straight into his eyes.

'What can I say? It's the truth. When we first met it didn't matter, we were just having a good time, but when I fell in love with you, I couldn't tell you in case I lost you.'

His eyes glittered with anger. 'You say you fell in love with me, but you still continued in your profession! You didn't love me enough to stop you taking other men to your bed.'

How could she explain? The fact that she had now stopped, and had found a job this week, seemed irrelevant. He would wonder why she had waited so long to do so. Indeed, she wondered that herself.

'I'm so sorry, Brad.'

'You lied to me. Did you lie about your parents too?'

She nodded. 'My father left my mother just before the war, though he *is* in Australia. Mum lives in Southampton. I left home after a row and I've not seen her since.' She saw the disappointment on his face. 'I wanted to impress you,' she cried.

'Why, for God's sake?'

'Because you come from a much better class than me. I wanted you to think well of me because I liked you – then I loved you. And that isn't a lie, Brad.'

He shook his head as he looked at her. 'Oh Rusty, class wasn't at all important. There was no need for all this subterfuge.'

She gave a bitter laugh. 'Oh really! My mother is a drunk! What's to be proud of?'

'Alcoholism is an illness, it isn't her fault. I've dealt with that in my practice, I know.'

'Have you dealt with prostitution too?' She glared at him defiantly.

'What made you become a prostitute, if I may ask? I'm trying to understand. Why that and not some other job?'

There was no way she could make him understand; it would sound so shallow. How could she tell him she had just wanted a good time and the opportunity arose one night and she just carried on from there, knowing she could make a mint of money?'

'It really doesn't matter why, Brad. I am what I am, and no one can change that.'

He was at a loss to know what to say, as his own feelings were in turmoil. He started the jeep's engine, reversed, turned and drove back to the town.

Rusty sat beside him, tears brimming in her eyes, knowing she'd lost the man who meant everything to her.

Brad stopped the vehicle outside the church where he'd met her. He didn't know what to say. He just looked at her.

She saw the pain etched on his face, and her heart was breaking. She touched his hand. 'I am *so* sorry. I wish it was a different story because I love you so very much.' She leaned forward and kissed his lips softly . . . then got out of the jeep and ran down the street.

Brad wanted to call after her, but he couldn't bring himself to do so. He put the car into gear and drove back to the camp.

During the next few weeks, Brad hardly had time to draw breath, which was his saving grace. Overlord was on, and D-Day was approaching. Southampton was packed with troops, lining up ready to cross the English Chanel to Normandy. The weather was bad, and Eisenhower had delayed the crossing for twenty-four hours.

Despite asking his commanding officer if he could be allowed to cross with his men, this had been denied. He was pivotal to the organization, he was told. 'We need you here.' He had to remain in the war room, surrounded by maps, with the plans for the invasion before him.

But when it was time for his men to leave, he spoke briefly

to them and wished them luck. As he watched them march out of the camp gates, he wondered just how many would be coming back. He saw Kowalski marching past. He wasn't unhappy to see the last of the man.

Kowalski saw the captain watching and smirked to himself. *Well, Captain*, he thought, *you got what was coming to you.*

But the GI got his as he stepped off the landing craft. He didn't even make the beach, as a single bullet caught him right between the eyes.

Rusty, now working as a shop assistant in Edwin Jones, wondered if Brad was among the troops that were marching through the streets. She was leading a very quiet life these days. She'd moved out of Canal Walk and was renting a small flat in the Polygon area, well away from the streets where she used to trade. Not a day passed that she didn't think of her lover and wish that things could have been different. If only she could have seen him just once more . . . Remembering how hurt he'd been, it was perhaps for the best, but she was deeply unhappy.

To her surprise, one day in mid June she looked up as a customer paused in front of her counter and saw it was Jenny. She didn't know what to do or how Jenny would be towards her, knowing that she was such a good friend of Brad's.

'Rusty!' said Jenny. 'How lovely to see you. How are you?'

With some relief, Rusty smiled back. 'I'm fine, how are you?'

They chatted about inconsequential things, and then Jenny asked, 'Do you get a break for lunch?'

'Yes, in about half an hour.'

'Good, let's go and get a sandwich together.' She saw Rusty hesitate. 'Please, I'd like to talk to you.'

They agreed to meet outside.

Once they were settled in a coffee shop and had ordered, Jenny turned to Rusty. 'I am so sorry to hear about you and Brad.' It was said with such sincerity that Rusty was taken by surprise.

'Well, so am I. But what could you expect?' She gazed at Jenny and decided it was useless to pretend. 'You know the reason why?'

'Yes, I do, but who am I to judge you, Rusty? After all, here I am, a married woman – having an affair!'

'Have you seen Brad? Has he been sent to France?'

'No, he's still at headquarters. I've seen him only once, he's been so busy since the invasion, but I can tell you he's not a happy man. He truly loved you, you know.'

'If only I'd stopped taking punters sooner, when I fell in love with him, but it's too late for regrets.' She pursed her lips. 'I am now working in a respectable job, as you saw. I've put my other life behind me, but it's too late for me and Brad. Oh, Jenny, if only I could turn back the clock.'

Seeing the unhappiness in the other woman's face only made Jenny wish there was something she could do.

'How's Chad?'

Jenny smiled. 'He's fine – busy, of course, because he works in Brad's office, but we meet when we can.'

'If you don't mind my asking, where do you see your situation going?'

'No, I don't mind, but to tell you the truth I don't know. Like you, I've fallen for an American, and I want to spend my life with him . . . but there's Adam.' She let out a deep sigh. 'I'm just living for each day at the moment.'

'Life's a bitch, isn't it?'

Jenny burst out laughing. 'I couldn't have put it better myself. Look, why don't you come over to my place for lunch on Sunday?' Seeing Rusty's worried expression she added, 'I'll be all on my own, and I'll be glad of the company, honestly. Please say you'll come.'

And Rusty agreed to do so.

But when Jenny arrived home and opened her mail, she realized that she now had a big problem. Adam was coming home. He'd been injured, not seriously, but he'd caught some shrapnel in his leg and had been flown home after an operation, to recover. He would be arriving on Monday.

She sat at the table in the kitchen and looked out of the window. She was sorry he'd been injured – of course she was – but the idea of having him here, wanting her to be at his beck and call, filled her with trepidation. The idea of sharing a bed with him made her go cold. She didn't want him to touch her, and when he was well enough she couldn't bear the idea of his making love to her. She knew she just couldn't do it. She closed her eyes, but the thoughts of the difficulties ahead would not go away. What on earth was she to do? She picked up the phone and called Chad.

Young Sarah was also suffering, but her pain was the birth of her baby. She was in her bedroom at Cherry Tree Farm, with the midwife and Ethel Brown, who was sponging the perspiration off her forehead.

'It won't be long now, my dear, and then this will all be over. You'll forget all about the pain when you hold the baby in your arms, I promise.'

Another contraction grabbed Sarah, and she let out a cry of pain. 'You'd better be right,' she said, 'because there will only be one child! I can't do this again.'

Ethel smiled to herself, remembering having similar thoughts herself, but when half an hour later Sarah was gazing lovingly at the baby boy in her arms, she knew the girl *would* forget, as she and many other mothers had.

Sarah studied the small face of her son and was amazed. So this was what she and Gunter had made. She thought the child looked a miniature of his father and wished with all her heart he could be here to see this miracle for himself. At least she could have a picture taken and send it to Gunter. She asked Ethel to pass her hairbrush to make herself look less frazzled from the birth, and then asked her to take a picture of them, to send to the father.

'He'll be so proud of you both,' said Ethel as she aimed the lens at the bed and its occupants.

'But when ever will he see little Hans?' They had both chosen names for their baby through letters.

'Don't start finding difficulties,' warned Ethel. 'You've both come through the birth, and you have a healthy child. You just tell yourself that sometime in the future you'll all be together, and that's what counts!'

At that moment there was a knock on the door, and Mr Brown asked if he could see the new arrival. He was ushered in.

He smiled at Sarah. 'Well done, girlie.' Then he leaned over the baby. 'Now, there is a handsome child if ever I saw one. Have you got a name for the little fellow?'

'Hans. Gunter and I chose it.'

'Yes, and it suits him,' he said. 'I'll leave you in peace now. But congratulations.'

That evening, Jenny opened the door to her lover and flew into his arms, in tears. 'Oh Chad, what am I going to do?' she cried.

He held her close and said, 'Hey, now, come on honey, calm down and we'll sort this out.' He led her into the drawing room and they sat on the settee. 'Now tell me what was in the letter.'

Jenny gave it to him to read.

He put down the letter and took her hand in his. 'Well, darlin', the time has come to decide the future – are we going to stay together . . . or not?'

She looked into his eyes and caressed the face of the man she was in love with. 'I can't live with Adam,' she said. 'I can't go back to my old life. I just can't!'

'Before you decide, you must face up to reality, Jenny honey. Can you put this comfortable life behind you? Because I'm not sure what I can offer you. I have enough money put aside to open a small ranch back home, but it will be real hard to begin with. There won't be any luxuries, not for a while, until I get established.'

'I don't care about that! I just want to spend the rest of my life with you, that's *all* I care about.'

But he was insistent. 'That's great, and you know that I want you with me, but life will be so very different. I'm just a cowboy from Wyoming, after all. I don't have the education or position that you have and are used to.'

'Do you think that matters a jot to me? You are so much more than just a cowboy; you have a gift that is amazing. I can't wait to see you use it again. I want to be part of your life, don't you believe me?'

He kissed her softly. 'Yes, I do, and I can't quite believe my luck, but what are you going to do when your husband comes home? You'll have to tell him. Are you prepared for that?'

Shaking her head she said, 'No, but it has to be done. I'll feel dreadful and Adam will be furious, but I can't lie to him, pretend that things are fine, because that wouldn't be right.'

'It may mean you'll lose everything,' said Chad. 'Your home, your friends . . . and we'll have to wait until the war is over before we can be together. It could be some time. I'm asking a lot from you, Jenny. Are you really sure? Don't you want time to think this thing through?'

She smiled fondly at him. 'I can't wait to see your world; it sounds so different. Sitting round a campfire, tending to the land, looking after the horses. Don't you see, Chad, to me it sounds like heaven.'

He laughed. 'That's your free spirit emerging; I told you a long way back you would eventually understand. The real you will blossom once we get to Wyoming, and I can't wait to see that woman.'

And as she lay in his arms that night, Jenny could hardly wait to start her new life, but she knew that before that happened she would have a very rocky ride. She had no idea how Adam would react to her news. *Would* she be ostracized by all their friends? So what if she was! She could put up with that; after all, she was a woman with a mind of her own, and she'd made a decision – and as far as the others were concerned, they could like it or lump it! Chad would no longer be her guilty pleasure; she would be able to meet him openly once she'd spoken to Adam.

She looked at the face of the man sleeping beside her and knew she'd made the right decision. Come what may.

Sixteen

When Rusty arrived at Jenny's house on the Sunday, she could see that there was something on Jenny's mind, and after making some coffee, Jenny explained her situation.

After listening carefully Rusty said, 'Well, at least you know you have a future with Chad, but I don't envy you having to tell Adam. Oh, Jenny, war is hell! It messes up so many lives. Without it we would both be going our own way as usual – without complications.'

With a rueful smile, Jenny said, 'I don't know about that!

Living with Adam was always complicated, and I'm sure your life had its moments too.'

Rusty chuckled softly. 'Oh yes, a few, I have to admit. But how will Adam take it, do you think?'

Pondering on this, Jenny said, 'I'm really not sure. When he was home last time he said I'd changed, that he didn't know me any more – and he was right, of course. I'd carved out a life for myself; I was at last my own person. Mind you, at that time I'd only seen Chad at the stables, we hadn't become lovers yet.'

'Will you still be able to stay here?'

'I've no idea. Adam is only home until he recovers from the operation. It's not the best time to be told his wife is in love with another man. But I don't have a choice.'

'Well, if you have to leave, I have a spare bedroom going at my flat. You're very welcome to move in with me.'

'Oh, Rusty, that's so good of you. I may have to take up your invitation for a while until I can sort myself out. Thank you. Anyway, let's put all this behind us. Whilst the lunch is cooking come and walk around the garden, it's looking lovely at the moment.'

They sat on the garden bench after and gazed around. 'Wyoming will be a very different landscape to this,' Jenny remarked quietly. 'America is so vast in comparison.'

'You'll find it strange to begin with, I'm sure,' Rusty agreed.

'Yes, but so exciting! I can hardly wait, but of course I'll have to.'

'That will be the hardest part. Then, when the war is over, the GIs will go home to be repatriated.' She looked at her hostess. 'I do hope you don't have to wait too long.'

Jenny put her hand over Rusty's. 'I only wish that you and Brad could make it up between you. You belong together.'

'Sadly, there is no hope of that. It's a shame because, like you with Chad, I would have followed him anywhere, without a backward glance.'

At the end of the day, as she was leaving, Rusty gave Jenny her address. 'You know where I work if you need to get in touch with me during the day.' She hugged her. 'I do hope when Adam comes home tomorrow that things won't be too difficult. Please let me know what happens, I'll be worrying about you, but remember you have a place to stay if you need it.'

As she watched Rusty walk down the path, Jenny thought: *What a marvellous girl*. If only she could talk to Brad and make him see sense. There were two people who were about to leave their life in ruins . . . for what? Rusty wasn't a bad woman; if only Brad could accept her past, they could be happy together. But as she closed the door, she knew that tomorrow she was going to have to face her husband, and she felt nauseous at the thought of what lay before her.

Adam Procter sat in the military ambulance as it took him out of the town towards Chilworth. His leg was sore from the operation, and after several sleepless nights, he was somewhat irritable. How good it would be to be home, in his own house with Jenny to care for him. The doctors had done a good job, apparently, and when he was recovered he would be recalled to duty.

He was able to walk with the aid of a stick and needed to exercise his leg – walking round the garden would do that to begin with. It should take about a month for the wound to heal, he'd been told. His own doctor had been informed and would be visiting him tomorrow to change the dressing.

As the vehicle turned into his driveway, he wondered how Jenny was. He hoped she'd no longer be involved with so many committees, as he needed her to care for him. She'd have to find the time for him whilst he was home, no matter what else she had to do.

Jenny waited at the front door as the ambulance drew up beside her. The driver got out and smiled at her as he walked around to the back of the vehicle and helped the patient down.

Adam looked better than she expected, she thought thankfully, and he seemed to be walking reasonably well. She went up to him and kissed him briefly on the cheek. 'How are you?' she asked.

'Weary, and a bit stiff.' He turned to thank the driver and then entered the house.

'Would you like a cup of tea?' she asked.

'No thanks, I want something a bit stronger. A large gin and tonic would be nice.'

'Are you allowed alcohol? I wondered if you were on any medication,' she added hastily when she saw the look of irritation on his face.

'I've finished all the antibiotics, so it's all right.' He lowered himself on to the settee. 'It's good to be home. They needed the bed so were quite happy to let me go. Dr Bailey is calling tomorrow to give me the once over,' he said as he took the glass from her. 'Aren't you having one?'

'No, it's a bit early for me. I have a coffee in the kitchen. I'll just go and get it.'

Once in the kitchen, Jenny took a deep breath. This wasn't going to be easy. She'd have to wait for the right moment to talk to him about Chad; she couldn't blurt it all out the minute he arrived. She picked up her cup and returned to the sitting room and sat in an armchair opposite her husband. 'How long do you think you'll be home?'

'They said about a month. It was quite a nasty wound, but they managed to get the pieces of shrapnel out eventually, and they grafted a bit of skin they took from my thigh to cover the gash in my leg.'

'I am sorry, that must have been very painful.'

'It wasn't a barrel of laughs, and at one stage it became infected – but at least I'm alive, unlike some poor devils.' He glanced through the window. 'The garden looks nice.'

'Well, the roses need deadheading, but the shrubs are fine.'

'And what have you been up to whilst I've been away?' He didn't give her chance to answer. 'I do hope you aren't as tied up as last time I was home because you'll need to look after me.'

Already his dictatorial tone was getting on her nerves, and Jenny wondered just how long she'd be able to tolerate it . . . But the man was wounded, she'd have to remember that and try to be patient.

'Well, I *am* still busy,' she told him, 'and we'll have to come to some arrangement when I know just exactly how much nursing you'll be needing. At least you can get about, which is great.'

'I wouldn't want to get in the way of your work,' he said with heavy sarcasm.

'Don't start, Adam! You've been in the house less than half an hour. Let us at least try to understand one another.'

'I forget you're used to living alone these days, and my return must seem like an intrusion, but do remember I've been fighting in the bloody war! You could take that into consideration.'

She didn't retaliate; what was the point? 'Are you hungry?' she asked. 'Only, I've got a shepherd's pie in the oven and there are a load of fresh vegetables from the garden. You'll feel better with a good meal inside you.'

'Yes, now you come to mention it, I'm ravenous. I didn't sleep well last night, so if you don't mind I'll go to our room after and take a nap.'

Lunch wasn't too difficult. Adam told her about the fighting he'd been involved with and how he was in one way pleased to be sent to a military hospital as he could get a bit of peace and a rest.

'We're all so tired,' he explained. 'At times you just grab a sleep when and where you can. I can't wait to put my head down in my own bed.' But when he eventually went upstairs and into their bedroom – with Jenny behind him, carrying his suitcase – he stopped short and frowned. 'What's this? There is only one set of pillows on my side.'

'I've moved into one of the spare rooms,' she said. 'I thought you'd sleep better on your own, and I'd be worried all the time that I might inadvertently knock your wound as I turned over.'

'Very thoughtful of you, and for a while that's probably wise. You can move back in when it's healed.'

She didn't answer.

Downstairs in the quiet of the kitchen, she sat and drank a fresh cup of coffee, thankful that Adam was now asleep. Of course she wouldn't be moving back into their bedroom, and by the time that Adam was that well recovered, she would have given him her news. She decided it was only fair to give him time to recover first. He had been through so much; it would be cruel in the extreme to tell him before he was on the road to recovery. Chad would surely understand that.

At headquarters, Chad kept glancing at his watch, wondering if Adam Procter had arrived home, and if he had, how things were going. He wanted to pick up the phone and call Jenny, but realized how unwise that would be at this moment. Jenny had said she would call the office when she could, and he'd have to be content to wait. But he was restless.

At lunchtime he couldn't face the canteen and walked to the edge of the camp, found a quiet spot and sat on the grass. He couldn't help but worry about the life that Jenny was giving up to be with him. Not her marriage. He'd been aware that was in trouble when first they met; otherwise, when he'd realized he was in love with her, he simply wouldn't have told her. She was such a classy woman, and the life they would share would be so simple in comparison. But deep down he knew she'd thrive on it. The difference in their ages had long ceased to be a problem. In fact, it had never been so with him. It had worried Jenny to begin with, he thought, but thankfully, not any longer.

He could picture them riding the range together, rounding up horses, sitting beneath the stars when they sometimes camped out. But before that could happen, there was many a fence to be jumped; not least Jenny having to tell her husband she was leaving him. Chad had suggested that he be with her when she did so, but Jenny had been adamant. She had to do it alone.

He got up and returned to his office.

The next few days were a nightmare for Jenny. The doctor had called and changed Adam's dressing. She glanced at the wound, which still looked quite nasty, and afterwards Adam had been his usual demanding self and she'd hardly had a moment to breathe. But today she'd driven him to his golf club, where he was going to meet old friends and stay for lunch. She delivered him safely and drove to the stables where Chad was waiting for her. She had managed to call him when she knew she'd be free.

As she drove into the yard, he was waiting for her. She parked the car and ran into his arms. 'Just hold me,' she cried. 'I need to feel safe.'

Chad could feel her trembling, and he tilted her chin upwards and kissed her. 'Calm down, honey, I'm here now.' He led her to the kitchen, where Beth had told him to take her so they could have some privacy to talk.

He poured them both a cup of coffee, then sat beside her. Putting a comforting arm around her he asked, 'Is it that bad, darlin'?'

She sipped her drink. 'Well, Adam is Adam. Nothing changes. I'm not sure just how long I can keep up this pretence. I'm sleeping in the spare room. I told him he would get a better night's sleep. I can't help feeling guilty, knowing what I plan to do.'

'If you feel that bad, Jenny, then sit down and tell him, as you said you would.'

'I thought I should wait until he's stronger. After all, he's been through a lot and it's going to come as a great shock to him.'

Chad gave her a hard stare. 'You haven't changed your mind, have you?'

'Oh my God, no! Seeing him again, I know that even if you were not in my life I couldn't live with Adam as his wife, not any more.'

He was relieved. 'You had me a mite worried there for a moment.'

She laughed and kissed him. 'You are stuck with me, you crazy cowboy, like it or not!'

The next three hours was heaven for Jenny. Being with Chad had given her an inner strength, and she drove to collect Adam with a much lighter heart, which he noticed when she walked into the club to collect him, but he didn't say anything until they were in the car.

'Well, you look happier than I've seen you since I arrived home. Where have you been to make such a change?'

She was somewhat startled by his remark. 'I went to see Beth at the stables, that's all.' But Adam didn't look convinced.

'Is that really all?'

'I didn't have time to go anywhere else,' she said tartly. Thinking she would have to be careful to hide her happiness if she saw Chad again.

At the prisoner of war camp at Bishop's Waltham, Gunter Reinhardt sat beaming with delight as he looked at the snaps of his new son, Hans. He blinked away tears of emotion as he gazed at Sarah holding the baby. Their son, how wonderful! He silently vowed that no matter what difficulties lay before them, he would be united with his family one day and his son would have a secure future. He put the letter and picture in his pocket and walked towards the main office, where he asked permission to see the officer in charge.

When eventually he was admitted, he stood to attention and made his request. 'Today, sir, I received a letter from my fiancée with a photograph of our son, born last week.'

The officer looked surprised. 'Your fiancée?'

'Yes, sir, we met when I was held in Southampton, and we fell in love. I asked Sarah to be my wife, and she accepted.'

'How the hell did you manage to make her pregnant if you were interned?'

'I was working on a small farm for several months, and the farmer allowed her to visit, sir.'

The officer murmured his disapproval. 'So why are you here?'

Gunter removed the photograph from his pocket and showed it to the man. 'Here they are, sir,' he said proudly. 'I was wondering if there was some way they could visit me so I could see them . . . just this once?' He hesitated, then added, 'I intend to take them to Germany after the war. I want to have my family with me, sir.'

The officer looked at the photograph. He had children of his own, and he'd heard the yearning in the young man's voice as he spoke. He had quickly looked at Gunter's papers when he was asked for the interview, had seen his background and the report from Farmer Brown about his work on his farm. He'd liked what he'd read. This young man was no threat to the country, just a soldier doing his job, as was he.

'Very well, Reinhardt. Seeing you have a new baby, I'll give my permission . . . Just this once, you understand? This is a one-off.'

Gunter beamed at him. 'Thank you, sir; I won't forget your kindness. Thank you.'

'Find out when they can come, and let me know. Dismiss!'

Gunter rushed to his room and wrote to Sarah, telling her the good news. He could hardly wait to see them both; it would help him tolerate being in captivity for the rest of the war. Now he had a family of his own, and it felt so good.

He lay on his bed and let his mind conjure pictures of the future. He would want to continue with his studies, if at all possible, and then when he'd passed all his exams, he'd open a practice or maybe join his father in his. They would have a nice house on the outskirts of Hamburg. He'd teach Sarah German. Little Hans would learn it at school, but they would speak English at home so the boy would be bilingual. And so he dreamed for the rest of the day until the camp lights were turned off. He slept with a smile, the smile of a new father.

Seventeen

Adam had been home for a week when everything came to a head. He had walked up to Jenny, put his arms around her, one hand on her breast as he nuzzled he neck – and she'd frozen!

'What's the matter?' he asked angrily as she pushed his hand away. 'I am your husband, after all.' He stepped towards her, but she put out her hand to stop him.

Taking a deep breath she said, 'Come into the sitting room, we need to talk.' She tucked her trembling hands into the pockets of her cardigan.

Adam sat on the settee and waited impatiently. 'Well, what the devil do we have to talk about?'

Jenny sat opposite him. 'I'm sorry, Adam, but I want a divorce.'

'You what?'

'I want a divorce.'

His face flushed with fury. 'I've never heard anything so ridiculous in all my life!'

'I'm in love with another man.' She thought he was going to have a fit.

'In love . . .' He rose from his chair and stomped up and down, then stopped in front of her. 'So who is this *other man*?'

'He's an American soldier.'

He scowled. 'Not Captain Jackson, the man you seem to meet up with all the time.'

'No, not Captain Jackson. His name is Chad Maxwell.'

'Another bloody officer, I suppose?'

Jenny tried to remain calm. 'No, as a matter of fact he's a corporal.'

'A bloody corporal? Are you serious?'

'To me his rank is of no importance. I love him for what he is.'

'And what is he exactly?'

'He's a horse whisperer; he tames wild horses.'

'He sounds like a bloody cowboy!'

Jenny stared straight at him. 'Yes, precisely. He's going to buy a ranch in Wyoming after the war and raise horses.'

He gazed at her in disbelief. 'You mean to say you'd give up all this –' he gestured with his hand around the room – 'to live on some ranch in the middle of nowhere with some cowboy? Have you completely lost your marbles?'

'I know it sounds strange to you, Adam, as you have always liked material things, but to live a simple life with Chad, riding the range, to me sounds like heaven.'

'Chad? What kind of name is that for God's sake?'

'It really doesn't matter. I'm sorry, Adam, none of this was planned, it just happened.'

He sat back down on the settee. 'I can't believe I'm hearing this. Christ, Jenny, we've been married for years. I thought you were happy.'

'I was to begin with, but as the years passed, it became just a routine.'

'Thanks a bunch!'

'You said when you came home last time that I had changed – well, it was true. I suddenly discovered I was a person, not an appendage. I like the woman I found, but unfortunately for you, I no longer want my old life. I no longer want to be your wife. I want a divorce.'

He suddenly realized she was serious, and anger took over from disbelief. 'If that's what you want, then go to your bloody cowboy. Pack your stuff and get out!'

'But what about you, Adam? You need looking after until you're better.'

'It's a little late to be concerned about my welfare, isn't it?' he said bitterly.

'I'm quite prepared to stay and look after you until you're well enough to return to your unit.'

'That's very big of you! No thanks. Do you think I would

want you around me knowing you would rather be with another man? No. I'll hire a nurse and a housekeeper. Now, I suggest you pack a bag.' He got out of the chair and limped out of the room to his study.

Jenny heard the door slam. Although she didn't regret her decision for a moment, she was sorry she'd had to break the news to Adam when he was still injured, but she'd had no choice. She couldn't bear him to touch her. Not now.

She went upstairs to her bedroom and, getting out a large suitcase, started to pack her clothes. She would collect the rest of her things when Adam had returned to his unit. She would go to Rusty's flat for a while until she sorted herself out – she would have to rent a flat and find a job. There were sufficient funds in her bank account to see her through until then. Although she and Adam had a joint account, she had always had an account in her own name – which, as things had turned out, was just as well.

Adam stood at the study window and watched Jenny put her case in the boot of her car and drive away, using the petrol she was allowed to do her war work. He was stunned. He could hardly believe what was happening. Jenny must be completely mad, he thought. How could she give up her comfortable way of life with him to go and live in Wyoming – with a bloody cowboy, for Christ's sake! What's more, she seemed completely enamoured with this man.

He lit a cigarette. *She'll soon come to her senses*, he told himself. The war would have to end first, then time would pass before she could go to the States. But if she changed her mind, did he even want her back? All these thoughts clouded his brain until he couldn't think straight. He'd call a taxi and go to his club for a meal, a couple of drinks, and then come home. Perhaps then he could make some sense of what happened. Tomorrow he'd call an agency and hire a housekeeper and get a nurse to look after his medical needs until he was well. Maybe by then Jenny would have come to her senses and he would then decide what to do about their marriage.

Jenny and Rusty sat in the small lounge of Rusty's flat, eating baked beans on toast, washed down by a not particularly good bottle of red wine.

'I'll have to look for a job tomorrow,' Jenny said.

'Doing what?'

'I'll look in the *Echo* and see what's on offer. I'm good at administration, so maybe something to do with the military. After all, I'm already working with them.'

'Why don't you have a word with Brad?'

'Yes, I could do that I suppose. I'll wait and see what's in the paper first. By the way, I rang Chad and told him I was here and gave him this address. I hope you don't mind?'

'Look, Jenny, this is your home for as long as you want it, and you have your own key, so stop worrying . . . and if you want Chad to stay overnight, that's fine too.' She chuckled softly. 'Mind you, it will be bit of a squeeze with two of you in a single bed!'

Thanks, Rusty, what would I do without you?'

'Don't be silly. You'd have done the same for me.' She rose to her feet. 'I'm off to bed; I have to be up for work in the morning.'

'I'll go shopping for food tomorrow. I've brought my ration book; I'll see what I can find. I'll have a meal ready for when you get home.'

'How lovely! And to have company. I've felt really lonely since I moved here.'

There was a plaintive note to her voice, and Jenny felt sorry that the situation between her friend and Brad was so bad. She wondered if there wasn't something she could do to change this.

The following morning Jenny caught the tram and went to army headquarters and asked to speak to Captain Jackson. Chad came from the outer office, grinned broadly at her and said, 'Would you come this way, Mrs Procter?'

Brad walked round his desk, kissed her on the cheek and said, 'Chad told me about your husband. Sit down, Jenny, what can I do for you?'

She explained her situation. 'I'm looking for a job. I wondered if you knew of anything.'

'As a matter of fact, I do! We've set up a department to deal with war brides –' he smiled at her – 'which is something I know that you will be interested in personally in the future. Several of our men have met British girls and have already married them, and others plan to do so in the near future. After the war is over, we will have to ship these women out to the States, of course, but there are several steps that have to be taken before this can happen. You will have to liaise with the Red Cross – and us, of course, but you do that already so know the drill. I'll bring some papers over to your place late this afternoon if you like, and we can go over them together so you'll understand just what I want from you.'

'That's marvellous! Thank you, Brad, I'll really enjoy doing that.' She gave him her new address without telling him that she was staying with Rusty.

On the way home, Jenny joined several queues for food and eventually returned with some sausages, a rabbit and some vegetables, thinking all the while of the vegetables growing in her garden at home, which would be going to waste. She would make a good rabbit stew for this evening, which would perhaps help to cheer her friend and fill in her time waiting for Brad to call.

The American arrived late in the afternoon, laden with coffee, eggs, fruit and butter. 'I thought this would help out,' he said as he unpacked the goods.

Jenny was most grateful and even more delighted when he produced a tin of ham.

They sat down together and went through the papers he'd brought with him, discussing the finer details and what would be required of Jenny.

'I only hope these girls realize what they're letting themselves in for,' he said. 'I'm sure that many of the men have shot their women a line about their homes and lives back in the States, and some, I'm sure, are in for a big disappointment when they get there. But that's out of my hands. We've talked to the guys about doing this, of course, but that's all we can do.'

'If they really love their man, they'll put up with a lot before quitting,' Jenny said with conviction.

He smiled at her. 'I don't think you have a thing to worry about with Chad – he's a great guy.'

'I think so.' As she spoke, Jenny heard the front door being opened.

Rusty walked into the room and was shocked to see Brad sitting there. They looked at each other in surprise.

'This is Rusty's flat,' Jenny explained. 'She offered me a room when Adam kicked me out. I'll go and make us some coffee.'

Left alone, neither Brad nor Rusty knew what to say. Brad broke the silence first. 'You're looking well. How've you been?'

'Fine, thanks.' Rusty felt her heart pounding, she wanted to reach out and touch him.

'Rusty's working at Edwin Jones,' called Jenny from the kitchen.

'Is that right?' Brad asked with surprise.

'Yes, I got the job just before the last time we met. As you can see, I've moved. I've started a new life altogether,' she said hopefully.

'That's good to hear.' Brad looked at his watch. 'I'd better be on my way.' Getting to his feet, he walked to the kitchen door 'I'll in touch, Jenny, when I've set you up with an office. Probably by Monday. Gotta fly.' He smiled across at Rusty. 'Good to see you again.' And he left the flat.

Jenny walked back into the room. Rusty was sitting looking devastated.

'That didn't turn out quite as I had hoped,' Jenny told her as she sat beside her. 'Sorry I didn't tell you Brad was coming. I hoped once he saw you . . .'

Her friend grimaced and forced a smile. 'It was a nice try, Jenny, and I thank you for the thought, but as you see, it really is over as far as Brad is concerned. Oh well! Any tea in that pot?' And the subject was closed.

Eighteen

Brad Jackson drove away from Rusty's flat, his equilibrium definitely shaken. The last person he'd expected to see was the beautiful redhead with whom he'd shared so many romantic and intimate moments. How well she looked, and how shocked she was to see him there, but once that moment had passed – how tenderly she had looked at him. He pulled over to the side of the road and looked over Southampton Water. He got out of the jeep, lit a cigarette and walked over the grass and perched on a large piece of stone, staring into space.

God! How he'd missed her! His life with her around had seemed so full. Without her, it had no purpose, and now she was working at a proper job and had been, apparently, since before their last meeting. But why had she waited so long to do so? Why didn't she do so when first they met – or at least when they became lovers? He mentally argued with himself for the next fifteen minutes before getting in the car and driving back to the flat and ringing the bell with great insistence.

'All right! I'm coming!' Rusty yelled as she went to open the door.

'Get your coat, you're coming with me!' Brad demanded.

Jenny watched in amazement as Rusty grabbed her overcoat and was hauled out of the room by Brad, who was looking more than a little determined.

Brad drove up the Avenue and parked the jeep outside the Cowherds Inn, on the edge of the common, which was now commandeered by the American forces. He stopped the jeep, turned off the engine, turned towards Rusty, took her into his arms and kissed her until neither of them could breathe.

Gasping for air, Rusty said, 'Bloody hell! Well, that was almost worth waiting so long for!'

'What do you mean . . . almost?' Brad asked, slightly put out.

'What I meant was it was a long time coming! Sooner would have been better.'

'We need to talk, Rusty,' he said.

'No, Brad, we don't. All you need to ask yourself is this: can you forget I was a prostitute, or will it be for ever between us? It's as simple as that. Do you love me enough to let it go?'

He gazed at her with admiration. 'Oh, Rusty, how simple you make life sound, you see life so clearly. Is it really that easy?'

'That's up to you, Brad. I gave that life up for you – for us. Now it's up to you to decide if we have a future or not.'

He looked into the brown eyes that challenged him. Eyes that were honest, with nothing more to hide . . . and were full of hope. How could he resist? Why would he even want to? He cupped her face in his hands and kissed her gently.

'I see a great future ahead of us, Rusty darling. Come on, let's celebrate! We'll see what they've got on the menu in the dining room,' and he climbed out of the car, collected her from the passenger side, and with a broad grin put his arm round her and walked towards the entrance.

Rusty was almost too afraid to breathe. Could this really be happening? Did Brad really mean what he said? When he had time to think, would he still be of the same mind? All these thoughts tumbled through her mind, but she pushed them aside as they walked into the dining room. The man she adored was with her again, she'd just take each day as it came . . . but with everything crossed!

Adam Procter was not so happy. It had been several days now since Jenny had packed her bag and driven away. He had no idea where she was, and when he went to his club to seek out some company he'd had to field questions about his wife.

'She's well, thank you. Jenny's really busy at the moment; you know how involved she's become with various committees.'

So far, no one knew she'd gone or the reason behind her leaving – and he planned to keep it that way.

He'd hired a housekeeper, an older woman who didn't ask questions, and a nurse who came in twice a day to change his dressings and see he took his medicine. He was able to fend for himself, other than that. He was well able to dress himself and give himself a good wash down. When his wound was healed, then he'd be able to take a bath. But with every day that passed his bitterness grew. How could Jenny turn her back on all they had built together to run off with a bloody Yank? What sort of man was he, this cowboy who had tempted his wife so strongly that she'd turned her back on him? His curiosity grew and grew until he had to meet this man himself. He remembered that Jenny had spoken about an American doing work at the stables . . . What had she called him? A horse whisperer – that was it. He'd go to the stables tomorrow and see if he couldn't arrange a meeting with this fellow. Perhaps then he could settle the matter once and for all and put a stop to this ridiculous nonsense!

Chad had a day's leave and was helping Beth settle a new mare which had been brought in to the stable by its owner who was no longer able to care for it. The mare was in foal and unsettled by the change. Beth had been concerned that the mare would be stressed enough to endanger the foal she was carrying, and Chad said he would help her settle down. He was in the stable working with the animal when Adam Procter arrived, having been given a lift by a friend.

Chad heard the man talking to Beth. He could hardly miss the loud and imperious tone of the voice as the stranger asked about the horse whisperer he'd heard about. He guessed immediately the identity of the speaker and walked out of the stable, closing the door behind him.

Walking up to the man, Chad said, 'I believe it's me you're looking for. I'm Chad Maxwell, and if I'm not mistaken you are Captain Procter.'

Adam could hardly hide his surprise when he looked at the American. He was much younger than he expected; he also appeared to be very calm, considering he was facing the husband of his lover! But before he could say anything, it was Chad that spoke.

'Captain Procter, I think we need to sit down and talk, man to man.' He looked at Beth who was standing by, looking more than a little perturbed. 'May we use your kitchen?' Chad asked her.

'Of course. Help yourself to tea or coffee.' She walked away and left them together.

Once in the kitchen, Chad filled the kettle and plugged it in. 'Tea or coffee?' he asked.

'Neither, thank you! This isn't a bloody social call. I've come to talk about my wife!'

Chad calmly sat down. 'Of course you have. Right, shoot!'

Adam looked at him in astonishment. 'Is that all you have to say? You Yanks really do take the cake! You steal my wife away from a marriage of nineteen happy years and sit there and say . . . shoot! This is serious stuff, not one of your Hollywood films. You are about to ruin her life, and I won't let you get away with it!'

'I can understand your anger, Captain, but I have to question you about your marriage being happy. It wasn't – at least, not for the latter years.'

'What the hell do you know about it?'

'I know that when I met your wife she was happy. After all, she was free to be her own person, do the things that really interested her – for once.'

'That is very presumptuous of you.'

'Not really. Your wife is a free spirit whose character had been swamped by living with you. She had completely lost her identity. Now, happily, she knows who she is and what she wants out of life. Fortunately for me, she wants to come to Wyoming.'

'What rubbish! Jenny has no idea what she wants.'

'Have you ever asked her?'

Adam became flustered. 'Of course not, she's my wife; I know what's best for her.'

Chad raised his eyebrows in surprise, then frowned. 'There you have the crux of your problem, Captain Procter. Her needs are secondary to your own. You have no idea what sort of woman you married.'

'Of course I do! Good God, man! I have been married to her long enough.'

'Then tell me this. What's her favourite flower?'

Adam didn't hesitate. 'She's a gardener, so she loves all sorts of flowers.'

'Wrong! The poppy is her favourite. What's her ambition?'

Here the man was completely flummoxed.

'You didn't know she had one did you? She wants to ride out with her favourite horse and camp beneath the stars.'

'Jenny would hate that! She likes her creature comforts.'

Chad just shook his head. 'I feel so sorry for you, sir. You have been married to the most wonderful woman for nineteen years, and yet you don't know or understand her – and what's more, you have never even tried. That takes tremendous arrogance. You don't deserve such a woman!'

'And you do?'

'Probably not, if I'm honest. I didn't plan to fall in love with Jenny or she with me, it just happened, but let me tell you, I feel the luckiest guy on this planet. Believe me, I won't waste a moment of the time that we are together, no siree!'

Adam looked at Chad with contempt. 'You really think she's coming to live with you, don't you? Well, let me put you in the picture, my young friend; Jenny has just been carried away by the moment, as so many other women in wartime have. I was away, and you, a younger man, paid her some attention, which was flattering to an older woman. She loves her home, her garden – being my wife. As soon as you go away, she'll come to her senses. This, this . . . thing with you will pass in time, and we will get over it and move on.'

'That's up to Jenny. I give you my word that I won't push her either way. It will be totally up to her, but I have to warn you, Captain Procter, you will be the loser, because I know what makes Jenny tick, and sadly, you have no idea!' He rose from the chair. 'Forgive me, but I have an unhappy mare to see to.'

Adam glared at the American. 'I suppose you think you can understand the human spirit as well as you can understand a sick animal?'

'I'm amazed that you even recognize the fact of a human spirit. Maybe there's hope for you yet, Captain, but sadly not with your own wife! You left that far too late!'

Adam sat in the kitchen chair, fuming. How dare this whippersnapper tell him he didn't understand his own wife! Well, one thing he was certain of was this young man was definitely not Jenny's type at all! That much he *did* know. Let her have her moment of madness. He'd shortly be back with his company, but the American must soon be sent to Europe; when eventually the war was over, time would sort them out. She'd be happy to come home. He could wait.

Beth saw Adam Procter leave the stable and wait at the gate to be picked up. She wandered over to the stable and seeing Chad asked, 'Everything all right?'

He shrugged. 'As far as I'm concerned, but I don't think the Captain would agree.' He smiled at her. 'Don't worry, Beth, no blood was drawn!'

She chuckled and walked away, thinking that no two men could be more different than Jenny's husband and her lover. She had no doubt about which man she preferred.

An hour later, Jenny arrived at the stables to help out. She soon found Chad and watched him work with the mare, who by now seemed more settled. She saw Chad feel the swollen stomach of the animal, talking softly as he did so. Then, with a final pat and stroke of the animal's mane, he left the stable. Seeing Jenny waiting, he took her into his arms and kissed her.

'How's my girl?'

'Fine, and how are you?'

'I'm real good. I had a visit from your husband today; we sat and chatted.'

Jenny looked shattered. 'Oh my God!'

'It's OK, honey, we sat and talked in a civilized manner.'

She didn't know what to say for a moment. 'And what happened?'

'The captain told me that in time you would go back to him. He inferred this was just a moment of madness on your part and you would get over it.'

'Do you believe that, Chad?'

'Not for one moment, but he does. Poor man, he doesn't know you at all after all these years, and that's partly your fault, Jenny.'

'Whatever do you mean?'

'You let him take you over without a fight. You should have stood your ground, been the person that I know you are deep down. You let him swamp you with his own personality.'

She gave a wry smile. 'But when we were first married he was very much my hero. He was determined, sure of himself; I admired him immensely.'

'And now, all these years later?'

'I suppose, anything for a quiet life. You get into a routine and just go with the flow. My God, that sounds so weak, doesn't it?'

'You said it honey, not me.'

'Then when he went away, I was free to do the things I wanted . . . and then of course I met you.' She gazed fondly at him. 'Then I wanted even more.'

Pulling her into his arms, Chad kissed her softly. 'I've finished here. I still have until late tonight and I want to make love to you, so why don't we go back to the flat and there we can be alone?' He held her even closer until she could feel his arousal. His hand gently caressed her backside, and she couldn't concentrate.

'Let's go,' she managed to whisper. And they left the stables.

Nineteen

Gunter Reinhardt was beside himself with excitement. Today he was to see his son for the very first time and Sarah, the mother of his baby and the woman he intended to marry, come what may!

Ethel Brown the farmer's wife was to accompany Sarah and baby Hans on the train, which was a great relief to him. The kindness of strangers, thought Gunter as he waited. After all, the Browns hardly knew him apart from the time he'd worked for them, but they had taken Sarah into their home when her own family had disowned her. How could he ever repay such kindness?

He was ushered into a small common room by one of the British soldiers on duty and told to wait. He tried to sit patiently, but before long he was pacing the small room until he heard the door open and there stood Sarah with a small bundle in her arms. She stood, smiling at him, with tears streaming down her face.

He stepped forward. '*Liebling*!' He carefully took her and her baby into his arms, kissing her first and then looking down at his firstborn. '*Mein Gott*! Is this really our son?'

'Yes, Gunter darling, this is Hans.' She handed the baby over to him. 'I think he looks a lot like you.'

He gazed at the baby, taking in every small detail. He gently held the baby's hand and was overcome when the tiny fingers closed around one of his. He looked up at Sarah with tears brimming his eyes. 'Did you see that?' He carefully placed the baby on his shoulder, breathing in the scent of him. 'He's wonderful. And how are you, my *liebling*?'

'I'm fine. The Browns are wonderful to us both. I help Ethel in the house; we get along very well.' He voice broke. 'Oh Gunter, I thought I'd never see you again.'

He caught hold of her hand. 'We are a family, Sarah. No one will ever come between us. No matter what, or how long it takes, we will be together after the war, I promise!' The baby gurgled. 'There! You see, little Hans totally agrees with me.'

Gunter looked up as one of the soldiers on guard came in

with a tray of tea. 'I thought your wife might need this after her long journey.'

Sarah smiled at the soldier. 'Thank you, that's so kind of you.'

He man shrugged. 'I have a baby myself, haven't seen him for several months.' He smiled and nodded at Gunter, then left them alone.

'What a nice gesture,' Sarah remarked. 'They obviously treat you well here.'

Gunter just nodded. He didn't tell her about the few sentries who treated the prisoners like dirt, who told them the only good German was a dead one. Of the insults he himself had suffered when it was known he had a child by an English girl – from his own kind, as well as from the guards. It was only a small nucleus of the men guarding them who treated them badly, but enough to make living there unpleasant.

The afternoon passed all too soon, and Sarah was told her time was up. With a voice choked with emotion she asked, 'When will I see you again?'

'I have no idea. This visit, I'm afraid, will not be repeated. I was fortunate to be allowed to see you and the baby at all. Never mind, *liebling*, we will write all the time, and one day we'll put all this behind us. You must be strong for our son.' He stood and held them both in his arms, kissing first the baby, then Sarah. 'Remember that I love you both, more than life itself.'

Sarah, too full of emotion for words, left the room to join Ethel Brown and journey home.

Gunter walked back to his room in a daze. There was joy after seeing his child and Sarah, but such sadness as he faced the fact that he might not see them again until the child was no longer a baby. He would miss seeing his son progress so much, but at least he had today. No one could take that away from him.

One of the other German prisoners put his head round the door. Seeing Gunter standing there, lost in thought, the man stepped inside. 'I hear you saw your bastard child today.'

Gunter hit him, sending him reeling into the corridor. He then shut the door.

Adam Procter had only another week left before he returned to his regiment. He had phoned Beth at the stables to ask for Jenny's address, as he had to see her to make arrangements before he left. Beth wouldn't give the address to him without Jenny's permission, but she said she would pass on the message, which she did – and Jenny had called her husband and arranged to go to the house to see him.

As she drove up the drive, she looked at her garden with a certain longing. She loved working in it when she'd been living there, and although it was tidy to a point, it was obvious to her that it needed someone who really cared about it. She drew up in front of the house, got out of the car and walked to the door. Here she paused; she had her own key, but it didn't seem right to just walk in, so she rang the bell.

Adam opened the door. He looked better she expected, and she was pleased. She had felt guilty leaving him when she did, but it had been his choice to get someone else in to look after his needs.

'Hello, Adam. You're looking well,' she said.

'Yes, well, no one is indispensable,' was his terse reply, and she knew that this meeting was going to be difficult.

They went into the sitting room. Adam went to the table in the window where the drinks were kept. 'Can I get you something?' he asked.

'Not for me, thanks.' She watched as he poured himself a large gin and tonic and guessed it wasn't the first one that day – and she waited.

'I'm due to join my regiment next week, so I thought we ought to discuss a few things.'

'Like what?'

Financial arrangements – after all, I *am* still your husband, and I must provide for you financially – and then there's the house.'

'What about the house?'

'I certainly don't want it left empty when I'm away. I don't want to sell it, and I certainly wouldn't dream of letting it to strangers.'

'So what are you suggesting?'

'That you move back in when I'm gone. It's been your home for many years, and I'm sure you wouldn't like to see it empty and neglected.'

'No, of course not!'

Adam was delighted. He hoped that once again residing in her home and seeing to the garden, which was her pride and joy, might eventually persuade Jenny that she had made a terrible mistake, wanting to leave.

'Good, I'm pleased you agree. It will also put a stop to any rumours that we've parted. I've certainly not told anyone, and I would appreciate it if you were discreet. I do *not* want to be the centre of local gossip. I will, of course, make a monthly payment into your account.'

'There's no need. I'm working and earning a living.'

He looked at her coldly. '*You* may have forgotten that you are a married woman and have a duty to me; however, I am different. As long as you are married to me, I will take care of you!'

She suddenly felt sorry for him. Adam lived his life by the rules. Rules were to be followed at all times, and now she had broken them and he didn't know how to cope.

'Thank you, Adam. Under the circumstances, I think you are being very noble.'

'The circumstances are not of my making, Jenny.' He dropped his guard for a moment. 'Can't you see what a terrible mistake you're making, how much you are throwing away? I beg you, think again before you ruin your life . . . and mine!'

'I am sorry, Adam, I really am. I have thought long and hard about what I'm doing, but I haven't changed my mind, and I don't want you to go away with any false hopes. After the war, I'm going to the States to start a new life. None of this was planned, it just happened, and I cannot let the opportunity pass. I'll always regret it if I do.'

His jaw tightened. 'If you continue down this road and it doesn't work, don't think you can come crawling back to me!'

She smiled softly. 'It will work, I am certain of that. Chad and I love each other.'

'We loved each other once!' His cry of anguish touched her deeply, but there was nothing she could do to alleviate his unhappiness.

'Yes, we did, and I will always remember those early days, but we all change. You will always have a special place in my heart.'

'Don't patronize me, Jenny! If you continue with this divorce nonsense, I'll have no choice but to sue on grounds of adultery.

Is that what you want . . . your dirty laundry spread all over the papers?'

'It's not ideal, but I don't have any choice.'

'Yes, you do! For God's sake woman, when are you going to come to your senses?'

She stood up. 'Look, Adam, this isn't getting us anywhere. I will come back and take care of the house until you return from the war, as you wish, and after that we will go our different ways. Just take care when you're over there, wherever that is. Here is my office number if you want to contact me during the day.' She handed him a card. 'Look after yourself,' she said and picking up her handbag she left.

Later that afternoon, Jenny was surprised when Brad knocked on her office door, then entered. They hadn't a meeting planned, and she wondered why he was there. 'Something wrong?' she asked.

He sat down. 'Not in the way that you mean, Jenny, but I do have some news.'

She frowned at the seriousness of his tone. 'I have a feeling I'm not going to like what you have to say.'

'I'm being shipped out, and Chad is coming with me.'

Jenny felt a chill creep up her spine as if she was sitting in a draught. It was the news she'd been dreading. 'Oh Brad, I am so sorry. When do you leave?'

'Next week. Obviously I can't tell you more, but it's a big operation. If it's a success it could bring an end to the war. That's a big if!'

'That would be wonderful! Have you told Rusty yet?'

'I haven't had the chance, and it's Rusty I want to talk to you about. You'll be alone once Chad and I have left. I just want to know you'll look after each other.'

She cast a critical glance at him. 'I do hope that you're not infer-ring that Rusty might go off the rails once you've left? Because if you are, I would be bitterly disappointed in you, Brad!'

'No, no, I don't mean that at all, but you'll be lonely and worried, you'll need one another for support.'

'I saw Adam earlier today, and he wants me to move back into the house when he goes to make sure it's kept up together. I had planned to ask Rusty to move in with me.'

'That would be great, Jenny. I'm sure she'd love it there.'

'Well, it's big enough, as you know, and she can help me with the garden – and as you say, we'll need one another. You just make sure my man comes back safely . . . and you too, of course!'

He rose from his seat. 'Both Chad and I have an overnight pass from tonight, so I guess I'll see you later.'

When she was alone, Jenny fought back her tears. Thousands of women had been through this sort of hell, that's what war did to people. She and Rusty would just have to get on with life, but she was so grateful to have her as a friend, especially at this time.

When Chad rang her a little later they decided to meet for a meal first to give Rusty and Brad some privacy as these final days together were so special. He rang again later with a change of plans.

'Pack an overnight bag, Jenny. I've booked us a room for the night; that way we can be totally alone. We have a lot to talk about before I leave, and I don't want any interruptions. Besides, I want to hold you, make love to you, without worrying about Rusty and Brad being in the next room. I'll pick you up at seven.'

Hearing his voice made the situation all the more poignant, and she couldn't wait to see him. He had become such a part of her everyday life, and Jenny knew that when Chad eventually left there would be an enormous void, as this extraordinary man had come to mean absolutely everything to her.

She longed to experience his world. The simplicity of it sounded wonderful, and the thought of living on a ranch, of riding in wonderful surroundings, was so exciting and so different to everything she was used to. Her one worry was that she would disappoint Chad. How awful it would be if she didn't live up to his expectations. Being lovers here and now in wartime was one thing. It had a certain edge to it, an excitement. But being settled in a home, being part of normal everyday life, was very different. Well, it would be a long time before that happened, anyway. Tonight might be the last time they would be together for a very long time, and she was going to make the most of every moment.

Twenty

Jenny arrived at Rusty's flat before Brad, so it was she who broke the bad news to the redhead, and it was she who comforted her when the tears began.

'Come on, Rusty, you don't want Brad to see you all red eyed and sad. These are the last few days you'll spend together for a while, so send him away with happy memories.'

Rusty looked at her with amazement. 'How can you be so calm?'

With a wry laugh, Jenny confessed: 'Don't you fret, I shed a bucketload of tears when Brad left my office, but I've had time to recover. Now I suggest you go and have a bath, wash your hair, put on your make-up and enjoy every moment you can; I intend to. Chad has booked us in to a hotel for the night, so you'll have your captain all to yourself.'

Rusty quickly wiped away her tears. 'You're right, of course.' She giggled mischievously. 'I'll give him the time of his life!'

'Before you go, there is an offer I'd like to make to you.' Jenny explained about her visit with Adam. 'So how would you like to move in with me? It would save rent on this place, and we'd have more room.'

'Oh my God, are you really asking me to live in that beautiful house?' Her eyes were bright with excitement.

'Absolutely, or I'd be rattling around on my own. Mind you, you'd have to help me with the garden.'

Rusty hugged her. 'How marvellous! We can keep each other's spirits up.' She went to say something else, but Jenny stopped her.

'We haven't time now. I'll take the bathroom first, we need to get ready.'

Chad was the first to arrive. He whistled when he saw the girls. 'My oh my, you two look good enough to eat! Are you ready, honey? Have you packed your overnight stuff?'

Jenny told him she had, and they left the flat. They drove to a restaurant in town where Chad had booked a table, neither of them saying a word about his leaving until they'd ordered and the wine had been poured.

Chad lifted his glass. 'To us, darlin', and to our long and happy future together.'

Jenny clinked hers with his. 'To us and our future.' She sipped her drink. 'I don't know how I'm going to manage when you leave.'

'You'll do just the same as all the women in your situation; you take it a day at a time, and write . . . often. But I just wanted to discuss with you my plans for after the war, so you'll know what you're letting yourself in for.'

Jenny held up her finger and hushed his flow of words. 'I don't need to know. I'll come to you wherever, whenever – the rest is just background.'

He smiled, gazed at her and shook his head in disbelief. 'You really do mean that, don't you?'

'Absolutely!'

'I don't deserve you, Jenny honey, but I promise you, you'll never ever regret what you are doing, what you are giving up for me. On that, you have my solemn oath.'

They talked about a million things during their meal. Jenny explained that she and Rusty were moving back into her house and the reason why.

'It makes good sense,' Chad agreed. 'It's a beautiful place, and I can understand why Adam wants you to look after it. It's the least you can do for him.'

They chatted about a million things until it was time to retire, and they drove to the hotel, where Chad signed the register as Mr and Mrs Maxwell, picked up the key and headed for the lift. When he found their room number, he swept Jenny up into his arms and carried her into the bedroom.

'Here we are, Mrs Maxwell, this is our trial honeymoon!' he said as he put her down.

'What do you mean, trial?'

'Well, if you don't cut the mustard and please me, I'll find me a nice little Mademoiselle to take your place!'

'You cheeky devil! I haven't heard you complain up till now!'

He pulled her close and kissed her softly. 'That's for sure. What's to complain about? You are everything I've ever wanted in a woman – and more.'

Brad arrived at the flat that evening, carrying a huge bouquet of crème roses and an extravagant box of chocolates.

'Good heavens, how on earth did you come by these?' Rusty asked as he handed them over.

He grinned broadly. 'I'm liable to be court-martialled. These were sent over from the States for the Colonel, but unfortunately they got lost in transit!'

She couldn't help but laugh. 'Oh Brad, thank you so much, you have no idea what a treat that is. Come in, I've made some coffee. What do you want to do this evening?'

He raised his eyebrows quizzically.

'Apart from that!' she scolded.

'As Chad and Jenny are elsewhere, I thought we'd stay in. I had one of the chefs make up a picnic for us.' He went over to the front door, opened it and brought in a box and a bottle of champagne. 'Tonight we'll celebrate.'

'I don't want to celebrate you leaving, Brad.'

'No, Rusty darling, we are going to celebrate my return – and our future.'

She put her arms around his neck. 'Are you absolutely sure that's what you want?'

'Definitely. Now put this bottle into the fridge, and let's see what the chef has done.'

They sat down to a sumptuous meal which, in the wartime conditions that prevailed, Rusty really appreciated. There was pâté to start with, followed by large prawns in a delicious sauce, a Waldorf salad, potato salad and something Brad called coleslaw – a mixture of carrot and white cabbage in mayonnaise that was really tasty. Freshly-baked bread rolls with real butter were carefully wrapped, and to finish there was a lemon cheesecake.

Rusty tucked in with great relish. 'My goodness, Brad, if the food in the States is like this, I'll pile on the pounds!'

'No, you won't, you'll soon get used to it. Anyway, you forget I'm a doctor. I'll keep an eye on you!'

As they ate, Brad told her all about Denver where they would live, about his parents, and how they would be able to spend their spare time together . . . and the children he hoped they would have.

This startled Rusty. With the life she'd been leading, children were the last thing she'd thought about; her one concern had been making sure that she didn't become pregnant. Her surprise must have shown on her face because he questioned her about it.

'Don't you want a family, Rusty?'

'To be honest I hadn't thought about it. You forget, Brad, I haven't been in a serious relationship for a very long time.' Then she stopped. Why the hell had she said that? It only brought up her past.

'But now you are. I've always envisaged my household filled with children when I eventually married, that's all.'

She realized that this was a serious issue with him. 'I'm twenty-eight; you don't think that's too late?'

He roared with laughter. 'Good God, Rusty, I've delivered babies whose mothers have been well into their thirties, and a few even in their early forties.' At her shocked expression he explained: 'This was usually at the beginning of the menopause and mostly unexpected, I have to say.' He held her gaze. 'Don't you want us to have children?'

She took hold of his hand. 'I would love to have your babies – but not too many!'

'I think six is a nice round figure.'

'What?' She looked horrified.

He started laughing again. 'I'm only joking, but at least two; I was an only child and often wished I had a sibling.'

'Me too. All right, two.'

'In which case, I think I need a bit of practice. Let's leave the dishes, this is far more important.' And he led her into the bedroom.

They didn't turn on the light, but kept the curtains open, letting the moonlight from the clear sky above shed its soft glow. 'Come here,' he said, taking her into his arms. His kisses, at first soft and gentle, intensified as he caressed her body and slowly removed her clothing. Then, when they were both naked, they lay on the bed together.

'I'm really going to miss you, darling,' he murmured as his

mouth moved down her body, kissing the soft mounds of her breasts. As he parted her legs, she tensed with pleasure and anticipation.

Brad's love-making was slow and sensuous, until she cried out for him to take her.

After, they lay sated and satisfied. Rusty let out a deep sigh. 'I really needed that,' she said softly.

He nuzzled her neck. 'I know just what you mean.'

They lay together, talking softly, until they fell asleep, entwined in each other's arms.

The following morning, Rusty awoke to the smell of bacon frying, and pulling on a dressing gown she wandered into the kitchen to see Brad standing at the stove. She stood behind him and put her arms around his waist. 'That smells amazing.'

'I brought some bacon with me; as you can see, I'm always prepared. Will you make some toast whilst I cook some eggs?'

'Eggs too! My, you know the way to a woman's heart.'

'There, and here was me thinking it was my good looks and bedroom technique!'

'Oh, that too,' she told him.

They sat eating their breakfast until he had to leave. 'I may not have a chance to see you again before we ship out,' he told her as he left. Holding her close, he said, 'You take care, you hear?'

Rusty sat finishing her coffee, looking out of the window, wondering just how long it would be before the war would be over and when that happened, she tried to visualize her new life as Mrs Brad Jackson, but somehow the picture wouldn't form in her mind at all. She supposed it was because it still seemed unreal that she could have survived her life on the streets, to find such a man who knew of her past and who still wanted her. She found herself crossing her fingers as she thought about the future.

In the two weeks that followed, the men couldn't get away, but phoned the girls as often as possible. Chad managed to escape for a couple of hours and suggested to Jenny that they take a couple of mounts from the stables and have one last ride together.

Knowing how much it meant to Chad to ride out into the woods, she was happy to accommodate him, calling her friend

Beth to save two horses for them. She, knowing the situation, was happy to oblige, and when they arrived at the stables it was to find the horses already saddled and waiting.

'Take as long as you like,' she told them and left them alone.

Neither of them spoke as they rode out of the stable, along the country road, then turning off into the wooded area they loved so much. When they reached the middle, Chad reined in his mount, indicating to Jenny to do the same. He tied the reins to a tree, took her hand and they walked even deeper into the wood, stopping soon after. They sat on an upturned log, and he gathered her into his arms.

'Don't you just love the peaceful atmosphere of this place?' he asked her.

'Yes, it's lovely. No one could imagine sitting here that there's a war on.'

'If only that were true, honey. But we must just try and think of how great a life we'll have in Wyoming.' He looked at her with eyes shining. 'I can't wait until that day comes. We are going to have such a good time, Jenny darlin'. I long to see you blossom like a flower as you learn to enjoy the freedom you'll have living there with me.' He drew her to him and kissed her longingly. Then looking at his watch, he pursed his lips. 'We have to go, I'm afraid.'

They rode back in silence, both lost in their own thoughts.

After unsaddling the horses, Chad said goodbye to Beth and drove Jenny home. He helped her out of the jeep and held her close. 'I wish we had more time, but I have to go now. You write me as often as you can, and I'll do the same.'

She was lost for words and just clung on to him as he kissed her goodbye.

Tears streamed down her face as she watched him drive away, then she ran inside the house to her room, where she lay on the bed sobbing.

Brad had even less time to spend with Rusty, but two days before he left he was able to spend a few hours with her at the flat. They went to bed together and made love. After, they lay in each other's arms talking.

'Have you any idea at all how much longer the war will last?' asked Rusty.

'I wish I had, darling. But, honestly, it can't be that much longer. As Brad got dressed, Rusty pulled on a dressing gown, then walked him to the door.

He held her close and ran his fingers through her hair. 'My redhead,' he whispered as he kissed her. 'Take care of yourself,' he told her. 'I'll write as often as I can, but during wartime mail delivery is uncertain, so if you don't hear for some time, don't worry. I'll be coming back for you, make no mistake!'

'You'd better, or I'll damned well come looking for you!'

He smiled at her. 'I love a woman with spirit.'

She stood at the window and watched him drive away. 'Don't you bloody well get yourself killed!' she said, then she went into the kitchen and made herself a coffee, her heart heavy, knowing it could be a very long time before they saw each other again.

Twenty-One

The following day, the two women moved into Jenny's old house. There was still a couple of weeks to go on the flat rental, but they both felt they needed to keep busy, knowing their men were due to leave these shores the following day. Neither of the women spoke of this as they moved all their belongings into the house at Chilworth.

Jenny showed Rusty to her bedroom, which was sizeable and at the back of the house, overlooking the garden.

The redhead was thrilled when she saw it. She rushed over to the window and looked out. 'Jenny, this is so beautiful, and the bedroom is so comfortable. I'll feel like a queen here.'

'I'll leave you to it,' Jenny said. 'I have to go and unpack myself.'

Adam had dismissed the housekeeper and the nurse just before he returned to his unit, so the house was clean and tidy, but in their bedroom Jenny felt saddened when she saw some of his clothes carefully draped over a chair. Poor Adam, she thought as she put them away, his world had changed, and she wondered how he would cope when eventually he came home for good, to an empty house and a wife who no longer wanted him.

She realized that she could no longer sleep in this room, the room where she'd spent so many years with him, so she moved her things into the bedroom that she and Chad had shared. There she felt more at ease. This room at least held nothing but good memories, memories that she knew would sustain her in the days and months to come. Thank God Rusty had agreed to move in with her, because she felt that she couldn't have stayed here alone.

When they'd unpacked, Jenny showed Rusty over the house, then they walked around the garden, looking at what needed doing and discussing how they would organize their day. Jenny would be able to drop Rusty at work every morning before she went to her own office, and then they could meet up to come home together.

Sitting together in the kitchen, Rusty looked around. 'You must really love Chad to give all this up,' she remarked.

Jenny dismissed her sentiment. 'This is just bricks and mortar. If I was happy with Adam, then it would be different, but with Chad, I'd happily sleep outside in the open air on a blanket, because I'd be content. Here with Adam, and the life I would have to continue to live, the house would be like a prison.' She smiled softly. 'Chad tells me I am someone special, and with him I feel as if I am. He's an extraordinary man, and I consider myself a very lucky woman.'

Rusty nodded. 'How both our lives have changed! Do you sometimes worry that you'll wake one morning to find it all a dream?'

'No, but I do wonder how long I could have gone on married to Adam. My life changed when Adam left – before I met Chad. Even without meeting him, I wanted out of my marriage, and that was a concern because I didn't know how I would manage. Now I don't have that worry. How about you?'

'My only concern is if Brad and I ever row, will he bring up my past? If he did, that could destroy us.'

'He made his decision when he came here for you, Rusty. He was an unhappy man without you. I know, because Chad told me.'

Neither of them brought up the possibility that either of the men might never return but would end up as a casualty of the war . . . or worse. That was the stuff of nightmares, and neither of them wanted to think about those consequences.

Whilst the women were getting settled in, their men had moved out of the Southampton base. Brad and his men had joined up with the 82nd Airborne division and were to be dropped at Groesbeek, near Nijmegen. Neither man had jumped before, and so they had taken a crash course with some others. 'Remember to bend those knees as you land,' was the voice ringing in their ears as they climbed into the aircraft taking the troops to the drop zone.

'Give me a rodeo any time, even with a mad old steer!' Chad remarked as he lowered himself to the floor beside Brad.

'I've never ridden in a rodeo, but I've been to plenty, and to be honest, I'll take the jump!' was Brad's retort.

Operation Market Garden was under way. The objective was to take and hold three bridges. One at Eindhoven, one at Nijmegen and the other at Arnhem. British, American and Polish forces would all take part, hoping that with their might, and that of the allies already on the ground, their task would be completed.

The red light came on in the interior of the plane, and every man got to their feet and shuffled forward, clipped the line of their parachutes to the overhead apparatus – and waited. When the light changed to green, men tumbled out of the aircraft, one after another. Chad went just before Brad and he heard Chad let out a loud whoop.

'Crazy cowboy!' he muttered as his parachute opened and tugged at his shoulders.

As the troops landed and stowed their chutes, it appeared chaotic for a while until the men gathered and eventually found their companies with the road to Nijmegen stretched ahead of them. The plan was to scout out the town and reconnoitre the two bridges to be taken from the Germans and held. But the enemy was well established, and the troops were driven back time after time.

As the company took cover in any building they could find, the men took a break whilst the officers in charge talked with headquarters about their next move.

Chad pushed his helmet to the back of his head and lit a cigarette. He offered one to Brad, who took it gratefully. 'Thanks. Jeez, I'm glad that's over for a bit.'

Chad agreed. 'That was hairy, man! Any minute I expected a bullet to take me out.'

'I didn't have time to worry. We should have some extra might when the next drop arrives tomorrow and the gliders with the Poles come in. We need more firepower.'

'We need more everything!' Chad looked around. 'Did we lose many men?'

'A few, and if things don't improve, we'll lose a few more.'

'You're a bundle of laughs, Captain Jackson!'

'You have no idea the responsibility on my shoulders. I promised Jenny I'd bring you safely home.'

'You make damned sure you do, you hear? Oops, we're off again.'

The men rose to their feet and gathered to make yet another attempt on the bridge.

'Come on, cowboy, you stick to me like glue.'

'I'm right behind you, Brad, so for Christ's sake keep your head down!'

The two women settled down at the house in Chilworth fairly quickly, neither encroaching on each other's privacy, yet coming together for meals and sharing the housework. Rusty knew nothing about gardening so was quickly shown the difference between a plant and a weed as she helped Jenny look after the outside.

As the days progressed, Jenny, now once more a resident at her old stomping ground, was surprised to find she was the centre of attention from several of the housewives in the area, who had learned about her friendship with the young GI. When they gathered together to plan a Winter Fête, with all the proceeds to go to the serving troops, this became very apparent.

After much discussion and planning, they broke for coffee, and two of the women wandered over to her.

'I suppose you're torn between the British and American troops when it comes to collecting funds and gifts for their well-being?'

Jenny frowned and looked puzzled. 'I beg your pardon?'

'Well, Jenny, we all know about you and the American horse whisperer.'

The second woman quickly interceded. 'Not that I blame you, darling, he's frightfully good-looking.'

The first woman was not so forgiving. 'I think it's disgusting! These Yanks come over here, they're overpaid and oversexed and women lose their heads – all for what?'

Jenny's hackles rose. 'You seem to be very well informed, Fiona – you tell me!'

The woman flushed. 'Very well, I will. Your husband is fighting for his country, and you are gallivanting around with another man – an American, at that. I think that's quite disgusting!'

'You can think what you like, Fiona, but frankly, what I do or don't do is none of your damned business, and I would appreciate you remembering that.'

'Well, I never did!'

'No, you probably never have, which is a great pity, it may have done you the world of good!' And she walked away, leaving the woman looking outraged.

Jenny stayed to the end of the meeting, as she had promised to help and felt duty bound to do so, but she was aware during the rest of the time there that several of the women were talking about her . . . and now she knew why. Fiona Haskins, a leading light among the local women, had been made to look a fool and she didn't like it! She was now hell bent on revenge.

One of the women on the committee was Ethel Brown, the farmer's wife, a thoroughly down-to-earth woman. At the end of the meeting she walked over to Jenny, and taking her aside, she had a quiet word with her.

'Don't you take any notice of those busybodies with too much time on their hands! We all have but one life to live, and I know how things can happen to change it beyond all reasoning.' She then proceeded to tell her about her young friend Sarah and Gunter, the German prisoner of war.

Jenny listened with interest. She was used to hearing all kinds of stories at work from the women who would be sailing after the war to the States as GI brides, but this, with Gunter being German, had a different twist. 'How kind of you to take her in when she was pregnant,' Jenny said.

'What else could I do, Mrs Procter? He is a good man, and they're in love. That made the difference. He wants to marry her, it wasn't just a fling, but now I do have a problem.'

Seeing the worried expression on the woman's face, Jenny asked: 'What is it?'

'My son is coming home. He's been wounded, and now he hates the Germans, hasn't a good word to say about them, which is understandable. How do you think he'll feel about Sarah and her baby, fathered by a German? I don't know what to do.'

'Let's go and have a cup of tea somewhere and talk about this. Perhaps between us we can come up with an answer.'

A week later, Sarah and her baby moved into the house in Chilworth. When Sarah was made aware of Ethel Brown's predicament, she was only too pleased to fit in with any plans that would house her and the baby and give her a living.

Jenny had met Sarah at the farm soon after her chat with Ethel Brown and, liking the girl, had put a proposition to her: 'I need someone to keep the house clean. Rusty and I are out all day, so keeping the house and garden up to scratch takes up so much time – time that we really do not have. Everything is getting out of hand, and we'll never catch up. Are you interested in a live-in job for you and of course your baby?'

Sarah was delighted and had agreed immediately – and Rusty had insisted that as Jenny wouldn't let her pay any rent, she would pay half of Sarah's wage.

Once Sarah had settled in and worked out a routine, she wrote to Gunter explaining what had happened and telling him it was perfectly all right for him to write to her at this new address.

The baby in the house added a new dimension for Rusty and Jenny, and they both made a fuss of Hans when they were home, so Sarah had plenty of willing hands to help mother her child.

As Rusty said, 'I need to practice because Brad wants a family once we get married.'

They were all content in their way, which didn't sit well with Fiona Haskins. She had discovered Rusty's past and the fact that the young girl who was now living in and working for Jenny Procter had a child and was not yet married. The sanctimonious busybody began a campaign against them all.

Twenty-Two

It was Rusty who was the first to realize that something was going on. She was working on the haberdashery counter at Edwin Jones. It was a busy morning, but out of the corner of her eye, as she served several customers, she was aware that she seemed to be a subject of interest to two women. They were pretending to inspect the reels of cotton, but they seemed more interested in her. They watched her, then chatted to each other as they did so. It became somewhat unnerving, and eventually she walked over to them.

'Good morning, ladies, can I help you?'

Her direct approach threw them for a moment, and they scrambled to buy some elastic and cotton, following her to the counter with their goods. Whilst they waited for her to package their buys, one of them addressed her.

'Excuse me, miss, but aren't you staying with Mrs Procter?' one asked.

'Yes, I am.' Rusty looked somewhat puzzled.

The two women looked at each other with satisfied expressions. The taller of the two smirked and said, 'Chilworth is a bit out of your league, isn't it?'

Warning bells sounded loudly in Rusty's mind. She'd been around long enough to sense a predator, and this woman in particular was out to attack. 'I'm afraid I don't follow your line of questioning, madam.'

The woman glared at her. 'I would have thought Canal Walk would be more suitable for you!'

Rusty froze. Canal Walk was where she used to do her business when she was on the game. She stared straight at the woman and dearly longed to swipe the sly grin off her face. She wrapped the goods that had been bought, handed out the change, then she said very quietly, but with a note of steel in her voice, 'Here you are, madam, thank you very much. Carry them carefully, because I would be loath to have to shove the bag down your throat for casting aspersions on my character!'

The woman looked shocked. This certainly was not the reaction she had been expecting, and for a moment she was speechless.

'Thank you, good morning,' Rusty said and moved away to see to another customer. But behind her she could hear the two women's outrage as they eventually reacted to her remarks, although this time they kept their voices to a whisper as they walked away.

Rusty told Jenny all about this strange encounter as they drove home at the end of the day.

'What were they like?' Jenny asked. 'Describe them to me.' She listened and pursed her lips in anger. 'Did the taller one have a plummy accent?'

'Oh, yes,' agreed Rusty, 'and so condescending. She obviously forgets she has to go to the lavatory like we all do! I wanted to thump her, Jenny, honestly, I don't know how I kept my hands to myself.'

With a chuckle Jenny said, 'Oh Rusty, my dear, I've been wanting to do that for years. That obviously was Fiona Haskins. We have crossed swords many times, but we did so very recently. She dared to remark on my affair with Chad. She's a sanctimonious old bitch!'

'But a dangerous one, Jenny, make no mistake about that. She's out to make trouble. She's found out about my past somehow, and she knows about Chad. No doubt before long she'll learn that Sarah has a bastard child fathered by a German. The bloody woman will have a field day! Are there many occasions when the two of you have to be together?'

'We are on several committees. In fact she chairs two of them. Make no mistake, this woman has a great deal of sway in this community.'

Rusty sat and thought for a moment. 'What's the worst she could do to you?'

'Destroy my reputation, what's left of it. After I told Adam I wanted a divorce and why, I went about openly with Chad, but she could get me ostracized by the various committees, which would be a pity as I do feel I make a major contribution.'

'But that won't kill you, will it?'

'No, but I would be really annoyed if that was to happen, all because of a spiteful woman who thinks she's better than she is!'

Rusty began to smile. 'Listen, no one is guilt free. Everyone has a guilty pleasure – we just have to find out which one is hers!'

Jenny started giggling. 'Fiona Haskins with a guilty pleasure! Are you sure she'd even know what one was?'

'Trust me! In my business I've learned so much about people, and it's usually the last one you would suspect who is the worst. Fiona fits that bill to perfection. We just need to keep digging!'

The opportunity came sooner than either woman could have wished for. The following Sunday morning, Fiona Haskins was opening her house for a coffee morning, for charity. And when Rusty saw the advertisement in the local post-office window, she pointed it out to Jenny. 'Here we are. Old frosty face is having a do, and we need to attend.'

'Are you serious?' Jenny looked appalled.

'I'm deadly serious! We have to face the enemy and try and find out how well armed they are and search out their weak position. Oh my God! You can tell I've spent too long with the military can't you?' and she doubled up laughing.

'Are you prepared for whatever she throws at us? She won't be able to help herself, she'll *have* to have a dig at me. She wouldn't be able to resist the opportunity.'

Rusty stood tall and defiant. 'I can match her any time, and so can you. Come on, Jenny, let's strike a blow for freedom.'

'Yes, let's! The old trout *will* be surprised when we walk in.'

So it was on the following Sunday morning that Jenny and Rusty walked up the drive to Fiona Haskins house and entered the open front door, following the arrows pointing to the room holding the coffee morning. It was very crowded.

'She's got a good turnout,' Rusty remarked.

'The Chilworth residents are very good when it comes to worthy causes,' Jenny told her, 'no matter who is holding the event.'

There was a table with two ladies serving coffee with boiling water from a large urn on a table at one end of the room; beside that, another table full of home-made cakes.

'Bloody hell!' Rusty exclaimed quietly. 'How did this lot happen with today's rationing?'

'I was wondering the same thing myself. It's really quite amazing.'

One or two of the local ladies started talking to Jenny, and Rusty slowly edged to the door. Once outside she found her way to the kitchen, just as someone emerged carrying yet another plate of cupcakes.

'I think I've died and gone to heaven!' Rusty cried. 'I've never seen so many delicious cakes since war was declared.'

The woman beamed. 'I know, isn't it marvellous? We couldn't possibly do it without Fiona – she has ways and means of getting things done!' And she winked.

'I bet she has,' muttered Rusty, now alone in the kitchen. She opened the fridge and peered inside. There were several packets of butter beside a large slab of cheese, a dozen eggs and a leg of lamb. In the cupboard beside there was plenty of tea, American coffee . . . and tinned fruit.

'Bloody hell! It looks as if she's raided a food warehouse.' Then she stood and smiled. 'Well, Fiona, this is your guilty pleasure! Gotcha!'

Rusty returned to the other room and sidled up to Jenny. 'I think it's time we tell our hostess just what a wonderful job she is doing, don't you? And don't forget to introduce me.' Seeing the look of concern Jenny gave her, she just grinned broadly. 'Trust me!'

They made their way carefully through the throng, clutching their coffee cups, until they found Fiona Haskins playing the lady bountiful in a loud voice.

'Fiona!' said Jenny, touching her arm.

The woman turned, and the smile froze on her lips.

'What a splendid turnout, you have done well. I believe you've already met my friend, Miss Dobbs?'

Rusty immediately spoke up. 'My goodness me, Mrs Haskins, I don't remember when I've seen such an array of cakes, and with rationing so very strict! All that butter and eggs needed for such a spread . . . and you still have so much left! This coffee is delicious; I've not tasted as good except when an American gave me some from their stores.'

Fiona turned pale.

Rusty put a hand on her arm and leaned closer. 'But then I always say it's who you know rather than what you know, in such times as these.' And she tapped the side of her nose and winked at her before moving away, with Jenny quickly walking behind her.

'What the hell was all that about? I thought Fiona was about to pass out!'

'Well, my dear Jenny, our illustrious hostess is up to her neck in the black market. Oh my God!' Rusty stopped dead as a man emerged from one of the rooms.

'Jenny, my dear, how lovely to see you. How's it going in there?'

'Very well, James. Are you going to join them?'

'Not bloody likely! I'm off to my study.'

'This is my friend Rusty.' But Rusty had walked away and was already halfway down the drive.

James Haskins followed her gaze and saw the redhead in the distance. 'Never mind, I'll meet her another time. Good to see you. Have you heard from Adam?'

'Not lately, but you know how difficult it is for mail to get through, then several letters arrive at the same time.'

'Well, take care, Jenny. Good to see you.'

She ran down the path to catch up with her friend. 'Why did you take off like that?'

'That man used to be one of my clients. What was he doing there?'

Jenny tried not to smile. 'How absolutely priceless! That is James, Fiona's husband!'

'No!'

'Yes, I'm afraid he is.'

'Oh, don't be afraid, Jenny, he was one of my favourites, a great lover. With him it was my pleasure, believe me!'

They both walked down the drive, their laughter echoing.

At the study window, James Haskins watched them and smiled softly to himself as he remembered.

His reverie was interrupted by his wife, who swept into the room in high dudgeon. She stormed around the room, complaining loudly about having her privacy invaded. Then, eventually, she sat down.

When James inquired as to the cause of her fury, she told him about Rusty's remarks.

Her husband chuckled. 'I did warn you about dealing in the black market, and you dismissed me, if I recall.'

'And that Jenny Procter has a cheek to show up here when we all know about her and that American GI!'

James looked intrigued. 'Are you implying that's she's having an affair?

'I'm not implying anything, it's a well-known fact!'

'Then good for her! I could never understand what she was doing with that pompous oaf Procter; she deserves much better.'

'James! What a terrible thing to say.'

'Not at all, my dear, and my advice to you is people in glass houses shouldn't throw stones. Just hope that Jenny's friend, that glamorous redhead, doesn't tell the authorities about you!' And he walked out of the room.

Twenty-Three

The men of the 82nd Airborne division were weary. Despite the fact that eighty per cent of their supplies had been recovered from several drops, the weather had deteriorated, stopping vital troops from gliding in. The company still had been unable to capture the bridge at Nijmegen and were now fighting to take control of the landing zone.

That evening, as Brad and Chad sat eating their K rations, they both admitted how tired they were.

'I'm beat,' said Chad as he lit a cigarette. 'God, I thought I was a really fit man, but I've never ever been so damned tired.'

Brad pushed his helmet to the back of his head and rubbed his eyes. 'Me too, buddy. What I wouldn't give for a hot bath and a comfortable bed. I'd sell my soul to the devil for it, given the opportunity!'

'No, you wouldn't, you're one of the good guys!'

Brad started laughing. 'Whatever gave you that idea?'

'I've gotten to know you pretty well since we came to Britain, but don't let it go to your head!'

Brad looked across at his friend. He had been made up to sergeant now and was very popular with the men. His way of handling them was different. He didn't yell or shout at them, there were no snide remarks about their inabilities as soldiers – he just showed them respect and understanding. No doubt helped by his experiences with horses, he understood the men's psyches. Nevertheless, when it was necessary, Chad could yell as well as the next sergeant.

The two men had been firm friends before they were sent to the war zone, but in battle real friendships are forged which last a lifetime, and these two men looked out for each other through friendship and mutual admiration.

They spent the rest of the evening talking about their plans for the future.

'When eventually I get my ranch up and running,' Chad said, 'you and Rusty ought to come out and stay for a vacation. After all, you're not that far away. The girls would love to spend some time together there.'

'That'd be great,' agreed Brad. 'Like you, I'll have to take time to set up my practice again.'

'But what about the patients that you had before. Won't they come back?'

'I doubt it! You forget how long it's been. They will, by now, feel comfortable with their new practitioner. The doctor-patient relationship is very personal, and that's important both for the doctor and the patient.'

'There you go,' Chad remarked with a grin. 'You're a people whisperer!'

Shaking his head, Brad smiled. 'How that lovely woman puts up with you, I'll never know!'

'To be honest, Brad, neither do I, but thank God she does. I feel the luckiest guy on the planet. Right, I'm off to get some sleep, see you in the morning. Let's hope it's an easier day than today.' And he made his way to his bed.

Back at home, Jenny and Rusty got on with their lives, watching the post every morning in the hopes of hearing from their men. When a letter did arrive, the recipient would go off in a quiet corner to read the contents before sharing whatever news with the other. Like their two men, they'd become firm friends and cheered each other when one felt low.

This particular evening, they were in the sitting room exchanging gossip when the telephone rang. 'Who on earth can that be?' Jenny said as she went to answer it. 'Yes, this is Jenny Procter. Yes, my husband is Captain Adam Procter.'

Rusty looked up and saw the shocked expression on Jenny's face.

'Where did you say he was?' Jenny listened for a moment and then asked: 'Can I go and see him?' After taking down some details, she replaced the receiver.

'Jenny! Whatever is the matter? You look terrible.'

She sank into the chair beside the phone. 'It's Adam! He's been injured and is in hospital.'

'Oh my God! Is he badly hurt?'

'They wouldn't say, just asked if I would go and see him and talk to his doctor.'

'Where is he?'

'In a military hospital in Basingstoke. I must find out the train times. I'll go up in the morning.'

'I'm coming with you!' said Rusty.

'But your job?'

'I'll ring in the morning. You can't go alone. Who knows what's happened!' She walked over to Jenny and put a comforting arm around her. 'Maybe it won't be too bad.'

Neither of the women slept well that night, wondering what they would face the following day. They left Southampton in the morning and eventually arrived at the hospital.

Jenny went up to the reception desk and spoke to the nurse on duty. 'I'm Mrs Jenny Procter. I received a call last night to say that my husband, Captain Adam Procter, had been brought here. I would like to see him, please.'

'One moment, Mrs Procter,' said the nurse and looked through several notes on her desk. She frowned and said, 'Yes, that's right, just one moment please.' She made a call to tell someone of Jenny's arrival, then asked her to take a seat for a moment.

As they sat waiting, Rusty took hold of Jenny's hand and squeezed it, but neither said a word.

Before very long they heard the sound of footsteps and saw a man wearing a white coat approaching. 'Which of you is Mrs Procter?' he asked.

Jenny stood up. 'I am.'

'Would you like to come with me, please?'

'I'd like my friend to come too. Is that all right?'

'Yes, of course,' he said quietly, 'just follow me.'

Jenny could feel her heart racing as she followed the man. He showed her into what appeared to be his consulting room and indicated that they should take a seat.

'I am Dr Braxton and have been attending to your husband.'

'Is he badly injured?' asked Jenny fearfully.

'I'm afraid so. He was injured by an explosion. He has mainly superficial injuries caused by shrapnel, but I'm so sorry to have to tell you that, due to the blast, he is blind.'

Jenny let out a cry of anguish and covered her mouth with her hand.

'Oh my God!' exclaimed Rusty.

'Is this a permanent thing?' asked Jenny. 'Is there any hope that he may regain his sight?'

'I'm afraid not. The optic nerves have been too badly damaged.'

Jenny sat, stunned by the news, unable to fully grasp the situation.

'What happens to Captain Procter now?' asked Rusty.

'He'll remain a patient here for a while until we can get him well. As you can imagine, he's been through a series of operations where we tried to save his sight and he's a sick man at the moment. When he's well enough, we'll send him to St Dunstan's, where they will train him to cope without his sight and teach him Braille – then he'll come home.'

'What sort of a life will he have then? He'll not be able to work, he'll have a terrible time. He'll hate every moment! You don't know my husband, Dr Braxton.' Jenny was beside herself with worry.

'He'll need a great deal of help, Mrs Procter, to get used to being blind. But you know it is possible to lead a good life if you are mentally strong. But I won't lie to you, it isn't going to be easy.'

'Can I see him?' asked Jenny.'

'Yes, of course, but I would ask you not to stay too long, not this time. I'm sure it will cheer the captain to hear your voice, but I don't want him tired. I'm sure you understand.'

'Of course.'

'I'll show you to his room. He's in a side ward where he can be quiet. Your friend can sit in the waiting room.'

Jenny tried to fight off the trepidation she felt as she was taken to see Adam. She had no idea what she was about to face.

At the door, the doctor left her. 'Half an hour at the longest,' he told her.

Jenny opened the door. The smell of ether and disinfectant seemed to invade her nostrils, making her feel nauseous. She stepped inside the room.

Adam was lying in bed, his eyes covered with bandages. He looked frail and thin. She walked over to the bed and gently took his hand. 'Adam, it's Jenny.'

He stirred just a little and moved his head straining to listen. 'Jenny, is that really you?'

'Yes, Adam, I'm so sorry to see you like this.'

'I wondered if you would come,' he said weakly. 'Thank you, it means so much to me.'

She could tell that talking was wearying him. 'Don't talk,' she said. 'They will only let me stay for a while.'

He squeezed her hand. 'Next time you can perhaps stay a little longer.' His voice faded, and he fell asleep.

She sat studying her husband. This was so unlike the man she knew. Adam had been a tour de force; now he looked weak and frail. How on earth would he be able to cope in the future? Thirty minutes later, she gently removed her hand from his and crept out of the room.

Rusty was walking up and down the waiting room, worried for her friend, wondering what was going to happen next. She stopped as Jenny walked in and held her friend as she dissolved into tears.

When Jenny had recovered, she told her friend about Adam. 'He looked so ill, it was all he could do to say a few words. Oh Rusty, what a terrible thing to happen to him. His life is in ruins!'

Although Rusty felt sympathy for the man lying in the hospital bed, she was more concerned about Jenny. *And your life is also in ruins*, she thought to herself.

The train journey home was taken in almost complete silence, both women sat lost in their own thoughts. Rusty anxiously watched her friend, whose shoulders were slumped and her face pale.

Jenny was trying to face the facts that had just been put before her, seeing her future happiness slowly and painfully fading away. 'I can't possibly leave him now!' she suddenly exclaimed and then burst into tears.

Rusty put an arm round Jenny, but couldn't find the words to comfort her. What could she say? What would she do if she was in that position? She honestly didn't know. If only Brad was here! With his medical background he would be able to assess the situation rationally. She felt completely hopeless and helpless.

Once they arrived at Southampton, they took a taxi home. Rusty put the kettle on and then poured Jenny a stiff brandy. 'Here, drink this, it's good for shock.' She poured herself one too, then made a pot of tea.

'There's no sense in making any decision until you know more about Adam's situation,' she said as she poured the steaming liquid into a cup.

'What more is there to know?' said Jenny. 'Adam is blind. He couldn't possibly manage without help for the rest of his life. How can I walk away from him, knowing that?'

'What about Chad, your plans for the future? Are you going to throw that all away?'

'What choice do I have? I *have* no choice!' she cried.

'Stop that!' Rusty shook Jenny by the shoulders. 'All your married life, Adam has made decisions for you. Now, you have to fight for what you want.' She stood up and stalked around the kitchen angrily. 'For Christ's sake, Jenny, for the first time in your life, stand up for yourself! Don't throw in the towel so easily!'

'You didn't see Adam or you wouldn't be so heartless!'

Rusty drew up a chair beside her. 'Look at me!' she demanded.

Somewhat startled by the ferocious tone of her voice, Jenny did as she was told.

'Don't think for one minute I'm not deeply sorry for Adam, because I am. My heart goes out to him, but I am more concerned about you at this moment. Adam will get the best medical treatment going, and though this may sound hard, he's not the first man to lose his sight. He'll be trained to cope, as have many others, and in time he will have a quality to his life – not the one he had hoped for, but a life that can be lived. But you . . . *you* will be destroyed! Now, that's not right in any man's language.'

'I know what you say is true, but I don't know if I'll be strong enough to walk away when the time comes.'

'At least give some consideration to the man who adores you!' Rusty let out a sigh of frustration. 'Chad will be devastated if you let him down. How can you live with that?'

'I'm not at all sure that I can. Oh Rusty – what a mess!'

'You listen to me. You'll have to see Adam, of course you will. He needs you now, and because of the years you've been together, you have to help him at this time.' She caught hold of Jenny's hand and gripped it tightly. 'But never *ever* let him think this is a permanent situation! If at any time he talks as if he thinks it is, you must gently remind him of your plans. Don't give him any false hopes. That way you'll be able to cope and he will be prepared for it.'

'You should be a psychologist! Where did you learn all this?'

Rusty chuckled. 'Mostly on my back, darling!'

Despite everything, Jenny had to laugh. 'Do you think I should write to Chad and explain the situation?'

Rusty looked appalled. 'What, and worry him to death? What would be the point? Goodness knows *when* the men will be home. Until that time you can do your duty by Adam, help get him on his feet, and then later, when this bloody war is over, we can all get on with our lives.'

'Thank goodness we met and became friends, Rusty, I'd be lost without you.'

'And where would I be at this moment if we'd not met? It was fate that brought us all together, and together we'll stay!'

'You are an extraordinary woman!'

Rusty just raised her eyebrows and smiled. 'So I've been told in the past!'

'And naughty!'

'That too! But I'm a survivor, I've had to be, but I've learned to fight for what I believe is right, and you must do the same. Do you think that Adam would want you to stay with him out of pity?'

'In the beginning I don't think he'd care as long as I was there, but later, no, he'd hate it . . . and what's more he'd let me know it.'

'And then you will have given up everything for nothing!'

'I'll just have to take it one step at a time, that's all.

'Then we'll take those steps together, Jenny, because I'm not sure I trust you to be strong!'

Jenny Procter didn't answer, but she knew that Rusty spoke the truth. She would feel it was her sense of duty to stay with Adam, and she needed someone to push her when the time came. How lucky she was, she thought, to have found such a friend.

Twenty-Four

The next two months were difficult for everybody. Adam battled with his health; Jenny tried to help by visiting twice a week, and more if she could get away from her job with the forces. When she tried to explain to her husband that she was working, sorting out the papers and details of the GI brides, he was scathing.

'That is more important than coming here to see me?'

'I have to make a living, and I'm paid to do this job . . . and I feel it's worthwhile.'

'You don't have to work! How many times must I tell you this? I will provide financially for you!'

Jenny breathed deeply to try and remain calm. 'Adam, there is no need to do so, especially under the circumstances.'

He put his hand up to the bandages covering his eyes in frustration. 'If only I could bloody well see, then we could talk sensibly!'

Thinking of Rusty and her advice, Jenny tried to be firm. 'Adam, not being able to see me makes no difference. You know what I mean, and nothing has changed.'

He cursed loudly. 'For me, *everything* has changed. For Christ's sake, woman, how can you sit there and say that?'

'That's not what I mean, and you know it.' She got up and walked to the window. She knew that it was never going to be easy, but why did it have to be *so* difficult? Then she chided herself for being so selfish; after all, she wasn't the one in the hospital bed. But how to handle Adam and at the same time be of help was beyond her. She decided to have a word with the doctor before she left and see what he had to say.

Dr Braxton tried to reassure Jenny. 'The first few months are the worst. I promise it will get better in time, but, to begin with, the realization that you will never be able to see again is a terrible thing. There is desolation, anger, frustration . . . and, eventually, acceptance. That's when we can really get to work and start rehabilitation. St Dunstan's comes in to its own then. In time the patient realizes that there is a sort of light at the end of the tunnel, even if they can't see one, and that all is not lost – then it's up to the individual.'

'How do you think my husband will cope, Doctor?'

The man shook his head. 'It's very difficult to say, Mrs Procter. If your marriage is a strong one, that'll help.'

Jenny's heart sank. 'I feel you should know all the facts, Doctor Braxton, as it might help in my husband's treatment. We are separated. I plan to get a divorce and move to the States when the war finally ends.'

'Ah.' The doctor smiled softly. 'That would explain his extreme anger. He's not only lost his sight, but you also.'

'I know, and don't think I don't feel guilty about this, because I do. We were married for a long time.'

'Forgive me, but I have to know – is there any chance that you might change your mind and stay with the captain?'

Shaking her head, Jenny said, 'No. At first I felt it was my duty to do so, but it just won't work. The war changes us all, and I'm afraid although I have a deep affection for him, I no longer love my husband. I know that once we were home together, then the rot would set in, and that wouldn't be good for Adam.'

'Then I suggest, Mrs Procter, that you don't visit the captain so often. The sooner he gets used to the idea that you won't be around, the sooner we can rehabilitate him. Now he's just confused and no doubt thinks that you will eventually stand by him, which will only make it harder for him when you leave for good.'

Jenny felt like a traitor. To walk away from Adam at such a time seemed cruel in the extreme. She looked at the man sitting opposite and met his gaze. 'Are you sure this is the way to go?'

'Absolutely positive. Forgive me for being blunt, but if you are leaving your husband for another man, the sooner you go the better for him.'

'You make it sound so callous! I was married to Adam for nineteen years, but I fell in love with an American. It wasn't planned, it just happened. Then this! Believe me, Doctor Braxton, I have been torn between the devil and the deep, but I know getting on with my life will ultimately be the right thing for both of us.'

'I'm not here to judge you, Mrs Procter; I'm just interested in what's best for my patient. Captain Procter will soon be moved to St Dunstan's, and I suggest you give him a month before you visit, which doesn't mean you can't write – a nurse will read out your letters to him – but please don't give him any false hopes about the future.'

Jenny rose from her seat and shook the doctor's hand. 'Thank you, you have been very helpful.'

The next three months flew by, and December was soon upon them. Adam was now at St Dunstan's and seemed at last to be settling down to a new regime. He was becoming more adept at walking around unaided once he knew the layout of his surroundings, which gave him a feeling of independence, and whenever Jenny did visit him he seemed more cheerful. But each time she saw him he told her he couldn't wait to come home, which filled her with a certain amount of trepidation as to how he would manage. Once again, Adam would have to hire staff to take care of him. In her heart, Jenny knew that Adam was hoping she would step into the breach, that her feeling of duty would overcome everything else.

Brad and Chad were still in Holland but no longer near Arnhem. It had been a bridge too far, and the American troops had had to retreat, eventually. The company had tried to cross the river to get to the bridge, but they'd had to use British boats, with which they were unfamiliar; there was also a shortage of paddles, which didn't help their cause. The men were using rifle butts in some cases, but the covering fire was heavy and the men had to fall back. As they did so, they were trapped in a pocket of land, with no possibility of escaping. They dug themselves in as quickly as possible.

Brad called for the radio operator and reported his position, hoping for covering gunfire; they were not any in position to help, but he was told that more troops would be sent to aid them.

Brad could hear Chad giving orders to his men as they returned fire, keeping their heads down as the bullets whizzed past them. They continued to hold their position until eventually more troops arrived with their added firepower. It was a great relief, and they were able to fall back to safety.

The two men had survived, and they wrote to the women they loved when they were able – never telling them of their narrow escape, of course, but about their hopes for the future, and about how the war could not possibly last for much longer.

Rusty liked to curl up in a chair and try to visualize her future. She had nothing to leave behind that meant anything at all to her, except perhaps for the friendship of Jenny Procter, but they would be in the same country and nearby states. They had vowed to keep in touch with each other once they were in America. It was a kind of safety line which they both would protect and treasure.

The girls had spoken about finding another flat to share now that Adam was back in England, but he wouldn't hear of it.

'How ridiculous! I've no idea how long I'll be at St Dunstan's, and in any case, the house is enormous, there's certainly room for us all. Besides, I'm not sure how long it'll be before I'm allowed home for good, so the house must be occupied when I'm not there.'

Jenny had finally agreed, with the understanding that once Adam was back home permanently, they would move out.

Christmas came at last. Jenny and Rusty spent the holiday at Beth's, helping with the horses and enjoying a family Christmas after all. On Boxing Day they all went out for a ride early in the morning through the woods, which looked like a fairyland with the hoar frost making the ferns look magical.

Jenny looked across at Rusty, sitting on her mount with confidence, and grinned at her friend. 'If Brad could see you now, he would be surprised. You sit there as if you know what you're doing!'

'I need to practice for when we are back at his place! You know how he loves to ride.'

'You'll be joining the hunt before you know it!' Jenny teased.

'Not bloody likely! I've watched the hunt in action; when a fox has been sighted, it's crazy. Everyone is off like a shot, jumping anything that gets in the way. That's too bloody dangerous for me, thank you!'

During the first week of January, Adam came home for a week to see how he would be able to cope. He had a male nurse in attendance who walked him round every room to familiarize him once again with the contents of his home.

During this time, Sarah took Hans to stay at Beth's. It was deemed too complicated to have Sarah stay, with little Hans running around and perhaps tripping Adam up, and Jenny wasn't sure how Adam would feel about having them living there, anyway.

Once he was settled in, on the day of his arrival, the nurse had a word with Jenny. 'Whatever you do, Mrs Procter, don't move any furniture or your husband could trip over it and hurt himself,' he told Jenny. 'He will have memorized everything in its place, and there it must stay.'

'I understand,' she told him.

It was an uncomfortable time for them all. Rusty felt she was intruding, Jenny felt even guiltier about leaving Adam, and Adam became more and more demanding as each day passed.

'I don't know where you get your patience from,' Jenny said to Jack the male nurse after Adam had been particularly unpleasant one morning.

'Ah well, Mrs Procter, I know my patient. He's proud, and now he feels less of a man because he's unable to see and so is not in control. And he's angry – even more so because of the state of his marriage, if you forgive me for saying so.'

'He's told you about us?' Jenny asked with surprise.

'Oh yes. In the beginning when the captain was first injured, he talked to me a lot. I think it was the only way he could cope. After all, he can't see me; that makes it so much easier to open up. If he was sighted, he would never have done so.'

'Yes, I understand.'

'What perhaps you don't understand, Mrs Procter, is that your husband honestly believes that when push comes to shove you'll stay with him. But that's not how you see it, is it?'

Jenny was horrified. 'I thought I made it very clear to Adam that my plans hadn't changed.'

'Oh, you did that, but you see that's not what he wants to hear, so he refuses to accept the fact. I have tried to make him see he's barking up the wrong tree, but he doesn't want to know.'

'What can I do about it?'

'Move out of the house. As long as you are installed here, the captain thinks you'll stay for good.'

'Thank you, Jack. When Adam returns to St Dunstan's, I'll find a flat.'

'It'll be for the best, Mrs Procter, in the long run.'

The following morning, Adam had just finished his breakfast when he heard the front doorbell ring. 'I'll go, Jack,' he said, pushing his chair back and reaching for his white stick. He liked to greet the postman these days and open the front door to those who called. He was feeling more confident in his own surroundings and wanted to show those who knew him that he could manage perfectly well, thank you!

'That you, postman?' he asked as he opened the door. 'Got anything interesting for me today?'

'Good morning, Captain Procter. I'm afraid I'm not the postman.'

Adam froze for a moment as he heard the American accent.

'It's Chad Maxwell; we met once before at the stables.'

'You're that bloody cowboy!'

There was a note of amusement in the American's voice when he answered. 'Well, sir, I guess you could put it like that.'

'What do you want?' Adam was brusque.

'I've called to see Jenny. I flew in from France a couple of hours ago and have to fly out again tonight.'

'There's no point in you seeing her, my man. As you can see I'm home now, and Jenny is taking care of me. She has decided that she needs to be with me, so any thoughts you might have of a future together with my wife, I'm afraid, are out of the question. She's decided her place is here with me.'

Chad was stunned. He had been taken by surprise when the

door was opened by Adam; then to see that he was blind, and now to be told that Jenny had decided to stay with her husband! She'd not written about Adam in her letters. Those had been full of love and affection, talking about their future together. What on earth was going on? 'Where is Jenny now?' Chad demanded.

'I have no idea,' Adam lied. 'She's away for the day and won't be back until this evening.'

'Leaving you alone?' he asked suspiciously.

'No, I have a male nurse in attendance to give Jenny a hand. As you can imagine, this takes some getting used to, and it would be too much to expect her to take me on by herself.'

'And where is Rusty? She and Jenny were staying here together; at least, that was what I was told in her letters.'

'Yes, that's right. Until I came home, of course, then she moved out to a flat.'

'Do you have her address?'

'What on earth would I want that for? Now, if you'll excuse me, I've to take some medication. I'm sorry things didn't work out for you, but frankly, I think it was only a temporary aberration on my wife's part. It was never going to last — you know how it is in wartime.' Adam turned away and closed the door.

Twenty-Five

Chad stood looking at the closed door, his mind in a whirl. He had been taken completely by surprise to see Adam and was shocked when he realized the poor guy was blind! How dreadful for him — and for Jenny. He'd been moving around France these past few weeks and hadn't received any mail from her, no doubt telling him about Adam's condition. But had she really thrown away a future with him to look after her husband, after everything they'd been to each other? As he walked to the jeep he told the driver to take him to the stables and gave him directions. Beth would know what was going on.

But when he arrived, it was to discover that Beth was away and wouldn't be back until that evening. There was no one there that he knew and could ask about Jenny. Unfortunately, Brad had been seconded to another company several weeks ago, so his other means of communication were closed. Rusty would have told Brad of any change in Jenny's plans.

On the way back to the camp, he got the driver to stop at a florists, where he ordered flowers for Jenny. On the card he wrote: *Sorry I missed you today, darling. Will be in touch. Love you like crazy. Chad xx*

He had to let her know that, for him, nothing had changed.

When the flowers were delivered, Jack took them to Adam. 'These flowers have just arrived for Mrs Procter. What shall I do with them?'

'Is there a card with them?'

'Yes, sir.'

'Open it and read it to me.'

Jack did so, and when he'd finished, Adam calmly said, 'Take them outside and put them in the dustbin! They never arrived, you understand?'

'Yes, sir.'

It was in Jenny's best interests, Adam told himself. Her obsession with this young man would pass; it was a wartime madness. She belonged with him in this house, and he'd be damned if he would let her waste her life with a bloody cowboy! But beneath his veneer, Adam was scared. Without Jenny, he didn't think he could cope. He realized, too, that his behaviour had been unreasonable during some of his stay, which was not the way to win her over.

Jenny, unaware of all the drama at Chilworth, was visiting a letting agency during her lunch hour. She'd told Rusty what Jack, the male nurse had advised, and her friend was only too pleased to move.

'To be honest, Jenny,' Rusty had said, 'I've felt very uncomfortable being in the house with Adam. I really felt I was intruding. But if he's still determined to keep you by his side, then Jack is right to suggest you move out.'

Jenny looked at a few flats and told the agent she'd bring her friend to look them over before deciding. One or two of them were perfectly adequate, as far as she was concerned, but Rusty would have to agree, it was only fair.

Knowing that Rusty had plans to visit friends that evening, Adam had Jack order dinner from a restaurant, delivered to the door. Jack laid the table and found two candlesticks and candles and set it out in readiness. When Jenny walked through the front door, the nurse informed her that dinner would be served in half an hour.

Taken somewhat by surprise, and feeling decidedly weary, she just smiled and said, 'How nice, I'll go and freshen up.'

When she eventually sat at the dining room table with Adam, she had to admit he handled eating his food very well. Jack told him where everything was on his plate, as if the plate was a clock face. His meat at eight o'clock, his potatoes at four, etc. Then he left them alone.

Jenny had forgotten how charming Adam could be. She enjoyed the chicken and the desert and found herself relaxing in the familiarity that the years spent together had fostered. Adam was recounting old scenarios that had caused them both such hilarity in times gone by.

He turned his head in her direction. 'It wasn't all bad, Jenny, was it?'

'No, of course not.' She gazed at her husband. He was still handsome; his hair greying at the temples made him look distinguished, and when he smiled she remembered the young man she'd fallen in love with so long ago. It broke her heart to see him now, dependent on others most of the time. She did realize that, as each week passed, Adam was becoming more confident and able to do more for himself, but he was a selfish man and she knew that, without a doubt, whoever was with him would be at his beck and call continuously – but it had been fun to reminisce.

Adam leaned forward towards her. 'Jenny, darling, don't throw what we had away. We can still have a good life together.'

The atmosphere of the evening changed in seconds. What had been fun and easy now became tense and edgy.

'Please, Adam, let's not go there. If this was your plan – to soften me up with dinner, candlelight and reminiscences about old times to get me to stay with you – then sadly it was all for nothing. It's a pity because, until now, I was enjoying it all.' She rose from the table. 'I'm off to bed. Thank you for the meal.'

Adam listened to her retreating footsteps and cursed to himself. He couldn't let her go without a fight. She was his wife, and they had spent too many years together to have some young Yank come along and ruin everything! He lit a cigarette. Was it about sex – was that what made the whole thing so exciting? But they had had a good sex life he had always thought.

But when he stopped to really think about it, it hadn't been special. Whenever he felt like it, he would reach for Jenny in bed. She rarely refused, and he was always satisfied, job done!

He stubbed his cigarette out angrily. Women! No man could ever understand them.

Upstairs in her bedroom, Jenny undressed and thought about the previous few hours. What a shame the whole dinner had been part of a plan, instead of just two people enjoying a meal and good conversation. But that was typical of Adam. He was always insistent on getting his own way; it was the manner of the man. As long as he was satisfied, that was what counted. It was the same in bed. Once Adam had reached his climax, nothing else mattered, he would turn over and sleep, whereas Chad was so thoughtful as a lover, making sure that she too was satisfied. How she longed for him at this moment.

It wasn't until the following morning that Beth was told about the American GI who had been asking for her. When Beth asked for a description of the soldier, she realized that it had to be Chad. She immediately rang Jenny at her office. 'So did you see Chad yesterday?' Beth asked as soon as Jenny answered the phone.

'What are you talking about?'

'A GI came looking for me yesterday, but I was out. His description fitted Chad so I was sure you had seen him.'

'No, I left the house early in the morning and didn't get back until late.' She hesitated, then swore softly.

'What is it?' asked Beth.

'Last night Adam arranged a candlelight dinner as a surprise to tempt me back, and now I know why. Chad must have gone to the house. Oh my God! What must he have thought to see Adam there?'

'That all depends if he saw Adam and if they spoke, I suppose.'

'If they did, I can imagine what was said. Adam is such a devious sod! He'd do anything to keep me here.'

'If that was the case, Chad would wait until he saw you, I'm sure, before believing any story. You just have to wait until you hear from him.'

'I can't do anything else, but I shall certainly have a word with Adam when I go home tonight. He can't run my life for me, and it's time to remind him of that!'

Adam was sitting by the fire in the living room, sipping a glass of brandy, when Jenny swept into the room that evening, bristling with indignation. 'So what lies did you tell Chad when he called?' she demanded.

At first he was startled, but then he just smiled. 'How did you find out he'd called?'

'He went looking for Beth. What did you say to him, Adam?'

'I told him you had decided to stay with me.'

'You what? How dare you! You had no right to do such a thing, and it was a lie.'

'At the moment it is, but I know you'll soon come to your senses. Then it'll be the truth.'

She couldn't believe what she was hearing. 'When will you accept that our marriage is over? Even if I never heard from Chad again, I wouldn't come back to you, Adam. You are a selfish, self-centred, controlling man who has never learned about humility, even now. I'm moving the rest of my stuff out tomorrow. You will need to arrange for someone else to care for the house. I no longer want anything to do with it – or you!'

The following day, Jenny and Rusty moved into a flat in Hill Lane. She went to the Post Office to fill in a form for change of address, as she didn't want any of her mail to go to the house. Adam was not to be trusted with any letters that might come from Chad, and now more than ever she needed to hear from her lover to find out if he believed Adam's lies.

She sat down before she went to bed and wrote a long letter to Chad, assuring him that she still loved him.

Nothing will come between us, my darling, she wrote. *At one time,*

I confess, I thought it was my duty to stay with Adam, but it wouldn't work, and I would wilt away to nothing without you beside me. I can't wait for this terrible war to be over so we can start our life together. Yours always, Jenny xxx

She prayed that Chad would receive the letter in the near future.

But Chad Maxwell was on an aircraft, flying to France once again. He had delivered his papers into the right hands and now was returning to his company. Surely this damned war had to be over soon? He couldn't wait to get out of uniform, back on a horse and the open country side without the sound of gunfire . . . with the woman he loved.

He wondered just where Brad was at this time. He really missed his company. He put his head back, closed his eyes and slept.

But at the stables, no one was asleep. Little Hans had become very poorly in the early evening, and his condition had worsened. Here, everyone was awake . . . and worried.

Twenty-Six

Captain Brad Jackson was war weary, as was every man in his company. They all wanted to pack up and go home to their families and a normal life. But, for many, normality would never be the case. So many servicemen would have their lives altered for ever, due to the injuries they received during the fighting. And, for some of them, death would have been kinder. Brad had to deal with these men and try and get them up and give them some kind of hope before he shipped them home.

As a doctor, he knew that it wasn't only his injured men who were the ones to suffer. Depending on the extent of the injuries, some of the soldiers' family members couldn't cope with sons or husbands who would return as different people, not the fit and healthy men they once knew.

Some of the men were courageous and mentally strong, accepting that things would never be the same, but determined to make the most of the help that was offered by the service hospitals, but others were unable to see a future and felt they had lost their livelihood and, consequently, their manhood.

In Southampton, Jenny was doing a similar job but with less brutal injuries. Some of the women who came into her office were in dire straits. Not all the women had been married to their GIs before they were sent to the battlefields, and many of them had illegitimate children to show for their liaisons with the men. Those who suffered most were the women with Negro babies. In many southern states of America it was illegal for a Negro to mix with a white woman, and to give her a child was a lynching offence.

In their own hometown, the women were looked down upon, and now they had no financial support from the father. This was the hardest part of Jenny's job, but she did what she could for the women, using the WVS to help with clothing for the babies, and begging, borrowing or stealing anything else she could from any organization that she thought could help.

Three weeks had passed since Chad had called, but Jenny had not heard from him. She couldn't imagine what was in his mind after calling at the house and seeing Adam there. Would he really have believed that she was back with her husband?

Rusty hadn't had a letter from Brad either, but it wasn't surprising – the war in Europe was still raging, but slowly the Germans were being beaten, and the bombing of Dresden had put fear into the hearts of the German people.

Eventually, in March, the US Army crossed the Rhine at Remagen. Brad was with the army as it finally drove over the bridge, which had been detonated by the Germans but had failed to explode. When General Bradley realized the fact, he sent everything he could across it.

A letter from Rusty had eventually caught up with Brad, but it had been written some time before, so he was unaware of Adam's status and the brief visitation of his buddy. But now the allies were across the Rhine and the Russians rapidly approaching Berlin, the general consensus of opinion was that the end was nigh, and Brad was content to wait to catch up with the woman he loved.

★　　★　　★

In the prisoner of war camp, Gunter listened to the news every night, praying for the end of the fighting so he could be repatriated and prepare a home for his family. He had written to his parents, but had not received a reply. They could be with his sister – or worse, beneath a pile of rubble. He had no way of knowing until he was able to return to Germany and see for himself.

In the camp, most of the prisoners realized that Germany was losing the war. Most by now just wanted it to end so they could be free, but the few dyed-in-the-wool Nazis were very bitter, and when, in April, Hitler committed suicide in a bunker in Berlin, they felt cheated and betrayed . . . but Gunter was filled with hope.

Chad was in Prague with the US Third Army when it took the city, but they were ordered to stay there to allow the Russians to take the rest of the country. None of the servicemen cared. They were happy to settle in for the time being, away from the fighting.

Chad sat quietly in a corner of a small cafe he had found, with a small glass of brandy which the owner had proudly produced as Chad sat at the table.

'God Bless America!' the man cried and grinning all over his face disappeared into the back.

Chad chuckled to himself and started a letter to Jenny.

Hello, darling. We are in Prague, and the fighting is over for a time and hopefully for good before too long. I've been moving around so have received no mail at all. I was in the UK briefly a few months ago and called at your house. I saw Adam. Poor guy, what a rotten shame. He told me that you were staying with him. I can understand that you think you have a duty to this man who you were married to for so long, but I am praying that you still want to be with me and come and live in Wyoming.

This makes me sound like a heel, with Adam being blind and all, but Jenny honey, I love you so much, and I can't bear to think of you dying inside as you surely would if you stayed in Chilworth with him.

I may not make it back to see you if an armistice is declared

in the near future. I may be shipped home first to be discharged,
but I want you to know, I'm coming back for you, darling,
however long it takes.
Yours always and forever,
Chad.

At last the war was over. There was dancing in the streets, street parties, the pubs were bursting at the seams with people celebrating VE day. But there were many who celebrated with heavy hearts. Pleased that the fighting was over, but knowing that their lives would never be the same again.

Rusty, Jenny and Sarah all celebrated at the stables with Beth. Sarah was dancing with little Hans, telling him that soon they would be seeing his father again. Jenny wondered how Adam was, as she'd not seen him for some time. He was back in the house, she knew that, and after going once to see him there, she haddn't returned.

Their visit had ended acrimoniously. He had accused her of betrayal to her marriage vows and to him and had ended up calling her a slut, which was when Jenny had walked out of the house – and out of his life.

The next two months passed quickly, but for Jenny and Rusty it was a fraught time. If they were to go to America, there was so much to be done officially. Passports to be obtained, two copies of birth certificates, a statement from the husband or fiancé, and in some cases letters from the man's family. Evidence that they could afford a train ticket at the other end of their journey. For both the women, much that was needed was from the men, who were not around and as yet had not been in contact.

It was Brad who surfaced first of all. He managed to beg a space on a plane leaving Europe for London. There was no time to get in touch with Rusty, and as the aircraft landed in England, Brad decided just to make his way to Southampton. After all, Rusty would be at work, so calling her on the telephone would be difficult.

It was mid-afternoon, and Rusty had just finished serving a customer and was carefully folding one of the rejected garments, looking down at it, focusing on making it neat, when a hand caught hold of her wrist. She looked up in surprise and saw Brad! She felt the blood drain from her body, and her knees buckled.

Brad leapt the counter. 'It's all right, everybody, I'm a doctor!' he cried. 'Someone get me a glass of water.'

A few minutes later, Rusty started to come round and felt something cold against her forehead. She opened her eyes. 'Brad, Brad, was that really you?' she murmured.

'Yes, darling, it really is. How are you feeling?'

Rusty looked up at him and gave a wan smile. 'You could have given me a heart attack!'

He smoothed her cheek. 'For one awful moment, I thought I had.'

She looked around and saw lots of concerned faces staring down at her. 'Oh my God,' she whispered.

'It's all right, folks, the young lady is fine. She just fainted.' To the senior manager of the department, who had arrived to see what all the commotion was about, he said, 'I'm taking Miss Dobbs home. I doubt if she will be back for a few days.'

Once outside, Brad took her into his arms and kissed her longingly. 'I've waited for what seems a lifetime to do that,' he said. 'I'm taking you home. Let's find a taxi. Are you still at Chilworth?'

Rusty gave him her new address, saying, 'It's a long story, I'll explain later.'

Once they arrived at the flat in Hill Lane, Rusty made a cup of coffee and a sandwich for both of them and they sat on the settee and caught up with each other's news. Every now and again one would reach out to touch the other, as if trying to convince themselves that the other person was real.

Brad was sympathetic when he heard the news about Adam. 'That's a really tough deal,' he said. 'How did Jenny take it?'

Rusty tried to explain how difficult a decision it had been for her to keep her promise to Chad and put aside her feelings of guilt.

'Well, darling, life is cruel, I'm afraid. It throws some diabolical curves your way, as if to say, now get out of that!' He pulled her towards him and looked into her eyes. 'I have to return to the States to be discharged, but I'm getting a special licence before I go, so we can be married.'

This took Rusty's breath away. 'Oh my God! Are you sure about this?'

'Absolutely! Why, have you any doubts?'

She threw her arms around his neck. 'Don't be ridiculous!' she cried – then she kissed him.

The next few days were frantic, trying to get ready for the wedding. Beth had offered to do the wedding breakfast as a present to the couple, and Jenny had one of her gowns altered for Rusty to wear. It was a coffee-coloured extravaganza bought before the war in an exclusive boutique in London. It was below the knee and fitted with a swathe across the neckline. It was very glamorous and expensive . . . and looked it.

Rusty, with her auburn hair, beneath a small straw hat with a veil, was a perfect foil against the coffee shade of the dress. She carried a small bouquet of cream roses. Jenny was her maid of honour in a soft pale-green gown.

As the girls sat together in the wedding car, taking them to St Mark's church in Archers Road and a vicar who made time for them, they held hands.

Rusty was trembling. 'Is this really happening to me, Jenny?'

'Indeed it is, and for goodness sake, try and relax! This is a special day for any woman, so enjoy it. Now come on,' Jenny gently chided, 'there is nothing to be nervous about. Brad loves you, and you'll have a wonderful life.'

'Oh, I do know that, it just seems too good to be true. Until he puts that ring on my finger and we are declared man and wife, I won't believe it! I just wish you'd heard from Chad and that he could be here too.'

Jenny leaned out of the window of the vehicle. She had hoped by now to have had a letter from her lover. She wondered if he was still in Europe, waiting to be sent home, or was he already in the States? But why hadn't he written?

Brad had tried to trace his whereabouts for her, but had not been able to get a result with troops being moved hither and thither. 'Try not to fret, Jenny,' he told her. 'Chad will get back to you, of that I'm certain.'

The wedding was a quiet one, with only a few friends attending. Rusty didn't invite her mother, and her father was still in Australia, but it was a small but happy gathering of friends who were dear to her that sat at the table at Beth's house after the ceremony.

And after the speeches and the cake cutting, they all got changed out of their finery and went riding. It was a truly perfect ending to the day, with much merriment as they all rode through the woods together.

Later that night, in the honeymoon suite of the Polygon Hotel, Brad drew his bride into his arms. 'When we get home, we'll have a grand reception for the family.'

'That'll be nice,' Rusty said, 'except there won't be anyone there to represent me.'

'We can invite Jenny and Chad,' he said, kissing her softly.

'What do you think has happened to him, Brad? I'm getting somewhat concerned for Jenny.'

'I've no idea, but I'm sure he's going to show up. He loves Jenny, he's not going to let her down.'

'But what if he believed Adam when he told Chad Jenny was staying with him?'

'Well, if I was in his shoes, Jenny would have to tell me to my face before I would believe it. Now, Mrs Jackson, your husband is waiting.' And he pulled her close.

Twenty-Seven

Little Hans had been fractious for a couple of days, and whatever Sarah tried to do seemed fruitless. The child wouldn't eat, he was restless and decidedly grumpy, and on the third day he started to cough and his temperature rose. He seemed to be having trouble with his breathing, and Sarah began to panic. She called to Beth to come and take a look at him.

Beth felt the baby's fevered forehead and noticed his laboured breathing. Calling for one of her staff to get the doctor, she took Sarah and the baby into the kitchen, where she boiled a kettle. When it was boiling, she made Sarah open an umbrella and hold it over her and Hans, making a canopy in which to hold the steam coming from the kettle. After a while, the child's breathing was easier, to everyone's relief, but the two women knew this was only a temporary measure. Hans was very poorly, and they were all relieved when, shortly after, the doctor arrived.

After examining the child, the doctor called an ambulance. 'Your baby is suffering with croup, and we need to get him to hospital and in a steam tent to relieve his breathing. This, hopefully, will help with the cough, and we need to get his temperature down. Has he eaten much?'

Sarah shook her head. 'He wouldn't take his milk or his cereal, nor would he drink the water in his bottle.'

The doctor frowned. 'He's probably dehydrated too.' Seeing the worried expression on Sarah's face, he lightly touched her arm. 'Try not to worry. In hospital they have all the equipment to get him better.'

But as she carried Hans into the ambulance, Sarah wasn't sure that that would be enough.

Beth had called Jenny's office the following morning to tell her about Hans and how poorly he was, so that evening she and Rusty went along to the hospital, armed with nightclothes for Sarah, who was sleeping in a chair next to the baby's cot; toiletries for her use; grapes and sandwiches to eat; and magazines to read.

Sarah looked distraught, and when she saw the two women she burst into tears.

Whilst Jenny was comforting the girl, Rusty poured a cup of strong tea from a flask and slipped two lumps of sugar in. She stirred this and handed it to Sarah. 'Here, drink this, love, it'll make you feel better.'

Whilst Sarah was resting, drinking her tea and having a snack – to build her strength, as she was told – the two friends were looking at Hans in his steam tent.

'Ah, bless him,' said Rusty. 'Will you just look at the little chap? He does look so pale, but this contraption seems to be working, as his breathing isn't too laboured.'

'He still has that hacking croupy cough,' Sarah told them. 'It sounds so awful, almost as if it's coming from his little boots.' She fished in her pocket and held out a crumpled sheet of paper. 'If

I give you the address, will you send this to Gunter for me? I need him to know about Hans. He is his father, and he has the right to know.'

Jenny took it from her. 'I'll catch the last post tonight,' she promised.

Gunter eagerly opened the letter the following afternoon, anxious to see what Sarah had to say. These letters were like a lifeline to him and kept him going during his imprisonment, but when he read the content he went pale. He quickly read it again, before heading for the office where the English captain, who was in charge of camp, was to be found. He asked permission to see him on compassionate grounds.

Once inside the office, he stood to attention.

'Well, Reinhardt, what is it that brings you here to see me?'

Gunter handed the officer the letter he'd just received.

The captain read the contents, frowned, handed back the letter and said, 'I'm sorry to hear about your son. I hope he gets better soon.'

'I would like your permission to go and see him, sir. I realize this is asking a lot, but he's only a few months old, and I've only seen him when he was very small. I've missed so much of him growing, and now he's really sick; you can imagine my concern.'

'Yes, of course I do. I have children myself. But I'm afraid that's not possible.' As Gunter started to protest, the officer interrupted him. 'I will, however, allow you to make one call to the hospital to find out for yourself exactly what the situation is – but Reinhardt, that is all I can do.'

'Very well, sir, thank you.'

Gunter was led into the outer office, where the clerk found the hospital number, dialled it, then handed the receiver over.

He was eventually put through to the ward where Hans was being cared for. 'My name is Gunter Reinhardt. I wish to know how my small son, Hans, is doing. He was brought in yesterday.'

'One moment, Mr Reinhardt, I'll get Matron.'

Gunter listened to the woman as she told him of Hans' condition. Gunter looked even more concerned as he listened, until the matron said, 'Would you like a word with your wife? She's here with the baby.'

'Thank you, I would appreciate that.'

'Hello?' There was a tentative note in Sarah's voice.

'Sarah, *liebling*, it's me, Gunter!'

'Gunter! When they said my husband was on the phone, I wondered who on earth it was. Oh Gunter, if only you were here. Hans is so poorly. They have him in a steam tent for his breathing, but his cough sounds awful!' She started to cry, which tore him apart.

He tried to comfort her, but felt absolutely hopeless. 'I am so sorry that you have to face this alone. I've asked to see Hans, but they won't let me, I was only allowed this call. Oh Sarah, try not to worry.'

Between sobs she told him that Jenny, Beth and Rusty were keeping her company. 'But the only person I want with me is you!'

Gunter was so frustrated. He desperately wanted to be there with Sarah and his son, and he wondered just how he'd get through the next few days, which the matron had said were crucial for the little baby.

'I have to go, Gunter, Hans is crying. I'll write to you every day. I love you.'

He didn't even have time to say goodbye. He handed back the receiver to the soldier on duty and walked back to his room, but he just couldn't settle. Eventually, he walked outside and wandered around. He had to get out of the camp somehow and see his boy.

Parked outside the camp kitchen was a lorry delivering vegetables to the cook. The driver picked up a large sack of potatoes and carried it into the kitchen. The German saw the name of the company on the side of the van, and when he saw it gave an address in Southampton, he made a quick decision. He swiftly climbed into the back of the lorry, saw an old mac on the floor and picked it up before burying himself beneath a pile of empty sacks. He heard the driver return, and he held his breath. To his relief, the man closed the back doors to the van and, climbing into the driver's seat, drove out of the camp.

Gunter had no idea where he was headed and how he would find his way to the hospital, but at least he was out of the camp, and somehow he *would* see his sick boy. He had the address of the hospital in the letter Sarah had sent.

The journey seemed to take a long time, and Gunter wondered when the vehicle would stop. Eventually, it did so, and he heard the driver get out and walk away. He carefully got to his feet and peered through the small windows of the door. They seemed to have stopped outside a warehouse, and he saw a man he presumed to be the driver walk into the vast interior.

Gunter quickly opened the doors of the van, closed them behind him and slipped inside the building. Fortunately, everyone inside seemed to be too busy to notice him, and when he saw a man emerge from a nearby room, he noticed through the open door a row of coats hanging. He waited, then walked over to the door casually and, with baited breath, opened it. Luckily for him, there was no one inside.

He quickly looked for a coat that would fit him. He tried one on and felt in the pocket, where to his delight he found some loose change. He swiftly went through the pockets of the others and soon had a small collection of coins. Opening the door of the cloakroom, he looked out and, seeing that no one seemed to be nearby, he slipped out and walked purposefully out of the building.

Once clear, he looked around for someone to ask about the hospital he wanted to visit. He approached an elderly lady and politely asked her. To his great relief he was in Southampton, as he hoped.

The unsuspecting woman gave him detailed instructions, even to which tram to catch – which would take him almost to the door. He thanked her and made his way to the tram stop.

Sarah was sitting by Hans – who, in his steam tent, was sleeping peacefully – turning the pages of a magazine. She looked up as she heard footsteps approaching. She frowned. That man walking down the ward looked just like Gunter, she thought, but how ridiculous! He was in civilian clothes, and Gunter was in Bishop's Waltham. But there was something about him that made her keep watching. She was about to cry out as he got nearer, but the man put his finger to his lips, so she covered her mouth to smother the sound which was rising in her throat.

When he reached her, he kissed her quickly and whispered, 'Don't say anything, *liebling*, I'm here. Let's make the most of the time we have together. Now let me see my son.'

Sarah could hardly believe what was happening, and after she'd told him the latest news of little Hans, and held on to Gunter's arm to make sure he was real, she couldn't wait any longer.

'Gunter, what on earth are you doing here? I thought you were unable to come.'

He held her to him. 'I escaped from the camp, and soon they'll discover I'm missing. They'll probably find me pretty soon, knowing my son is sick, so we may not have much time.' He gazed into her eyes and kissed her passionately. 'I had to come. How could I let you face this without me?'

'You'll be in so much trouble!' she exclaimed.

'What can they do to me, Sarah? I am already a prisoner. But I had to see Hans and you.'

'The doctor says that probably tomorrow Hans can come out of the tent, as his breathing is so much better.'

'That's marvellous news,' he said, reaching in the tent to hold his baby's hand. He smiled as he looked at his son. 'He has grown so much, it's amazing.'

Gunter was still there in the late afternoon when Rusty and Jenny called into the ward. Sarah introduced them, saying, 'He won't be here long, as they will have discovered he's missing at roll call this evening.'

Jenny looked at the happy expression on Sarah's face, but she knew that the situation wasn't good. 'May I make a suggestion?'

They looked at her with puzzled expressions.

'It would be better for Gunter if he went back to the camp under his own steam. The consequences would not be so severe. I'd be happy to drive him back there. What do you think? After all, these are compassionate grounds. If he goes back without waiting for them to come and get him, they may look upon the whole thing more kindly.'

Gunter looked at Sarah and smiled. 'Your friend makes sense, *liebling*. Now I've seen you and Hans, I can sleep at night without worry.'

She hugged him. 'Go, darling, I don't want you to get into too much trouble. It was wonderful to see you, but you need to leave now before it's too late.'

And so Jenny and Rusty bundled the young man into the back of the car and drove out to Bishop's Waltham.

Jenny stopped just short of the camp and let the German out. 'Please don't worry about your family,' she told him. 'Whilst Rusty and I are about, we'll make sure she and the baby are fine.'

'Thank you so much, I don't know what to say. Sarah is so lucky to have such good friends.'

'You had better go,' said Jenny. 'With a bit of luck no one has yet left to search for you, which will only help your cause.'

The two women watched him walk up to the gate and be stopped by the guard. As they let him through, Gunter turned and smiled.

'Nice chap,' said Jenny as she drove away. 'I'm so pleased we met him, because now we know that Sarah has a good man.'

'Nothing's easy though, is it?' said Rusty wryly. 'There he is, supposedly the enemy, now with an English wife and baby. Her parents have disowned her, and who knows how his family will react to his situation once he's repatriated?'

'From what I saw today, if his parents didn't approve, I don't think it would make any difference to Gunter. Did you see the way he looked at Sarah? And he's naturally crazy about his son. No, nothing will keep them apart but time!'

Apart from a serious reprimand, Gunter Reinhardt was spared further punishment. The fact he returned voluntarily, and before the military police had been sent to find him, stood him in good stead. He was able to write to Sarah and tell her the good news. A few days after, she was able to write and tell him that little Hans was being allowed home, which was a great relief to all.

Twenty-Eight

Chad Maxwell had been in a military hospital in Southern France, suffering with a severe bout of bronchitis, which had laid him low. He'd been too ill to enjoy the celebrations when the end of the war was declared; all he knew was that he had to get better. But before he was fully recovered, he was shipped home, spending the voyage in the ship's hospital.

When the liner docked in New York, he made the journey home to Wyoming, staying with his parents until he was better. There he told them about the wonderful girl he was going to marry.

'So when do we get to meet this Jenny?' asked his father.

'When I have a home to offer her, Dad. I need to buy a ranch so we can raise horses. She's given up so much for me, I want her to be happy.'

'She needs a ranch to make her happy?' asked the elder Maxwell.

'Hell no! She said she would sleep on a blanket in the open as long as she's with me.'

'Then why the devil are you wasting your time? Bring her out here!'

'It's not that simple, Dad. She's married and has to get a divorce, and there is a great deal of paperwork to get done before we can be together.'

'She knows you're home, son?'

'I've not had the opportunity to write. First I was ill, then I was on a ship, now the journey here.'

'You're taking a chance, aren't you, my boy? How do you know she's still waiting for you?'

'I don't, Dad, and to be honest it scares the hell out of me.' He then explained to his father the predicament he discovered when he saw Adam.

His father frowned. 'Well, Chad, do you believe the man?'

'To be honest, I don't know. I realize that Jenny would feel she had a duty to stay with him, under the circumstances, but I also know how we felt about each other. I want her with me, but I feel a louse to even think of her leaving a man who has lost his sight!'

'Then you must go back there and sort this out! Once you've been discharged, you must go back to England. You can't get on with your life, Chad, until you do. You know that, don't you?'

'You're right, of course. But first I have to get my discharge. Then I'll sort it, I promise.'

Back in Southampton, Jenny carried on working, sorting out the paperwork and getting the GI brides ready for the voyage that would send them off to a new country and a new life, all the time wishing it were her that was going.

She and Brad had pulled a few strings to enable Rusty to stay in the flat, instead of joining the other brides at Tidworth camp, whilst awaiting passage to America. He had now left the country and was home, discharged from the army and setting up his practice once again.

Rusty was kept informed of his every move by letters which came regularly, which only made it more difficult for Jenny, who had heard nothing from Chad. Jenny had also been served divorce papers by Adam's solicitor and was visiting her own solicitor to enable the case to go to court, but it was a long and arduous task. As she wasn't disputing the charge of adultery, she wouldn't have to appear in court, for which she was eternally grateful.

Meantime, Chad was having a hard time booking a cabin on one of the *Queens* to travel from New York to Southampton. The bookings were full, and he was on a waiting list. He'd written to Jenny, telling her of his plans . . . but this letter wasn't readdressed to her, because the time had run out at the post office, and it landed in Adam's hands, who put it in the dustbin, unopened.

It was now September, and Jenny had still had no word from the horse whisperer, but she tried not to be too disheartened. She couldn't help the doubts which kept creeping into her mind that once Chad had arrived home things had changed, but deep down she really believed she'd see him again. There had been a sincerity about the American that was unshakeable in her mind, and on the darkest days she clung to this hope.

She spent her spare time at the stables with Beth. For Jenny it was cathartic, cleaning out the stables, rubbing the horses down and taking them out on exercise, letting them gallop, feeling the wind through her hair – being alone with her thoughts.

Today she'd been out with one of the stallions for a good hour, giving him a thorough workout and then a run, and she rode back into the stables in good spirits, having benefited as much as the animal. She slipped out of the saddle, watered the horse, then led him into his stable where she removed the saddle and the rest of the tack, wiping him down after she'd done so. All the time talking softly to the horse, engrossed in what she was doing.

'I do believe I could train you to do my job.'

Jenny froze. She could hardly believe her ears. Turning, she saw Chad leaning over the stable door, grinning broadly at her.

'Hello, Jenny honey. Sorry it took me so long to get here, but here I am.'

With a loud cry of delight, Jenny ran to the door which Chad had now opened, to be lifted off her feet as she flew into his arms.

'I knew you'd come!' she cried as she rained kisses on him.

Beth and the others came running at the sounds of excitement, and Chad was made welcome by them all.

'Hey, it's great to be back and see you guys again,' he said, all the time keeping his arm around Jenny.

She looked at Chad and frowned.

'What's the matter, honey?' he asked.

'I'm trying to think what's different, but of course, you're not in uniform, that's what's different!'

Chad was wearing a pair of dark-brown trousers and a tan leather coat. He looked very smart, but it did seem strange to see him out of uniform.

Beth sent them into the house so they could be together and alone. 'But you can make us all a cup of tea in half an hour,' she told him as she walked away, laughing.

Once in the kitchen, Chad took Jenny into his arms. 'Here, let me look at you,' he said as he caressed her face. 'God! How

I've missed you. I was almost afraid to come here this morning in case you sent me away.'

'Did you believe what Adam said, then?' asked Jenny.

'I didn't want to, but you know, the poor guy was blind. That's why I sent the flowers, to let you know I still felt the same.'

'What flowers?'

'After I saw Adam, I went to the florist and sent flowers with a message.'

Jenny shook her head. 'I never did see them. Adam must have got rid of them.'

Pulling her close to him, Chad said quietly, 'You couldn't blame him, honey. He was fighting to keep you. I'd have probably done the same.' He gazed fondly at her. 'My folks are very anxious to meet you.'

'Do they know I'm married, waiting on a divorce?'

'Yes, they know. They also know that I love you and we are going to be together.'

'How long are you here for?' Jenny asked.

'As long as it takes to get the situation sorted. I'm not leaving here until you can come with me.'

'My divorce comes up next week. Then I'll have to wait six weeks before it's finalized and I get my decree nisi. I don't have to go, as I'm not contesting it. I'm afraid he named you, Chad, as the man I was consorting with.'

He grinned broadly. 'Consorting, eh? Well, I guess that's one way of putting it. What say we make Beth her tea and then go back to your place and consort?'

Jenny started to laugh. 'It makes sex sound kind of legal, doesn't it?'

He kissed her soundly. 'I don't care how it sounds, honey. Let's just go and do it before I lose my mind waiting. It's been a long time.'

After the divorce, Jenny and Chad waited for six weeks for the decree nisi and then they were married by special licence at the registry office in Southampton. Rusty and Beth were witnesses as the two of them took their vows. After which the four of them went to the Dolphin Hotel for a champagne lunch.

Chad reached for Jenny's hand. 'Sorry this wasn't perhaps the wedding you dreamed of, darlin', but when we get home we'll have a church blessing with the family and friends.'

'It really isn't important, Chad.' She held out her hand and gazed at her shiny new wedding ring. 'What's important is that we are married. The rest is all just stuff!'

'I love this woman!' he joked. 'I'll never have to spend a fortune on her, she said she'd live with me on a blanket outside if need be. Well, Jenny honey, I took you at your word. At home I bought us a couple of Indian blankets! Who needs a home – it's just stuff!'

Gunter Reinhardt had returned to Germany with the other prisoners and like the Americans had been discharged from the army. To his delight, when he returned to his hometown, he found his home intact and the office where he was training was still in business. His parents were alive; his father had survived the fighting, and his mother had escaped the worst of the raids by staying with relatives.

They were somewhat shocked to discover that he had fathered a son with an English girl, but when he showed them the pictures of young Hans and Sarah that she'd sent to him, they were intrigued by their grandson.

As soon as he was able, Gunter arrived back in Southampton to take Sarah to Germany to be married. She introduced him to Beth and all the staff at the stables, and then they travelled by bus to visit the Browns.

Ethel Brown was delighted to see them and made a great fuss of Hans. She insisted they stay, and when Gunter queried the wisdom of this, she said, 'The war is over! The sooner we get over it the better!'

At lunchtime when the farmer returned with his son, Sarah and Gunter were a bit apprehensive, but the young man surprised them. He shook Gunter by the hand. 'My dad is always telling me how hard you worked whilst you were here and that he couldn't have managed without you, so thanks for that. No hard feelings?'

'No, indeed. Your parents were wonderful to me and to Sarah. I will always be in their debt.'

'That's enough of that,' Arthur Brown said. 'Let's eat. I'm starving!'

The following week, Gunter took Sarah and their son across the channel by ferry and on the train to his home and family, where they were greeted warmly. Fortunately for her, his parents spoke English, but as his mother said, 'Once you get settled in and married, you will have to shop, so you'll need to learn the language.' At the look of trepidation on Sarah's face, she smiled. 'Don't worry, being in the country will help you to pick it up, but you must speak English to little Hans, then he'll grow up knowing both languages automatically. I'll help you.'

And she did. By the time Gunter had found a house for them and arranged a wedding, Sarah was already making progress with the language and finding that Gunter's family accepted her without difficulty. For once, she felt part of a real family, and she blossomed.

It was January that they were married in a little local church with his family and friends assembled. Farmer Brown and his wife had travelled there, with Beth to give Sarah some support. Rusty and Jenny would have gone too, but Rusty was booked on a ship to take her to New York, and Chad was trying to get himself and Jenny a berth on the *Aquitania*, but they sent gifts and a telegram of good wishes.

Sarah sent her father a picture of her wedding and of Hans, but she ignored her mother. As far as Sarah was concerned, she didn't have one.

The day arrived when Rusty left Southampton and, with the hundreds of other GI brides, sailed out of the port for New York and a new life. For some, when they reached their destination, it would be like being in heaven; sadly, for others it would be like hell on earth. But as the ship left the harbour, every one of them had a head full of dreams.

Beth, Chad and Jenny waved to Rusty from the quayside. Brad was meeting her in New York, and he'd invited Chad and Jenny to visit at any time. Rusty made her promise she'd keep in touch and that when they were both in the States they would visit each other at least once a year. She had given her word.

It took some further three weeks until Chad and Jenny were due to leave England for Wyoming. They had been to the American Embassy in London, filled in all the necessary papers, taken the medical and satisfied the authorities that financially they were secure. Chad's father stood as guarantee for Jenny over and above his son, her husband. The American Embassy demanded a lot before they gave Mrs Chad Maxwell her visa.

Beth gave them a small farewell dinner, which was attended by the staff and a few friends. It was a happy occasion, and as they walked around the stables after, they talked about their first meeting and how their lives had changed.

'It's the crazy war, Jenny honey. Everything changes in one way or another. Some changes are for the good, and others, not so. It brought me you, so I was the lucky one. And believe me I'm going to make sure I deserved the break. We are going to have a great life together. You will learn to love my country as I learned to love yours, and we'll come back now and again to see it.'

'Can we do that, really?'

'Sure we can. This is where your roots are and will always be. No one can take that away from you ever, nor should they want to.'

She put her arms around his neck. 'Mr Maxwell, you have a great understanding of what goes on in the mind.'

'Of course I do, Jenny honey, I'm a horse whisperer, it's part of the job!'

'I just can't wait to use those Indian blankets you bought,' she teased.

'I can't wait to see you among my friends with your quaint English ways. Wait until you introduce them to teatime!'

Laughing she said, 'With cucumber sandwiches, scones and crumpets.'

'What the hell are crumpets? It sounds like an illness.'

She laughed loudly. 'You have a lot to learn, cowboy!'

He chuckled. 'You think so? Wait until you come on a round-up and have to cook on a chuck wagon!' He drew her to him and kissed her. 'We are going to have so much fun, you and I.

And when we are old and grey, we'll sit on our porch in the twilight and reminisce of how we met and the trials and tribulations we went through to be together.'

She smiled softly. She would always think affectionately of Chad as her guilty pleasure, which sounded a little naughty to her still, although they were now married. She hoped that one day Adam would find a little of the happiness she felt; then it would be a really fitting end to everything. She was now Mrs Chad Maxwell, and that was enough for her.